CLINT EASTWO

EDWARD GALLAFENT

CLINT EASTWOOD

Actor and Director

STUDIO
VISTA

A Studio Vista Book

First published in the UK 1994
by Studio Vista
Villiers House
41/47 Strand
London WC2N 5JE

Distributed in Australia
by Capricorn Link (Australia) Pty Ltd
2/13 Carrington Road, Castle Hill
NSW 2154

Briitish Library Cataloguing-in-Publication Data
A catalogue record for this book is available
from the British Library

ISBN 0-289-80115-X

A Movie Book
Edited and designed by Ian Cameron

Produced by Cameron Books
PO Box 1, Moffat
Dumfriesshire DG10 9SU, Scotland

Filmset by Cameron Books, Moffat

Printed and bound in Britain by
Hartnolls, Bodmin, Cornwall

*Frontispiece: Clint Eastwood as William Munny
practising to improve his rusty skill with a pistol
in* Unforgiven.

This book is for Jean, Robert and Lillian, and in memory of Andrew Britton.

CONTENTS

Acknowledgements and Note on Sources   6

INTRODUCTION: ECHOES AND ESCAPADES   7

1. THE DOLLARS FILMS   11
   A Fistful of Dollars—For a Few Dollars More—
   The Good, the Bad and the Ugly

2. THE CALLAHAN FILMS   35
   Dirty Harry—Magnum Force—The Enforcer—Sudden Impact—
   The Dead Pool—Tightrope

3. SENTIMENTAL AND OTHERWISE   73
   The Beguiled—Play Misty for Me—Breezy

4. THE LATER WESTERNS   102
   Hang 'Em High—Two Mules for Sister Sara—Paint Your
   Wagon—Joe Kidd—High Plains Drifter—The Outlaw Josey
   Wales—Pale Rider

5. THE WAR MOVIES   138
   Where Eagles Dare—Kelly's Heroes—Escape from Alcatraz—
   Firefox—Heartbreak Ridge

6. EASTWOOD'S TRAVELS: THE ROAD MOVIES   156
   Coogan's Bluff—Thunderbolt and Lightfoot—The Gauntlet—
   Every Which Way But Loose—Any Which Way You Can—
   Bronco Billy—Honkytonk Man—Pink Cadillac

7. AMERICAN LIVES   199
   Bird—White Hunter, Black Heart

8. THE IDEA OF ORDER AT BIG WHISKEY   217
   Unforgiven—In the Line of Fire

9. THE RAGGED PROMISED LAND   231

Filmography   238

Bibliography   252

Index   254

Acknowledgements

Part of this book was written on sabbatical leave from the University of Warwick English Department in the academic year 1991-92; I would like to thank past and present Chairmen of the department for their support for a project which is not, as Huckleberry Finn might have put it, in their line.

In its first years at Warwick, Film Studies was lucky enough to be represented by Robin Wood and Andrew Britton; to them I owe the incalculable debt of early inspiration. More recently colleagues have been personally generous and intellectually vital: my contacts with staff and with students in Film Studies have been a continuous pleasure.

I have also benefited from talking with other colleagues at Warwick, and with the members of the editorial board of *Movie*: I would especially like to thank John Fletcher, Douglas Pye, Helen Taylor and Michael Walker. I must acknowledge a more general intellectual debt, to the critical work of Stanley Cavell and the access that it has given to me to ways of thinking about movies; I hope that I have made some sense of what I have read.

To my editor Ian Cameron many thanks are due for his general encouragement of this project, for his taming of the moments of incomprehensibility in the text, and to him and Jill Hollis for all their skill and hard work.

Finally I come to two names where personal and intellectual friendship are inextricable – Clive Bush and V.F. Perkins. I hope that they know how grateful I am to them, and what pleasure it gives me to say so.

A Note on Sources

The title of the introduction is taken from a source in classic American literature, the footnote to Walt Whitman's entry on names and naming in *Specimen Days in America*. With typical expansiveness, Whitman lists twenty-eight rejected titles for his book –'Echoes and Escapades' is one of these.

The title of the third chapter is borrowed from Thackeray – it is a chapter title in *Vanity Fair*.

The description of America as 'the ragged promised land' which I borrow for my conclusion is taken from Chapter 12 of Jack Kerouac's *On the Road*. At this point Kerouac is actually remembering Joel McCrea and Veronica Lake in *Sullivan's Travels*; the words are his description of Hollywood.

INTRODUCTION
ECHOES AND ESCAPADES

'There are scenes of all sorts; some dreadful combats, some grand and lofty horse-riding, some scenes of high life, and some of very middling indeed; some lovemaking for the sentimental, and some light comic business; the whole accompanied by appropriate scenery, and brilliantly illuminated with the Author's own candles.'

Of course, these words were not written as a description of the disparate body of film-making assembled by Clint Eastwood over the last quarter century; they are taken from the author's prologue to a nineteenth-century novel, William Thackeray's *Vanity Fair*. I reproduce them here not just for the fun of their aptness, but to indicate something of the spirit of my account of Eastwood's films and my interest in viewing them as characterisations or commentaries on a series of worlds. Thackeray underlined his perspective by subtitling *Vanity Fair* 'A novel without a Hero'; I will be considering what kind of figure, or hero, it is possible for Eastwood to be, and at the same time exploring a number of subjects in Eastwood's films from *A Fistful of Dollars*, which was made in 1964, to *In the Line of Fire*, released in 1993.

I can begin to suggest what these subjects are and where I find them by taking a short sequence as an example. It occurs a little way into the opening of Eastwood's penultimate western to date, *Pale Rider* – some thugs are beating up an unarmed man. The presentation of this violence is alarming; while little evident harm has been done as yet, the worst is to be anticipated as the man tries to crawl under his wagon and is dragged out again to be finished off, while one of the thugs is about to set light to the wagon. At this moment, from just behind the camera's point of view, a bucketful of water is thrown, by a hitherto invisible hand. It soaks the perpetrator of the arson – the accompanying line is 'You shouldn't play with matches.' Nonplussed by something – the reference of this admonition to the precepts of the nursery, or the fact that these tough guys find that they have allowed themselves to be crept up on – the men turn to find Eastwood, for it is he. A fight now follows, but it has a totally different tone from the previous violence. As if mesmerised by Eastwood's presence, the men – seven of them – allow themselves to be knocked out neatly, one by one.

I produce this sequence because I recollect that while watching it on the release of the film in 1985 I first considered the possibility of a study of Eastwood's films. What does it propose? Of course a rescue, the perpetrators of violence punished and humiliated, something that we wish to see. But this is brought about not by superior skill, but by magic, by grace and speed triumphing over brute force, by a kind of vaudeville act – Eastwood's hat is possibly evidence of this quality here – by something that is in part a joke, in part a spell. This is indicative of the kind of world that a significant part of Eastwood's work occupies, or wishes to occupy, with varying degrees of success and acknowledgement of difficulty. It is a world in which a rescuer can literally – the larger plot of this film – appear from nowhere as the answer to a young girl's prayer, a world which can move easily from one kind of meaning to another, from realistic surfaces to figures and acts that we can approach through an understanding of the myths that they embody.

Throughout his career, Eastwood has been attracted to material which is overtly the stuff of myth and legend – the western, the war movie and the lives of famous creative artists. Other material offers an accessible, mundane world to the viewer – a contemporary landscape – but continually explores the effect of characters assigning themselves to mythic roles: rescuer, thief, lover. Different subjects are foregrounded in different genres; different examples of a genre may offer various ways in which a role and its limitations are felt. For this reason I have grouped the films, not by their order of production, but by their more or less obvious generic bases. Part of my interest here has been in the constituents of the less self-evident groupings. Any organisational principle has its drawbacks and advantages – it has seemed useful to trace the trajectory, or look for it, in Eastwood's use of various worlds, but I have necessarily been unable to give full emphasis to connections between movies in different genres made in the same period. I address this issue briefly in the concluding chapter.

Any idea of the self is inseparable from the kind of society in which it is conceived. It is a truism that Eastwood's work, and his star persona, are intimately involved with his national culture. Apart from a brief period in disguise in *Firefox*, he has never played anything but an unmistakable American, and I have aimed to explore his concern with what I could call the possibilities of life in America. Given the period spanned by Eastwood's career, a first feature directed in 1971 at the height of the Vietnam war and the protest against it, through the Watergate conspiracies and the Carter and Reagan/Bush presidencies, this needs a further gloss. I am tempted to revise my formulation and say that Eastwood explores the impossibility of life in America, but that would also not be quite accurate. Part of my interest in Eastwood's work is in the way he dramatises the fantasies of representative Americans (or considers the conditions in which these fantasies are able to exist), working this subject out during a historical period when the remoteness of real power from ordinary American lives has arguably never been more complete.

In referring to fantasies, I do not mean some separate world of unattainable desires. My premise is that there is a quality particular to American culture of fascination with dreamers, not for the way in which a preoccupation with dreams divides the dreamer from his or her society, but for the journeys towards wishes or satisfactions which it seems, even now, American society might just possibly fulfil. To paraphrase F. Scott Fitzgerald, these are dreams that seem so close that the dreamer can hardly fail to grasp them. One element of this will be films dealing with showmen of different kinds, whose fantasies become acts in the world, *Bronco Billy* and *White Hunter, Black Heart*. (For a more eloquent discussion of this view of fantasy, see Stanley Cavell's comments on *Vertigo* in Chapter 13 of *The World Viewed*. Cavell's formulation there is that 'fantasy is precisely what reality can be confused with.')

Alongside my aims here, I am aware of what F.O. Matthiessen in the introduction to his *American Renaissance* called 'the important books I have not written'. The conditions which have applied to the great part of Eastwood's work – his control of Malpaso, his own production company, and thus his influence over the shape of the product even when he was not its director – are central to these films and to the consistency of interest that I will be examining. Yet this book is not an account of those conditions. Though I do not deny their importance, it seems to me that they can be thought of essentially as opportunities – the question is, what has been done with them. I do not attempt to give a developed account of Eastwood's career and the reception of individual films, nor do I deal with the cultural significance of the different ways in which Eastwood has been promoted to us outside his actual products as a film-maker and actor. Accepting that stars are constructed in many ways means that I am contributing to the study of Eastwood as a star only from a single point of view. In the light of Richard Dyer's comment in *Heavenly Bodies: Film Stars and Society* that 'a star's films are likely to have a privileged place in her or his image', this does not sound too bad an area on which to concentrate, as long as one is prepared, if not content, to admit that any story is not the whole story.

The subject of authorship requires more explanation. I have not made a sharp division between films directed by Eastwood and those by others. In this I am partly following Eastwood himself, who has frequently stressed the largely collaborative nature of his film-making and the contributions made by long-standing members of the Malpaso production and technical crews. In interview, he has described what determines his decision whether or not to direct a Malpaso film with the Emersonian term 'whim'. The difficulty of making distinctions is increased by Eastwood's use of directors who have emerged from his own group – for example, Jim Fargo, who was assistant director on a number of Malpaso films before directing *The Enforcer* and *Every Which Way But Loose*. Eastwood has also made films with directors outside the Malpaso team. Apart from those directed by Sergio Leone before the formation of Malpaso, the most prominent names are Michael Cimino (*Thunderbolt and Lightfoot*), Richard Benjamin (*City Heat*), Wolfgang Petersen (*In the Line of Fire*) and Don Siegel, who directed four Eastwood films. The interest of these films, at least in the context of this book, varies considerably. I have discussed the films made by Siegel and Cimino at length and the Petersen film briefly, but not in terms of their directors' visions; *City Heat* seems to be of relatively minor interest.

In the following chapters, my frame of reference in my discussions of Eastwood is that of other products of American culture. I have not confined myself to film culture – I wish among other things to think of Eastwood's work as continuous with, although not of course identical to, the America expressed in the vision of a Mark Twain or a Henry David Thoreau. With reference to other film-makers' work, the case is a little different. Sometimes, it has been helpful to approach Eastwood's work by looking across at films being produced at the same time by other studios and directors. Elsewhere, it has been helpful to think of the work of Douglas Sirk and Frank Capra as a way of situating the themes of Eastwood's work and of considering differences in approach. This does not express a crude archaeology of influence – I am not especially interested in pursuing the issue of whether or not Eastwood has seen particular films. But I think that it illuminates his work to consider how it echoes and inflects the subjects of earlier films and film-makers.

Over the period of writing this book, a frequent response to my explaining what I was doing was an enquiry as to whether or not the project would involve meeting the star himself. It was clearly felt that this would be a great thing, almost a justification. Equally, if this was not my object, the enquirers implied, they were quite unable to understand what I could be up to.

Clint Eastwood is not to be met with in these pages, at least not in the way that I assume was being thought of: some version of the 'reality' of a star served up at second hand. What I am attempting to offer is a different kind of exploration. The roles that Eastwood has played, and the films that he has directed, cannot be disentangled from the nature of the American culture of the last quarter century, its fantasies and its realities.

CHAPTER ONE
THE DOLLARS FILMS

The first line delivered by Eastwood as star of a feature film is spoken a few minutes into the running time of *A Fistful of Dollars*. Watering his mule at a well on the edge of town, the Stranger, played by Eastwood, has watched a gunman mistreat a peasant and his small child. As he rides into the middle of town, he is told, 'It's not smart to go wandering so far from home'. Other gunfighters start to shoot at his mule's feet. When the animal bolts, the Stranger grabs hold of a signpost; as he swings in the air, he encounters the gaze of Silvanito (Jose Calvo), an old man who keeps the town's saloon. Eastwood's line is 'Hello'.

To consider what exactly is being acknowledged here involves us in contemplating Sergio Leone's film in more than one way. From the perspective of the other end of Eastwood's career, of our knowledge of him as a major star and filmmaker, the scene has something of the status of an announcement – the point to which we look back as marking his arrival as a star. A comparable instance is John Wayne's appearance as the Ringo Kid in *Stagecoach*, again not by any means the first sight of the actor, but the moment when some of the crucial elements that make up the star's persona converge for the first time, and the star's significance begins to be clear.

But this is a kind of illusion, a reading backwards from our position in the present, as if the star were playing in a biopic of his own career. These moments are not in fact the beginnings of careers, but are already influenced by what led up to them. We need to address the question of how this moment worked for its original audiences, to ask what factors rendered it possible.

I am not thinking here of the ten movies of the 'fifties in which Eastwood had small parts. Neither these movies in themselves nor Eastwood's function in them would appear to be of much interest other than as an example of the apprentice work that any young male film actor of the period might have undertaken. Possibly the only significance of these parts is that they made the offer of work in a new western TV series in 1959 an attractive prospect.

Eastwood's decision to take a part in the series *Rawhide* (CBS, 1959-66) was not unique for film actors of his generation. James Garner accepted the starring role in *Maverick* (WB-TV, 1957-62) and Steve McQueen that in *Wanted: Dead or Alive* (CBS, 1958-61). Both actors made the decision after being cast in relatively minor parts in insignificant feature films in the earlier 'fifties. The logic of these decisions and the possibilities represented by such roles reflect the brief dominance of western series on American TV networks. Inevitably, television westerns influenced the ways in which the cinematic genre developed in the 'sixties, and thus there is a relation to Eastwood's roles in the Dollars films which extends beyond his appearance in a specific TV series.

Before 1956, TV western series for adult viewing did not, in effect, exist. In 1952 there were only two series in the evening schedules, *The Lone Ranger* (1949-57) and *The Gene Autry Show* (1950-56), screened at 7 or 7.30 p.m. and aimed at an audience of children. *Gunsmoke* (1955-75), first shown at 10 p.m. on Saturday nights, was the first series aimed at adults and relating directly to the more prestigious forms of western cinema – CBS had attempted to persuade John Wayne to take the part played in the series by James Arness. ABC followed a year later with *Cheyenne* (1956-62), and, with the ratings competition between the networks, the popularity of the series led to one group (*Have Gun Will Travel*, *Maverick*, *Wagon Train*, *The Restless Gun*) starting in 1957 and another (*Wanted: Dead or Alive*, *The Rifleman*) in 1958. At this point, rumours that the big-money televised game shows were 'fixed', which eventually culminated in the widely publicised admissions made by the contestant Charles Van Doren before a House of Representatives sub-committee in November 1959, prompted their withdrawal and the appearance of another group of westerns, among them *Rawhide* (1959-66) in January and *Bonanza* (1959-73) in the autumn.

Thus, by Christmas 1959, network television was saturated with western series including the ten mentioned above as well as a number of others. The situation was short-lived: four of the ten had disappeared by the end of 1962, and another four by the end of 1966. The only survivors through the years of the Vietnam war were westerns centred on a settled world, the family ranch of *Bonanza*, and the Dodge City of *Gunsmoke*.

Detailed investigation of how the television series affected western features in the cinema is beyond the scope of this book; I will offer only one general point, and elaborate it in connection with *Rawhide*.

An obvious difference between TV westerns and western feature films is the series format. In the late 'fifties, there were no significant numbers of made-for-TV features or mini-series; the only TV westerns that were not part of a larger whole seem to have been pilot features for series that were subsequently abandoned. The series format clearly has implications for what such narratives can actually address. The larger questions, of how the variations of episodes in series relate to the concept of genre and of differences between the material bases of television and cinema, have been discussed by Stanley Cavell in his essay 'The Fact of Television'. Towards the end of that essay, he writes:

'If classical narrative can be pictured as the progress from the establishing of one stable situation, through an event of difference, to the re-establishing of a stable situation related to the original one, serial procedure can be thought of as the establishing of a stable condition punctuated by repeated crises or events that are not developments of the situation requiring a single resolution, but intrusions or emergencies – of humour, or adventure, or talent, or misery – each of which runs a natural course and thereupon rejoins the realm of the uneventful; which is perhaps to say, serial procedure is undialectical.' (*Themes out of School*, p.258)

This description seems to work well for TV westerns, in which the stable condition that is the *donnée* of a particular series either locates the action in an unspecific historical present, or offers a simple cyclical pattern based around the seasons of TV scheduling. (Thus, *Wagon Train* followed the route from St Louis to California each TV season.) In the context of Eastwood's work, this distinction can be seen in the relation between *Rawhide* and the film that apparently served it in part as a model, Howard Hawks's *Red River* (1948).

Hawks's film addresses a number of moments in American history through an emblematic story. There are obvious biblical overtones in the creation of a great herd through the union of the bull belonging to Tom Dunson (John Wayne) and the cow belonging to Matthew Garth (Montgomery Clift), and the trajectory of the film is from this heroic age, embodied in Wayne, to the new times of the postwar southwest, represented partly in historical events (the opening up of the Chisholm Trail, the arrival of the railhead at Abilene). Historical change is also signified in the different quality of masculinity embodied in Clift and in the treatment of women: the film begins with Wayne stoically losing his girl, and ends with Clift winning his Hawksian heroine. It ends by implying a future (in however tentative and Hawksian a set of terms) that posits continuity – the marriage of Garth and Tess Millay (Joanne Dru) and their inheriting of the ranch after the death of the pioneer Dunson would make a narrative which can, in broad terms, be traced back to James Fenimore Cooper's *The Pioneers* (1823).

Rawhide dehistoricises this material. The relationship between the two men, Gil Favor (Eric Fleming) and Rowdy Yates (Eastwood) is still central, but now it is expressive largely only of age and the politics of the family, the difference between an older authority figure and a young subordinate. History cannot give meaning to the different possibilities of what these two characters could do or be, because the 'stable condition' of the series has no way of, or perhaps interest in, addressing this. Most obviously, no liaison with a woman can be permanent – and neither of them can die. They reach the end of the cattle drive (*Rawhide* roughly followed the cyclical pattern of *Wagon Train*) only to begin it again next season. No great moment of change can be evoked, no emphasis on the uniqueness of any specific event in history (which can be a crucial element in the drama of the western), no movement between the different qualities of past and future.

This is clearly implied in the formula followed by the titles of the first season of *Rawhide*, where episodes were called 'Incident of the Tumbleweed Wagon' (ep.1), 'Incident of the Curious Street' (ep.13), etc. The episodes were essentially anecdotes, set in the western context, but borrowing elements of their structure from other generic models, such as the family melodrama or even on occasion the horror story. The potency of this formula may have rested on offering 'history' without its uncertainties and anxieties, either in terms of doubts about the history of the westward expansion or contemporary nervousness about the Cold War: it provides a world where events happen, but nothing changes.

The final question here is exactly how appearance in a serial like *Rawhide* might affect the formation of a star persona and the way in which this is perceived. It seems uncontentious that in classical narrative the re-establishing of the stable situation that Cavell describes can be brought about by a change or new understanding on the part of the hero, so that he is transformed in some way by the narrative – he becomes the same but different. The series format might offer a different model, where the constant quality of the star is measured against the 'intrusions or emergencies' of each episode – he is part of what is relied upon to remain exactly the same. This may produce a different attitude to the star's persona. Rather than seeing any variations in his presentation as evidence

Rowdy Yates in disguise: Eastwood as the Stranger, with the cigar and poncho of the Dollars movies, in A Fistful of Dollars.

of actual or potential changes, we see them as disguises, as masks underneath which lies something that is not alterable. Of course, this may produce an interesting dynamic in situations in which such a figure is used to dramatise a desire for change and the forces that work against this desire.

A Fistful of Dollars

As we watch the beginning of *A Fistful of Dollars*, an important question to ask – that is, one that the film itself seems to insist on – is a simple one: Where are we? The answer – not in the United States – is something we can observe in a number of different ways. The landscape itself, the white adobe houses between which the little boy runs in the opening moments, and the street of such houses down which the Stranger (Eastwood) rides, the costumes of gunman and peasant, send a message that seems familiar – these signify Mexico. But alongside this we are presented with more obscure data. The relative crudeness of the credits (as well as the names we see) suggests that one of the Americas absent here is Hollywood – we are looking at the product of another film industry. It is difficult to guess what proportion of an American audience in 1967 might have known or cared where the film was made, but the appearance of the term 'spaghetti' as a qualifier of 'western' says something about how little any exactitude about this was felt to matter. There are further complications to this idea of foreignness. If what we are seeing is not Hollywood, then this Mexico is not what Hollywood uses for Mexico (Southern California or Mexico itself) but somewhere else (actually Almería, a province of Spain that would presumably have meant little or nothing to many Americans).

The effect of this is to accentuate the remoteness of this film's Mexico, to put it in a different relationship to the United States from that found in the Hollywood western. There, Mexico can be an image of benign escape, a refuge from the 'blessings of civilisation', the irony articulated by Doc (Thomas Mitchell) as Ringo (John Wayne) and Dallas (Claire Trevor) head for the border at the end of *Stagecoach*. Or later it can be an image of more ambiguous change, the region into which characters wander as an expression of failure of their relation to American civilisation, its dominant use in films such as Sam Peckinpah's *Major Dundee* and *The Wild Bunch*. In Peckinpah's work this is understood in a complex way. Mexican civilisation is seen as older, more mature, than that of the USA, but it is also felt as alien; it becomes the site of fulfilment, despair and loss. (The connection between this and the American imagination of Europe in the work of Henry James and Edith Wharton is not all that remote.)

The Mexico of Leone's film is quite different, a place of collapse and death which has no positive qualities and is placed firmly beyond the possibility of redemption. San Miguel, the town of *A Fistful of Dollars*, is not to be confused with a place taken over by bad men, a community terrorised by figures who will be routed by the benign gunfighter or sheriff, the bottled-up towns of *Rio Bravo* or *High Noon*. Here the town consists of a few briefly seen widows, two old men (the bar-keeper and the coffin-maker), and two families locked into mutually destructive conflict. Leone presents the Rohos and the Baxters as disintegrating families, unable to do more than glimpse a world that might arrest their collapse into sterile violence. The central figure in this drama is Marisol (Marianne Koch), the only young woman in the film, an icon who represents the possibility of restoring life to these families. One version of such an outcome would couple her with Ramon (Gian Maria Volonté), the dominant brother of the Roho family – the other, barely articulated in the film but clearly implicit, with the son of the Baxter family. In fact both routes are blocked. Marisol is married to a Mexican peasant and already has a son, the small boy who appears in the opening moments of the film. Attempting to impose his solution, Ramon has abducted Marisol, but is apparently unwilling to do serious physical harm to her husband and son.

Leone's presentation of these blockages is at its clearest in a scene at the centre of the film, involving all the principal actors, in which Marisol and the Baxter son, each held as a prisoner by the opposing side, are exchanged in the town square. The movements – the Baxter son returns to a mother who slaps his face, Marisol embraces her husband and son briefly before reluctantly going back to her role as Ramon's unwilling mistress – express the pathos of this situation, where the collapse of these dynasties can end only in death. The force of the scene is underlined in two ways. One is through music – the sonorous melody that is played over the whole sequence is crucial to its tone, and exemplary of the importance of Ennio Morricone's score in supplying a kind of gravitas to the whole film. Alongside this is one of Leone's mannerisms as a director, the cutting between close-ups of the faces, or even just the eyes, of the principal figures at moments when the action is allowed to pause. The result here is not only to stress tension – as it might be in a gunfight sequence – but also contemplation. The effect of this is to suggest the possibility that the characters see themselves as actors in a drama that they cannot control, able to sense the meaning of the moment but not to transform it. (In the gunfight, the subject that the characters contemplate is the possibility of their own deaths.) By the end of the film all the members of both families are dead, the Baxters destroyed by the Rohos, and the Roho brothers killed by the Stranger in the final gunfight.

The scene of exchange of prisoners in the square also expresses something about how the character played by Eastwood relates to the drama of the two families. He does have a small active role in the sequence – when one of the Roho men threatens to kill Marisol's husband, he is stopped by the saloon keeper Silvanito, and the Stranger indicates (Leone uses a shot of Eastwood's eyes) – that he will support the old man against the young one. He also defuses

Collapsing dynasties in A Fistful of Dollars. *In the town square, Marisol (Marianne Koch) is returned to the Rohos.*

the situation, telling Marisol to hurry back to Ramon and the husband to get the little boy off the street.

The Americanness presented by Eastwood in this film is expressed in two very traditional impulses of the western hero – to support the little (powerless, unarmed or old) man against the threat of the gunman, and to defend the family. The latter is implied in his gaze as he watches the violence towards the father and son in the film's opening moments, but it is not only a matter of freeing the family group, literally sending them away from this deadly place, in an inversion of *Stagecoach*, across the border into America. It is also the defence of a view of sexual order, expressed in the opposition between the Stranger's attitudes and the sexual predatoriness embodied in Ramon. Gian Maria Volonté's performance stresses the particular quality of this character's violence, his enjoyment of killing – for example in the shots of his face as he massacres the troops by the Rio Grande – as a displaced form of sexual energy, something which will become much more marked in the next film in the group. The climax of the film is not the rescue of the family, but the showdown between the two men who embody different attitudes to it.

The climactic gunfight takes place in the absence of any actual woman whom either of these men might claim, or win, or steal, or any community that can be defended or revived. Is this important? In the absence of a past that can be retrieved, or a civilisation that can be defended, what remains is the belief in the difference between Ramon and the Stranger. This can be understood by them only through a confrontation in which one of them will die, but in which the victor's situation will be changed in no significant way by the death of the other. The bleakness of this context is reflected in a trope that might seem quirky or trivial were it not for its reverberations in Eastwood's later films: the connection of his invulnerability with the idea of the character already being dead. As the final showdown begins, Ramon, unaware of the thick steel breastplate under the Stranger's poncho, shoots him apparently in the heart and cries in triumph, 'The Americano is dead.' But the Stranger gets up and keeps coming. As shot after shot is fired at the heart and the Stranger falls with the impact but rises again and again, Ramon is unnerved not by the idea that the shots are missing their target, but that they are striking it, that the Stranger cannot be killed, and thus that Ramon's idea of himself as the victor cannot be substantiated.

Finally the poncho is thrown aside and the invulnerability is revealed as a prop, or a piece of ingenuity. But the point of the scene remains Ramon's insight that it is not the Stranger's skill, his speed as a gunslinger, which is truly at issue, but his unbridgeable distance from the world of San Miguel. A figure with no past or future related to the town, he is envisioned for a moment as a gothic avenger from some other plane of being, a subject which Eastwood will go on to exploit, in different ways, in *High Plains Drifter* and in *Pale Rider* and which has its relevance even to *Unforgiven*.

The suggestive factor here is the attitude of the Stranger to the values he defends. His exchanges with the Rohos on the subjects of home ('I never found home that great') and peace ('It's not very easy to like something you know nothing about') suggest the distance and reserve with which these dreams are treated. His contact with Marisol is reduced to a gesture, or a joke – the only scene in the film in which they would have been alone begins with the Stranger

Above: saved – Marisol and her family in A Fistful of Dollars. *Opposite: Ramon (Gian Maria Volonté) in his final confrontation with the Stranger.*

accidentally knocking her unconscious. Only once is there a more direct expression of commitment. As Marisol and her family leave for America, she asks the Stranger why he is helping them. He replies: 'Why? Because I knew someone like you once – and there was no-one there to help. Now get moving. [*Impatiently*] Get moving – get out of here!'

Is this autobiography? 'I knew someone like you once' is not very specific and certainly does not have the kind of substance that, say, a flashback might have offered. The vagueness and the impatience here may be more than simply the gruffness of a man committing an act of generosity. They point to the degree to which the impulse to defend the 'traditional' values now floats entirely free of any place with which it can be firmly identified or any narrative that can be realised, or remembered – it has indeed to operate in the face of a surrounding world of unrelieved brutality. In a downbeat inflection, an analogous figure in the period might be that of the Cold War spy, caught between national power bases and entirely without commitment. Alec Leamas (Richard Burton) in *The*

Spy Who Came in from the Cold (Martin Ritt, 1966) is such a figure, who asks 'When can I go wherever home is?'

I have argued that the effect of a star persona constructed through the series format might be to present apparent differences in the star not as change but as disguise of something unaltered, and this may in part be true of the figure in *A Fistful of Dollars*. The physical details that characterise the Stranger – the cigar, the poncho – are very much externals. Eastwood is neither aged nor made to look younger, and the beard had appeared intermittently in *Rawhide*. Alongside these factors is his evident Americanness, expressed in both the quality of his language and the fact that his speech is undubbed. The detail of Eastwood's language expresses more than just the national identity of the character. From the beginning, his speech is used to suggest control of situations not just by acts of violence, but by language. The conceit about the mule ('You see, my mule don't like people laughing, he gets the crazy idea you're laughing at him') as he faces the first group of gunmen is typical, their unease springing as much from puzzlement at his words as from fear of his guns. Elsewhere he appropriates and ironises a cliché so as to turn it into something almost like one of the tag-lines that mark the Callahan movies: 'Sometimes a man's life depends on a scrap of information.' And a speech is used at the beginning of the film and in effect repeated at the end of it, as if to emphasise that the predicament of this man (the subject of both speeches is being caught between two opposing forces) is unchanged, as is his attitude to that predicament.

Thus we see a plot in which a lone American, caught in a place that is both alien and deadly, proves to contain within himself the impulse towards benign action, thus characterising America as a place of safe refuge. The potency of such a plot for American audiences may have been affected by a matter of dates; when Italian audiences were first exposed to the film (31st December 1964), 267 Americans had died in Vietnam, and there were 23,000 American troops stationed there. By the end of 1966 these figures had become 6,644 dead and a presence of 385,000 troops – *A Fistful of Dollars*, delayed by legal problems connected with American rights to one of its sources, did not open in the United States until February 1967. For Italian audiences, Eastwood may have been 'El Cigarillo', but a nineteen-year-old American, watching the film in 1967, was likely to have been exposed to Rowdy Yates's cattle drive every Tuesday evening from his eleventh to his eighteen year. The sense of a benign past, intimately experienced through the series format and now in eclipse, may have been a crucial factor in the way the Eastwood character was received.

For a Few Dollars More
The figures quoted for the budgets of the Dollars films in biographies of Eastwood are $200,000 (*A Fistful of Dollars*), $600,000 (*For a Few Dollars More*), and $1,200,000 (*The Good, the Bad and the Ugly*). It was presumably at least in part the much larger budget for the second feature that enabled Leone to make a film using sets that present to us a recognisable image of the United States. As with the first film, the stress on the subject of foreignness versus Americanness is felt from the opening moments, but in a different way. The film could now be more direct about its origins – the names on the credits make less attempt to conceal its European cast and crew through anglicisation or pseudonym. But

the claim is also to more immediate Americanness. The images with which it opens, a train, a drummer, clerks and porters, an 'Indian' extra, an arrival at a tiny halt and a conversation with a ticket collector, are familiar elements of the iconography of the Hollywood western.

Yet the quality of their presentation here is not quite the same as in Hollywood production. In his account of the Dollars films in his *Spaghetti Westerns*, Christopher Frayling discusses Leone's interest in this iconography and characterises it as 'a "peep-show" attitude to the social context', arguing that 'Leone and other Spaghetti directors emphasise these details *because* the Cinecittà context is so "inauthentic" ' (p.170). This may accurately locate the impulse, but the effect of the emphasis is paradoxical. Perhaps because of the frequent reminders of foreign origin in the form of dubbed speech, the western iconography has the air of triumphant reproduction of an idiom, of loving quotation of something experienced at a distance. I think that this is not a matter of accuracy or anachronism – the subject is covered thoroughly by Frayling – but rather that the opportunities for film-making in Spain and Cinecittà, at least for Leone in these circumstances, can produce a plausibly authentic Mexico but a West that knows it own distance from Hollywood. An acknowledgement of this distance might be related to some of the expressionist details: a Wanted poster of Indio which shows him roaring – or screaming – with laughter and the comic sequence in which a passing train causes a whole set to shake into pieces.

Another way in which the western detail shifts the emphasis of this film is in the sense of the extensiveness of its imagined context. Leone is now able briefly to sketch a populated world where the principal players perform against a background of extras – saloon girls, gamblers, children – part of whose function is to present the indifference of the wider civilisation to any one set of private lives and motivations. To say this is not to suggest that the film offers the wider civilisation as benign, as moving away from old ways towards a humane future. The America that is the background to the action is still one without law, where the calculations of all the principal players are based solely on money, and in which almost no benign form of behaviour is seen to exist.

A comparison of the plots of the two films indicates another difference. Whereas in the central act of *A Fistful of Dollars* a memory of the past is behind an act of rescue, the comparable impulse in this film, a redemption in the present, again relating to a past moment where there was nobody around to help a woman, is now a response to an atrocity that can be revenged but not redeemed in the present. There is no woman in this film through whom the past can be given symbolic reembodiment and release. It is also significant that the relationship to the past and the woman in it is given here not to the figure played by Eastwood, but to another kind of American.

The literal details are these. The film shows us two bounty hunters, a young man played by Eastwood in his poncho-and-cigar Stranger persona from *A Fistful of Dollars*, and a Confederate army officer, Colonel Mortimer, played as a fifty-year-old man by Lee Van Cleef. As these men hunt for the bandit Indio (Gian Maria Volonté) and his gang, it emerges that at some unspecified point in the now distant past, Indio raped Mortimer's sister. (According to Frayling, a sequence cut from the final print showed the sister's suicide.) In a final confrontation, Mortimer kills Indio.

Above: the malign all-male group - the Stranger with Indio's band in For a Few Dollars More. *Right: in Agua Caliente, the Stranger (Eastwood) and Indio (Gian Maria Volonté) look on as Mortimer (Lee Van Cleef) opens the safe.*

The meaning of Southernness is important here. Mortimer is associated, through costume and prop – the fob watch which holds a photograph of the sister – with the ambiguities of his past. He evokes civilisation and elegance, but also a cause that was lost and a society the fall of which is related in many other contexts to the failure of its regulation of both male and female sexuality. (The subject is returned to in a later Eastwood film, *The Beguiled*.) Then there is the casting of Lee Van Cleef, a player of villains in westerns (*High Noon, The Man Who Shot Liberty Valance*), and his association in the film with the impersonality of technology, the collection of high-accuracy rifles that is prominent in the opening bounty hunt. The result is a figure whose act of revenge is only the last gesture of a civilisation gone irreparably wrong, a hero who might remind us of the doomed patriarchs of William Faulkner's novels.

The other side of this gothic scenario is exactly provided by the conception of Indio, and the qualities of Gian Maria Volonté's performance. The frustrations of *A Fistful of Dollars* were based on a perception of the limits of power, specifically power over a woman – Ramon can make Marisol his mistress, but not his wife, not the reviver of the fortunes of his family. Here the family has vanished, the brothers replaced by the entirely malign all-male group that is Indio's band. In flashback, we see the mere sight of a legitimate couple driving Indio to murder,

rape and theft. That Indio and Mortimer are linked through this moment is expressed by the identical fob watches – it is implied that Indio stole one of the pair from the raped sister. Both of them are trapped in the past, doomed to relive the moment represented by the tune which plays when the watch is opened, an image both of time running out (clockwork running down), and something inescapable, a tune which haunts the brain.

Indio is presented as a figure who understands his act of rape and murder not as a triumphant accession to villainy but as an admission of his own damnation. His actions – he continually, hysterically, kills men and has nothing whatever to do with women – invite the vengeance for his original act that no man has yet been able to provide by killing him. His first extended scene, in which he orders a man's wife and child to be killed and then invites the man to a gunfight timed by the running down of the musical watch, offers a scenario which is a clear example of this, an invitation to a man to kill him as punishment for violence to a woman.

The same impulse governs the trajectory of Indio's actions in the film. He accepts the Eastwood figure into the gang; he will later say, 'I knew he was one [a bounty killer] from the first moment he arrived.' After robbing the bank in El Paso, he retreats with his gang to Agua Caliente, a place he describes as 'like a morgue', where the gang will shatter into murderous factions before Indio's final confrontation with Mortimer. This resembles a familiar gothic scenario of a flight to a place where nature is at an extreme of hot or cold, and where death can at last be welcomed. (The use of sterile space on the edge of the city in the

Callahan films, which I will consider further in the next chapter, is loosely analogous to it.)

In Gian Maria Volonté's performance, Indio is an alternately moody and giggling neurotic. Where Leone stresses the efficiency or stony indifference with which the two bounty hunters carry out executions, he shows that for Indio murder is an act of carnality, an expression of the erotic charge that he carries. Compared with either Mortimer or the Stranger, Indio represents – of course in negative terms – the eroticised male, villain but potential lover and associated with a culture that is not American. This reverberates both inside the narrative, where Indio's Mexicanness is contrasted with the Americanness of the two other principals, and outside it, as a European actor displaying the power of the sensual to American audiences. (Loosely parallel figures would be Hollywood romantic stars whose Europeanness is part of their star personas, Charles Boyer or Louis Jourdan.) It is possibly not surprising to find Volonté's performance as Romeo at the Arena di Verona in 1960 quoted as the starting point of his career.

An obvious distinction between the first two Dollars films is the role played in the plot by the Eastwood figure. In *A Fistful of Dollars*, it is the Eastwood figure who destroys the villain played by Volonté, whereas here he dies at the hand of Mortimer, and the relation of the Stranger to the revenge plot is never more than circumspect. He is shown in the opening scenes as an effective bounty hunter, and his motive for destroying Indio's gang is simply a financial one. An opportunity for something else is specifically rejected in the scene in which Mortimer and the Stranger form a partnership in pursuit of Indio. The Stranger has asked Mortimer for an explanation of his past and been refused on the grounds that 'the question wasn't indiscreet, but the answer might be'. In contrast to the strategy of the first film, Leone inserts the flashback sequence here to explain Mortimer's and Indio's story only to the audience. Framed between shots of Indio's face, it pointedly avoids suggesting that the fact of the sister's rape becomes known to the Stranger.

The Stranger's role, then, is partly that of spectator. This is one of the repeated configurations of this film – the confrontation between Mortimer and the Hunchback (Klaus Kinski) in the saloon, and the last part of the gunfight between Mortimer and Indio are examples of it, with the Stranger as witness to passions for which he has no explanation. The fact that the dead woman in the photographs inside the watches is Mortimer's sister is confirmed to the Stranger only after the final gunfight. But this is not quite all. The scenes between Mortimer and the Stranger have a dynamic to do with the family, a consciousness on both sides that the two men are metaphorical father and son. This takes the form of ironic address, calling each other 'son' and 'old man'. That such a relationship can be benign is hinted at in the comic scenes between the Stranger and the film's more apparent old men, the madman in the hut by the railroad and the telegraph operator cooking breakfast. This contrasts with Indio's relationship to father figures; he begins the film by betraying and murdering the old man who is his fellow prisoner. The idea that the Stranger might be inserting himself into a family as a metaphorical son is closest to the surface at the end of the film, when he rescues Mortimer from certain death at Indio's hands, and sets up the final gunfight, as he returns the watch that Mortimer has dropped: 'Very careless of you, old man.'

But although this banter continues into the very last exchanges in the film, nothing of substance comes of it. The Stranger's response to Indio's death is a dour 'bravo' – he had greeted an earlier exhibition of Mortimer's shooting with the same word. Mortimer's watch and the Stranger's gunbelt are returned to their original owners after the fight, and Mortimer underlines the true purpose of his mission (and his difference from the Stranger) by departing, leaving the other to collect all the bounty.

I argued that the defence of civilisation in *A Fistful of Dollars* amounted to sending a family away to America, a potent image. There is also a subdued possibility of some release from the world of the film for the Stranger – there is a border across which he too could pass. The movement of *For a Few Dollars More* is from a bleak America to a dead Mexico. The possibility of civilisation amounts to a memory, a series of images associated with the past. The central one is clearly the photograph, the black and white image of a woman long dead. Allied to this is the world before the trains came – 'when all this was prairie'. The old man (Josef Egger) who recollects this time describes himself variously as mad and dead in the scene in which his home is shaken to pieces by the 'damned good-for-nothing trains'. It is to the grimness of the present that the figure played by Eastwood acts as a witness, without any real hope of change or progress. His position at the end, with his wagonload of corpses and the suggestion by Mortimer that he is now a rich man, points towards a resonant irony in American culture: the way in which an idea of 'success', presented through the image of the American dream of becoming rich, is to be understood in the context of a world in which nothing suggests how these riches might be realised or enjoyed.

The Good, the Bad and the Ugly

One of the impulses behind the western in the late 'sixties seems to have been the desire to call its seriousness into question. There had, of course, always been the possibilities of comedy in westerns, from comic elements and characters to full-scale burlesque, but the period 1965-70 produced a strikingly large number of features that announce themselves in various ways as comedies. A possible starting point for these is a section of an otherwise sombre western, John Ford's *Cheyenne Autumn* (1964), the sequence known as the Dodge City interlude. One of the themes of Ford's film is the distance between the lives of the Indians and the way in which they are perceived by an industrialising America to which they are increasingly irrelevant. In the Dodge City interlude, Ford extends this point to suggest that white characters who were once central actors in the drama of the West are now unable to be taken, or to take themselves, seriously. The presentation of the figures of Wyatt Earp (James Stewart) and Doc Holliday (Arthur Kennedy) is a measure of the distance travelled from the subject matter and possibilities of the world of Ford's own *My Darling Clementine* (1946). Typically, there is a moment where this distance is interrogated and could collapse: the point at which a scalp is flung down in front of Earp dramatises the choice between the reconstitution of the seriousness of these figures and an escape into festive rowdiness, which is what happens.

The casting in western comedies of actors such as James Stewart, who had played major roles in westerns, is an important part of what is being addressed here, the invocation of the seriousness of the genre in the past, and a questioning of elements of that seriousness. The parallel cases are the use of Lee Marvin in *Cat Ballou* (1965), Robert Mitchum and George Kennedy in *The Good Guys and the Bad Guys* (1969) and James Stewart and Henry Fonda in *The Cheyenne Social Club* (1970). Television western comedies also appear to use the same strategy – for example, the feature *The Over the Hill Gang* (Thomas Spelling Productions, 1969) included Pat O'Brien, Walter Brennan and Andy Devine in its cast, and *The Over the Hill Gang Rides Again* (1970) used largely the same actors.

There were also other forms of comedy in westerns. The comedian Don Knotts starred in *The Shakiest Gun in the West* (1967), a remake of *Paleface*, and James Garner exploited the comic elements of his persona from *Maverick* in *Support Your Local Sheriff* (1968). Comedy western series on television did not feature western stars – *Pistols 'n' Petticoats* (U-TV, 1966-67) starred Ann Sheridan, and *Rango* (Thomas Spelling Productions, 1967) starred Tim Conway.

Eastwood's first two Italian westerns had used individual gags, like the number of coffins the Stranger orders before and after the gunfight in the opening of *A Fistful of Dollars*, but neither film can be described in terms of its structure or mood as a comedy. Part of the shift between these films and the final Italian western is a shift into overt comedy, and in this change and its central strategy of framing the comedy around the casting of an actor not simply perceived as a comic, Leone is taking part in the broad appropriation of the possibilities of the western as comedy.

A number of other characteristics distinguish *The Good, the Bad and the Ugly* from the earlier Dollars films. In part, it is an exercise in the representation of the specific historical period of the American Civil War rather than a more general evocation of western landscape – again the increased budget was no doubt instrumental in making this a possibility. It is hardly interested at all in the histories of its characters, or actions that spring from or depend on pieties seen to be learned from another time. Rather, it is an account of behaviour based on a calculation of immediate gain – a caper movie. And where other comedy westerns refer back to the history of western production through the use of major stars, Leone plays with a smaller but related canvas, exploiting his audience's assumed knowledge of the earlier Dollars movies.

The film reveals itself as a comedy initially in oblique terms. It is of a piece with the group of comedy westerns that I have outlined in that the casting does not crudely signal it. Eastwood and Lee Van Cleef propose a continuation of the moods of the earlier films. The third leading actor is Eli Wallach, whose previous credits in westerns (*The Magnificent Seven*, *The Misfits*, *How the West Was Won*) are not comedies, although his film role immediately previous to this one had been in a caper movie, William Wyler's *How to Steal a Million*. Perhaps the only immediate hint is in Ennio Morricone's music; as it plays over the opening credits, it seems to have moments of overt parody of the earlier scores, but it is difficult for a non-musician to be sure of this, or to know how to express it.

The opening sequences of the film itself are not indicative of comedy. Leone appears to be repeating the strategy used in *For a Few Dollars More*, of giving each of his main players a sequence in which the role is established before any interaction takes place, formalising it here by moving through these sequences towards a freeze-frame in which the actor is given his sobriquet in a subtitle, the words appearing in Italian even apparently on the American prints. He begins with Tuco (Wallach) – *Il Brutto*, The Ugly – in a sequence which implies a condition of violence and a failed civilisation, a gunfight in a 'ghost town' western set, in which Tuco appears to kill all his pursuers. This is followed by the introduction of Angel Eyes (Lee Van Cleef) in another sequence terminating in a gunfight. This time, Leone appears to evoke the images and the pieties of *A Fistful of Dollars*. Angel Eyes is a paid assassin, who dispatches a nervous Mexican paterfamilias and his elder son in a way that invites us to see him as a violator of the rituals of the benign Mexican peasant world. The sequence has opened with a little boy drawing water from a well, and the father is killed by a shot delivered by Angel Eyes who is eating at the man's table. Immediately after this, we see Angel Eyes kill again, this time an old man who is suffocated and then shot to death through a pillow.

At this point, the subtitle *Il Cattivo* (The Bad) appears, leaving us to anticipate the actor who will be *Il Buono*. Leone cuts to a desert set in which Tuco is set upon by bounty hunters, shot from his horse in a way similar to the pre-credits sequence of *For a Few Dollars More*. Eastwood now appears, but his entrance is distinct from those in the earlier films in several ways. Most importantly, the first sign of his presence is not his body, either in the sense of a figure that these men see or one that is in front of the camera. His voice announces his presence, through an initial admonitory line, replying to something said to another: 'Yeah, but you don't look like the one who'll collect it [the reward money]'. I will return to the subject of the distinctiveness and the importance of Eastwood's voice – here it announces the threat that can be carried even by his disembodied presence and is actually expressed in that disembodiment, the strange fact that none of these men appear to see him until he speaks.

Eastwood is no longer identified through his costume with the idea of disguise, as in the earlier Dollars films. In *For a Few Dollars More*, Leone made this the subject of an irony, introducing the Stranger by showing him riding into town in his poncho in the pouring rain. Now Eastwood wears clothes more associated with the western gunslinger, the long coat of the rider across the plains, a costume Leone used again to striking effect in the opening sequence of his *Once Upon a Time in the West*. He is not at this point given his subtitled nickname, although an obvious cue exists for it – Leone apparently wants to tell us something else.

It may be now that the comedy starts very indirectly to declare itself, in Tuco's stream of inventive insult, as Blondy (Eastwood) ties him up and takes him into town to collect the bounty money. We next see Tuco mounted on a horse with a rope around his neck. At exactly the crucial moment, Blondy shoots through the rope, Tuco gallops off on the horse, and we see the two dividing up the reward money. It emerges that they are heading for another town to pull off the same stunt again.

It only becomes clear at this point that Blondy and Tuco are versions of the confidence trickster, a figure who can be traced back in American culture to Edgar Allan Poe's 1843 essay on *Diddling Considered as One of the Exact Sciences* and to the hero of Herman Melville's 1857 novel, *The Confidence Man*. As a couple, operating in a spirit of mutual, comedic mistrust, the type can equally be traced to the figures of the King and the Duke in Mark Twain's *The Adventures*

'Sorry, Shorty.' Tuco (Eli Wallach) captures Blondy (Eastwood) as he aims at the noose around his partner's neck in The Good, the Bad and the Ugly.

of Huckleberry Finn (1884), through the Bob Hope/Bing Crosby Road movies, which span the period 1940 to 1962. The joke, or potential for comedy, springs here from the degree of ironised recrimination, alongside a sublime self-confidence or self-reliance. Consider this moment of comic betrayal. Blondy is abandoning Tuco to probable death in the desert. As Tuco rages and vows revenge, Blondy shakes his head: 'such ingratitude, after all the times I've saved your life'. It is at this point, as if to confirm that the mode of comedy is finally firmly established and the nicknames are to be read in part as ironies, that the actor gets his subtitle of *Il Buono* – The Good.

To describe the film as an ironic comedy distances it from the Hope/Crosby movies and the majority of western comedies which play with the comedic inflection of star personas. It can be linked more closely with the satirical elements of the literature of the confidence trickster, with Melville's novel and the darker elements of Twain's work: the essentially hostile world in which death is omnipresent, often imminent and casually accepted as sooner or later inevitable. A scene in which Tuco captures Blondy as he is practising the same con-trick with another outlaw is an exemplary piece of business. We never see the outlaw, but we know he is about to hang. Blondy asks Tuco permission to shoot through the rope, and Tuco refuses. At that point the moment dissolves into a gag – Blondy apologises to his partner, who is now hanged: 'Sorry, Shorty'. The distance between the apology and the nature of what is happening is clearly the source of the comedy, but also an observation about its demonic tone. The film shares with *Measure for Measure* the fact that every male figure in its world is at some point under threat of death.

This mood is sustained through the first half of the film, in which Blondy and Tuco first con the townspeople and then turn on each other in scenes of betrayal and revenge. Each time the threat of death is lifted, it is by something both random and expressive of a more pervasive social violence. At the point when Tuco is trying to hang Blondy, a shell falls nearby and demolishes the building. Later, when Tuco is enjoying the spectacle of Blondy's death from exposure in the desert, the appearance of a shot-up Confederate Army stagecoach full of dead and dying men again diverts the action, and a plot twist gives Tuco a sudden reason to keep Blondy alive.

The plot twist is this. One of the dying soldiers is a thief who has buried a massive treasure in a graveyard – he tells Tuco the name of the graveyard, but Blondy the name on the grave. Tuco, with festivity and rapaciousness, is going about the routine business of robbing the dead, only to be diverted into a frenzy of greed and frustration as he realises that he has nearly gained the key to a fortune and now must try to revive the man he has recently been torturing to death. This is one of the most successfully sustained scenes of comedy in the film and firmly establishes Tuco in the line of comic villains whose gusto in the enactment of his own rascality can be allowed to redeem him. (There is a tradition for this in comedy that includes Falstaff in *The Merry Wives of Windsor* and Macheath in *The Beggar's Opera*.)

The second half, which is the caper movie, begins with this plot twist. A caper movie may be defined as one in which a group of characters make their way to (and sometimes from) the site of riches which they may or may not succeed in stealing. One essential element of the type is that while the thieves obviously have no legitimate claim on the loot, its actual ownership – by a museum, a bank, a discredited regime – is not defended in the film and no individual is necessarily the loser by the theft. Another element is the importance of comic contrasts found within its group of villains, and Leone makes obvious use of the different qualities (both physical and in the mannerisms of their characters) of Eastwood and Wallach. There is some evidence that this was a plausible commercial angle – Leone could not have been unaware of a recent United Artists release, Jules Dassin's *Topkapi*, a jewels-in-museum caper which had won Peter Ustinov an Academy Award for Best Supporting Actor in 1964.

In this half, the American Civil War is important as background to the caper movie. Earlier, it had figured only as a convenient plot-device to save Blondy, and as a provider of local colour – a minor part is given to a Confederate soldier who is a double amputee, but nothing hangs on his military status. Now Tuco's and Blondy's journey to find the stolen money takes them into a context where the war is omnipresent. Tuco takes Blondy to recuperate in a monastery full of Confederate wounded – on leaving it they are almost immediately captured by Union troops.

Leone's presentation of the Civil War must be considered in the light of its date. The film was completed in 1967 and released in America late in 1968, when reactions to the Vietnam war would have affected anyone making – or viewing – movies in Europe or America. Leone's position partakes of both liberal protest and anti-war satire. There is a consistent commitment to the view that the two sides cannot be distinguished and that only a pragmatic choice governs allegiance to one or the other. This is first hinted at in the image of the Union officer brushing his uniform, revealing the dark blue underneath the dust that has caused Tuco to mistake him for a Confederate. The point is carried through to the final major action sequence, the defence of Langstone Bridge, where it is clear that the two armies are exactly, pointlessly balanced, able to inflict death on each other but otherwise identical.

There is also the sense of an interrogation of the images of 'official' war history. We see a figure engaged in wet plate photography of a group of officers, but also the images that the still camera could not record – the anecdote of a thief executed by firing squad and bundled quickly into his coffin. Officers are given the role of liberal protest against the war; the type represented by the commander of the prison camp who protests to Angel Eyes about the corruption and maltreatment of the prisoners reappears, shifted a little further towards 'sixties anti-war satire, in the drunk commander of the forces at the bridge, who denounces the waste and loss of warfare. In both cases, Leone gives this clarity of vision to men who will not survive the war – the camp commander is dying of gangrene, and the commander at the bridge is wounded and dies in the course of the sequence.

Does the war have anything to do with the caper plot, or does it function only as a visual pleasure, the kind of 'exotic' background that often seems appropriate to caper movies? The only point when the war is experienced by Blondy and Tuco other than as an extension of the condition of omnipresent violence which licenses their actions is in the bridge sequence. Prompted by the commander's ironic instructions, the couple wire the bridge with explosives and blow it. Their apparent motive is to cause the troops to go elsewhere so they can cross the river, but it is implied that Blondy at least wishes to prevent more loss of life on both sides. Earlier, watching the fighting, he has said 'I've never seen so many men wasted so badly.'

This impulse, which cannot save life but expresses a disgust at the pointless loss of it, is underscored in a scene which immediately follows the destruction of the bridge, and which is Leone's final invocation of the war. After crossing the river, the two men briefly separate, and Blondy, in a burnt-out building, a set which is possibly chapel-like, finds a dying young soldier. He offers the man his cigar, a gesture which has been firmly established earlier in the film as its trope of human contact, the only appetite Blondy can share. (It is an idea that will reappear in *Coogan's Bluff*.) The soldier dies, and Blondy shrouds the body in his coat, picking up an alternative lying nearby. Leone's camera, and the triumphant motif in the score, only offer hints as to exactly what this is, but we are prepared for the moment when we see Blondy later, dressed in the poncho of the previous two films. The act of humanity, the only 'good' gesture to an innocent party in the entire film, is associated with the return of the persona of the earlier movies, and the resonance in 1968 of the pathos of death of a young American in wartime was obviously considerable. The poncho functions now not as a disguise, but as a revelation, that this character is essentially the same figure that the audience has seen in the earlier Dollars movies.

Moments later, the film reaches its final setting, a huge circular military

Leone's Civil War: Blondy and Tuco in the battle zone.

graveyard. The strange sterility of this set and the mood of hysteria induced both in the score and in Leone's camerawork, as Tuco runs in circles through the graves looking for the name that Blondy has given him, makes the scene feel like a blackly ironic version of a caper, the goal of the quest turning into a *tour abolie*, a hoax or an absence.

It is at this point that the terms of the presence of the Eastwood persona are reprised. In a sequence which recalls his first appearance in this film, Blondy appears at the graveside, at first in the form of a shadow; then a spade is flung down in front of Tuco with the admonitory line, 'It'll be a lot easier with that.'

Only when Tuco looks up does Leone show us the icon directly – the star in his uniform, the 'trademark' of the poncho.

That this humane figure must now defeat the force of evil in the film is a conventional requirement. Angel Eyes now arrives, identified through the matched form of his appearance as Blondy's evil double. He throws down a second spade in front of the two men, and a gunfight ensues. This is a strange moment, since it clearly meets a generic imperative, but has a quite different relationship to the plot of the film from that of the previous two Dollars movies. In both those cases, the protagonist/antagonist couple of the fight was clearly identified through the narratives, which also explained the Stranger's role as non-combatant witness of the fight in *For a Few Dollars More*. Here it makes sense only as the fulfilment of a generic imperative, in that there is little connection between Angel Eyes and Blondy, no motivation from revenge or justice, no sense that Blondy is even aware of the acts that define Angel Eyes as 'the Bad' in the opening of the film, any more than Angel Eyes is aware of the humane moment with the soldier which is its obverse at the film's end. Some sense can be made of this only by the audience who have seen these moments and the earlier Dollars films – Leone even quotes the musical chimes of the watches from the previous film in the score here.

After Angel Eyes is shot dead and the money recovered, the film faces the question of what to do with Tuco. After all, he is a rascal, who is guilty of every sort of crime (we have heard the lists read out earlier), and Blondy is the good, the moral agent of this comedy. So Tuco looks up from the grave to find that Blondy has rigged up a noose. In Gay's *The Beggar's Opera* (1728), a play which shares with this film a perception of an unreformably corrupt and venal world, the ending, in which the highwayman Macheath is about to be hanged, becomes a moment for the contemplation of the requirements and expectations of this particular kind of comedy. The action pauses as the Beggar, the author of the play, discusses its outcome with the Player. The Beggar is for hanging Macheath in the name of 'strict poetical justice' until he is reminded by the player that 'the catastrophe is manifestly wrong, for an opera must end happily', and Macheath is duly reprieved.

Of course there is no such discussion in Leone's film, but the same imperatives operate in it. Blondy leaves Tuco hanging, his feet on an increasingly wobbly cross as he shouts imprecations at his retreating partner. At the very last moment Blondy shoots through the rope, and Tuco is reprieved, his cries of revenge absorbed into the closing notes of Morricone's score. Like Gay's, Leone's world is too satirically conceived for the punishment of its festive villain to be appropriate – there is no suggestion that the world would have been perceptibly affected for good or ill by Tuco's death.

How can we sum up what it is that Eastwood takes forward from the Dollars movies to his American feature films? We know two things about him. One is that he is an American. As an Italian director's visions of different Americas – an America in the mind, an America in decline, an America at war – the films use the combination of American star and European vision continually to keep in play the issue of what the United States is and what being an American means.

Then there is the question of the kind of American that Eastwood plays. His role is not that of leadership, nor is it informed by the vision of a future, of land

Comic gusto: Blondy prepares to hang Tuco in the graveyard.

or a woman, that is vouchsafed to the pioneer. His relationship to power is significant; he is a marginal figure, someone passed over, without a past or a future involving possessions or place. He is at a remove from the social world in which identity can be conferred, however ambiguously, by someone else. The albeit ironic possibilities contained in becoming, say, *The Man Who Shot Liberty Valance* are negated here in the phrase which has come to be used to cover Eastwood's parts in all three films – The Man with No Name.

His skill as a gunfighter does not reform this civilisation – rather it is exercised in the knowledge that the world around him may possibly be descending into chaos or decay. His commitment is only to himself, to a conception that he has of himself, to a limited idea of justice that finally might have to acknowledge that a wider understanding of the concept has to depend on some other kind of energy within the society, not on men like himself, and that this kind of justice – call it Law – is nowhere to be found. The attenuation of Leone's visions of America – including the America of the first film, which exists only inside the stranger's head – is central. It is related to the stylistic motif I have already mentioned, the emphasis in the photography, at moments of tension or climax, of close-ups of faces or eyes. The point is about the irrelevance of the social – the world exists only as an inhospitable landscape or as consciousness, a set of visions existing behind the eyes framed in such a shot. The constructed world, the world in which any kind of civilisation – or even just an alien, rowdy vitality – might be signalled, becomes either absent or indifferent.

Women are both centrally important to this vision and very largely physically absent from it. Women are the linchpins of the plots of the first two movies but their importance is massively more to do with what these men think about them than anything that they themselves can do or be. Their importance in the third film is that a part of the demonic quality of the comedy depends on its being set in a world from which women are virtually totally absent.

Is there the possibility of change in this world? Not for the Stranger. In *For a Few Dollars More*, the moment in which Mortimer kills Indio is the unique 'event of difference', in Cavell's phrase, which satisfies the expectations of classical narrative – there is only one man in the world who has raped his sister. For the Eastwood figure, Ramon Roho and Angel Eyes do not have this function, having no possibility of unique connection with a man who has no significant relation to them in the past. They are only 'the Bad', and there will always be more of them; they exist not as individuals, but as a condition. In a much later film, Eastwood's character will express something similar, saying in response to a question about what it is that brings the crazies out, 'They are always out.' Hence his triumph in the film is expressed not by changing, but by being unalterable, and the repetitions – of lines, of costumes – insist on this.

But this is not a uniformly dark vision. If the Stranger cannot redeem the world, he does not for certain know that it is doomed, and his self-reliance is seen to be a form of positive energy and a source of comedy. This is Poe's definition of the confidence man in the essay that I mentioned earlier: '. . . a compound, of which the ingredients are minuteness, interest, perseverance, ingenuity, audacity, nonchalance, originality, impertinence, and grin.'

This does not seem too far from the positive qualities that Eastwood's persona carries forward, qualities for survival within a starkly imagined America.

34

CHAPTER TWO
THE CALLAHAN FILMS

There are nine movies up to *The Dead Pool* (1988) in which Clint Eastwood plays a law enforcement officer. In five, he plays the same role, Inspector Harry Callahan: *Dirty Harry, Magnum Force, The Enforcer, Sudden Impact* and *The Dead Pool*. To identify what, apart from Eastwood's role, these films have in common, and what their project is, I will attempt a general description that fits, with some small exceptions, the first three films in the cycle and the first half of *Sudden Impact*.

We might start here where several of them start, as do many films of this type – in the air, hovering over the city, which is San Francisco. The aerial shots do not just announce that these are films set in an urban world. The city we see is huge, so huge that it can be viewed more or less whole only from the air, and from this perspective it is impossible to interpret detail. What we see is a landscape of towers and canyons with hardly any comprehensible relation to individual human activity, and this is confirmed in what these films show us on the ground. There is little or no sense of a city in which different zones represent different styles of living or economic or racial groupings – and little sense of it as a place where money is made. What we are shown consists mainly of sites dedicated to the satisfaction of different needs: the diner, the liquor and drug stores, the bars and massage parlours. There is no sense of specific architecture or date – if this city has an 'old' quarter, it is never emphasised visually, and its monsters are not gothic in that they do not spring from any connection to the past. Time is important only for the distinction between the daylight hours and the dark, and the different appetites that can be satisfied at different hours. The image of the domestic in any direct form is absent. The figures who might be particularly associated with homes – children, old people – are almost entirely absent except as victims, and none of the action dealing with them is given a domestic setting. Even the apartments of those who live alone are rarely seen and are then presented as relatively anonymous spaces.

The Harry Callahan movies also share obvious narrative elements. They begin with an exposition of the difficulty that is being experienced by the city authorities in bringing wrongdoers to justice. In *Dirty Harry* an anonymous assassin is holding the city to ransom; in *Magnum Force* the trial of a mob boss collapses; in *Sudden Impact* a judge declares the evidence against some young hoodlums to be inadmissible. The settings for these scenes are places where we might expect the power of law to be felt: the Mayor's office, the steps of the courthouse building, a courtroom itself. In the next scene, we see Callahan fulfilling a need that seems to substitute for the absent domestic world in these films – he goes to a lunch counter. But in this public place, he is interrupted by a criminal act, a situation which he does not create but which develops around him. In the resulting shoot-out, he kills or disarms the hoodlums. In no case is the incident directly connected to the main plot of the film, but rather serves to establish a contrast between the problems of law enforcement to which the main narrative is addressed, and the simplicities and satisfactions of the gunfight in which the participants face each other over a few feet of space, where the result depends purely on the qualities of the gunman – calmness, skill with the weapon.

The subject of the major plot is always to bring a law-breaking element, either a single figure or a small group, to the point where he or they can be confronted and destroyed by Callahan. Two points seem essential here. One is that the central figure is always a killer and, more specifically, seen to be a killer of women as well as men. The other – familiar from many cop narratives – is that the figure cannot be destroyed in the populated centre of the city, but will die, either alone or as the last of the small group, in a landscape on the edge of it, emptied of other people. In the four central films, these locales are a cement mill in *Dirty Harry* (it is never specifically identified, but I think this is what it is), a deserted tanker in *Magnum Force*, the abandoned prison of Alcatraz in *The Enforcer* and a funfair, empty because it is night, in *Sudden Impact*.

I suppose there to be some reason for this over and above the obvious excitement to be found in a chase sequence around a complex and spectacular set. One way of understanding it is to relate it back to the openings of the films, to see a movement from the impersonal public spaces at the centre of the city to spaces not just impersonal but actively inimical to human presence, sites associated with dangerous heavy industrial processes in the first two films, and with heavy plant abandoned or shut down in the latter two. This movement is part of a larger shape in the films, the shift from the public to the private, from a role played out for an audience of grateful onlookers in the diner shootings to an insistence on the final killing as an act suggestive of a kind of privacy or intimacy. We might also say that the final act takes place in a context apparently profoundly opposite to the natural, to the setting of the 'green world' outside the city towards which the resolution of comedy traditionally moves. This 'sterile space' is perhaps related to nature tangentially by the presence of water – the space on the edge of the city is the waterfront in each case, and, in two, the film ends with the killer dead in the water.

All four films end in long shot, the credits rolling as the image becomes a view of the whole landscape. The destruction of the killer is located in surroundings of complete devastation, in which only Callahan remains. The first three films in the cycle all take the position that the killer may be dead, but the wider corruption is unreformable. In *Dirty Harry*, the water receives not only the body of the killer but also Callahan's police inspector's star. In both *Magnum Force* and *The Enforcer*, the whole police organisation has been exposed as weak or corrupt, and while there are notional differences (in the former Callahan's corrupt superior dies, in the latter the feeble mayor is saved), they are less significant than the effectively identical landscapes, strewn with debris and scarred by fire, that are presented to the viewer. In the first two films Callahan walks away, but the narrative offers no indication of where he might be going. In *The Enforcer*, he is left standing over the dead body of his partner. Only in *Sudden Impact*, the fourth film of the Callahan cycle, is there finally a movement away from this pattern – I will look at it in detail later.

It is important to consider what is implied by these endings. A related kind of narrative might argue that there is clearly a benign world, a world of pleasures and ambitions which are felt to have value, but that this world cannot be saved or protected by the enforcement of law. This is not the argument here, and neither is it the case that such a world is established, then challenged in the film and exposed as some kind of sham, as not worth saving. Rather, the films take the position of describing a condition in which more positive values become almost unthinkable. Thus, the enforcement of law approaches a situation cut off from purpose or logic, inexplicable because it is not underpinned by ideas of the civilised or of the future. I say approaches because the existence of another world, however far it may recede, never quite vanishes – the films all display the traces of what another life might be like, or might have been like, inflected differently in each case.

Is it paradoxical to say, in the light of this, that these films are certainly about pleasure? They clearly allude to the pleasure of killing. We are repeatedly told explicitly that the distinguishing characteristic of the central villain is that he actively enjoys the business of murder. Where the film is structured around a single killer (*Dirty Harry*, *Tightrope*), this insight is given to the Eastwood figure. Where the central murderer is part of a gang, the speaker is usually a forensic technician (*Magnum Force*, *The Enforcer*).

A dominant image of the city in the films is as a system dedicated to the provision of pleasure, and specifically sexual pleasure for men. The acts of the murderers can be read as the products of this culture rather than protests against it. It is for this reason that all the major villains are seen to kill women, and in no case is the death of the woman offered as clearly deserved. When men in the Callahan films kill men, this can be motivated by something other than pleasure. At one extreme, the shooting of a pimp whom we have just seen gruesomely poison a woman in *Magnum Force* is clearly offered as rough justice. The other end of the scale is marked by the deaths of the policemen or security guards who are killed in action, doing the job that they are paid for – this is not justice, but we can understand it as the product of an acknowledged risk. But the deaths of the women in the films, very strongly associated with their actual or near nudity in many cases, is shown simultaneously as a punishment for the pleasure of others and as a pleasure in itself for the killer. It is in this area that the divide between Callahan and those he pursues is located, and it is a central issue in the cycle. What is at stake here is the relationships that these different men might possibly have with women, or perhaps the proposition that having different relationships to women makes them different men. So, of course, the films must ask what relationships between men and women remain possible in the contemporary context that is addressed.

The contemporary is also raised in another way. In several of the films, there is a point at which Callahan is called something implying that he is the last fragment of a lost past – 'about to become extinct' (*Magnum Force*), a 'Neanderthal' (*The Enforcer*), a 'dinosaur', an 'endangered species' (*Sudden Impact*). The superficial meaning here, that his methods or skills are not appropriate to the contemporary world, carries with it another question, that to be thus described is to be a monster, a creature so out of step with the everyday as to have no place in it. I will return to this subject in due course.

These general observations tell only a small part of a tale. The detail of the films tells more, particularly of how the possibilities of the material are explored through variations related in part to the changing historical and political background to their production. This brings me to looking at a – necessarily limited – range of moments in the films.

Dirty Harry

In the credits sequence of *Dirty Harry*, we see an anonymous gunman, staked out on a rooftop, use a rifle with a telescopic sight to kill a woman who is alone in a swimming pool situated on the top of another tall building. The killing is nominally a matter of extortion, and we see Callahan find a note demanding money from the city with the threat of further killings. This premise, that a killer is stalking random victims as a way of holding the city to ransom, addresses both anxieties and areas of reassurance for us. Don Siegel cuts to the Mayor's office and a discussion between Callahan, the Mayor (John Vernon), the Police Chief (John Larch) and Captain Bressler (Harry Guardino). Their anxieties here are about motive – that the killer's victims are innocent citizens – and about technology: the difficulty of locating a killer who does not have to approach his victims in order to destroy them. There is also the problem of the scale of the city, the difficulty of tracking a single sniper from the air in a landscape of tall buildings.

Against all this is posed the reassuring category of the psychopath. While it is perfectly possible that random killings might have been coolly conceived as a means of extracting money from a city administration, this killer is constructed as a psychopath first and a blackmailer only incidentally. The visual representation of this is the extortion note, now projected on a screen in the Mayor's office, which explains the sniper through comfortable categories. He is poorly educated (the note has a number of deletions) and racist (the note refers to killing a 'nigger' next). The Mayor confirms the judgement, telling Callahan that there is 'a madman loose'. To define the problem this way is to situate it as a technical problem, subject to solution via known methods of analysis. The Chief of Police will later explain it: 'You see, these sick guys have behaviour patterns.'

This placing of the sniper is extended by the comic exchange with which the scene ends. It is an anecdote about establishing criminal intent. The Mayor, nervous of Callahan's methods, asks him how he had known a particular suspect in an earlier case intended rape. This is the reply:

Callahan [*at the door*]: When a naked man is chasing a woman through an alley with a butcher knife and a hard-on, I figure he isn't out collecting for the Red Cross [*exits*].
Mayor: 'I think he has a point'.

The important issue here is the violence against women. The guarantee of Callahan's action rests on his standing against the combination of violence and sexual excitement – the butcher knife and the hard-on. His attitude to the killer, particularly in the second half of the film, will be legitimated in these terms.

This scene is followed by the gunfight at the diner, where Callahan acts alone to foil a bank robbery, the action hero at his most effective but caught inside the circuits of ordinary domestic activity, as if such activity is – as of course it is – inevitable. A series of scenes now serves to emphasise this – Callahan is a man foiling a bank robbery while still chewing the last mouthful of a sandwich, saving his $29.50 trousers from the scissors while having his wounds dressed, arguing with Bressler about haircuts while discussing police business back at the station.

What is wanted is a context in which the man of action can place his need to eat, to grumble about money and time – we might say, to be sustained in his belief that a man who has killed others is not necessarily a monster. Such a context might be provided through an actual marriage or a stable relationship to a woman, but Callahan has already used the word 'nobody' in reply to the Mayor's interrogative 'Wife, sweetheart?' in the earlier scene. Bressler now says to him, 'You need a partner,' and he is introduced to Chico Gonzales (Reni Santoni) in Bressler's office.

To locate the difference between a wife and a partner in these narratives we might say that a wife, unless drawn into the plot by the actions of the villains, waits at home to hear whether or not her husband has been shot. She can neither defend him, nor is she at risk herself. A partner introduces new aspects of risk and of protection – both parties are liable to be shot, and both can save the other's life or fail to save it. Thus there is always the danger that the presence of a partner might simply confirm the business of policing as deadly, and this is Callahan's history. He reminds Bressler, 'You know what happened to the guys that I've worked with. Dietrich's still in the hospital with a bullet in his gut and Fanducci's dead.' When Chico queries this, Callahan replies as a tough guy: 'So if I need a partner, I'll get me someone who knows what the hell he's doing.' But the authorities insist on the pairing with Chico, and, like so many narratives constructed around a pair of antagonistic figures forced into proximity, this hints at a comedy of education, a matter of learning through the other to understand something about yourself. The ways in which Chico is thought by his new partner to be unsuited for his role – he is young, college-educated, and Mexican – imply a process for Callahan of re-learning what qualities are needed to do his job, and where those qualities might be found.

A great deal of the central section of *Dirty Harry* is set at night, and until the final confrontation, all the significant scenes with the killer and Harry take place in the dark. Part of the point here is that the city which the film is interested in, the city in darkness, is immediately suggestive of sexual pleasure, both legitimate and illegitimate. As Harry and Chico cruise the streets on night patrol, Siegel shows us a familiar scenario in which the role of the cops is to contemplate the sleaze. But he extends this to look at Harry's reaction to more acceptable forms of sexual pleasure. This begins as comedy, when a wrong guess about the contents of a suitcase causes Harry to be taken for a Peeping Tom and beaten by a group of outraged citizens. He is rescued by Chico, and Siegel includes a little bit of business here to underline the double entendre made in the film's title.

This leads to a related incident the following night. Chico and Harry are staked out on a rooftop waiting for the killer to appear on the roof of another building, when Harry's concentration wavers. His gaze through the binoculars moves across the uncurtained windows of the building, picks out a middle-aged couple arguing, then pauses on a lighted stage, an empty room. A girl in a bikini walks across it, disappears, and returns a moment later entirely nude. We then see her open her door to admit a couple, whose clothes suggest alternative/hippie

culture. Harry watches as the nude girl shakes hands with the visitor, a moment of comically grave propriety in the circumstances. Harry's response to this little silent comedy is not censorious; he addresses himself: 'You owe it to yourself to live a little, Harry' – a rueful acknowledgement of a lack without any strategy for action. But the point is to establish Harry as a man who wants to 'live a little', rather than a figure opposed to all forms of sexual pleasure.

The killer's second victim – a black child, again shot from a roof — underlines the sense of a psychopath preying on the defenceless. The third victim is introduced through a scene in which we see Bressler looking at a series of snapshots of a young girl. The snapshots are obviously amateur shots supplied by the girl's family. Images of a mundane domestic felicity, they are signs of what has been destroyed, confirmed by contents of the box sent to the mayor – the girl's bra, a hank of hair, a tooth. We are never to learn whether Harry is right when he says to Bressler, 'You know she's dead already, don't you.' But a course of action has to be pursued, posited on the possibility that the girl might still be saved. That Harry follows this through even though he believes the girl to be in all probability dead is part of the darkness of the film at this point, a black variation of the 'Kill me and you'll never know my secret' plot used for comedy in *The Good, the Bad and the Ugly*.

The defence of the family – implicitly of the daughters in many a citizen's book of family snapshots – is shown as increasingly desperate. When Harry goes

Opposite: 'You owe it to yourself to live a little' – Inspector 'Dirty' Harry Callahan (Eastwood) and his binoculars. Below: defending the family – watched by Bressler (Harry Guardino), Callahan tapes the knife to his leg in Dirty Harry.

Absolute loss: the body of Ann Mary Deacon is recovered in Dirty Harry.

late at night to Bressler's office to pick up the money which will supposedly ransom the girl, Ann Mary Deacon, he asks Bressler for sticky tape so he can attach a knife to his leg. In the frame, we see the blade across the image of Bressler's face, as he sits at the desk next to a framed photograph, apparently of his own daughters. Watching Harry, Bressler says, 'You know, it's disgusting that a police officer should know how to use a weapon like that.'

The matter does not end triumphantly, but moves towards a world in which the innocent cannot be saved and the guilty go unpunished. Although Harry is able to inflict a knife wound which will result in tracking down the killer, the girl is dead, at least by the point at which the police can reach her. The moment of dawn, as the nude body of the girl is pulled out of the hole in which the killer had placed her – it appears to be a drain or something similar – is a moment of complete loss, one of the bleakest in the whole cycle. It is followed by a further irony, that running roughshod over procedure in the rush to get to the girl has resulted in the evidence being inadmissible and the killer going free. The scene in which this is argued makes the anxiety about the inability to defend the family even more explicit. On the District Attorney's desk is another photograph of children, snapshots stuffed into its corners. He tells Callahan, 'I've got a wife and three kids. I don't want him on the streets any more than you do.'

The effect of this on Harry is clear in his conversation with Chico's wife; he acknowledges the rightness of Chico's quitting the police force, and seems to admit that his past, represented by the accidental death of his own wife – 'there was no reason for it, really' – makes no sense. Nor does his present; when she asks him why he continues to do the job he replies, 'I don't know. I really don't.'

Against this, there remains the comforting fact that the psychopath is constructed by the film as compulsive, that he will finally be destroyed by the hero exactly because he cannot quit. We can read his final act of terrorism – he commandeers a school bus and takes the driver and children hostage – as an act of irrational exposure, of rendering himself liable to attack rather than using the size of the city to conceal himself. Siegel's final confrontation scene turns, as will several other similar moments in the cycle, on a repetition. What is repeated is the speech made to a hood as he lies wounded and contemplating whether or not to reach for his gun one more time. We are taken back to the moment at the end of the diner shoot out, in which Harry wonders out loud whether he has fired six shots or only five – the speech which ends with the line about feeling lucky: 'Well, do you – punk?' Earlier, the punk had backed down – this punk feels lucky and goes for his gun, and Harry kills him. The force of this moment seems to be the reassurance that this killer is no staggering monster but just another lawbreaker, and at the same time that the magic works, that in the case of a murderer – as opposed to the bank robber earlier, when Callahan's gun was in fact empty – there will always be one last bullet in the chamber.

Is it also a way for the hero to assert that he is the same figure as when he gave this speech earlier. The decision to go after the killer for this last time has marked a complete break with police and the Mayor's orders, and Harry's throwing of his inspector's star into the water after the killer's death acknowledges this. The point of the speech inviting the punk to try his luck was always that it was quite outside police procedure, a way of converting self reliance into a mode of behaviour, of saying that he has the conviction that luck is on his side. The reassurance is that Harry can still make the speech – the anxiety is that rather than standing within the society which the killer has attacked, he remains on the fringes of it, or rather of what can be imagined of it.

Irrational exposure: Scorpio (Andy Robinson) commandeers a bus in Dirty Harry.

Magnum Force

Dirty Harry was released the year before the major withdrawal of American ground troops from Vietnam. In taking as its subject the enemy who is known but cannot be seen, the difficulty of dealing with a sniper who moves across a landscape that can be policed only inefficiently by helicopter, it addresses an anxiety loosely related to the problems of the war. Two years later, the premise around which the second film in the cycle is built obviously follows changes in the preoccupations of its American public. Previously the figures senior to Callahan – the Mayor, the police chief – are identified as hesitant but not corrupt. In the early months of 1973, after the withdrawal of American ground troops from Vietnam, the Watergate scandal was beginning to break, with the convictions of the original burglars and the Senate vote for an investigation in the January and February respectively. The script for *Magnum Force*, by John Milius and Michael Cimino, reflects this in locating the corruption firmly inside an organisation – Callahan is an honest cop in a corrupt force. The reasons for the failure of law enforcement are no longer to do only with the properties of the city as landscape, but of the city as bureaucracy, incapable of engaging successfully with organised crime. The dispensers of 'justice' here, vigilantes engaged in systematically shooting the crime bosses, are a group of young motor-cycle cops led by a bureaucrat, Lt Briggs (Hal Holbrook).

The contrast between *Dirty Harry* and *Magnum Force* can be registered by looking at the sequences in which people die. One such scene in *Magnum Force* takes place in a penthouse apartment. We see a young couple lying on a bed, evidently taking cocaine. They are both nude. The girl teases a third figure, an older man in a dressing gown: the crime Boss. He treats the couple with contempt, but joins the girl on the bed. Meanwhile a figure in the uniform of a motor-cycle cop, his face obscured by the helmet, enters the building and kills the guard outside the apartment. He bursts in and shoots both men. We now see the girl from the waist up from his point of view. He shoots her several times, and the impact sends her naked body through the window, and she falls from penthouse height to street level. The reward of such a scene is in our anticipation, our awareness of the dramatic irony that while these figures are being casually vicious, they are actually about to die at a time and place not of their choosing. That the place seems to be so often a bedroom or pool or other occasion of female nudity works in several ways. One element of it is the familiar idea that any mobster might be unarmed and vulnerable when with a woman. Another is that the specific relationships to women that we are shown are themselves suspect – part of the corruption that is being punished. Finally, the use of women in these scenes is part of the spectacle offered to the audience, but possibly also part of the critique of the killers, in that while the guilt of the gangsters is assumed, the role of their women is never so clear.

This configuration, of moments of anticipation followed by the violent death of the corrupt, is repeated a sufficient number of times in *Magnum Force* that we might call it the central effect. In contrast, the opening shot of *Dirty Harry* is the only occasion when we anticipate a mortal threat of which the subject is unaware, and there the point is the pathos of a helpless – and in that case clearly innocent – victim. The body of the second victim in *Dirty Harry* is never shown, and we glimpse the corpse of Ann Mary Deacon only briefly. In *Dirty*

Harry, the vision of death is a matter of horror, as we see when Chico is literally sickened by the sight of the dead child. After the first killings in *Magnum Force*, we see the same subject treated as comedy in Callahan's new partner's loss of appetite in the diner scene.

For much of its length, *Magnum Force* operates as a relatively straightforward and in parts obnoxious thriller, showing us the killings by a masked figure and asking us to guess his identity while participating in the spectacle of the execution of the 'guilty'. Within this structure, it takes up a number of the subjects of the earlier film, but its attitude to them is almost uniformly deeply pessimistic.

An example is its idea of the domestic world. We have seen how in *Dirty Harry* this expresses what Callahan wants of the world, or would like to want. In *Magnum Force*, this world becomes more substantial – we actually enter a home – but more negative. As in the earlier film, a form of access to it is through other cops close to Callahan and their wives. The main figure here is Charlie McCoy (Mitch Ryan), a figure obviously parallel to Callahan. We are told that they are both ex-marines, and it is implied that they are around the same age. We learn that McCoy has a wife and children, but is separated from them, and it is clear in his only scene with Callahan that McCoy is cracking up. Partly this serves a plot function, to offer us a plausible candidate for the masked assassin, but it also constructs the family as negative, a further pressure rather than a refuge. This is confirmed when we see Callahan at dinner with McCoy's wife Carol (Christine White) and her children. The focus of the scene is on the conflict between the wife's desire and family life – her attempt to initiate a seduction of Callahan is blocked by the presence of the children. Her line to him at this point – 'With all these kids, do you think I'll ever get laid?' – dovetails with a call from the station for Callahan. Eastwood's performance here presents Callahan as emotionally frozen, wanting to be responsive but relaxed only for a moment with the youngest child. The effect is to present both parties as trapped in their roles, as mother, as cop, both on duty – unable to effect a mutual seduction that might have been what one or both of them wanted.

Later in *Magnum Force*, Callahan does appear to have a 'young lady friend' (the term is his) but this tends rather to confirm the gloom of the film. The manner of their first encounter (she says: 'What does a girl have to do to go to bed with you?' and he replies 'Try knocking on the door') seems to imply that a sexual relationship is most possible when it has least context, when the only thing at stake is desire. The affair is never more than gestural, an encounter taking place, significantly, in the dark, in the apartment which contains the unexplained photograph of Callahan and a woman – implicitly the real, lost, relationship. The girl's only other function in the film is to be the woman saved by Callahan (from the bomb planted by the corrupt cops in his mail box). If there is an echo here, it comes from the casting of Adele Yoshioka as the girl and is of the American soldier finding solace with the Vietnamese bar girl, a configuration that is often eloquently expressive of a sense of loneliness and distance from a domestic America.

Callahan also has a partner, this time a black figure, Early Smith (Felton Perry). Very sketchily, the same issues are raised through this figure as in *Dirty Harry*: the idea of the partner as a route to some acceptable form of the domestic. But Callahan refuses Early's invitation to his home. We glimpse Early's wife only

A figure of death? Callahan in shades in Magnum Force.

in one sequence – in the police shooting tournament, the moment when Callahan mistakenly shoots a 'policeman' target is followed by a shot of her looking at her husband, as if realising that as Callahan's partner he, too, is at risk, and he does indeed die before the end of the film.

All these subjects, the domestic world and sexual relationships, the figures of McCoy and Early, can be read as feeding into one question, initiated in *Dirty Harry* but much more pressing here. We might say that it is announced in the credit sequence of *Magnum Force*, which has Callahan speaking a version of his 'Do you feel lucky?' speech from the previous movie, but this time directly at the audience that is at the other end of his gun barrel. The question is – is this man in fact a monster, a figure of death?

This question is confronted in two ways in the first scene in which Callahan appears. One is in the narrative – Callahan tells Early that a group of cops are 'probably giving odds on how long you'll stay alive, being my partner'. The other way is via a visual image. This is a film in which the bringer of death has

– traditionally enough – no face, the eyes of the various motorcycle cops being concealed behind a sun visor or shades. Eastwood's appearance as Callahan in the movie is shaped by the scenes in which he appears with his eyes concealed and those in which his face is bare. His first appearance, at the scene of the multiple murder of a gang boss and his hoods, is played entirely in shades, and he wears them periodically in the first half of the film. The pivotal point is after the death of McCoy, who is shot by one of the corrupt young cops, Davis (David Soul). The body is taken to the airport, and Davis and Callahan, both with eyes concealed behind sunglasses, stand with Carol McCoy on the tarmac. The fare-well reminds us of Callahan's emotional impassivity, his inability to respond to Carol earlier. Now she leaves, and the two men stand for a moment in conver-sation side by side, neither looking at the other. This scene is the last time we see Callahan conceal his face. When he is confronted later by the visored cops in a basement garage, he appears barefaced and refuses to join them.

The importance of this might be to recognise that, in a world as deranged as the world of this film, Callahan's appearance, our image of him, is almost the only possible thing that can be changed. No reassurance can be summoned from a plot in which the figures Eastwood has to kill are not hoods but policemen, and

The corrupt patrolman: Callahan looks at Davis (David Soul) in Magnum Force.

also young men. Another reference to the shock of Vietnam is the implication in the film that covert operations on the fringes of the main military engagement may produce alienated veterans – the cadre of sharpshooters has met in the ambiguously named 'special forces'. In making a distinction between members of such a force and the ex-Marines (Callahan, McCoy), the film is subscribing to an important myth of the post-Vietnam period, of war experience as potentially both good and bad depending which war, or which part of the same war, an individual has experienced.

The Enforcer

The difference that I have outlined between the world of *Dirty Harry* and that of *Magnum Force* can be located more precisely if we look at the two obviously analogous scenes in which Callahan is interrupted by crime. In *Dirty Harry*, this happens in a mid-town burger bar opposite a bank. The hoods holding up the bank are not taking hostages or terrorising women. Is bank robbery possibly an agreeable form of crime, potentially a setting for comedy? Certainly the bank job, with its roots in the western, has the nature of an American tradition, as we see in *Thunderbolt and Lightfoot*. Callahan's line here may be an acknowledgement of this: 'Now, if they'll [the robbers] just wait for the cavalry to arrive.'

Opposite: a deranged world – Lt Briggs (Hal Holbrook) at the end of Magnum Force. *Below: a double act – Callahan and his partner DiGeorgio (John Mitchum) in* The Enforcer.

The viciousness of the world of *Magnum Force* is marked in the shift from this to an airport lunch-counter and a crime of particular modernity, the hijacking of an airliner by terrorists. The bank robbery is replaced by the fearsome image of hundreds of people caught up in the political brutalities of the modern world and finding themselves hostage to a technology capable of delivering them to a horrible death. The impersonality of a massive technology is followed through in the scene's treatment of the terrorists as just targets to be wordlessly destroyed by the hero. The verbal double act of cop and hood, which governs the end of the first gunfight in *Dirty Harry* – the hood whispers a request, he has to know if Harry's gun was still loaded or not – has entirely fallen away.

The Enforcer takes us back to something like the world of *Dirty Harry*, only one that is in some respects more obviously comedic. What we might call the diner scene now falls into two parts. In the first, Callahan and his partner DiGeorgio (John Mitchum) are passing a smart restaurant where there is some kind of emergency. It appears that one of the clientele has suffered a heart attack. We see the brutal Callahan drag the man to his feet – the gag is that this is a con man, Freddie the Fainter (he is so described in the closing credits), who eats a hearty meal and then fakes illness. As he is sent on his way by Callahan, Freddie is moaning – he admits that he has got his free meal, but he always enjoys the ride in the ambulance.

Two things are new here – one is the acknowledgement that villainy might be comic, that cops and hoods are not just a double act but sometimes a comic one. The other is that the joke is partly on Callahan, or rather our view of him – Dirty Harry Callahan has a reputation with the audience which might include kicking heart-attack victims.

We cut to a liquor store robbery. This looks like the routine sequence to establish the action hero's credentials, his use of both brute power (surprising the hoods by driving a car through the window of the store) and skill (the usual accuracy of aim). But it also plays jokes. It ends, rather than begins, with a parody of a moment of visual heroics, when the hero emerges from a cloud of smoke or dust or spray. Here Callahan emerges waving uselessly at the cloud sent up by the police smoke bomb. Similarly the complaint, now clearly set up from the earlier movies, that Callahan's methods are too brutal, is given a comic inflection when his superior Captain McKay (Bradford Dillman) begins the next scene not by discussing methods but by itemising the bill for the damage that Callahan's heroics have caused.

The hoods in *The Enforcer* are a group of young 'terrorists' who raid an arms factory. They blackmail the city by threatening to use the stolen weaponry, then kidnap the Mayor and hold him for ransom. We can judge this group to be less disturbing in many respects than their equivalents in *Dirty Harry* and *Magnum Force*. Take the treatment of the gang's motives. Although they announce themselves to be the People's Revolutionary Strike Force, we are told that their political aims are a transparent cover for blackmail – the political dressing is just disguise, like the killer's peace badge in *Dirty Harry*. There is also a pat explanation to hand for such figures: their war experience. We are told that they met in Vietnam, and so the war can now be seen to be responsible for common crime rather than for the vigilantism of *Magnum Force*. It is implied that the war is also responsible for turning the central villain, Bobby Maxwell (De Veren Bookwalter) into a psychopath, which in turn exonerates the city – so the city's sleaze, implicitly behind the killer's behaviour in *Dirty Harry*, can now be played for humour.

The scenes in the bars and on the strip in Siegel's film are replaced in *The Enforcer* by comic routines such as Callahan pretending to be a rural hick when he visits a massage parlour in search of a suspect, or the moment in one of the chase sequences where pursuer and pursued fall through a skylight into the set where a pornographic film is being shot. The fact that sleaze is treated comically is related to the treatment of City Hall – the lawyer who runs the massage parlour is presented in terms that are not really much different from the politicians manipulating the public in another sphere. The moment where the Mayor announces ruefully that he has to fix the press – 'I'll just go down there and jerk 'em off' – offers a language that operates in both worlds. A range of attitude from mild distaste to strong disgust is registered in all these scenes, but the major distinction lies elsewhere, in the difference between the exploitation of women here and the mortal violence towards them elsewhere, of which the 'lady with a shotgun stuck in her ear' in the liquor store robbery is a symbol.

There is a pattern initiated in the pre-credits sequence, in which a sexy hitch-hiker entices two men to their deaths, a pattern formed around women and death. In outline, it is this. The gang includes two women. (An audience seeing the film on its release in 1976 might have been expected to recall the Patty Hearst affair two years previously, and one of the women seems to be physically modelled on Hearst.) The women are the first members of the gang to die. In the raid on the arms factory, the blonde Miki (Jocelyn Jones) is shot by DiGeorgio, in an unaimed shot which he fires as he is stabbed by Bobby Maxwell. She is not killed outright, but an attempt by another gang member to rescue her is stopped by Maxwell, who shoots her to death. DiGeorgio later dies in hospital, and the new partner assigned to Callahan is a woman, Inspector Moore (Tyne Daly). We learn that the second female gang member, Wanda (Samantha Doane),

A new partner for Callahan: Officer Kate Moore (Tyne Daly) in The Enforcer.

has murdered an innocent civilian, the bridge operator held at gun point during the abduction of the Mayor. The confirmation of Moore's effectiveness as Callahan's partner comes when she saves his life by shooting this second woman. Immediately afterwards, Moore accompanies Callahan to Alcatraz in the final action sequence. She corners one of the hoods, who cannot believe he is being threatened by a woman. She replies to his incredulity: 'You laugh at me, you bastard, and I'll shoot you where you stand.' He goes for his gun, and she does shoot him dead. A few moments later she is herself killed by Maxwell as a result of shouting a warning to Callahan. The film now ends with Callahan killing Maxwell.

Analysing this we may see how the distinction between cops and hoods turns on violence to women. Male cops do not kill women here – DiGeorgio only wounds Miki by accident, and Wanda is shot by Moore. Killing women is the defining act of the hoods, and in particular of Maxwell, who early in the film kills Miki and at the end kills Moore. Women enter the world of *The Enforcer* as combatants, not victims, as in the earlier films of the cycle – all three women die, but two of them also kill, and the third is an accomplice to murder.

The film does not ask us to be interested in the two women gang members beyond the fact of understanding that they are not innocent – we view their deaths in the light of earlier deaths which they have directly or indirectly caused. Our interest is focused on the figure through whom the relationship to women of the action hero might be resolved, the woman who might be a partner to Callahan – a double entendre that the film clearly recognises.

The introduction of Moore places her firmly inside the terms set up in earlier movies in the cycle. Callahan, temporarily demoted from Homicide, is put on a panel that is interviewing for Inspectorships. A woman representative of the Mayor's office indirectly calls him a 'Neanderthal', and the appearance of Tyne Daly as Officer Moore, a candidate for a partnership with another officer, offers an obvious trajectory, a comedy in which the couple will be seen to be taking on the same professional task, but in which the values of the woman will redeem those of the man, rescue him from his cave-man status and confirm a modified version of his authority as acceptable. There are echoes of the Spencer Tracy/ Katharine Hepburn cycle here – is it coincidence that Moore's first name is Kate?

The detail of the interview sequence supports this. Callahan's first question is, 'How fast do you run the hundred?' – Moore's last answer is to respond to a legal technicality in great and apparently accurate detail. In other words, he asks her if she is fit, and she tells him that she is bright. Between these moments, Callahan gives a familiar speech about the responsibilities and risks of a police partner. So they both claim to know what they are talking about – the argument is about the right qualifications for this life.

But such a comedic subject cannot be sustained in a world as dark as this one. There are two important sequences in which we are asked to think about what involvement in the other's world means for Callahan and Moore. The first is when they go to the morgue to attend the autopsy on Callahan's last partner. Moore refuses Callahan's suggestion that she wait outside. We see her face as she contemplates the dissected body of DiGeorgio, which we cannot see. The autopsy surgeon announces, 'We're going into the brain now.' In a convention familiar to any viewer of pre-1980s horror movies, shadows on the wall represent the bone saw cutting through the skull, and the removal of the brain. Here perhaps the convention works to suggest Moore's direct gaze – she has to watch what we may not. The surgeon carries on with some technical dictation, and then this:

Surgeon [faking great surprise]: Say, Harry, look at this – damnedest thing I ever saw!
Callahan: What's that?
Surgeon [looking down at brain]: What it says here – 'Eat At Luigi's!'

There is a shot of the surgeon roaring with laughter – visually a mad scientist from a horror film. Moore stumbles out. We see Callahan's face – he is not laughing. We cut to Moore outside, leaning against a pillar – a shot of Tyne Daly in right profile which strongly emphasises her beauty. Callahan contemplates her for a moment and speaks a line from *Dirty Harry*: 'Welcome to Homicide.'

The line could be described as a reminder of what homicide is, a division of police work which deals with the world where people kill each other, and of how this means living both with the physical results of it – the visual grossness of damaged bodies – and the psychological results, making it bearable by deflecting your response in some way. The grotesque joke is only one strategy – the violence and the irony that we see in Callahan are another part of it.

It is also a world in which you may well be killed – this is the context of the 'Welcome to Homicide' line when it is spoken in *Dirty Harry* – and at risk of having to kill. The final truth of being in Homicide is preparedness to kill in order to protect your partner, and this moment is a decisive point in our appreciation of Moore's position, and her understanding of it.

The incident happens in a church, where Callahan is questioning the priest about the whereabouts of the gang. A 'nun' enters, and we see that she is concealing a shot gun. Before she can kill Callahan we cut to Moore, who has just shot the nun dead, and she cries, 'Look at her hands, look at her hands!' We see the red nails of the dead woman as Callahan picks up the shotgun, and we recognise her as the remaining female gang member.

Moore's line about the nun's hands is in practical terms more or less redundant – there is no need to draw attention to the red nails of a nun who was carrying a shotgun. The cry is one of justification, a moment of insistence on the guilt of the woman that Moore has just killed, an acknowledgement here that she has, in a grim sense, now truly joined Homicide. The hood who thinks that a woman will not shoot him in the Alcatraz sequence will now be proved wrong, but equally being a woman no longer confers special status, and she dies in the final gunfight in a way much like most of Callahan's previous partners.

Only one scene interrupts the descent to this point. It occurs after Callahan has been suspended from the force for talking back to McKay and the Mayor. He and Moore walk in a park, stare at some water and take a drink together. He asks her why she does this job – it is important that she does not ask him. What she does is to indicate what she knows. This is the dialogue:

Moore: Every other cop in the city is satisfied with a 38 or a 357. What do you have to carry that cannon for?
Callahan: 'Cos I hit what I aim at, that's why. A 357's a good weapon but I've seen 38s careen off windshields, no good in a city like this.
Moore: I see – so it's for the penetration.
Callahan [smiling]: Does everything have a sexual connotation with you?
Moore [smiling back]: Only sometimes . . .

Why is this not tactless? Is she not explaining a piece of sexual display, some meaning that the action hero must conceal (with talk of careening and windshields), letting him know that she knows? That this seems to be taken as a favour rather than as a transgression implies that this is how he wishes to be understood. A moment earlier she tells him that she has made up a name for him: 'Cold Bold Callahan, with his great big forty-four', a name that makes him sound like a character from a Wild West show. He does not deny this identification, but he cannot embrace it, and so the understanding through comedy of himself and his desire, which this might have led to, never happens. The setting of the scene outside the city is suggestive – wind gusts on the soundtrack as the couple talk on an autumnal hillside. After a while they will go down again to 'a city like this', and Moore will die.

Sudden Impact

Seven years separate the release of *The Enforcer* and *Sudden Impact*. In the interim, Eastwood had made seven other films, and the fourth Harry Callahan movie has to be read partly in the light of this, and also with an awareness that the film was conceived under very different conditions in 1983 from those that had operated for the first films in the series. As well as changes in the costs and structures of production, I am thinking about the substantial success in the late 'seventies and early 'eighties of film cycles dealing with rape and revenge, which form the material of part of *Sudden Impact*.

A basic question of strategy is raised by the conception of another Callahan movie at this point, even though the film is offering a figure identified with that of the earlier movies. After the first film established the character, the sequels placed Callahan within various sets of circumstances. Although those circumstances reflect the historical specifics of making the film, the narratives do not particularly refer to each other – except very briefly on the subject of Callahan's partners – and the character himself is not seen over time: he does not age.

Another way of putting this is to say that up to this point a sense of the past is not important. In *Dirty Harry*, it hardly exists at all, and in *Magnum Force* and

The older Callahan: testing a new weapon in Sudden Impact.

Dispatching the gulity: Callahan and his Smith & Wesson in Sudden Impact.

The Enforcer only minimally, as an explanatory footnote to villainy, in the allusions to Vietnam. Callahan's physical age has only a small place in *Magnum Force*, in the interpretation of the defeat of the rookie cops as the defeat of the young sons by the father: Callahan's epigraphic line is, 'Briggs was right, you guys don't have enough experience.'

The issue is different in *Sudden Impact*. The character as played by Eastwood is clearly older and is contrasted with the first hoods we see, who are much younger than he is. When these hoods are freed at the beginning of the film on the grounds that Callahan's evidence has been obtained by illegal search, the judge says, 'This is an old story.' Then there is old age, represented in the Mafia godfather Threlkis, whom Callahan visits at his granddaughter's wedding. In both cases these figures use the perspective of their youth or age to express contempt for Callahan, but they do not last long. Callahan fools Threlkis into believing that he has failed effectively to silence a crucial witness against him, and the old man suffers a fatal cardiac arrest. The young hoods attack Callahan in his car, are outmanoeuvred and drown when they crash their car into San Francisco Bay. Both these moments occur in the early part of the film and the link is that Callahan does not act directly – the guilty are destroyed by old age and inexperience respectively.

This can be linked with that invariable indicator of the mood of these films, the diner scene. Here again is reference to the passing of time. Every day for the last nine years, we learn, Callahan has had a large unsugared black coffee in this diner. Today, the waitress puts a lot of sugar in it. Callahan takes his first sip of the coffee while walking along the street and, prompted by this signal, he returns to dispatch the hoods who are holding up the place. The dialogue is suggestive:

Callahan: We're not just going to let you walk out of here.
Hood [*incredulous*]: Who's we, sucker?
Callahan [*reaching for his gun*]: Smith – and Wesson – and me.

Invoking the names of the famous gunsmiths allies Callahan with technical accuracy and skill as well as with the historical past. As previously, the moment at the end of the ensuing gunfight is emblematic. Here Callahan faces down the last hood with a speech from which we can clearly measure the distance in mood from *Dirty Harry*. The confident teasing of 'Do you feel lucky?' is replaced with a plea to the hood – to try for a shoot-out – that has become notorious: 'Make my day!' The only pleasure left, it seems, is dispatching the guilty – the disappointment is that nowadays the opportunities for this are so few.

The itch to kill in this scene is not answered in what immediately follows. With the three groups of the guilty in the next part of the film, Callahan's role as gunfighter is confirmed only once, not by the deaths of Threlkis and the young hoods, but in the sequence with the men avenging Threlkis's death. Here, however, while the gunfight is direct, the satisfaction is minimal. Dispatching the professional hitmen for the mob offers no answer to anger directed at young hoodlums or (to use Callahan's description of Threlkis) old scumbags.

At this point, Callahan's superiors send him out of the city. An aerial shot of San Francisco harbour ends the Callahan film as we have previously seen it. The two premises that were central to it no longer operate: that the major crime under scrutiny is a product of the particular nature of space and organisation in a large city, and that the life of a homicide detective in this place is expressed by how he treats his partner, and who his partner is. Callahan does have one scene with a partner-like figure, Horace (Albert Popwell), but the character is not developed and seems to be here for a plot reason. The death of Horace in the second half of the movie will give Callahan a personal motive for revenge.

Callahan goes to San Paulo, following up a lead on an unsolved homicide in San Francisco. This is a familiar landscape, the small town as centre of gothic excess. The plot depends on an event in the past: the rape of a young woman, Jennifer Spencer (Sondra Locke), and her sister by a group of local youths ten years earlier. Seeing one of the rapists by chance in San Francisco, Spencer was prompted to follow and kill him – the unsolved case that Callahan is following up. She now returns to San Paulo and starts to execute the rapists one by one.

I want to set discussion of this part of *Sudden Impact* in context by considering some groups of films that might be described as or related to revenge-for-rape narratives. Although the history of this subject in film is very extensive, we may consider it from the point in the early 1970s when the relaxation of censorship restrictions allowed for greater graphic presentation of violence associated with sex of some kind. The films can be grouped as follows:

1) Films in which male members of a family act to avenge the violation of a female member of it: *Straw Dogs* (Sam Peckinpah, 1971), *Last House on the Left* (Wes Craven, 1973), *Death Wish* (Michael Winner, 1974) and *Death Wish II* (Winner, 1981).

2) Films in which women revenge acts of rape against themselves and/or their sisters: *Lipstick* (Lamont Johnson, 1976), *I Spit on Your Grave* (1980), *Ms.45/ Angel of Vengeance* (Abel Ferrara, 1981) and *Sudden Impact*.

3) Films involving serial killings of women and men, predominantly in the context of sexual activity of some kind: The *Friday the Thirteenth* series (three films of the series were released before *Sudden Impact*, between 1980 and 1982) and the *Halloween* series (three films between 1978 and 1982).

These groups are, of course, indicative rather than exhaustive. There are a number of things to say about them. Some of the films were very profitable. Domestic box-office receipts for the six films in group three were just over $80 million, and the figure for the two *Death Wish* films was over $17 million. In the case of very graphic products outside the mainstream, such as *Last House on the Left* and *I Spit on Your Grave*, the films were notorious. These last two were at the centre of the row over 'video nasties' which took place in the UK in the year of *Sudden Impact*'s release. *Sudden Impact* itself was strikingly successful commercially, with a US domestic gross of $34.6 million.

The common elements that became immensely popular and profitable in the period following *Halloween* are the gothic small town, the darkness from the past returning, and a narrative regularly punctuated by deaths. In the *Halloween* and *Friday the Thirteenth* cycles a psychotic figure punishes the innocent; in the revenge-for-rape movies, the avenger punishes the guilty. What is common to all these films is that the discrimination between guilty and innocent parties is very clear and we are not invited to question it. Rape might be said to occupy the same ground as psychosis in providing an unquestioned guarantee of our understanding the reasons for the killings.

One particular quality of the revenge-for-rape film is the construction of rape as a 'private' crime, one that is often presented in the same settings as other sexual encounters (inside, or in the darkness). The reason that the victim cannot seek redress other than through direct action is not only the lack of witnesses or the indifference of the police, but the presentation of rape as an intimate wrong that can be answered only by an equally intimate act of revenge. It is for this reason that recognition is so important – the case requires not only that the avenger should kill the rapist, but that the denial of individual will invoked in the rape should be redeemed by the moment in which the rapist understands who is killing him and why. The use of flashback is important here, a cinematic device allowing the revenge to be placed next to the original violation, so that time is briefly eclipsed. Such recognition occurs in every case where we see the revenge in detail in *Sudden Impact*; with Jennifer Spencer's penultimate target, the son of police chief Jannings (Pat Hingle), the impossibility of this recognition – the figure is catatonic after a car accident – precludes revenge. Jannings understands this in his rueful line, 'Now you're here and he doesn't even know it.'

A narrative in which a woman revenges her rape obviously gives legitimacy to her use of a gun, but not without some difficulty. One possible problem is that of presenting the character as both permanently traumatised by the rape and yet able to assume power and take revenge. In *Sudden Impact* (and earlier in *Lipstick* in a slightly different way), this is addressed by splitting the character into two raped sisters. We hear Jennifer's account of the first revenge killing in a scene in which she tells it to her sister Elizabeth (Lisa Britt), who has been rendered catatonic by the injuries associated with her rape. The sight of Elizabeth is clearly a further assurance to us that Jennifer is justified in killing. There is reassurance, too, in Jennifer's profession. *Sudden Impact* shows her as an artist

Victims of rape: Jennifer Spencer (Sondra Locke) with her catatonic sister Elizabeth (Lisa Britt) in Sudden Impact.

and restorer. The metaphor of her restoration work in 'making old ugly things right again' is obvious enough, but her other work as a painter is also part of her careful positioning in the film. That she can be associated with creativity is positive, but her actual work – we see a head of a woman which seems to owe a lot to the work of Edvard Munch – offers the myth of the 'tortured' artist, neurosis placed in an acceptable social category.

How this may be related to Callahan and the concerns I have so far discussed will become clearer if we look at the way that the setting of San Paulo and the origins of the hoods is signalled to the audience. We are shown the benign small town, represented by the bright young cop whose life Callahan saves within moments of his arrival, and the comedic elements of Callahan's first meeting with Jennifer Spencer. Set against this is the small town at night, shown through the bar which Callahan visits in his attempts to follow up his murder enquiry. Whereas the comparable world in the city had to do with commodified sex, here there is sexual dysfunction rather than prostitution.

The rape is presented as a hysterical attempt to assert masculine potency, particularly on the part of the central villain Mike (Paul Drake). A number of opportunities are taken to emphasise his possible impotence, and queries are raised for us about the other rapists' potency. Where men are seen as inadequate, masculine aggression is displaced; it reappears in the highly negative treatment of the two women associated with the rapists. The central figure is Ray Parkins (Audrie J. Neenan). We see her first in a bar, where she tries to pick up Callahan with a combination of violence and sexual aggression. The failure to assume supposedly feminine qualities also applies to the widow of the second rapist to die, Kruger. When Callahan comes to question Mrs Kruger (Nancy Parsons), she sees him off with a loaded shotgun. His exit line – 'I'll come back when you're less bereaved' – ironises her failure to feel appropriately 'feminine' emotions. Just before Jennifer kills Ray Parkins, we are given a flashback to the moment when the sisters were invited by Ray to the party that turned into the rape. It appears from this that the whole idea was Ray's from the beginning, that women were to blame for all this after all.

Or women and class. In the flashback, in which we learn that Jennifer is a 'college girl', she hesitates at the invitation and Ray asks 'What's the matter – us locals not good enough for you?' The rape is seen to grow out of the element of small-town culture expressed in the red-lit bar scene, all the rapists being signalled as proletarian, apart from the only one to be traumatised by the rape, Jannings's son. Part of the subject here is the image of the small town in the hands of the violent redneck. We see this in Mike and his two cronies from Kruger's fish business, who invade the collapsed middle-class home (that of Jannings, whose wife died in childbirth, and the catatonic son) and kill the patriarch.

At this point in *Sudden Impact*, Jennifer has killed all the rapists apart from Jannings's son, and Mike. She is captured by Mike and his cronies, and taken to the funfair, the site of the original rape. Earlier they have beaten Callahan badly and believe that they have drowned him. Now Callahan reappears – in back-lit shadow – to the words 'Holy shit' from one hood. He kills the two sidekicks and finally Mike. Callahan now manages a piece of business with guns which will lay all the earlier deaths at Mike's door, and the couple are left together. Roberta Flack sings 'This Side of Forever' over the closing credits.

This reinstatement of the couple – or rather symbolically of the family, for the young cop whose life Callahan saved earlier is included in the frame – follows the pattern of the end of a horror movie. The visual identification of Mike with monstrosity comes when he is shot and falls so that he is impaled on the horn of the roundabout unicorn – staked like any other vampire. The young cop's line to Callahan is, 'Is it over, then?' He is assured that it is.

In the opening of *Sudden Impact*, Callahan's perception of America is expressed in a conversation with Horace about bullet-proof limousines. He says, 'They're making those, these days, for sheiks, and business executives, and hoods – impregnable to about anything but artillery.' If this grouping, which clearly departs from the simplicities of the world in which all lawbreakers were different kinds of punks, is representative of Callahan's understanding of his situation in the first half of the film – and I think it is – then the project of the second half is to associate him with an area and a figure linked with other, more clearly legitimate forms of innocence and guilt. Callahan's attitudes can then in turn be legitimised by our seeing them as support for Jennifer, the two of them as having the same perceptions of law and justice. Jennifer's final speech – 'Where was all this concern for my rights when I was being beaten and mauled?' – is nominally spoken in opposition to Callahan. But, in truth, it is an appropriation of his rhetoric, from the moment in *Dirty Harry* when he spoke to the District Attorney of Ann Mary Deacon: 'What about her rights? She's raped and left in a hole to die. Who speaks for her?'

Thus, in a reversal of the terms of the previous films, here the couple can become lovers, Callahan can take over Jennifer's cause, execute Mike and rescue his woman at the same moment. The questioning of the limits of the power of the action hero has all but disappeared, to be replaced by a reassuring fable of the dispatch of a monster.

The Dead Pool

Eastwood apparently said that this, the fifth Callahan movie, would be the last. The qualities of the city and the relationship to the partner were the organising premises of the first films in the Callahan cycle, and although *The Dead Pool* returns to these premises, it now interprets them entirely as jokes. Callahan's opposition to the city authorities as represented by his superiors, or the figure of the Mayor in the earlier films is a case of this, where ways of criticising him have now become exaggerated to the point of parody. Take the notion of Callahan as spending city money. In *The Enforcer*, he is busted from Homicide to Personnel for wrecking a city vehicle. At the beginning of *The Dead Pool*, he wrecks another in a shoot-out, and we hear that: 'City vehicles cost $13,000 – and you wrecked three last month.' The change of tone is related to another point. Callahan is no longer in opposition to the rest of the force – for the first time he is a hero, and the film begins with the successful prosecution of a gangster. The sense of the possibility of failure or frustration that remains up to the end of the first half of *Sudden Impact* has completely gone, and the Callahan figure is at its closest to that of James Bond: licensed to kill for an audience of admiring sidekicks. His remark to his boss Donnelly after he has killed the film's major villain with a harpoon – 'I guess you'll find him hanging around over there' – has the smart-aleck quality of lines on the dead in the James Bond cycle. The construction of sequences around a technological gimmick, such as the long chase sequence here between Callahan and a model car wired up as a bomb, seems closely related to the same source.

Other elements of the movie have also lost any dimension that might imply a problem. The narrative of Callahan's finding a woman in the city is treated as unproblematic. It takes a form close to that in *Coogan's Bluff*, from a first meeting as antagonists – this time the woman is a reporter, Samantha Walker (Patricia Clarkson) – to the invitation to dinner, to their becoming lovers, and ultimately to constructing the woman as final target of the killer, to be rescued by Callahan. Other areas are resolved in outright comedy, such as the idea that Callahan is a target for Mob revenge. He visits the prison, and uses a trick to terrify the Boss, after which the hit-men still pursue Callahan – but to act as his bodyguards.

The matter of the partner is similar. The new partner is a Chinese-American teamed with Callahan for public relations reasons, and almost nothing is made of their dependence on or responsibility for each other. When the partner is injured, but not seriously, it raises no question as to whether the job can be worthwhile. When this question is raised, it comes typically as a gag. Harry has been taking Samantha to dinner, when they are trapped and sprayed with bullets by hoods. They survive, and Samantha sits on a bench to deliver her one liner: 'Whatever they're paying you, Harry, it isn't enough.'

One aspect of *The Dead Pool* repays a little attention. The central villain is a psychotic obsessed with an icon of glamour in the shape of Peter Swan (Liam Neeson), a director of exploitation horror movies. His killings are an attempt to frame Swan in revenge for Swan 'stealing my nightmares'. Described as 'without a personality' by the film's doctor, the villain is obsessed by the idea of the glamour of fame as promoted through the mass media. Related to this feeling is the only rewarding sequence in the film, in which an unconsidered citizen is threatening to commit suicide (by setting himself on fire) unless he can tell 'his story' on the evening news. He demands a reporter and gets to talk to Samantha, who tells him that bid for attention is doomed. 'Nobody is going to watch you die on the six o'clock news.' But he accidentally sets himself alight anyway.

The man we see pretending to act as cameraman in this little incident is, of course, Callahan himself. The moment comes shortly after a sequence in which Callahan nearly shoots two men who turn out simply to want his autograph. Samantha reminds him of Andy Warhol's dictum that in the future everyone will be famous for fifteen minutes. I do not wish to make too much of this, but the film has some sense of the brutality and emptiness of the public realm in a culture where the private is continually marginalised or unimaginable. In an incident at the very beginning of *The Dead Pool*, Callahan asks the cop responsible for public relations (he has been using language like 'maximising your public relations value') a question: 'Do you have any kids, lieutenant?' The cop does not appear to understand this, as if such a question were a gross irrelevance, rather than an attempt to define a world where such thinking would really do damage. He replies, 'No', and Harry offers a nice absurdity: 'Lucky for them . . .'

Callahan and TV reporter Samantha Walker (Patricia Clarkson) in The Dead Pool.

Tightrope

Tightrope was written and directed by Richard Tuggle, the screenwriter of *Escape from Alcatraz*. I consider it the most distinguished of this group of Eastwood's films. Like the Callahan cycle, it begins with an aerial shot of a city, but the city is New Orleans, a place with particular meanings. The name suggests foreignness, to this city as a place of immigrations, of Creoles (catholic, Francophone culture) and of Cajuns (French-Canadian immigrants from the late eighteenth century). This is the stage for an encounter between plain Americanness and the foreign. Eastwood plays a cop called Wes Block, originally from out of town. He is to meet a woman whose name is Beryl Thibodeaux, played by the French-Canadian Geneviève Bujold.

The different strains of Francophone culture relate to the familiar idea of New Orleans as the site of a licensed and historically legitimated freedom of sexual activity. The sale of sexual pleasure by women in the Callahan cycle was part of the sleaze of the city, treated either seriously, as in *Dirty Harry*, or more comically, in *The Enforcer*. The New Orleans setting offers it as something the women do for themselves – the figure of the male pimp and, with it, the sense of the city's prostitution as an industry (a particularly modern form of an old corruption), have almost disappeared. This is related to the way in which we are shown the places where the women make their living: the absolute distinction between the homes we never saw and the brothels and street corners where the women work has begun to blur.

The idea of New Orleans as a city in which the buying and selling of sexual favours has a historical legitimacy means that it is in effect no longer outside the law. So the women are no longer in opposition to the cops – the common scene in which we see a bored or angry prostitute, dragged into the police station either on a charge or as a witness of crime, makes only one very brief appearance in this film, and the women treat cops as just another group of clients.

The final association we make with New Orleans can be given in one word – carnival. If this city represents a zone where the bounds of what is acceptable sexual practice are changed, we can read Mardi Gras as an expression of this freedom, an attempt to extend it, and as carrying one of its more unsettling consequences, a world of disguise proving to be a world of satyrs as well as one of clowns. The masked procession of Mardi Gras, an occasion for public expression of pleasure, also paradoxically expresses nervousness at the public gaze, acknowledging the necessity of cloaking the self. This is particularly important in *Tightrope* because the film reverses the terms of the Callahan series. We move from a cycle in which the domestic world can never be satisfactorily realised to a film insistently concerned with the domestic: with home and what is meant by being in it, what can and cannot happen there.

We can see this in the presentation of the first murder. The film opens with a familiar scenario of the 'stalker'. A woman is walking alone through the gothic space of the city, with dripping alleyways, darkened church and fog. She is pursued by a man in sneakers. At the climax of the sequence, she reaches her gate and confronts a man, who appears to be a cop – but we see his sneakers, and know

Half in shadow: Detective Inspector Wes Block (Eastwood) in the New Orleans night in Tightrope.

'Going out to look for something' – Block and prostitute Becky Jacklin (Rebecca Perle) in Tightrope.

he is her pursuer. She has said to him, 'I live right here, could you watch to make sure I get in.' She is at home.

A sequence introducing Block is placed here – I will return to it shortly. When it ends, we cut directly to the interior of the woman's home, where she has been found dead, raped and strangled. Next to the bed on which she has died is a half-eaten brownie and an empty cup of coffee. The forensic scientist confirms to Block that the killer has indeed made himself a cup of coffee. He cannot understand this, cannot imagine it. In a line echoing a subject in the Callahan movies, Block explains, 'He was starting to enjoy himself.' We have learned earlier that the struggle took place at 9.15 p.m., but the woman was not actually killed until three hours later.

The presentation of murder, where the murderer is a stranger to the victim, can be a way of reinforcing a distinction between the safety of home and the dangers of the street, the vulnerability of being outside. The murders in *Dirty Harry*, where the victims all die outside their homes, are just such a case. Equally, murder can be presented as a terrible irruption of the non-domestic world into the home. This does not simply mean the figure who breaks in, kills and leaves. The point here turns on what he does in the home, on whether it relates to the domestic world in an oppositional way. Thus, smashing up the place becomes a reassurance – this is what we expect, or hope, killers would do. Its opposite is something which signals a mind making connections between the fact of killing and other possible relations to a woman and her space. Perhaps the famous historical case for American culture still remains that of Albert DeSalvo, the Boston Strangler, who arranged an article of clothing in the form of a bow around the bodies of some of his victims.

Thus the brownie, a snack half-consumed and left for no apparent reason, announces a subject of this film. We might be right to see this as a horrible re-interpretation of the sight of Harry Callahan chewing a burger or drinking a coffee as he goes into action in the diner scenes in the Callahan cycle, for the subject is not unrelated; both this murderer and Callahan are men whose world contains continuities between drinking, eating and killing other people.

The sequence which occupies the space in which the murder would have been presented is the one which introduces Eastwood in his role as Detective Inspector Wes Block. It opens not at the precinct or the diner but in a street, where Block is seen playing football with his two children. The street that is sufficiently safe for informal sport is a common image of benign suburbia – what follows is a simple anecdote indicating the value of this world. A mangy dog is rooting in the trash cans. Block and his two daughters approach it. The younger one, of course, wants to rescue it. Block replies that it would be better to 'take him to the pound, they'll find him a good home.' The younger child, who has the traditional role of speaking unadorned truth, asks, 'What happens if they don't?' The exchange of looks which follows between Block and his elder daughter Amanda (Alison Eastwood) announces that we know the answer to this, and the next sequence shows Block feeding the dog (there turn out to be two others) in his kitchen. So, a home can provide nurture, the ability to effect an unproblematic, almost magical rescue symbolised in the animal saved from death. The rest of the sequence is less positive, showing a family with one parent, with the father's plans to take the daughters to the football game interrupted by the call to a murder scene and the care of the family handed over to the baby-sitter. The context of a strain of exploitation movies at this time might exactly suggest that the baby-sitter operates as a signal to audiences of the dangers facing the household when, or rather because, the members of the family associated with safety, order and control are absent.

After his visit to the murder scene, Block returns to his home. He appears as a figure of order, sending the baby-sitter off and tucking in the daughters. But the sequence also explores what this home does not contain. When he reaches his own bedroom, the other occupant of the bed is the dog. Momentarily, the absence of the wife is offered as comedy, but the next morning, as the daughters leave to visit their mother and her new partner, it is figured as loss, as humiliation. The children are driven off in an expensive car while Block sits on the child's bed, forlornly holding a toy.

The wife's departure is the condition of the main action of *Tightrope*. While his daughters are away with their mother, Block does what he will later describe to Amanda as going 'out to look for something'. He interrogates a friend of the murdered girl, another prostitute, and ends up having sex with her. At the same time, the killer is with a different prostitute, a girl who works in a jacuzzi house, and he kills her. The scenario of Block's visiting the 'working girls' of New Orleans and his interrogation turning into a sexual encounter is repeated twice, with the difference that it is now these women whom the killer targets, and both die shortly after their encounter with Block. As this action develops, another detail becomes explicit, that the sex Block has with the women involves some form of bondage. In the case of a third woman, it appears that Block has handcuffed her.

I do not think that this presents a simple parallel between sex involving bondage and sex culminating in death – the argument that the killer is acting out the fantasies that Block cannot admit to. This idea certainly exists in the film; it is presented as the killer's assertion, his claim that Block is like him and wants to do what he does, and the crude analysis of the psychiatrist who offers Block banalities like, 'There's a darkness inside all of us.'

But the film proposes something else. It can best be approached by considering how it explores the idea of orderliness. We are shown a family consisting of a father and two daughters, one of whom is a small child. The other is of an age where she can take on some of the roles abandoned by her mother, such as cooking food. The role she cannot take on, of course, is the sexual one. She sleeps next to her father only once in the film, when he has drunk himself unconscious on the sofa.

Block's desire for women has to be satisfied firmly outside the house. That we are to understand this is clear in a number of significant details, such as the speech of the first 'friend' – the word is Block's – who begins her seduction by announcing the wife's departure as a condition of it. The fact of desire cannot even be acknowledged to the younger child. The expression of this is a scene in which, having overheard something, she asks what a hard-on is. Block's attempt at explanation is a failure – it is Amanda who says to him, 'Dad – forget it.'

The visits to the women represent an important combination of the orderly and the anarchic. In some ways Block retains, or tries to retain, control. Since these are women in the business of providing sexual pleasure, no commitment is called for from him, just – presumably – some money. The demarcation between their world and the world of the daughters would seem to be complete, and he will not be inviting any of these women home. The suggestion of bondage might seem to fit into this, as a metaphor for a sexual act shorn of the threat of being held or touched. But it is exactly those things that Block uses to impose control which turn out to escape it, in a series of mistakes – we might call them Freudian slips. As he leaves the first woman, he realises that he has forgotten his tie, and with the third, he leaves his handcuffs in the booth.

Alongside these encounters is a developing interest in another woman, Beryl Thibodeaux. She is linked to the other women through Block's fascination with women's physical power, feeling the need to restrain it on the one hand, and here drawn to a woman who displays it, or is at ease with it. Her job is running a rape centre which teaches self-defence to women, and Block finally asks her out after watching her exercise in a gym. She is also a woman who can manipulate language; in their first meetings it is she who shows intelligence and wit.

The affair which now develops offers a route back, an opportunity again to make love in the context of the home. Earlier Tuggle had implied the connection – and the blockage – by cutting from a shot of Beryl watching Block at a public performance, a press conference) to a private moment, the scene in which the little girl tries to discover what a hard-on is. The subject returns, or is returned to, after Block has been on his first date with Beryl. He arrives home, implies a

Physical power: Block and Beryl (Geneviève Bujold) in the gym in Tightrope.

possible new order in moving the sleeping girls from his bed to their own, and the phone rings. The little girl is prompted to say, 'I'll bet that's her right now, and she wants to see you again, and you can have a hard-on any time you want.' Of course nobody in the family can reply: the truth cannot be acknowledged, any more than there can be an overt admission that Beryl is the stronger party, that Block is the one needing help. But it is implied. Earlier the pair have had a conversation about Beryl helping men as well as women. This is the dialogue which opens the sequence that will end with his bringing her home:

Wes: Can I see you tonight?
Beryl: I've got some work.
Wes: Can it wait?
Beryl: Are you OK?
Wes: I don't know.

The reversal of conventional gender roles in the speeches here is clear enough. During this moment, Beryl is in the self-defence centre. She is shown next to a poster which reads 'Speak out, you're not alone'.

Above: control – Block, Beryl and the handcuffs in Tightrope. *Opposite: the masked self – Block and the psychopath (Marco St John).*

Finally the couple arrive in the bedroom. They have an exchange about domestic disorder. When Wes asks her to excuse the mess, she replies, 'You should see my place sometimes', perhaps implying that there is no need to fuss over disorderliness, that it is not as threatening as Block thinks it is, and that it is not her job to clear it up.

A crucial moment in the film follows. She picks up Wes's handcuffs from the bedside table, and they discuss why the killer uses cuffs – Wes says, for 'control'. It has been made clear that we are looking at an intelligent woman, and Beryl knows as we do that they are also talking about Block's sense of feeling threatened, of vulnerability to others. Beryl locks the cuffs around one wrist, holds out her hands to Wes. His face is lit so that half of it is in shadow (this device is pervasive in *Tightrope*); hers is fully lit.

The scene is finely performed, the expression of interest on Eastwood's face giving us no reading of whether he will now cuff the other wrist or take the handcuffs off. I think it is important that we understand that Beryl does not know this either. She is finding out what he wants, or can allow himself to want, of her, and she has the confidence to offer him a real choice.

He takes the handcuff off. But if he does not want to control this woman, wants her to touch him, it is not as simple as that. As she reaches out to touch his face, he flinches. What happens now is interestingly obscure. The sequence ends without making it clear whether or not they now make love. The cut is to a masked figure attacking the sleeping Beryl. The figure tries to strangle her, and she tears off the mask to reveal Wes's face. This is a nightmare – the next shot, of Wes sitting up in bed bathed in sweat, locates it as his dream.

Again we need to probe the crude explanation – that Wes 'really' wants to kill Beryl and is repressing his wish. Perhaps it is worth noticing that the sequence is not shot subjectively from either combatant's point of view. We might also consider here Freud's argument that dreams 'of the death of persons of whom the dreamer is fond' represent a wish that the person may die only in the case where the dreamer is 'deeply pained by the death and may even weep bitterly in his sleep' (*The Interpretation of Dreams*, p.347). Such is not the case here, where the dreamer awakes clearly in a state of terror.

The dream sequence can be understood if we connect it back to the right detail, not the moment with the handcuffs, but Beryl's gesture of touching Wes's face a few seconds later. Over their first meal, Beryl said 'I'd like to find out what's underneath the front you put on.' They have now reached a point where she might find out, but encounters his fear of being touched. I take his dream to be a continuation of this flinching, the imagining of unmasking as a horror, a revelation of himself to himself as homicidal. In other words, he does not know if he is or is not the man described by the killer – he dreams that he might be that man, but the film is not arguing that he is.

So far the action has achieved the introduction of the woman into the home. The climax of *Tightrope* involves the actual intrusion of the murderer into it, as the killer attacks the occupants of two houses, first Block's daughters and then Beryl.

The thinking of the killer is clear at this point. He destroys the pretence of the domestic world to offer order and protection, killing the baby-sitter and two of the dogs. But his main business is with Amanda. We see him take Amanda from

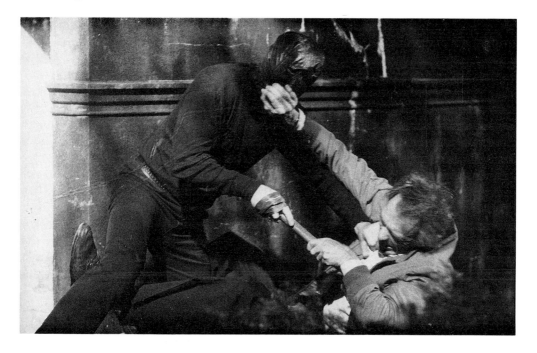

The assertive woman: Beryl in her office in Tightrope.

her bed; he is eating one of the brownies that she has made earlier. Block returns home, finds Amanda gone, moves through the house to his own bedroom. The shot shows a figure lying on her side on his bed, her back to the viewer and the legs uncovered almost to the buttocks – it is Amanda. The significance of this, the obvious display of Amanda as a woman, is as a challenge to Block's picture of the different spaces occupied by daughters and sexual partners. Block's tucking up the daughter in her own bed has been replaced by tying her up and placing her in the father's, with the implied invitation to violate the taboos of incest and rape.

This is the second moment when Wes demonstrates his difference from the killer. The man who has earlier put aside the handcuffs now releases Amanda, and sets out in pursuit of the killer, who escapes. Accompanying Amanda in the ambulance and later in the hospital, Block is silent. The failure of the father and the domestic order that he controls to protect the daughters is eloquently expressed in the next sequence, where he returns from the hospital to the now-empty house. For the last time in the film, he moves through it, tidying and or-dering. He picks up Amanda's football yet again (as a domestic detail expressive of the value and at the same time the interminable disorderliness of family life, it might be seen as a descendant of the loose top of the banister post in the Bailey home in Frank Capra's *It's a Wonderful Life*). He moves to his own bedroom and adjusts the position of the bedside lamp twice before throwing it across the room and tearing the covers off the bed. Again, the impulse to express anger at the disruption of a precarious domestic order by tearing it to pieces may be familiar. Another man returned to 'all I had in the way of a home' to find an invitation to sexual corruption in his bed – there it was in the form of the naked Carmen Sternwood. He responded by throwing her out and trashing the bed: this was Marlowe in Raymond Chandler's novel, *The Big Sleep*.

The wrecking of the domestic ends through the agent that introduced the subject in the film – Wes stops when he meets a puzzled stare from the dog. This begins the re-establishment of a revised domestic order, as Tuggle now cuts to Beryl's house, where the little girl is sleeping. We now see the image of the couple in bed, or rather on Beryl's bed, for the first time, resting together. Wes is covered with an old sweater of Beryl's. The camera pans to the bedside table, where the handcuffs and gun have been put aside.

A major subject of the film, Wes's fear that he may be like the killer and the killer's assertion that this is so, effectively ends at this point. Tuggle cuts to the police headquarters, where the man is immediately identified as a rapist who was arrested by Block and who has recently been released from prison. So the figure now diminishes into a literal hood with a name, his reason for revenge on Block explained. What follows is largely a routine thriller, where Block rescues Beryl just as the killer is about to succeed in strangling her, and tracks him into the sterile space in which he can be faced and destroyed. The ending obviously stresses the physical similarity between the two men fighting, but this is now not a threat – Wes can accept the similarity because he has demonstrated the difference between them.

After the killer is dead, Wes walks away, and the scene seems about to go into the kind of long shot that would recollect the endings of the earlier Callahan movies. But Beryl appears and stands in front of Wes, her face, as ever, clearly and fully lit. She reaches out to touch his cheek. He can now accept this and they walk off together – part of the quality of this moment is that they do so without speaking. It relates back to an earlier moment. Wes has come to the hospital with the younger daughter, and he brings two things for Amanda. One is, of course, the football. The other is a necklace; he says, 'My mother used to wear this, maybe you'd like to wear it too.' It is a charm, a positive image to stand against the film's many references to strangulation – a little magic around the neck. He stares out of the window. When the camera returns to the room, it is evidently some hours later, near dark, and the mother sits watching over the two sleeping daughters – the only moment when the members of the original family are all seen in the same space. The sequence ends without anyone speaking.

Silence and eloquence in *Tightrope* can be read in another way. Death in the Callahan movies is mainly brought about by gunshot. *Tightrope* – of course, this pun is implicit in its title – takes strangulation as its central act. We can take this – if substantiation were necessary, it could be provided by the concluding acts of *Othello* or *King Lear* – as a desire to deprive the victim not only of life, but particularly of speech: to prevent women from talking. Thus the figure of Beryl is an appropriate heroine, combining both assertive female speech and a confident and assertive sexuality, against the speechless killer.

Where does Block stand in relation to the assertive woman? When they first meet, in the police headquarters, Beryl's words to him are 'Welcome back'. He has been telling his staff to lie to her, to tell her that he is out of town; the words record her knowledge of the lie, confront him with it and imply an arrival, a point from which something will need to follow. This is their next dialogue:

Block: Look, I'm not particularly eager to talk to women who go around with chips on their shoulder, tell everybody I'm doing a lousy job, and get everybody pissed off at me.

Beryl: Oh, I wouldn't be eager to talk to them, either. On the other hand, I'm really not eager to talk to cops who have a chip on their shoulder, stereotype women from rape centres and then go to just about any lengths to avoid them. I'm sure you don't care for those kinds of cops either.

She is telling him who he is – you might say, a cop like Harry Callahan – and offering him an alternative to this. The film acknowledges a potential price to be paid for giving up control, both in the dream after the release of Beryl from the handcuffs, and in the later sequence in which Wes moves around the brewery, hallucinating moments from his past encounters. The danger of madness, or rather of coming to believe one is insane, can be related to earlier views of the madness of the paterfamilias for whom the domestic order is unsustainable – again the figure of George Bailey (James Stewart) in *It's a Wonderful Life* is the central case. *Tightrope* can be thought of as a revision of Capra's film, one in which the breakdown of the nuclear family has actually happened and a new family can be tentatively assembled only through a new relation to the sexuality of the 'liberated' woman. The figure of Violet Bick (Gloria Grahame), who is never quite allowed to disrupt the family in Capra's narrative, is recast in Beryl's role here.

The ending of *Tightrope* does not show us the united, or reunited, family. In the final minutes it looks as if the encounter between the two men will take place in a graveyard, but in the last moments they move on, into a shunting yard where one is killed and his remains are whisked away by a train. It is the only example in these films where Eastwood is neither the deliberate agent of his central opponent's death nor its cool witness. The fact that it is the killer and not Wes who dies is offered as apparently a matter of chance as the two bodies roll towards the tracks.

At the beginning of *Tightrope*, Block and another cop emerge from the dead woman's home and look up at the moon. When the cop says, 'Think it brings the crazies out?' Block replies, 'They're always out.' This states violence as a permanent condition, not a moment of gothic excess. A particular aspect of this is picked up later, in the moment when Amanda, apparently at the centre of domestic security (she is in the Block kitchen, doing nothing particular), opens an envelope from the forensic lab containing images of death, the glossy prints of the dead girls. She stuffs this horror back into its envelope, but asks her father, 'Dad . . . do you get hurt?'

This might sum up for us the interest of the whole cycle, the question of the nature of cops – particularly homicide cops – and their presentation to us as figures who must see and do things that are proscribed for most people. Further, it identifies the role of cinema as allowing us to contemplate such acts and such sights. The consistent question in the cop cycle is whether the cop's life is peculiarly damaging – we might follow Amanda and say hurtful – and what kinds of pleasure such a man might feel he owes himself. Depending as it does on Eastwood's previous roles as Callahan, *Tightrope* is the culmination of the cycle, the most searching exploration of these questions.

CHAPTER THREE
SENTIMENTAL
AND OTHERWISE

The groups of films that dominate our perception of the first part of Eastwood's career are the westerns and the Callahan cycle, but there is another influential group constituted by Don Siegel's *The Beguiled*, and Eastwood's *Play Misty for Me* and *Breezy*.

There are several connections between the three. In each case, the major subject is the hero's relationship to women. In *The Beguiled*, we see a world of women, a world controlled by them, and there is no significant living male figure in the film other than the Eastwood character. The other two films deal with a pair of lovers, showing them precariously surviving different forms of threat. These two, *Play Misty for Me* and *Breezy*, are Eastwood's first and third films as a director (the second is *High Plains Drifter*). *The Beguiled* and *Breezy* are also linked in a way unusual in Eastwood's work at this time: they were both unsuccessful at the box office. The films are anomalous in other ways – *The Beguiled* is the only film before *Honkytonk Man* in 1982 in which the Eastwood character dies, and *Breezy* is the only film until *Bird* (1988) which Eastwood directs but in which he does not appear.

In the light of the settings of spaghetti westerns it is sensible to notice that these three films are set in America. We know immediately where we are, in a world locked into the particular trajectories of collapse that belong to southern melodrama in *The Beguiled*, and addressing contemporary anxieties in the other two films, which are both set in the California of their present day.

The nature of the violence in these films also sets them apart. Guns are not important here – peripheral in *The Beguiled*, unseen in *Play Misty for Me* and not thought of in *Breezy*. The violence which these films address is not connected with crime and money (another contrast to the spaghetti westerns is that money has almost no direct role), but what is referred to as 'domestic' violence. Its weapons are the humdrum items found in the home, literally to hand in a moment of need – the kitchen knife, the pair of scissors, razors. It can dispense with weapons altogether – a man is pushed and falls the length of a staircase, a single blow causes a woman to fall to her death. Even at its most premeditated, violence is still associated with the domestic arts – the one careful execution in these films is carried out by administering poison at a formal meal.

These moments occur in *The Beguiled* and *Play Misty for Me*. The violence in *Breezy* is not strictly domestic, but it is ordinary enough: the instantaneous horror of car accidents which disrupts routine lives. The opening human gesture in *Breezy* is the rescue of an animal lying in the gutter after it has been hit by a car; the resolution of the plot comes about when the hero learns of a car accident in which a minor character has died.

Breezy is the only film in this group where we do not see violence perpetrated by women. *The Beguiled* and *Play Misty for Me* can be linked – and placed in opposition to the westerns or the Callahan cycle – by the image of a woman with a knife (or other 'domestic' weapon), rather than a man with a gun. In this respect they are part of the development in the representation of women and the effects of their violence as it appeared on screen during the early 'seventies which came about as a result of the the relaxation of actual or implicit censorship restrictions and was facilitated by special effects that offered the possibility of representing the work of knife or razor more convincingly than before.

This has a wider context than I can address here, stretching clearly into the images on American screens in the 'seventies from underground or independent film-making, or from European art cinema. In the area of images associating women with violence that mainstream producers considered could be suitably certificated and likely to show a profit, *The Beguiled* and *Play Misty for Me* can be linked with *The Legend of Lylah Clare* (Robert Aldrich, 1968), *Sisters* (Brian De Palma, 1973, but shot in the spring of 1972) and *Carrie* (Brian De Palma, 1976, based on Stephen King's 1974 novel). Elements of horror are important in all these films, and there are again links to the cycle of horror movies in this period which are more 'explicit' in terms of both censorship and special effects, among them the contemporary Hammer productions, *Lust for a Vampire* (Jimmy Sangster, 1971) and *Dr Jekyll and Sister Hyde* (Roy Ward Baker, 1971).

A list like this can do no more than suggest the currency of a particular subject or image, an opportunity for filming. It is part of the history of Eastwood's reputation that writers giving the films a cursory treatment at this time were liable to abstract the image from its context, producing a necessarily distorted version of it and of the films. A representative position can be found in Marjorie Rosen's *Popcorn Venus: Women, Movies and the American Dream* (1973). Arguing in a chapter entitled 'Clinicians of Decadence' that contemporary moviemakers have 'equated female sexuality with psychopathy' – Rosen quotes as two of her examples: 'the bunch of seething, hungry seminary girls in *The Beguiled* (1971), repaying the fickle attentions of wounded Clint Eastwood by cutting him up in tiny pieces; Jessica Walter, rejected by Clint Eastwood in *Play Misty for Me* (1972), manically attempting to stab him and girlfriend Donna Mills.'

My interest here is not particularly in the accuracy or otherwise of the descriptions of the films – although *The Beguiled* is hardly recognisable in this gloss – but the point of the underlying argument. In the same chapter, Rosen states that 'the appearance of brute strength on screen has paralleled the growth of female autonomy off [screen]', and refers to women having 'seized on a more productive lifestyle than ever before'. I am not sure what is meant by 'productive lifestyle', but the point would appear to be one about threat, that the films are intended to respond to the threatening idea of women as possessors of some kind of new power by labelling them as maniacs.

But the image of the woman with the knife is no more innately a negative image of woman than that of the man with the gun is necessarily a simply negative image of man. Siegel's and Eastwood's films describe the conditions of societies in apparent or concealed crisis – the American South of the Civil War, the Cali-

74

fornia of the last years of the Vietnam war – and these conditions determine both the nature of the violence and responses to it for both men and women. But we should look at the detail of the films to consider what Eastwood makes of this, his use of the image of the woman with the knife.

The Beguiled

The apparently unsurprising opening of *The Beguiled* – the credits sequence announcing that this is another Eastwood war film, this time set in the Civil War – soon turns unfamiliar. A badly injured Union soldier, Corporal John McBurney (Eastwood), is rescued from death by a little girl and taken to the comparative safety of a nearby Southern plantation house which is a school for young ladies. He does not make the unlikely, swift recovery familiar in the narrative of the action hero. He plays the first half of the film bedridden or hobbling on crutches, and, except in flashbacks, we never see him able to move easily, or away from the setting of this house.

Other elements in the opening of the film seem very recognisable, even though the audience of 1971 might not have expected to find them in an Eastwood movie. The mansion and its inhabitants embody a set of familiar elements which describe the social order defeated by the Union in the Civil War. They are commonly presented in a way which both offers a criticism of that order and mourns its passing, and this is true here. The building and its furniture, fittings and artworks present a vision of an aristocratic culture implicitly associated with Europeanness and a non-anglophone world – in the opening moments we see the girls being given a French lesson – a world seen as both splendid and useless. The collapse of this culture is frequently associated in Southern texts with transgressive sexual acts, miscegenation and incest, and we soon learn that the head of the school, Martha Farnsworth (Geraldine Page), has committed incest with her brother. (By the end of the film we know that the same brother also attempted the rape of a black servant.) The revelation of incest is introduced by a shot of one of the artworks of the mansion, a painting of the brother and sister couple – the point seems to be that the order expressed by the work of art is either a downright lie or a vacuous assertion of a lost past.

The first half of the film is built around the image of McBurney's enforced passivity in this world of women, and the speculations of the different women who assign him a role, or sketch out a future for him. For Martha Farnsworth, he will take the place of her brother, substituting Northernness and legitimate desire for the degeneracy of Southern masculinity. She believes that he can be made to wish to stay on when the war ends, and his potency is conceived as redeeming the past. This configuration, in which an older woman situated at the centre of a Southern plantation gone to seed looks for redemption from the past through a younger male stranger, has a substantial antecedent in American texts: Joanna Burden and Joe Christmas, the couple in William Faulkner's *Light in August* (1934). In Faulkner's novel the couple do become lovers; this does not redeem but exposes further negative qualities. Joanna's sexual desire becomes nymphomania, and her responses to Joe unlock the psychosis which leads him finally to kill her. At the centre of the fantasy of redemption is an image of the renewal of fertility which links the restoration of the land to the birth of a new family. In *Light in August* Joanna believes that Joe has made her pregnant, but

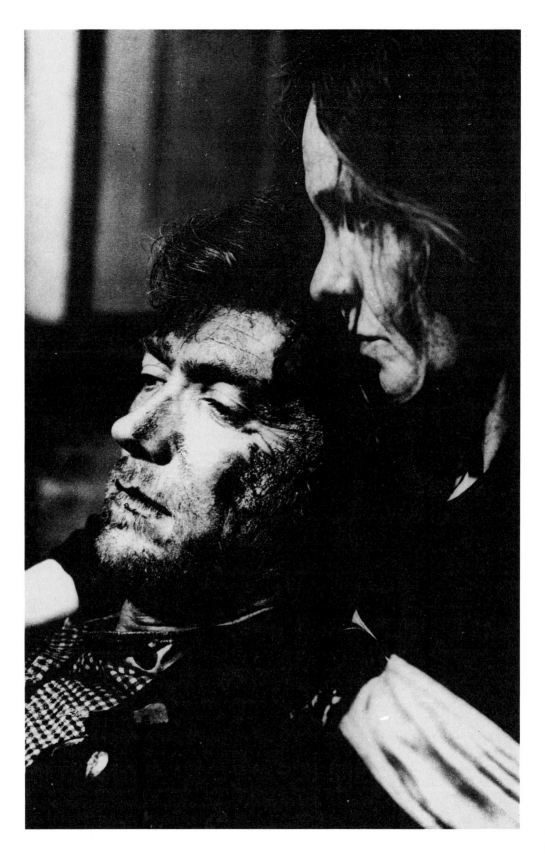

the couple are literally as well as metaphorically infertile, for her missed periods are brought about by her menopause.

In *The Beguiled*, the attempt at reconstruction of the family is initiated by reassigning roles within the mansion. Martha takes McBurney's presence as a prompt to remove the sign designating the place as a school, and in the same sequence she approaches her young teacher, Edwina (Elizabeth Hartman), with an offer of a partnership that will eventually lead to her inheriting everything. This looks like a way of positioning Edwina firmly as a metaphorical daughter rather than as a rival for possession of McBurney.

The film shows us the forces that bring about the collapse of Martha's fantasy. Despite her actions, there is competition for McBurney's affections. The plain and shy Edwina, presented with an opportunity for initially unthreatening contact with a man of around her own age, responds to his charm. Further, the sexual frisson engendered in the schoolgirls by the arrival of the soldier incites one of the older ones, Carol (Jo Anne Harris), to attempt to prove her attractiveness to herself by seducing him.

McBurney's behaviour among these women is significant in terms of both the subjects of *The Beguiled* and our appreciation of Eastwood's persona as a star at the time. His response is that of someone who makes no very profound calculations. Wishing to avoid being sent to a Confederate prison once he is well, he uses his charm on the various women who tend him, but there is no evidence that his motives are more complex than this, or that he contemplates their attitudes to each other. When McBurney is talking to women, Siegel uses flashbacks that contradict his words to define him as a casual liar, a sexual con man with no thought beyond exploiting the situation for his immediate convenience.

There is also the matter of social class. In one of the first screenplays in Eastwood's work where class differences have a clear role, the Eastwood figure is a corporal, not a lieutenant. The effect of this is twofold. On the one hand, he embodies for these genteel Southern women the myth of the potency of the proletarian. But while they are excited by him, he distrusts them. In this context, it is fitting that he first has sex with Carol, the woman who is constructed as the least genteel, even contemptuous of the culture (foreign languages and the right way to use a napkin) taught in the school. Jo Anne Harris's performance stresses Carol's crudeness, with a distinct Southern accent and verbal mannerisms.

The tensions arising from McBurney's attempted manipulations are concisely explored in a scene between McBurney and Hallie (Mae Mercer), the school's black servant, in which she has been instructed to shave the invalid. The occasion involves recognition of the attraction between the two, as she strokes his beard and jokes about his 'rooster blood', and is shot through with the ironies (already established in an earlier scene) of their positions respectively as slave and prisoner. Hallie mentions her lost black lover, and McBurney instantly offers a bargain: he will find the lover if she will help him escape. It is doubtful if he expects to be believed, or taken seriously, but it is a plea for some kind of complicity. As he concludes, 'You trust me now, huh?', Siegel cuts from Hallie's face to a shot of her hand picking up the cut-throat razor to shave him.

The female plantation owner and the male stranger: Martha Farnsworth (Geraldine Page) and Corporal John McBurney (Eastwood) in The Beguiled.

In cameo, this is an expression of a central subject of the film – the easy appropriation by the man of a situation (or a history) of a woman's pain or loss, and the visual sign of her anger (and also of her power over him) in an object which is simultaneously a domestic tool and a weapon.

A subsequent sequence writes this large. The narrative reaches the point where the three women – Martha, Edwina, Carol – have made their approaches or propositions to McBurney, and he has encouraged all of them. He is also regaining his strength and thus returning to a world where his sexual desires might pose an actual threat. As night falls, Siegel gives a little hint of this: the house is visited by Confederate soldiers who are reluctant to leave without 'paying their compliments' to the young ladies. It is time for the almost well McBurney to be positioned firmly within the family structure, and Martha now makes the direct offer to him that he stay on to run the plantation and become her lover.

McBurney's final choice seems to be made not out of a strong preference but as a result of crude pragmatism. On his way to Edwina's room he encounters Carol and makes love with her as a way of protecting himself from the consequences of her jealousy – finding him with Edwina earlier, she has tried to have him handed over to the Confederate soldiers.

But the privacy of a sexual act lasts only for a moment. Edwina's discovery of the couple, and her causing McBurney to fall down the stairs, precipitates him again into a situation where his wounded body – his injured leg has been broken in the fall – is the focus of the whole group of women and girls. They take him into the dining room – the central space where we see him with them all – and after the young girls are sent away, the principal women (Martha, Edwina, Hallie, Carol) experience together an intense physical relationship to his body.

I am being deliberately suggestive here. The act that they are engaged in is not group lovemaking, but the amputation of the soldier's leg – the film's insistence on the link between the two is clear if we refer back to the sequence immediately before McBurney chooses. It is a dream sequence – a painting of women with the body of Christ that hangs in Martha's room is translated in her unconscious into a scenario in which she and Edwina share the pleasures of McBurney's body, and acknowledge their mutual desire for each other in a kiss. (This is in contrast to the sequence showing McBurney's sexual imaginings – he recalls the occasions of kissing the three women as entirely separate.) The painting is a sanctioned way for a naked man to be surrounded by women. Martha's dream translates it into an expression of sexual satisfaction – the dream ends with the figures posed as in the painting, spelling out the connection to the audience.

What emerges through the amputation scene is the impossibility of satisfying the wish expressed in the dream, except in the form of this horrific parallel, or parody. For if the mansion cannot be turned into a family headed by the couple of McBurney and Martha or some more polymorphous grouping, then it reverts to its function as a disciplining institution – school, prison and hospital – in which a man can be shared between women only as an invalid to be nursed, or a body to be operated upon, or a corpse to be laid out.

The effect of the amputation is in part to return the situation to its earlier terms. McBurney is back in bed, visited by the same women as before. But there are also important differences. The experience of the initial wounding was something that happened outside, off the plantation, in the war between men. The

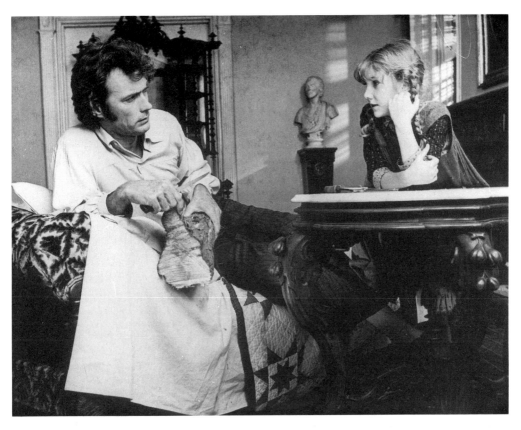

The good father-figure: McBurney with Amy (Pamelyn Ferdin) early in The Beguiled.

amputation is something these women did to this man in the house, and it is the basis of a new intimacy as real as that of lovers. (Or perhaps even more intense, in the case of his relationship to Martha. His attitude to Carol, who assures him that his crippling 'won't hinder you romantically', seems the least affected). At this stage, the Confederate army has retreated, and, as the soldier becomes convalescent for the second time, he has become less an intruder about to be handed over to the authorities and more of a stock figure of Southern myth, the victim whose impotent relationship to the forces destroying this civilisation is expressed in his or her crippled body. Not surprisingly, given its visual impact, this is striking in theatrical and cinematic contexts, rather than in the novel. Laura Wingfield in Tennessee Williams's play, *The Glass Menagerie*, is the famous case of it; the most closely analogous case to *The Beguiled* is in the most distinguished Southern film melodrama of the 'seventies, Richard Fleischer's *Mandingo* (1975), where both the father (James Mason) and the son (Perry King) are partly crippled.

What happens now feels a lot like self-pity, a licence to behave badly by one who feels badly used. Breaking into Martha's room, McBurney steals a pistol, threatens the women and goes to the cellar to get drunk. He has also stolen the brother's letters, and, learning in them of the incest, he confronts the assembled women. The scene takes place in an informal social space, not in the dining room but in the kitchen. McBurney seems to believe that he can expose Martha to the girls as morally bankrupt and unfit to teach them, but this misfires. He

Above: lesson time – supervised by Edwina (Elizabeth Hartman) and Martha, the children sew McBurney's body into its shroud in The Beguiled. *Opposite: the gentleman caller – McBurney charming Martha and Edwina.*

taunts her with the letters and a portrait locket, but Geraldine Page plays Martha's facing of her past with intense pathos, so that the value, rather than the corruptness, of the relationship is affirmed. The looked-for condemnation never materialises, and, as McBurney begins to try to spell it out, he is interrupted by Amy, the little girl who initially saved his life, looking for help with her pet tortoise. McBurney's act of killing the pet by drunkenly hurling it to the floor is the first of many moments in which the adequacy of a literally or metaphorically 'parental' character played by Eastwood – his ability to take on a role of caring or protection – is a crucial issue. This is followed by immediate remorse, but it is too late. He has failed in his attempt to act the patriarch condemning the corrupt mother, and then failed in the worst way to take an opportunity to show simple nurturing kindness. His awareness of this – ironically his now demonstrated affinity with the Southern culture of failed masculinity – is made explicit in his next line to Martha, which uses a word we have been waiting to hear: 'Condemned me, that's what you've done . . . why the hell didn't you just castrate me?'

The plot has one final twist. The pathos of McBurney's collapse moves Edwina to go to him – she locks them into his room, and they make love. They now plan to marry and leave the mansion. Simultaneously, the rest of the women conclude that they will be safe only when McBurney is dead. This is achieved appropriately by placing him at the head of the household at a formal meal that starts with him saying grace and ends with his death from eating a dish of poisonous mushrooms picked by Amy. The important quality of the sequence is its ordinariness – the young ladies of the seminary watch quietly while McBurney, sober and with his good humour restored, takes his poison and makes polite conversation. Martha's gesture to Edwina, indicating that she must not eat the mushrooms, is eloquent – the act of murder is treated as if it were a minor breach of manners, and the scene of sewing McBurney's body into its shroud, with which Siegel ends the film, is a mundane occasion utilised to teach one of the girls a new stitch. The gates of the seminary open. A little girl skips out, following the others carrying the corpse, and the credits roll.

This is not comedy, although it is at moments close to it, and neither are these figures gothic horrors. The presentation of incest in the film is exemplary – while, as ever, it stands as emblematic of the collapse of the Southern plantation family, it is also treated as a lost recollection of passion, and McBurney's attempt to use it to humiliate Martha fails. Just as incest fails to be a gothic horror, the conventional gothic scenario, in which the hero would flee with Edwina as the mansion burned to the ground, fails to materialise.

The entrance of a figure with the qualities of easy charm and simple motivations into a sexually charged situation of Southern culture inevitably recalls *The Glass Menagerie*, and the connection with Tennessee Williams's work is underlined through the casting of Geraldine Page, who was well known at the time for her stage interpretations of the plays. In his notes to *The Glass Menagerie*, Williams, with an irony that the play delicately articulates, calls the Gentleman

Caller 'a nice, ordinary young man'. This – including the irony – is Eastwood's role, a gentleman caller able neither to control the world into which he is inserted, nor to maintain his separateness from it.

Ultimately Siegel's film takes up a thread which we can find in Williams's work and elsewhere in American culture, where the critique of family life, the impossibility of sustaining a humane version of it in a particular set of cultural circumstances, is reflected through the presentation of the nature of the spaces in which the characters are seen to live and move. *The Glass Menagerie* shows a woman without a private place to sleep; the Wingfield living room doubles as Laura's bedroom. This is true again in *A Streetcar Named Desire*, in which Blanche is put up in a room which is 'primarily a kitchen'. The plantation house set in *The Beguiled* is only apparently the opposite. The house is huge, but the space occupied by McBurney is subject to continuous observation, or the possibility of it – children peep through the shutters, the various women enter the room at will to attend to his wounds, and the amputation is carried out not in a bedroom but in one of the public spaces of the house. Privacy can be achieved only briefly, in negative circumstances and with a struggle. When McBurney and Edwina are finally going to make love, we see her drag a heavy sofa across the doorway.

Play Misty for Me
Eastwood's debut as a director, *Play Misty for Me,* immediately follows *The Beguiled* and immediately precedes *Dirty Harry*. The milieu, as we are introduced to it in the credits sequence, is a recognisable form of the good life. A single man, driving a classic British sports car along a road which winds through the spectacle of the California seascape, is an image of freedom and modernity, set in a place which is neither the gothic South nor the lethal city. Almost the whole action takes place in or around a small town, identified in the film as Carmel. Eastwood does not characterise it in great depth – it is not the assertively benign small town commonly signified by the presence of happy children, but it seems to be free of conflicts prompted by race or class. Minor characters under-line this reassurance. Its silver-haired police sergeant, McCallum (John Larch), represents the pieties of the past: when he is thanked for his diligence, he winks at the speaker and replies 'Public servant'. The gay man who is the friend and confidant of the girl who will be the object of violence also has this function. This figure, whose role is to assure us that benign friendships are possible in the precarious world of this movie, has the status of a stereotype and can be traced up to the present – the gay characters in *Frankie and Johnny* (Garry Marshall, 1991) or *Single White Female* (Barbet Schroeder, 1992) are more recent examples.

The first building that we see in the film is this girl's house, a modest place, but set strikingly into the cliffs, its balcony looking directly down to the sea. There is nobody at home; the caller at the house is Dave Garver (Eastwood). He looks into the living room from the balcony at himself, or rather, at a portrait of himself. Then he drives off to his job – this is the credits sequence – and we learn that he is a disc jockey at the local radio station.

The portrait is perhaps the first clear sign of what the subject of the film is to be. It is an image that is both glamorised and threadbare, obviously not an artwork of very startling quality. Like other famous portraits in Hollywood melodrama – a celebrated example is the portrait of Gene Tierney in *Laura* – it is both a recognisable portrait of a star we can name and a hint of some reservation or anxiety. At stake is both the status of painting (the sense that the painting is obviously inferior to the photographed presence of the star) and the impulse towards possession. The idea that a painting can be owned announces the subject of a desire for possession of a beloved as absolute as the possession of his/her painted image.

We learn that Dave's show is a late-night one. His spiel offers 'a little verse, a little talk, and five hours of music to be very, very nice to each other by', casting him in the role both of a benevolent master of revels and a ghostly lover, a voice on the airwaves around whom fantasy can be constructed. His conversation with his fellow DJ Al Monte (James MacEachin) confirms his reputation as a lover, both off air – his ability to charm a female music producer is the subject of Al's irony – and on air, when the woman known to both men as 'your little Misty chick', calls with her usual request.

The self-deprecating grin that Eastwood gives to Dave when his sexual prowess is mentioned links the persona here with the cockiness of McBurney in the opening of *The Beguiled*; he is a man who has yet to feel that there are any potential problems in taking advantage of all the sexual opportunities that happen to come his way. We now see such a piece of serendipity, when, after work, he heads for his usual bar, meets a girl who turns out to be the 'Misty chick' and goes back to her place, where they make love. This girl will turn out to be the obsessive lover whose violence nearly destroys Dave and his girlfriend.

The nature of this initial meeting is important, and more subtle than the bald description of it suggests. When Dave arrives at the bar, the girl, Evelyn Draper (Jessica Walter), is alone. He asks the barman, Murphy (Don Siegel), about her, and is told that 'guys've been striking out all night'. The metaphor is continued, for Murphy and Dave now apparently begin to play a game with corks and counters that they call 'Cry Bastard'. More than one game is being played – Eastwood offers a series of carefully composed shots in which Evelyn is held in the frame with these two men as she first watches and then approaches them. The game turns out to be a piece of trumpery, a device to bring Evelyn over – Dave 'wins' when she accepts a drink from him, and Murphy tells her this as the images split up the threesome, offering Murphy alone and Evelyn and Dave as a couple.

There are ironies here. It later becomes clear that the manoeuvres of these two men are unnecessary, as Evelyn had come to the bar specifically to pick up Dave. This is almost an outright joke about the idea of control, given that one of the men is played by a veteran film director and the other by the neophyte director of this film. They think to frame or position Evelyn – her seduction of Dave is equally deliberate.

The scene at Evelyn's home which leads up to their making love for the first time is expressive of the film's relation to the subjects of sexuality and possession through its use of space. Eastwood shoots the couple in a set that seems cramped – small rooms shuttered against the outside world – but contains a framed image of space, the picture of the tea-clipper over the fireplace. The direction reinforces this, as the orderly compositions of the bar sequence give way to photography which is never less than medium close-up and emphasises the couple's awkward closeness – the shot of Dave kneeling to light the fire, where our view is partly obscured by Evelyn's body close to camera, is exemplary.

Above: framed by two directors – Evelyn Draper (Jessica Walter) watches Dave Garver (Eastwood) and barman Murphy (Don Siegel) at their game in Play Misty for Me. *Opposite: awkward closeness – Evelyn tries to hold on to Dave.*

When the couple has made love, the dissolve is to a shot which represents space – the calm, open sea, an image of peace or of sexual release. It is followed immediately by a shot of Evelyn inside her home, watching through her window as Dave drives away.

These oppositions structure what follows, a series of encounters in which Evelyn arrives unannounced at Dave's home or bullies him into coming to her place. The scenes revolve around food – bringing it to his house, inviting him to late-night supper – it is as if she believes that eating together in a domestic context might create an intimacy more substantial than that of a casual sexual union. It is outside their homes that Evelyn feels her hold on Dave to be weakest, and the initial moments when her anxiety spills over into rage all take place outside. She screams at a neighbour, then at a couple leaving Murphy's bar, and finally at Dave's business contact, an older woman whom she finds with Dave in a context that we understand by now must seem hatefully threatening; they are having lunch together alfresco. Jessica Walter's performance in this scene is exemplary – much of the film up to this point works around the sense that she communicates of Evelyn's state, as her project of transforming a voice heard on the radio into a lasting love-affair collapses into self disgust and vulnerability and desperation.

The film offers an alternative image of woman. Tobie Williams (Donna Mills) is certainly to be read as the film's 'good' girl, just as the dominant reading of Evelyn is as its murderous *femme fatale*, but the terms of her presentation are pointed in ways that can be linked with what the film expresses through Evelyn.

Tobie is Dave's long-standing girlfriend. She has been out of town in order to consider how she feels about her own desires for exclusive possession of him – she is the painter of the portrait which opens the film. But Dave and Tobie, as Eastwood presents and photographs them, rather than being a answer to the unhappy pairing of Dave and Evelyn, seem also to express some reservations about the idea of the couple.

If Evelyn is over-anxious for domesticity, Dave and Tobie seem consistently to exclude themselves from it. This is both part of the plotting – Tobie continually blocks the occasions when she and Dave might enjoy privacy by importing a series of female paying guests into her house – and part of the direction. We see the couple together almost exclusively outside, on the beach or wandering the coastal woods, as if they can feel at ease with each other only in such places. At the opposite pole from the scenes with Evelyn, the camerawork emphasises distance and space – their conversations are frequently shown with the couple in long shot.

The mood created by this is continued into the sequence which confirms Tobie's role as benign heroine: Eastwood shows the couple making love as a Roberta Flack ballad is played on the soundtrack. The sequence takes place after Evelyn has seen them together, and the collapse of her fantasy of intimacy has given way to a violent desire to destroy it. She is discovered by the maid wrecking Dave's home. After attacking the maid, she collapses, and the police take her away. Dave and Tobie's lovemaking now takes place neither in her place nor in

his but in the woods – the point (it is reflected in the lyric of the song) seems to be that only some kind of Edenic fantasy of an initial moment of desire is actually satisfactory. Eastwood seems to hint that this couple can no more make the journey to an actual domestic milieu than could Evelyn and Dave. If there is a lack of conviction here, perhaps it can be related to something that we know from *film noir* – the great difficulty in making the good woman as glamorous (or as touching) as the bad.

In another respect, too, the film can be illuminated by considering it in the light of *film noir*. I have already suggested that Dave's job is a glamorous one, seen as bringing him into potentially erotic contact with women. In this respect, he is a little like the *noir* private eye, a figure whose work may mean that he cannot possibly be domesticated, or can at best be projected into a domestic milieu that will occur after the end of the narrative and that we cannot quite imagine. Tobie's expression to Dave of her anxieties on this score, of other women as one of the job's hazards – 'Maybe he's run himself off a cliff, or maybe he's run into a blonde' – is a direct descendant of the ironic coupling of women and danger for the private eye; Velda's line to Mike Hammer in Robert Aldrich's *Kiss Me, Deadly*, 'Be careful, someone might blow you a kiss', is as concise as this point can get.

If we accept that there is a problem being stated, or rather restated, here, then the last part of *Play Misty for Me* can be read as an attempt to find a solution. In part, this is a disappointment – Evelyn changes from a desperate woman, aware of the hopelessness of her fantasy, to a simple incarnation of rage. The result is to move the plot more towards that of a thriller in which the home is under threat from a psychotic, and the man's role becomes the affirmation of the rightness of the good couple by destroying the intruder. But, even here, there are signs of tentativeness, or reservation. The fact that Tobie invites Evelyn into her home – under the alias of Annabel she is the latest of the paying guests – shows trust at the point where it meets foolishness. Evelyn's line to Tobie at the point when the alias is penetrated – 'God, you're dumb' – is hard for the audience to contradict, and Tobie's next appearance is as literally dumb, bound and gagged by Evelyn.

Of course, Eastwood does have Dave turn out all right in the end, a satisfactory man of action who strikes the blow which results in Evelyn's death, and thus saves Tobie and himself from her knife. But the authority with which he acts can be measured only if we look at his behaviour in the whole movie.

An important moment is the point which we take as the first sign that there is going to be trouble, when Evelyn turns up uninvited at Dave's home with her arms full of groceries. He attempts to teach her a lesson:

Dave: I'm trying to say that there's a telephone, and I pick it up and I dial, and you answer and I say, 'Hey what are you doing?'
Evelyn: And I say, 'I'll be right over.'
Dave: Fine, next time why don't we do it that way . . .

A moment earlier, Dave has explained why the telephone call might be necessary – 'what if he and I had been doing a little business, or I'd been entertaining some female company.' The telephone is offered as a way of structuring the world, dividing business from pleasure, or separating one girl from another. It can be taken as a refusal of any intimacy other than the immediate pleasure of lovemaking – after which the parties retreat to the ends of the telephone line, waiting to call or be called.

That Dave likes this relationship to women, or that it is all that he can bear of them, is indicated by his response to the real intimacy which Evelyn offers, that is, her rage. His numb puzzlement and lack of response to her public outbursts climaxes in the scene in which she cuts her wrists in his bathroom. It is followed by a sequence in which, in a sadly ironic inversion of Evelyn's earlier attempts to make for a domestic moment by feeding him, he now feeds her. It is arguably one of the more relaxed times that they have together, but it also indicates their similarity. Like Evelyn, Dave substitutes a dumb show of nurture for any more probing relation, any attempt to talk or listen.

The happy couple? Dave with Tobie (Donna Mills), the good girl in Play Misty for Me.

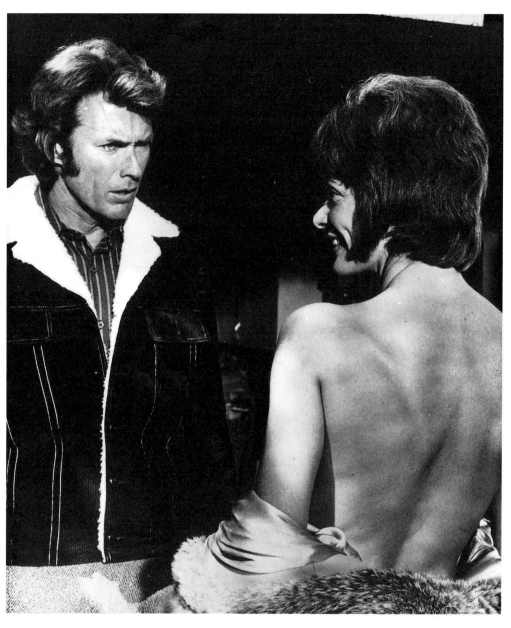

Bad behaviour: Evelyn and Dave in Play Misty for Me.

The confirmation of this similarity comes in the sequence in which Dave returns to his house to find the police there after Evelyn's attack on the maid. His lack of reaction to the stabbing and the wreck of his home is as marked as Evelyn's rage has been earlier. He makes no attempt to talk to Evelyn; he offers a modern platitude to Sergeant McCallum – 'What she needs is psychiatric help' – and McCallum's ironic 'Really?' signals for us the inadequacy here.

This is the last time that Dave sees Evelyn until the final scene in Tobie's house. Eastwood neatly ties the closing images of his film in with its opening, intercutting Evelyn's slashing of the portrait with Dave's high-speed drive from studio to house. The final encounter emphasises Dave's vulnerability as he is repeatedly slashed and stabbed by Evelyn, his desperate awkwardness indicated by a nasty effect when he grabs the blade of the knife. He lashes out with a fist, knocks her through the window on to the balcony, and she falls backwards over the rail to her death. It is the fall rather than the blow which kills her.

Compare with this a moment in a film released in the same year, the climax of *Klute*. There again, the final confrontation between hero and psychopath results in death but not exactly in execution. Physically the moment is not dissimilar, with the psychopath hurling himself through a window, falling from a huge height as John Klute (Donald Sutherland) comes to the rescue of his girl, Bree Daniels (Jane Fonda). In both cases, the impression is of the source of threat suddenly whisked from the scene, leaving a couple whose future is not entirely secured by this release. Klute and Bree Daniels leave her apartment and New York together, but her last line to her off-screen analyst is 'You'll probably see me next week', and the closing image is of their empty apartment, the nearest thing that the film has offered to a home, now stripped bare.

Dave and Tobie do not speak. Eastwood has them shuffle out on to the balcony – she is supporting him – and the camera follows their gaze, picking out Evelyn's body floating in the water. On the soundtrack, we hear the radio. A tape of one of Dave's earlier shows is playing. As they emerge into the open air, his voice announces a dedication to Evelyn, and the credits play over Errol Garner's 'Misty'.

In *Play Misty for Me*, the reservations about the future of the romantic couple are explicitly placed against something that we know from the movies, that the idea of the perfect couple is best expressed by 'their' tune, the melody which erases all literal difficulties by associating them with timelessness, with the 'classic'. The film that most famously promotes this idea, that the lovers' status is asserted through the theme tune, is *Casablanca*, where the lovers' re-encountering each other is celebrated by the direct playing of the tune. Eastwood's film can be associated with other material produced at about the same time which recalls *Casablanca* directly and registers its distance from the present. I am thinking of Herbert Ross's *Play It Again, Sam* (1972), in which the subject becomes a source of comedy for Woody Allen.

Eastwood's film, punctuated by telephone calls between the principals, is not a fable intended to elevate Dave's healthy self over Evelyn's sick one, but shows them both as trapped within technology that controls or determines the self. Evelyn does not know how to encounter Dave other than as a voice on the radio – she can think of only one thing to do, which is to suggest that they sleep together. This is exactly matched in the limits of Dave's control and competence when being that voice, or that self – when he encounters a woman seduced by it, he can think only of the same, one thing to do. The integrity certainly of the first half of *Play Misty for Me* lies in Eastwood's preparedness to allow the parallel between Dave and Evelyn to emerge in the scenes in which her rage and anger are matched by his, in the violence of his reaction to the discovery that he cannot control this woman any more than she can control him. In the sequences in his home, and particularly in his bedroom, leading up to and away from Evelyn's suicide attempt, he is completely impotent in the face of the dominance of her fantasy of their closeness. In the yellow bedroom – the colour is closely associated with Evelyn in the film – this closeness comes to seem inescapable. The dissolve between images of his face, separated by the hours Evelyn spends asleep in his arms, is a pointed parody of a convention of romance.

Their final conversation confirms them as mutual victims. Evelyn phones Dave's radio programme, pretending that she is leaving town. She asks for and seems to be given forgiveness. Dave asks her if she is near a radio, and her reply is close to *Casablanca*: 'No. But play it for me, anyway.' Their assumption of their roles as 'fan' and 'star' is unhesitating, but we do not hear its result until the last seconds of the movie. This moment, the final dedication and playing of 'Misty', taped and then reproduced on Tobie's radio, is a final indication of the inexorable quality of the technology among which these figures are situated.

Breezy

Play Misty for Me partly works by describing a world in which we see characters with almost no social context at all – the principals are never shown to fit into (or stand out from) milieux which involve friends or acquaintances, and perhaps a shared past. The radio station, as we see it, is simply a single set in which Dave Garver and one other DJ are seen talking into the machines – there are no managers, no secretaries, no public world of any kind. It is a world based on recognition by signs. The purest example of this in the film is the piece of business in which Dave follows a girl believing her to be Tobie. It turns out that he has misidentified her because she is wearing Tobie's distinctive sweater. The girl at once guesses what has happened and in turn correctly identifies him through his mistake. Dave's voice, or the words 'Play Misty for Me' on Evelyn's lips are other such signs, and the film is an account of their inadequacy, or dangerousness.

Breezy repeats the idea of the reluctant encounter of a male hero with a woman, but it is interested in locating the two within specific social milieux. Both films originate from Jo Heims, the storywriter and collaborator on the screen-play of *Play Misty for Me*, and the screenwriter here. Her particular subject in *Breezy* was topical in 1973, the relation of the 'straight' (bourgeois, employed) world to the world of the 'hippie'. This involves several overlapping matters – the assumptions that we make about these contexts, the ways in which they present themselves to the people who are within them, the ways in which either world appears to the other.

The opening shot of the movie puts us into some relation to the hippie world. Eastwood opens with his camera tracking across an interior – the shot shows a guitar, passes over various posters and a purple peace symbol. Finally, it finds a couple in bed. The girl, who wakes, is Breezy (Kay Lenz). She is clearly at ease in this environment, although it is not her home. We see her exploring it, her awareness of its squalor – she tries unsuccessfully to find some toothpaste. She dresses, there is a brief exchange with the man about money (which serves to establish that neither of them has any) and she leaves after a moment of dialogue shows that the man does not even know her name. A credits sequence follows in which she walks the streets in the sunshine to the accompaniment of a song by Marilyn and Alan Bergman about freedom.

Our introduction to the hero is in a sequence which offers itself for comparison to the first. Another couple are parting after a night together – a middle-aged man, Frank Harmon (William Holden), is despatching his date of the previous night into a taxi. It is an arid passage. Holden's acting of odious

The odd couple: Breezy (Kay Lenz) and Frank Harmon (William Holden).

heartiness conveys exactly Frank's impatience to get rid of the girl, and the actress playing the overnight date (Lynn Borden) suggests her miserable awareness of his feeling. The nature of her situation is important for the rest of the film, although this character does not appear again. It is clear that she is not a hooker – rather, she is a woman of Frank's class and social set who might reasonably hope that his interest in her would extend beyond this one-night stand, but has no sense of how to create the conditions in which this might happen. Even as she insists on giving Frank her telephone number, it is obvious to both of them that he will never call her.

The qualities of these two sequences seem to point to an obvious movie. Frank and Breezy will meet, and a scenario will develop in which the vigour and energy of a figure who is not a settled bourgeois will emotionally revitalise a static bourgeois life. This is roughly true – a chance encounter leads to others by design, Breezy falls in love with Frank, Frank loves her. Drama is then generated by his struggle between this feeling and his sense, in which age and class play a part, that what he is doing is foolish or improper. He loses her – Breezy's words are 'throwing us away' – and finds her again.

This is a familiar plot, but neither of the two opening incidents I have described seems to offer a context felt to be benign. Part of the interest of *Breezy* is in understanding how the two milieux that form the background to it were viewed in 1973, how they relate to the love affair, and from where, if not from these contexts, the affair is to find its positive qualities.

A paradigm for this can be established by looking at an analogous melodrama of the romance emerging from milieux where the values are very clearly defined for audience and characters, Douglas Sirk's *All that Heaven Allows* (1955), in which the settled bourgeois figure is female. In Sirk's film, the virtues of the country club part of the small town in which Cary (Jane Wyman) is a recent widow are, at best, routine friendship and affection; at its worst, it is explicitly corrupt, and sexually both predatory and sterile. Against it, Sirk poses the non-bourgeois world of Ron Kirby (Rock Hudson). This revolves around a close relation to nature (growing trees) and benign American culture (reading Henry David Thoreau). It is not an exclusively Anglophone world, and is focused around a couple who have abandoned an explicitly city-based and bourgeois pursuit, the advertising business. Sirk further expresses this difference through his direction and use of sets – the two worlds look very different.

The matter of choice between these two milieux is not difficult – I mean the audience's choice, not Cary's decision – as is partly emphasised by the apparent insularity of the two. Except insofar as the plot brings them into collision, the worlds seem to touch at almost no point – the town doctor is the only possible transitional figure. Otherwise they are blind to each other – the matron who claims never to have met Ron, and greets his reminder that he has been pruning trees in her garden for years as a social solecism, makes this blindness, represented in terms of social class, absolutely explicit.

Another way of putting this is that the two worlds of *All that Heaven Allows* are alike in their hauteur – while individuals might decamp from one side to the other, both assume the values of their own group to be unassailable. In *Breezy*, Eastwood offers neither world to the audience as ideal, and part of what is wrong in the bourgeois world is that it knows this, perceives its own inadequacy and stares uneasily at a world which looks to have different priorities. The hippies do not do this, but it is implied that this is out of narcissism rather than conviction. Part of the criticism of them here is their indifference to everything outside themselves.

The world of the hippies is probably the simpler case – we see less of it, and the signals are clear ones. We are shown the escape from bourgeois conditions as uniformly negative. Non-possessive sex is presented as indifference – the boy with whom Breezy is sleeping in the opening shot appears for a moment in a later scene designed only to show that he does not remember her. For women, the conditions of hippie life are represented by Breezy's friend Marcy (Jamie Smith Jackson). Here is both sexism – we are told more than once that her boyfriend 'gets pissed off if I'm not where I'm supposed to be' – and the negative elements of drug culture. Another boy appears in one scene only to emphasise selfishness. These are crude annotations, though not untypical of their time – the smiling, empty hippies who live opposite Marlowe (Elliott Gould) in Robert Altman's *The Long Goodbye* (1973) speak to the same prejudices.

What is perhaps more remarkable, and certainly more extensive, is the treatment of the film's bourgeois world. I have already described how we are introduced to it through a scene with a woman – this subject is taken up and elaborated in the sequence in which we see Frank at his work as a real estate agent. He has a lunch date with Betty (Marj Dusay), a woman whom he has been seeing for some months. On their way, Frank has to view a house which is to be sold. The couple wander through the empty rooms, and the woman speaks of her ambitions '. . . I suppose I could be hysterically happy in a house like this.' She goes on to outline her awareness of Frank's indifference to her, and tells him that she is accepting a marriage proposal from another man, whom she does not love.

The final figure of this kind is Frank's divorced wife, Paula (Joan Hotchkis). Her single appearance is a chance encounter with Frank and Breezy in a restaurant, where she drunkenly denounces Frank's reliability. She does not attack Breezy – her only comment is an astonished 'You're so young.'

It is not suggested that any of these women are stupid or unattractive. The link between them is that in each case they acknowledge the collapse of any context in which they might be able to make some sexual choice that would be satisfying and more than temporary – their world still calls this choice marriage. The result is a submission to their own betrayal and humiliation which they nervously acknowledge – Eastwood seems able, in his direction of these actors, to elicit performances that dramatise the misery of the speaker and the sense of the narrowness of opportunity offered by the whole milieu. And these women are representative – there is no example of a happy or successful marriage in the film.

In *All that Heaven Allows*, the limitations of even the benign side of the bourgeois world are embodied in Cary's best friend Sara Warren (Agnes Moorehead). In *Breezy*, this perspective is similarly embodied in a best friend, here Bob Henderson (Roger C. Carmel). Bob is yet another victim of the failure of marriage – reduced to crude sparring with his wife, he fantasises about an affair with a young girl, an image of sexual revival in which longing is mixed with self-disgust. Just as with the women, what is striking about Bob's role is the acknowledgement of weakness and misery, of fantasies that will not be fulfilled, of the sense of a man waking in middle age to an overwhelming feeling of betrayal. The character could be said to make the point for men that has been made by the trio of unhappy women, that the conditions of this milieu are massively unable to provide satisfaction for anyone who inhabits it.

In the light of this, it is interesting to compare the forces which motivate the plot in the last parts of *Breezy* with those operative in *All that Heaven Allows*. The plots are broadly similar in form – the bourgeois figure rejects the lover, realises that this is mistaken, and the lovers are reunited in the closing moments. In Sirk's film, Cary has to reject Ron not because he cannot be accepted into the bourgeois world (a party sequence where he tangles with the local lecher demonstrates this, although it was never truly his project), but rather because, even if Cary can leave that world, she cannot entirely sever her ties with it. We

Above: at the movies – Frank and Breezy go to see High Plains Drifter.
Opposite: not just a dirty joke – Frank and Breezy in his bed.

understand the crucial issue to be the gossip in the small town as it affects her children – her happiness cannot be allowed to make them unhappy.

Compare this with the set of comparable moments in *Breezy*. There is no scene in which Breezy's oppositeness to the 'straight' world is demonstrated – there is a party sequence, but Frank leaves Breezy at home. The point of this sequence is simply to demonstrate how appalling bourgeois life is, as a contrast to the possibility of life with Breezy: she and Frank make love for the first time when he returns home from this macabre occasion. When Frank and Breezy do confront Frank's friends, it is in a suggestively modern setting – they run into them by chance at the movies. Again this is not a stage for violent antagonism, but rather the opposite. Frank flees the occasion because of his shame at the probability of Breezy's being accepted by the group in a spirit of voyeuristic, lustful fascination.

A way of putting the contrast is that Cary rejects Ron because of her mistaken care for others. Frank rejects Breezy because of his self-contempt, his fear that Bob's seedy fantasy actually describes what he and Breezy amount to. His line to her is 'All we add up to is a dirty joke.' (This is a fear exactly articulated, and dismissed, in an early moment of the romance in *All that Heaven Allows*. Cary has agreed to go on a dinner date with Ron to meet his friends Kay and Ned Scott. As they arrive, Cary sees Ron lean forward to Ned and say something sotto voce, and Ned looks at her and laughs. Later, Cary questions Ron; he answers,

'I said, you had the prettiest legs I'd ever seen.' So Sirk explicitly offers a world where the erotic can be celebrated among friends, where the joke is not dirty.)

Between the parting of the lovers and their finding each other again in the final moments of the film, Sirk shows us Cary's discovery that her children no longer need her to be their mother, no longer need the security represented by the family home and thus by her position in it – their indifference is happily her freedom. Having cleared away this issue, Sirk then uses two conventions – the first, taken from the Hollywood women's film, is a scene in which a doctor is the mouthpiece telling a woman what she wants, and it is followed by an accident which brings Cary to Ron's bedside.

In *Breezy*, Eastwood plays with similar conventions. A midnight telephone call from hospital brings Frank to a bedside. This seems like the familiar accident which will unite the couple in a context of physical damage or disfigurement and which might be taken to promise a release from the old social world, a resolution of such differences that can be traced at least as far back as *Jane Eyre*. But when Eastwood's camera finally reveals the face in the hospital bed, it is not Breezy but Betty, the survivor of a car accident which has killed her new husband. Her story seems to have two points – that happiness might be found in unpromising contexts and that it should be seized for as much or as little time as it lasts. When he finds Breezy again, Frank now tells her, 'If we're lucky we might last a year.' Breezy's reply – 'A year. Just think of it Frank, a whole year.' – converts the uncertainty into a mild gag.

What I have left out of this account of *Breezy* is what the film offers as positive values in the light of its view that both the straight and the hippie worlds

are insupportable. Mostly, this is constructed around the casting of William Holden and the setting given to him. Frank's house, which sets him off from the other bourgeois, is isolated 'up in the hills' above Los Angeles. The building is a vernacular version of western architecture, perhaps owing something to some of the domestic work of Frank Lloyd Wright in the early decades of the century. In emphasising its glass walls and, later on, the importance of its massive fireplace, Eastwood is showing us a home which, rather than offering the domestic setting as excluding the natural, suggests a benign relationship to nature, incorporating light and fire into the domestic space. (Ron's restored mill, with its fire and huge window, in the closing sequence of *All That Heaven Allows* is an analogous case; Sirk's film ends with a line of dialogue about home, but the image is of nature, a shot of a deer grazing just outside the glass wall of the mill.) The effect is one of the modernisation of the ideal of the frontier cabin, rather than that of the family mansion, which Thoreau likened to the family tomb.

The scenes with Frank and Breezy in the house can be read for the contrasts with Breezy's past. Instead of the empty toothpaste tube at Bruno's, we are shown Frank's palatial showering facilities, the first thing Breezy wants to try. Equally, the more distant past can be evoked – seeing Frank's fireplace, Breezy tells him, 'We used to have one at home but it was a phoney, you know, electric, you had to plug it in.' At this point, we are asked to see her not as a hippie, but as a girl from deprived small-town America, finally discovering that the authenticity of the camp-fire can be contained inside the domestic world.

Of the other opportunities for domestic pleasure offered by the house, the most important is the nurturing of a pet. The role of the film's pet, a big dog, is as follows. Frank's first contact with Breezy – he gives her a lift – ends when she insists that they stop to help a dog lying in the gutter. Frank announces that the dog is dead, and Breezy runs off in despair. He then sees that there are still signs of life and reluctantly takes the dog to the veterinary hospital. Later, he promises Breezy a surprise, and takes her to the hospital where they find the dog restored to health. It becomes part of their life as a couple, on the beach, in the park, on the bed.

Some of the point to this is not difficult. In the film's first incident Breezy hitches a ride with a sexually predatory driver who tells her a story of a punishment for non-cooperation, 'I gave her something to remember and threw her out the car.' This makes the connection between the possibilities of Breezy's life and those of an injured animal in the gutter sufficiently clear. It is pursued in Frank's response to Breezy – in her first visits to his house, she is just a stray he is taking in and feeding. The film annotates this in simple ways, like her lack of concern at her own nakedness as she prepares to use Frank's shower.

The casual exposure of Breezy's body to the camera in the first half of the film is important. (Interestingly, it resulted in a censorship rating that may have damaged the commercial prospects of the film.) It contradicts what the two men initially assume, that she is some kind of whore, that she intends that her body be used as the basis of some kind of exchange. The malign version of this is clearly presented in the driver who propositions her, but Frank is equally convinced of her motives when she first comes to his house. The object of the

In the gutter: Breezy escapes from a predatory male driver.

shower scene is to establish that he is wrong – they cannot have the relationship either of hooker and client, or of owner and pet, and Breezy leaves.

When she returns, or rather is returned, by the local police, it is as a different person. 'Elizabeth Alice Breezerman' is the name on the cop's lips, and with a different relation – she has told them that she is Harmon's niece. She wishes to be part of this family. His acceptance of or rather complicity in this lie is an

Below: public pleasures – Frank and Breezy with her candyfloss. Right: the dominant male – Frank dressing for his bourgeois life.

acknowledgement that he wants it too. After this, he periodically refers to her as 'Elizabeth Alice'.

The restored dog is reintroduced here as a gift from Frank to Breezy – she gives it an absurd name. Its function has now changed from being a parallel or analogue to Breezy to being a symbol of the possible continuity of the couple, a substitute for, or promise of, children. When Frank rejects Breezy and she leaves his house, she tells him that he must keep the dog, as she could not afford to feed it, adding, 'Do me one favour – don't teach him to roll over and play dead.'

The significance of this moment is that it so exactly reminds us of the conditions under which this couple can exist at all. At first, Frank's money was used, as if by magic, to restore the pet from the dead. Breezy's parting line here makes the point that the some power of control still rests firmly with Frank.

A look at the detail of one final sequence will substantiate this and offer an example of the subtlety of *Breezy*. The scene takes place shortly after the couple have become lovers, when they are finding ways of declaring their new status. One element of Breezy's power is her body – finding candy floss on the front of her sweater, she dares Frank to the public eroticism of brushing it off. Now they pass a shop and, with a joke about Howard Hughes, he offers to buy her clothes, a scane that has the status of a commonplace – we might connect it back to *The Palm Beach Story* or forward to *Pretty Woman*.

Inside the shop, Eastwood does not show Breezy trying on different outfits for Frank's – and the audience's – pleasure and judgement. There is another customer, a woman of roughly Harmon's age, accompanied by a little boy with a toy gun, the only weapon in this film. He 'shoots' Frank, who obligingly plays the western role: 'You got me, partner.' This is sufficient introduction for him to turn to the woman, who is hesitating over a dress, and shake his head. A dumb show follows, in which she chooses another dress, he rejects it, and finally gestures approval of a third. Breezy now appears in her new outfit, replying to his compliment that she can see her beauty in her eyes. The saleswoman completes the transaction, assuming that the two are father and daughter.

These are all hints in the same direction. The fact that Frank and the woman customer do not speak underlines that it is merely by being the male in this room that he has the power to determine her choice, just as he is an honourable target for the little boy's western fantasy. Breezy's sense of her own beauty rests on her view of Frank's view of it – the saleswoman positions the two in a different narrative of the power of the rich, older man accompanied by the young woman. The scene demonstrates concisely how completely power devolves on the man – the wider film describes the limits of his ability to cope with its burden. The casting of William Holden is exactly appropriate. Holden's recent high-profile role had been as Pike Bishop in *The Wild Bunch* (Sam Peckinpah, 1969), where he is associated explicitly with the final moments of exhaustion of the traditions and vision of the western.

My readings of these three films have attempted to argue that in each case we are introduced to a context in which massively powerful forces operate against the formation of a couple with anything like hopes of happiness. In *The Beguiled*, a whole culture is collapsing around the players. The plot turns on variations in the positioning of the man within the corrupt categories of the Southern plantation world – proletarian redeemer, castrated patriarch – and finally acknowledges the appropriateness of his death as an ultimate metaphor of the impotence of any man in this situation. In denying the effect of the mushrooms – 'Maybe his heart just gave out' – Martha stresses this point for us. We are to see McBurney's death as not so much a literal poisoning as the result of the insoluble combination of his sexual energies with the historical situation of plantation society.

The specific modern historical moment is also important here. 1971 was an important year in the implementation of Richard Nixon's policy of withdrawing US military personnel from Vietnam. The number of troops there fell by half, from just over 300,000 to just over 150,000, but the cumulative total of those wounded in action for the whole war stood at 302,000 by the end of the year. The resonance of the figure of the wounded soldier, and an imagining of an America of women into which he cannot be reintegrated, must have formed some part of the context of the reception of *The Beguiled*.

Play Misty for Me proposes a totally different set of conditions, but their effect is no less absolute. Raymond Carney, in his masterful *American Vision: The Films of Frank Capra* (1986), has described in detail the development in Capra's work through *Mr Smith Goes to Washington* and *Meet John Doe* to *State of the Union*, arguing that Capra explores the terms in which the 'self was overwhelmed by the narrative and technological systems around it'. It is to this tradition that *Play Misty for Me* belongs, a cinema in which individuals are subject to technology and the categories and assumptions that arise from it. The refuges from such a situation in this film are violence and madness – but while Evelyn is certainly seen to become a psychopath, the film insists not on the competence of any version of masculinity to deal with her, but its near impotence. The traditional cop is useless, despatched in one blow, and Dave's final triumph is the result of a lucky blow, landed, in effect, on the edge of a massive precipice – it is the fall that does the job of disposing of Evelyn.

To think about the ending of a film with a couple poised over a vertiginous drop is to prompt the recall of a famous moment, the end of Alfred Hitchcock's *North by Northwest* (1959). Stanley Cavell has described the positive qualities of this moment: 'Thornhill (Cary Grant) lifts Eve (Eva Marie Stuart) directly from the isolation of the monument's ledge to the isolation of the marriage bed, as if identifying both places as the scene of cliff-hangers and declaring that they are at home in both' (*Themes out of School*, p.172).

Play Misty for Me is also a cliff-hanger. but an unhappily opposite one, where the despatching of the *femme fatale* leaves the couple together but not truly at home, staring aghast down a drop which could be taken to express the instability or precariousness of their world. Eastwood does not photograph them turning to re-enter the house.

Breezy is eventually only a little more happy, or optimistic. Perhaps more directly than either of the other films, it describes a culture in which power – specifically power over the domestic, with a central character in the business of selling homes – rests with men, and desirability is defined in relation to them. The pain of its minor female figures, recognising their submission to this, links them closely to Evelyn; they differ only in not possessing her violence. Breezy can find love only inside the same set of terms, and the only security of her position is arguably that she is on the fringes of this society. She is thus able to risk being 'hysterically happy' – to use Betty's resonant phrase – for a time.

A final way of describing the crisis, or situation, that all three films address is to see them as films in which a couple is given the task of getting past the fact of making love into some kind of context where the sexual act might evolve into something else. Clearly this is impossible in *The Beguiled*, where one sexual act leads to injury, and the other, taking place in the barricaded centre of the house, precedes the death of the man.

In both *Play Misty for Me* and *Breezy*, the celebration of the benign couple is not a celebration of home, but of space. This is most marked in *Play Misty for Me* in ways I have already described, but, even in *Breezy*, the ease of the lovers outside, at the ocean's edge or finally reconciled in the park, is in marked contrast to their behaviour in Frank's house, where always at least the potential for the negative effects of bourgeois power is lurking. This emerges in a subject which links all three films, the function of meals. To be positioned at the head of the table is literally a death sentence for McBurney, and rejections of both Evelyn and Breezy take place as they prepare food in the man's house. The fear which this moment engenders in the man (Frank's line to Breezy here is, 'I cannot cope with it. I cannot cope with any of it.') may work for us because of a directness which a meal on screen possesses, as distinct from a scene of making love. This is, I think, because we experience lovemaking on screen as more or less always simulated, but preparing food or eating it as real, with the actors handling real food. Certainly it is an activity which proposes a closeness, or possibly suggests a continuity, that cannot be sustained in the worlds of these films.

CHAPTER FOUR
THE LATER WESTERNS

Since the release of the Dollars trilogy in America in 1967, Eastwood has starred in eight westerns. These fall loosely into two chronological groups. The first, *Hang 'Em High*, (Ted Post, 1968), *Two Mules for Sister Sara* (Don Siegel, 1970) and *Joe Kidd* (John Sturges, 1972), relates firmly back to the history of western production in the context of both Eastwood's own career to this point and those of the directors. Ted Post, Siegel and John Sturges had all directed western features in the 'fifties, and Post, who worked extensively in television, was one of the most frequent directors of episodes of *Rawhide*. In their use of Eastwood, the films also rely on elements familiar from the Dollars movies. This is most apparent in the role of Mexico. *Two Mules for Sister Sara* announces both its connection with and its departure from the Dollars movies in the words 'Filmed in Mexico' in the opening credits, and so offers itself as a somehow more authentic version of the configuration of the American mercenary in a foreign land, the role that Eastwood reprises. But this signalling is ambiguous – if it is important to the audience to know that we are actually looking at Mexico and not Spain, we are still listening to a version of Mexican music composed by Ennio Morricone, the composer for all three Dollars films.

Joe Kidd is set in New Mexico. Its plot again turns on the relationship of Americans to Mexicans, placing the Eastwood figure between a group of Mexican farmers and a villainous American landowner. Although the action is set entirely in the United States, there is a stress on the difference between the two cultures, exemplified in a moment of confrontation, when a challenge made to the Mexicans by the landowner is repeated in Spanish by one of his men so as to make sure that it has been understood.

Hang 'Em High at first appears to be entirely unrelated to such issues, in that it is set in Oklahoma and Eastwood plays a lawman, a Federal Marshal. Certainly, this film does not place Eastwood in opposition to an alien culture – remarkably, for a film set in nineteenth-century Oklahoma, there are almost no Indians to be seen. Instead, it is built around a revenge plot. Perhaps what links it to Eastwood's earlier films is that after its opening minute it is not about achieved settlement. The Oklahoma we see dates from before statehood, a territory of outlaws and thieves, and there is not a positive shot of a home in the whole film.

A film closely related to this group is *Coogan's Bluff* (1968), also directed by Don Siegel. It uses the very firmly established persona of Eastwood as cowboy at this time to construct a comedy by setting him down, in the role of an Arizona sheriff, in another alien environment, contemporary New York.

The exceptional case among the westerns of the late 'sixties and early 'seventies is the musical *Paint Your Wagon* (Joshua Logan, 1969). It is of little interest as a western; Logan, whose main work was with musicals on stage and film, had no previous experience with the genre. Eastwood reportedly disliked making the film, and it lost money.

The second group of westerns consists of *High Plains Drifter* (1973), *The Outlaw Josey Wales* (1976), *Pale Rider* (1985) and *Unforgiven* (1992). These four have the obvious connection that they were all directed by Eastwood, but there is also a more specific historical issue. From their release dates, we might say that the first two were made and viewed in a period in which the 'decline' of the western was widely registered. This is a complex matter, for the feeling of decline covers various overlapping areas. There are the discussions of the possible decline of the western in critical accounts of the genre in the 'seventies, although, as Philip French points out, in his *Westerns* (1973), such arguments can be found in 'sixties and even 'fifties writings on the western. Another account might arise from our readings of the work of particular filmmakers, say the movement registered in Sam Peckinpah's work, from *Major Dundee* (1965) and *The Wild Bunch* (1969) through to *The Ballad of Cable Hogue* (1970) and *Pat Garrett and Billy the Kid* (1973). Finally, the perception on the production side of Hollywood was that westerns had become increasingly difficult to market and thus to finance. Steven Bach's discussion in *Final Cut* of the attitude of the studio in 1978 to a project then called *The Johnson County War* (later to be retitled *Heaven's Gate*) is indicative. It is clear from Bach's account that the studio's nervousness at Michael Cimino's proposal, long before the problems that the actual shooting was to encounter, related to the marketability of westerns, even modestly budgeted ones.

There is no magic year or pivotal film from which we can date the decline of the western. What we can say is that the context of making and marketing westerns changed substantially in the seventeen years between the release of *Hang 'Em High* and that of *Pale Rider*, and that in the case of the later westerns Eastwood's presence as a star, if not as an *auteur*, is crucial. The audience of the later films came to them with knowledge of Eastwood's roles in other genres, and the films make use both of the conventions of the western and of audiences' expectations of the star.

Hang 'Em High

The film begins with an image which would have been familiar to the audience of *Rawhide*. The clean-cut, clean-shaven Eastwood is seen driving a few head of cattle across a river, rescuing a weak calf from the water. The plot which follows – I sketch only the first part of it – does not sound particularly unusual. As he reaches the bank of the river, Jed Cooper (Eastwood) is surrounded by a group of men who accuse him of rustling the cattle. He protests his innocence, but after a few questions the leader of the gang Captain Wilson (Ed Begley) pronounces him guilty with the words 'Hang him'. They do so and ride off – this is the pre-credits sequence. He is now cut down in the nick of time by US Marshal Bliss (Ben Johnson), who puts him into a paddy wagon with some other miscreants and takes him back to the town. As he arrives in town he sees the female star of the film, Rachel (Inger Stevens). She is looking into the paddy wagon, searching for someone. He is now delivered up to the judgement of the law in the shape of Judge Fenton (Pat Hingle). The judge checks out his story, releases him and offers him a job as a Federal Marshal, part of his brief being to track down those who lynched him and bring them to justice.

The expectations raised by this point in the plot would clearly involve some resolution of the revenge plot, and of Rachel's mysterious search, and a final establishment of Jed and Rachel as the pioneer couple expressing the benefits of marriage and settlement. Such resolutions might be expected to be built around an acceptance of a movement, however imperfect, in which an ethic of individual revenge is seen to give way to the rule of law.

Had the film been made in 1958 rather than 1968, these expectations might have been more clearly met. Although we might accept that the revision of the western by the late 'sixties produced a re-thinking of what elements of westerns mean, the nature of the changes may be clearer in some types of western than in others. If we take the western built around encounters between white 'civilisation' and an Indian world, we can look for what Douglas Pye has called 'the almost complete reversal of moral poles' (*Movie* 27/28, p.79). The comment is made in the context of a comparison between Arthur Penn's *Little Big Man* (1970) and Robert Aldrich's *Ulzana's Raid* (1972), both part of a group of features dealing with the Indian that use the Indian/white polarity as an opportunity to make a political statement of contemporary relevance.

But what of the western in which there are no Indians, to be shown as better, or at least not worse, than whites? The strain of westerns I am thinking of meditate on the costs of settlement and on those energies and qualities that need to be excluded or abandoned if 'progress' is to happen. Obviously the narratives about reforming or cleaning up a town are central here, the expulsion of gunslingers, whores (and, of course, Indians) that is at the centre of a group of famous westerns including *My Darling Clementine* (John Ford, 1946), *High Noon* (Fred Zinnemann, 1952) and *The Man Who Shot Liberty Valance* (Ford, 1962). This context is important in that *Hang 'Em High* can be read as a related narrative, not with its terms reversed, but lacking the concepts of civilisation and progress that underpinned the earlier films.

Much of the detail of *Hang 'Em High* is suggestive here; the limits of what law can do and what civilisation looks like are established very early. On his way back to town with his prisoners in the paddy wagon, the Marshal pulls into a small, unnamed settlement to pick up another prisoner. The appearance of the set here is something that will be repeated in Eastwood's own later westerns; it is an image of the tiny settlement already in decline, human energies failing in the face of nature, or possibly in the face of the culture represented by the small town. The shabby buildings, the dirt, the noise of the wind on the soundtrack and a central visual image for this, the tumbleweed blowing around in the street, all point in this direction. We see the Marshal being told that the prisoner is in the food and grain store. This turns out to be an abandoned shop, deep in filth, where a man has been chained hand and foot. This community has produced not a criminal but an insane 'prophet'. The marking of a community as benign through its ability to include the deranged – we might think of Mose (Hank Worden) and his rocking chair in *The Searchers* – has been reduced to this moment. The man breaks from the Marshal and runs into the street. There is a parody of the main street showdown: he ignores the command to stop, and, egged

Frontier law: Jed Cooper (Eastwood) and Judge Fenton (Pat Hingle) in Eastwood's first American film as a star, Hang 'Em High.

on by the men in the paddy wagon, the Marshal first wounds him in the leg and then shoots him dead. The Marshal's parting line to the men of the town – 'You chained him, now you bury him' – seems to place the blame firmly on their treatment of the man, but the inability of the law to address itself to a figure who refuses the role of criminal is clear.

The next thing we see is the set of the territory's most important town. At one end of main street is the whorehouse; at the other is the courthouse, an imposing clean brick building, which we are obviously asked to see as new. At the centre of town, overlooked by the courthouse windows, is the gallows – punishment married to technology, a device of ropes and weights capable of executing six men at once.

In the course of the scene in which Jed is appointed as US Marshal by Judge Fenton, a man is led out to the gallows and hanged. To understand how this shows the system of law represented by Fenton, we need to consider the meaning of hanging and particularly its relationship to issues of masculinity and desire. The presentation of hanging was covered by the Production Code, and some of *Hang 'Em High* would not have passed the censor during the 'forties or early 'fifties. Interestingly, many of the same issues are raised explicitly in another film released in the same year, but working out of a very different tradition of both filmmaking and censorship, Nagisa Oshima's *Death by Hanging* (1968).

The film's approach is defined when Jed is hanged at the beginning. The group who lynch him are all men. Two of the most prominent in his interrogation are Captain Wilson and Maddow (Charles McGraw). Both are at least middle-aged, and the actors who play younger men in the group are certainly not chosen for conventional physical handsomeness – Dennis Hopper, Bruce Dern, L.Q. Jones. Eastwood, in contrast, is shown as the glamorous, eroticised young settler or cowhand. The interrogation before the hanging turns on the identity of the man from whom Jed claims to have bought his cattle. Jed, who has been fooled by an impersonation, claims that the man, Johannssen, is about thirty. One of the old men tells him that Johannssen, who has been murdered, was about sixty. What emerges here is that the hanging of Jed can be read as an attack by older men on a figure of youth and sexual vigour, who is mistakenly constructed as a killer of another old man. The point of hanging – as opposed to shooting Jed where he stands – becomes the defiling of the masculine beauty he represents, a ritual sexual humiliation. In that Jed survives the hanging, it comes to have a function not unlike that of a woman's rape in revenge-for-rape narratives.

This configuration is repeated in town, when the man who killed Johannssen is led out to the gallows and hanged. The man is in westerner's clothes. The judge, in shirt and tie, watches from his window and gives the sign to the hangman (Bert Freed), who is an icon of bureaucratic power replacing sexual potency – heavy, white-haired, dressed in an immaculate grey suit.

So justice in *Hang 'Em High* seems to mean the humiliation and destruction of masculinity, and in some cases explicitly the execution of members of a younger generation by representatives of an older one. Jed's role as Marshal is conceived around this issue, diverting his private desire for vengeance, which would mean tracking down and facing the members of the lynching party as a gunfighter. Replacing this is the Judge's insistence on their being brought to trial, and thus the humiliation of public hanging.

The implications are worked out in a series of events in the middle of the film. Jed is interrupted in his hunt for the lynching party by another apparent case of cattle rustling and murder. When the guilty are captured, they turn out to include one member of the original lynching party, Miller (Bruce Dern) and two brothers, blond innocents caught up in the rustling through a moment's stupidity, but not guilty of murder. Jed knows that all three must stand trial and takes the three men across the desert landscape back towards town. At one point Miller loosens his bonds and jumps Jed; after his recapture in a vicious fight sequence, he pleads with Jed to kill him there and then. Jed achieves the feat of bringing all three prisoners in alone. The moment that he rides into town underlines the emptiness of the idea of community in the film. It takes place at night, with Jed collapsing into Judge Fenton's arms as the Judge shouts his praises to the empty street.

Jed assumes that his testimony will save the two boys from the gallows. But the Judge finds them guilty, and explains to Jed why this is necessary:

'Why . . . because of you, Cooper – because of that beautiful magnificent journey you took to bring three killers to justice, because if the law didn't hang 'em, the next posse that goes out'd say hang 'em and hang 'em high. There's no justice in Fort Grant. And if there's no justice in Fort Grant, Cooper, there'll be no statehood for this territory.'

This statement is followed by a sequence in which the townspeople crowd into the square to watch six men, including the brothers, being hanged. The treatment of the crowd is substantially negative.

The speech and the subsequent executions combine elements that can be traced back in American culture to Hermann Melville's *Billy Budd*. The 'legend' of Jed's ride is shown to be literally murderous, the brothers seen as pathetic inheritors of the role of the Handsome Sailor in Melville's novella, condemned to death by the same appreciation of public feeling that is understood when Captain Vere, Billy's judge in the story, talks of the necessity of the hanging as an example to other men, who 'have not that kind of intelligent responsiveness that might qualify them to comprehend and discriminate'. Beneath this in the film is the ambiguous motive of political ambition, Fenton's belief that the apparent triumph of the rule of law will result in statehood for Oklahoma.

Taking a prompt from Melville and the oppositions which structure *Billy Budd*, we might hope that Jed would represent the possession of a vitality that would counter the dryness of Judge Fenton. This would obviously be provided by the romance of Jed and Rachel, but, again, the detail of *Hang 'Em High* is difficult to read as anything other than a very partial affirmation of the couple.

The first building we see in Fort Grant is the whorehouse; the state of censorship in 1968 meant that this could be stated unambiguously. It is to a girl in the whorehouse that Fenton takes Jed after his collapse at the end of his legendary ride. At the point of the brothers' execution, Jed picks the same girl out of the crowd and takes her to bed again, this time unsuccessfully. It is at this moment that Captain Wilson and two other members of the original lynching party burst in and shoot Jed. Only now does Rachel become interested in him, nursing him back to fragile health. She does this in one of the whorehouse's garish bedrooms – the couple are never seen in her home. Rachel's sexual reserve and her

The tentative couple: Jed and Rachel (Inger Stevens) in Hang 'Em High.

inspections of the prisoners brought into Fort Grant are now explained in a tale of the past. It emerges that she was raped and her husband murdered before the beginning of the narrative. The resolution here is more or less immediate but very partial. She tells the story of her past while the couple are on a picnic. It rains, they are soaked, and the convalescent Jed becomes ill again. They take shelter in an abandoned, filthy cabin – the visual connection seems to be with the wretched prisoner in the store at the beginning of the film. Rachel, in a moment of apparent reference to Howard Hughes's similar scene in *The Outlaw*, lies next to Jed to warm him with her body. When they wake, a sexual act is implied, with as much delicacy as if this were still 1942.

Rachel proposes that they should both now abandon their obsessions with the past, but Jed refuses. He pursues Captain Wilson and his two accomplices to Wilson's ranch; all three die. The sequence takes place at night, with Jed killing the two men in the grounds of the house and stalking Wilson through the gothic, empty house only to find that he has killed himself. Jed returns to town intending to give up his star, but Fenton tempts him with warrants for the last two lynchers still at large and a pardon for Jenkins, the old man who had argued for clemency at the original lynching. Jed accepts and rides out.

If there is a pattern here, it is that the world of settlement and marriage is continually referred to, but in terms which acknowledge its fragility, its inability to survive in a context where the level of violence is effectively uncontainable. Couples and families are mentioned only to announce their violent destruction, from Rachel and her husband (Rachel raped, the husband killed) through the Johanssens (both murdered) to the family killed during the rustling by Miller. The nearest thing to a family in the actual narrative is Wilson and his two meta-phorical sons, the young men Tommy and Loomis, who stick by him when a plan to buy off Jed's vengeance fails. The scene, which occurs immediately before the hanging of the brothers, is striking in the sympathy and pathos allowed to figures otherwise constructed as the film's villains. This is Loomis's speech:

'I'm thirty-seven, thirty-eight, I don't rightly know for sure. Started drifting when I was just a kid. These last few years, working for you, first home I ever knew. Saved a few dollars, thinking of finding myself a woman, staking out a few acres of my own, when this came up . . .'

This smashed dream ends with Loomis's death at Jed's hands in the grounds of the Wilson ranch. This is a final monstrous distortion of something which ought to represent the domestic: the sterile, gothic house in darkness, in which the three men make their last stand, and where Jed kills Loomis and Tommy, and Wilson hangs himself in terror.

When Jed rides out at the end of *Hang 'Em High*, he is not seen as the wandering, pioneering rider who backs a benign infant civilisation and its other, more domestically inclined, men and women. His departure from the town does not have the pathos associated with leaving something of value, or being rejected by it, or some combination of these things. In common with horror films of the time – 1968 was the year of release of George Romero's *Night of the Living Dead* and Roman Polanski's *Rosemary's Baby* – the film presents a civilisation arguably incapable of being sustained or renewed. A measure of this is the closing shot. Jed rides past the gallows, down the main street and out of town. A positive statement might have been implied by having Rachel, or even the judge, watch him depart. But no one pays any attention whatever.

Joe Kidd

Joe Kidd addresses a familiar subject for the western: the conflict between small farmers and big landowners or land dealers. In such narratives, the film is invariably on the side of the small farmer. In the simplest case, the small farm is seen to represent the values of family and community, and the big landowner stands for the destruction of this world in the name of profit. Within such a structure, a number of inflections are possible. The big landowner can represent legally sanctioned violence, as opposed to the pacifist or unarmed, or less well-armed farmer, or he can be presented as the impersonal face of capitalist bureaucracy; sometimes this force is simply known as 'the bank'. Perhaps the former is stressed more commonly in the western, the latter in the populist farming narrative of which *The Grapes of Wrath* (John Steinbeck's novel, 1939, and John Ford's film, 1940) is still the most famous example.

The version proposed in *Joe Kidd* is this. The setting is the town of Sinola, New Mexico, and the 'little men' here are Spanish-American smallholders. As

Spanish-Americans, they are associated with qualities relating to both the English-speaking settlers and the Indians. Like the Indians, their claim to the land stretches back historically to long before the English-speakers arrived. But they are seen as Americans, included in understandings of citizenship in a way that the Indians are not. The ambiguities here find expression in the unstable sense of otherness of race or skin colour – the leader of the Spanish Americans, Luis Chama, appears white-skinned and is played by John Saxon, an actor whose offstage name is Carmen Orrico, while his girl, Helen Sanchez (Stella Garcia), is at times more obviously Latin in appearance.

She can be contrasted with the petite blonde girl who is the mistress of Frank Harlan (Robert Duvall), the landowner who arrives in Sinola with the express intention of breaking the farmers' spirit by killing Chama. At the point of their arrival Harlan and his 'associates' are seen as gangsters. This emerges in their dress, language and weapons, as well as in plot detail – the first communication Harlan receives is a telegram from Chicago. But Harlan also manifests the lack of emotion of a man whose interest in Chama is purely financial. While trying to recruit Joe Kidd (Eastwood) to the hunting party, he tells him that he has no interest in who kills Chama. The whole enterprise is seen as a matter of business efficiency; Harlan says, 'I don't have time for court hearings.'

To understand how the figure of Joe Kidd is poised between these two groups, we must look in detail at the character. The film opens with Joe, dressed in a way that will be later described as 'like some town dude', in gaol on three charges: poaching, disorderly conduct and resisting arrest. In the subsequent courtroom scene, the sheriff tells the judge that the conduct charge relates to Joe's threat to urinate on the courthouse building. The judge's line to Joe – 'You do just about anything you feel like' – canvasses the impoverishment of the idea of freedom to the point where it means not only hunting where you like but the 'right' to bad behaviour and drunkenness. Later, we learn that Joe has a little ranch ('a one-loop outfit in Big Wash you work when you're not out hunting') and that he was once a bounty hunter. He tells Harlan this 'was a long time ago'.

Without the image of Eastwood before us, this sounds as if it describes an old man, an outmoded pioneer whose life has witnessed the contraction of the frontier, like a combination of the drunken Indian and the old Natty Bumppo in J. Fenimore Cooper's Leatherstocking novels. In Cooper's work – the obvious text is *The Pioneers* (1823) – the definition of the pioneers' freedom as outmoded and the assertion of a positive view of progress are achieved by linking the pioneer's world to the life of an elderly man, with the narrative's young man representing new, essentially domestic values. Interestingly, the figure of the young yet ragged hunter does appear in the opening of the novel, but it turns out to be the hero in disguise, a man playing the role at its point of eclipse. Breaking this connection between outmoded freedoms and old age, Sturges and his scriptwriter, Elmore Leonard, open up the question of what happens when the end of an era cannot be neatly written off via the presentation of the approaching or actual death of an elderly character.

Usually what happens is an attempt to return to the past, to halt the passage of time with one last hunt, or expedition. In its opening moments, the hunt for Chama seems to offer something of this, as both Joe and Harlan are seen to have changed out of their town clothes and are dressed as hunters. A reason for

Joe to join the gang is also given: Chama's band steal the horses from his ranch and one of them tortures his foreman. But as it develops, Sturges's film emphasises the negative qualities of this hunt. The emotionlessness of Harlan is linked with the view through the high-precision telescopic sights of rifles that can kill or maim at great distance, and the idea of attacking Chama without facing him is continued in the development of the action, when Harlan's group capture a small village and threaten to start shooting the people unless Chama surrenders to them.

Where Harlan's gang is associated with 'modern' weaponry, Joe's violence is associated with another order of skills. Precision of aim is treated largely as a negative quality – we see this at its clearest in Mingo, one of Harlan's hit-men, taking bets on his ability to hit a particular button on the coat of a man he is about to shoot down in cold blood. Joe begins the film by braining a teasing fellow prisoner in the gaol with one blow from a saucepan. Elsewhere, he dispatches Harlan's villains not by gunshot but by surprise – a man falls through a trap door, another is knocked out by a blow from a swinging pot. A typical moment in the series of encounters between Joe and Lamar (Don Stroud), one of Harlan's hoods, comes when Joe has been disarmed at the Mexican village and Lamar taunts him – 'without his gun he looks like a hick farm boy' – and invites him to shoot it out by grabbing a gun from a pile on a table next to them. Joe does so and bests Lamar not by firing the gun but using it as a club to strike him down. In all these moments, the emphasis is on physical skills allied with the mythical stealth learned from the Indians – only once does aim become important, when Joe kills Mingo with a captured precision rifle.

The difficulties in resolving this narrative are perhaps unsurprising in a film made in 1972, and can be seen as reflecting the problems of constructing any kind of 'commitment' film at the point of maximum awareness of the debacle of the Vietnam war. In this context, it can be linked to *Magnum Force*, made in the next year. No possibility of Joe simply defeating Harlan and joining Chama's group exists, in that the Spanish American leader is shown as unsatisfactory. This is true both of his strategy (he is prepared to sacrifice the innocent villagers to the cause) and significantly of his relations to his woman (when Helen Sanchez challenges him, he dismisses her with a sexist insult). It can be related to a larger concern in the depiction of Chama's group, which seems to exist simply as a guerrilla band – we never see these men associated with positive images of whatever homes they might be supposed to be defending. But the totally bleak ending in which Kidd would have turned his back on both groups is, just, avoided. Joe persuades Chama to let himself be taken in to Sinola 'to take his chances with the law'. Such an appeal to an abstract concept of justice is given no support anywhere else in the film, and it is difficult to accept that Chama and his men suddenly agree to it. Both sides return to Sinola, where the climax of the shoot-out is in the courthouse when Harlan, back in his eastern/gangster clothes, is shot dead by Joe Kidd, still dressed as hunter and firing his revolver from the judge's chair.

The implication of all this is a pressure at once towards a belief in progress – that some newly ideal version of law will uphold the justice of Chama's claims if he just gives it a chance. But alongside it is the belief in gun law, that Harlan can only be defeated by the older West in the shape of Joe Kidd's bullet. The inability of the law to engage with Harlan directly is made very clear in the complete impotence of the sheriff. The problem with this is that if modernity is represented convincingly by anything in *Joe Kidd*, it is by Harlan and his hoods rather than by an idea of an improved post-frontier justice.

High Plains Drifter

References to *High Plains Drifter* often take the form of bracketing it with other films and cycles prominent in the early 1970s – the 'apocalyptic phase' of the western, the group of films dealing with the devil and diabolic possession, and peripherally with the disaster movie cycle. It can further be associated with a group of films that includes the first two Callahan movies, made in 1971 and 1973, in which the narrative of the film is about tracking down a criminal (if the hero is a cop) or avenging some kind of indisputable wrong (if the hero is a private eye) but the background is a society felt to be malign. The common feature is that if there is a benign society, it has been marginalised to the point of complete absence. We see no homes, no families, except very marginally as victims; the pathos of even bad families and bad family relations is absent. Even in narratives in which the aims of the hero are achieved, this has no positive effect. Nothing is redeemed to any purpose – the hero survives, but still has nowhere to go at the end. A related effect is created by the subdued but distinct suggestion in *High Plains Drifter* that the Stranger figure (Eastwood) is a ghost, with no possibility at all of any connection with the society of the town.

Part of this context can be traced to the writer of *High Plains Drifter*, Ernest Tidyman. Tidyman was a novelist, the script-writer of William Friedkin's *The French Connection* (1971) and of the three *Shaft* films (1971-1973), which have a black detective played by Richard Roundtree and broadly share the positions that I have outlined. They are based on Tidyman's own novel, *Shaft* (published in 1970), which, in common with some other early 'seventies hard-boiled detective fiction, specifically locates Shaft as a Vietnam veteran.

These contexts present features which I wish to explore in some detail in relation to *High Plains Drifter*. These are the way in which the film uses the revenge narrative, and the positioning of the Eastwood figure as returned from the dead.

Revenge is, of course, a common subject in western narratives and appeared earlier in Eastwood's work, in *For a Few Dollars More* and *Hang 'Em High*. Revenge narratives seem to divide into a number of loose groupings. There are those in which the death or terrorisation of one member of a family is avenged by another member of the same family, as when parents avenge the deaths of children or one sibling avenges the death of another (as in *For a Few Dollars More*). Closely related are narratives in which the victim and avenger are not linked by blood but have another kind of closeness, as in one partner's revenge for the death of the other. Then there are narratives in which the victim of injustice does not die and comes to take his or her own revenge; this may be for physical abuse, such as a rape, or the lynching at the opening of *Hang 'Em High*, or for a betrayal resulting in imprisonment.

The exact nature of the scene of violation or murder in revenge narratives is clearly important, in that it can point to types and degrees of guilt. When offered such moments in flashback we are often being asked to make judgements – flashbacks in courtroom dramas are an obvious, if not necessarily simple, case of this. Where the act that we are watching is in some sense a public one (which might simply mean that it involves more than a single victim and a single perpetrator), an important distinction is often not simply between guilt and innocence but between the clearly guilty perpetrator and the implicitly guilty witnesses. Characters who fail to intervene or fail to do so effectively may be as important to the narrative as those whose guilt is clearly established.

The plot of *High Plains Drifter* is a further variant on the revenge narrative, which takes it into the area of the fantastic. The victim is dead, but nonetheless takes revenge, for the figure who acts as avenger is not a sibling or a parent or a child, but seen to be a version of the man who died. By this I mean a figure whose existence relates entirely to that of the dead man, but who is not simply that man undead.

This will become clearer if we reconstruct part of the background of the film's action. A group of men who hold some kind of power in an isolated town named Lago hire three contract hoods to kill the town Marshal, Jim Duncan. These men ride into town at night, call the Marshal on to the street, and whip him to death. Some of the townspeople are witnesses to this. The killers are framed with a false charge of robbery and sent to gaol for one year, and Jim Duncan is buried in an unmarked grave. A day or so before the killers are due to be released, a Stranger (Eastwood) rides into town. It emerges slowly for us that he is in some occult sense Duncan, returned to revenge himself on the killers and on the town. Of course, he does not look like Duncan. We may say that this is for plot reasons, that it is necessary that the townspeople do not recognise who they are encountering. It also expresses another difference, that Duncan was a vulnerable man, who allowed himself to be surprised and killed without so much as wounding any of his assailants. His reincarnation is invulnerable, a man who goes through the film without a scratch, something which is not necessarily the case for Eastwood in his action roles.

The obvious shape of a plot like this would be one which anticipates the moment when the revenger will finally encounter his quarry. The interest would lie in the preparations made by the avenger for the confrontation, the dramatic irony of the situation of the villains as they approach the town not knowing what they will encounter, and the climax, the moment of revelation, with some kind of flashback in which, at the point of execution, the hood recognises who is killing him and why – *For a Few Dollars More* provides an instance of it, and elements of this are present in *Sudden Impact*.

There are some substantial ways in which *High Plains Drifter* diverges from this model. One is in the role of the town. Eastwood described the situation in interview as '*High Noon*, only what happens if the sheriff's been killed.' The community of guilty witnesses becomes the central issue here, and the interest in the situation of the three gunmen who actually committed the murder is relatively peripheral. This is clear in the presentation of the three as vicious but essentially uninteresting, their status as evil men only established in the most routine ways. It is underlined in the treatment of their deaths, which do not involve a flashback. There is little interest in showing whether they realise that this is revenge for Duncan's death. Their deaths are presented as just another encounter between gunfighters, a repetition of the killings of the three gunfighters who die at the Stranger's hand in the opening minutes of the film. All these

Inverting the commercial order: the Stranger (Eastwood) gives blankets to the Indian
in High Plains Drifter.

figures are largely undifferentiated, just gunslingers who must always either kill
or die when they encounter another gunman.

But perhaps most importantly, the common polarity between the innocence
and justification of the avenger and the guilt of the subjects of the vengeance is not
a simple or clear one. This depends both on our reading of the Stranger as a dead
man, and thus in some sense possibly a thing of horror, and our interpretation
of the central business of the film, which is what he actually does in Lago.

The film begins with the Stranger moving slowly through the town set. He
goes to the saloon and encounters the local gunfighters, then to the barbershop
for a shave and a bath. The gunfighters pursue him there, and there is a fight in
which he kills all three of them. The way in which the figures are situated and
identified in terms of masculinity at this point is entirely familiar and conventional
– the shrinking, terrified barber, the old bartender, the inadequate gunslingers,
and the hero and star, the fastest gun.

In the next sequence, the roles diverge from simple expectations. We see the
Stranger encounter a girl in the street – like the gunfighters earlier, she insults
him. We might expect some mild comeuppance for her – a crushing verbal response from the Stranger, or a revelation of her duplicity, the admission that her
aggressiveness is a cover for a desire to seduce – something that might place her
behaviour in a context which would allow us to identify her character as corrupt

or immoral, possibly in relation to another figure offered as the 'good' woman.

No further context is given at this point. What happens is that the Stranger drags her off to the nearest barn and rapes her. Although he will later claim that 'as I recall, she enjoyed that quite a bit', there is no shot establishing any such shift from horror to pleasure. The incident is linked with the killing of the gunslingers – in both cases, as the Stranger emerges into the exterior, the town's dwarf, Mordecai (Billy Curtis), presents him with a cigar.

In the next sequence involving the girl, the Stranger is having a bath. She bursts in and tries ineffectively to shoot him. When she has been subdued and removed, there is this exchange:

Stranger: Wonder why it took her so long to get mad . . .
Mordecai: Because maybe you didn't go back for more . . .

At the same moment as this exchange is taking place, the girl is asking: 'Isn't forcible rape in broad daylight a misdemeanour in this town?'

The point here is to establish the quality of the town as something more than being subject to various different groups of gunfighters. It emerges that the raped girl, Callie Travers (Mariana Hill), is the girlfriend of one of the group of men in power in the town. The failure to protect her, or even to be very interested in her treatment – whether or not she resisted the rape is clearly immaterial to the men's reaction – is expressive of a comprehensive disgust for women that is glossed in Mordecai's line about her. Her treatment at the Stranger's hands is his way of exposing what the town conceals: its inability or refusal to act, and its attitude to women. The rape becomes a kind of replay of the death of Duncan, another outrage that the town will ignore.

It is generally true of the Stranger's relationship to the people of Lago that the outrages he perpetrates seem to be less for his benefit than for theirs, ways of letting them experience their impotence. At this point, the sheriff offers the Stranger 'anything' if he will defend them against the three killers. This is not a Faustian contract, but a chance for the Stranger to expose exactly what 'anything' in this community might mean.

He allows the storekeepers to experience how it feels to give away their stock – the drygoods man is forced to give blankets and sweets to the despised Indian customer, the bootmaker to give his best work to the Stranger, the saloonkeeper to allow drinks on the house. Then the idea that the town controls the civic order is demolished: the Stranger makes Mordecai both sheriff and mayor.

A familiar idea in the western is the group of meek citizens who learn to defend themselves under the tutelage of a gunfighter. The Stranger attempts to do this, and we see the formation of the 'City of Lago Volunteers', with the men of the town positioned as snipers under the Stranger's command, to practise defending themselves. They rehearse the arrival of the killers by shooting at dummies driven through the town on the back of a wagon. The contrast is intense – the citizens are totally inept, cannot aim at all, while the Stranger immaculately picks the heads off the three dummies with three shots. The moment when the Stranger realises this – that his charisma, or authority, cannot transmit itself to these men – is explicitly comic. In such a scene, the organising gunfighter clearly has a function which makes him a surrogate for the film's director, and a part of the comedy depends on knowing as we do that Eastwood is actually the director of this film, all-knowing and magically competent but unable to elicit the right 'performance' from his cast.

This understanding, of the Stranger as playing, or playing with, a role as the film's director in the events that follow, helps in reading what has proved to be one of the more obscure sections of the film. We are presented with a series of literal interpretations of figures of speech. When the stranger shoots the dummies, a delighted citizen exclaims, 'This is going to be a picnic.' Alongside the snipers, the Stranger now tests out another scenario, ordering picnic tables to be built and set up in the main street. There is a sign reading 'Welcome Home Boys' quite as if we have strayed into the wrong narrative. The other action seems to proceed from a phrase not spoken, but implied: to paint the town red. From here, there is an easy connection. One of the men required to colour the town with red paint comments, 'When we get done, this place is going to look like hell.' And Hell is indeed what the Stranger renames the town.

What does all this mean? It can possibly be explained by looking more generally at the qualities of the set that Eastwood built for the film, and what the set itself might be made to express about the bankruptcy of the idea of settlement. The viewer of the opening sequence of the film might be struck by the emphasis on glass, which is, I think, unusually marked for a western. It is established for the viewer as another screen, as we watch the movement of reflections on the clean panes in bright sunlight. Windows in westerns, as elsewhere, define the world inside and divide it from the world of the open air, as occasions when the distinction is literally smashed by a body falling through the glass frequently underline. (There is such a point in the opening gunfight here.) When the Stranger rides into town, it is difficult not to be conscious of these distinctions, of settlement seen as a construction of a world of interiors in a region of huge open spaces. One of the first objects we see close up in Lago is an icon of this issue, the complete but unclad frame of an building, an uncompleted promise of the expansion of settlement.

Obviously the distinction established by the emphasis on windows carries with it a series of implications that go with the differentiation of the various interiors, as announced by the sign-writing that is often prominent in western sets. The Stranger's actions in ordering the painting of the town might be interpreted as a way of announcing that the town's differences are subject to being erased with equal ease. This is underlined as the painting is to begin, when the Parson asks, 'You can't possibly mean the church too?' The stranger's reply is: 'I mean especially the church.' The painting draws attention to the degree to which the distinctions that the community lays claim to might not have any substance beyond the signs – some are painted over, some not – that proclaim them. We might also say that the director is drawing our attention to the idea that this western town set is only a set, capable of being repainted, torn down, blown up – all these things are instigated by the Stranger in the course of the narrative – and finally torched by the three killers when they return.

The idea that the Stranger is Duncan returned from the dead is not particularly prominent in the film, emerging more or less clearly towards the end, in a conversation about Duncan, and in a final exchange. François Guérif comments in his book, *Clint Eastwood*, that in the version of the film first released in France – presumably with a dubbed soundtrack – the Stranger was given the identity of

'This is going to be a picnic': the gunmen arrive in Lago in High Plains Drifter.

Duncan's brother. That it was possible to do this suggests how little the film insists on the elements of the fantastic.

Consider for a moment what the meaning might be of a narrative in which the Stranger was indeed the brother. In the film, we are told nothing about Duncan; he is never seen except at the moment of his death. Revenge would be therefore less a matter of celebrating his unexamined virtues and more one of defending family honour – a standard subject of revenge narratives from Jacobean drama onwards and, as I suggested earlier, a dominant subject in westerns dealing with revenge. It is family ties or the bond of marriage which give the right to revenge, and the value of such ties is thus implicitly promoted.

The result of making the revenging figure not a brother but a double is to nullify this. The Stranger cannot be said to avenge Duncan out of love, or for the honour of a family – he functions only as a horrific emanation of Duncan's dying curse, representing the negative elements of pioneering that produce both gunmen and those who hire them. The double that is the Stranger could be said to represent not so much Duncan's consciousness reinstated in another body, but rather Duncan as he would be with a different experience behind him. The title is important here, defining the Stranger not as the reincarnated Marshal but as the Drifter, an alarming product of a famous American condition that is present in the work of Melville and Poe, the horror of uncontrolled movement through uncontained space.

The idea of the horrific double as a product of a life lived under different conditions has a number of precedents. One suggestive case in American culture is Henry James's tale 'The Jolly Corner' (1908). James dramatises the encounter

'. . . to me he was no horror': the Stranger and Sarah Belding (Verna Bloom) in
High Plains Drifter.

between a humane, cultured American who has spent many years abroad, and his
ghostly double, the billionaire he would have become had he stayed in America,
a 'black stranger'. The story places both men in relation to a woman. It is only
the woman who knows what the stranger is: 'He's grim, he's worn – and things
have happened to him' says James's heroine, who offers the figure acceptance
and pity. She says, 'I could have liked him . . . and to me he was no horror.'

In Eastwood's film, Mrs Belding (Verna Bloom), the wife of the hotel keeper,
has something of this relation to the Stranger. She is the only person we see in
flashback to be appalled at Duncan's murder. For reasons that she does not seem
to understand – possibly because with her he treats the terrors of his violence and
sexual appetite as comedy – she sleeps with him. Afterwards she intuits that he has
something to do with Duncan; apart from the moment at the very end of the film
with Mordecai, which is clearly offered as a piece of prompting for the audience,
nobody else in the town realises in such clear terms who he is. Mrs Belding is the
only character who draws a smile from the Stranger, and the only one to smile
at him. At the end of the film, she is the only one apart from him to leave Lago.

The setting of James's 1908 tale is a familiar gothic space, a huge empty
family home, the New York mansion of the hero's childhood which is about to
be chopped into flats. A final suggestion I want to make, prompted by thinking
about the story and the film again, deals with ways of seeing, what a constructed

world looks like in the light of the evacuation of the values that were supposed to inform it. This is the James passage:

'It seemed to him he had waited an age for some stir of the great grim hush; the life of the town was itself under a spell – so unnaturally, up and down the whole prospect of known and rather ugly objects, the blankness and the silence lasted. Had they ever, he asked himself, the hard-faced houses, which had begun to look livid in the dim dawn, had they ever spoken so little to any need of his spirit? Great built voids, great crowded stillnesses put on often, in the heart of cities, for the small hours, a sort of sinister mask . . .'

We need to remember how central an ingredient of American gothic is the fear of emptiness, rather than just that of the monstrous or perverted or decadent. Of course, James's is an urban world – the horror of 'crowded stillness' is replaced in the West by the sense of how fragile the settlement is, how few people actually inhabit its stillness. Exterior photography in *High Plains Drifter* continually stresses the remoteness and emptiness of the whole region – the area actually used by Eastwood is Lake Mono, close to the Yosemite National Park on the California/Nevada border. The well-known reference here is the photographic work of Ansel Adams – his images of remote vast snow-covered mountains – and Adams had photographed Lake Mono in the 1940s.

We can also note the detail that the place has nothing to do with the benign context of farming the land. Lago is a mining town, although even here the narrative's interest in mining is that of Joseph Conrad's *Nostromo* – in the conduct of the town rather than in the mine or miners themselves.

One sequence expressive of emptiness leads up to the moment when the Stranger orders the town to be painted red. It takes place in the graveyard overlooking the town, and deals with a central image, the unmarked grave. The townspeople have new bodies to bury. Someone says, 'I don't know if we shouldn't mark the graves somehow.' But the ex-sheriff replies, 'I don't see any need. Ain't likely anybody going to cry over 'em anyhow.' In the frame now is the Stranger painting the word Hell over the sign that reads 'Lago'. This scene, as much as the 'apocalyptic' sequences with the return of the gunslingers, signals the end-point of a tradition of presenting the pioneering community as worth defending. The point is not that the people of Lago are particularly evil or corrupt, but that they are empty. The argument is that the values of the community in the western were always a gesture, just as gravestones would be here, a gesture for which people like these cannot imagine the need.

Eastwood moves out of his narrative with a series of steps that exactly mirror its opening. The death of the three gunmen repeats the opening gunfight; the ride out of town, again in brilliant sunlight, but now past windowless smoking shells of buildings, mirrors the ride in. The effect is less of a community destroyed than one of an illusion of a community exploded.

The Outlaw Josey Wales

A cogent description of the condition of becoming a particular kind of outlaw in America is provided by Mark Twain's *The Adventures of Huckleberry Finn*. At the beginning of the narrative, Tom Sawyer is forming a band of robbers. As ever, he has plentiful data for this business, but there are problems of interpretation.

Two details are suggestive. One is the moment when Huck Finn is almost excluded from the band. It emerges that a condition of the blood oath that the boys are about to swear is that an outlaw should have a family, to be killed in the event of any recidivism. Pap Finn is ruled too drunk to be acceptable, and Huck has to think of a substitute, the pious old maid who has taken him in, Miss Watson. This is agreed, and the boys start to discuss the details of robbery and murder. The dialogue ends like this:

' . . . do we kill the women, too?

'Well, Ben Rogers, if I was as ignorant as you I wouldn't let on. Kill the women? No – nobody ever saw anything in the books like that. You fetch them to the cave, and you're always as polite as pie to them; and by-and-by they fall in love with you and never want to go home any more.'

'Well, if that's the way, I'm agreed, but I don't take no stock in it. Mighty soon we'll have the cave so cluttered up with women, and fellows waiting to be ransomed, that there won't be no place for the robbers . . .'

What is acknowledged here is that the position of this outlaw begins and ends with the family, that in order to be such a figure you must be positioned in relation to the family, even if, like Huck, you seem to be outside it. Also, the activity of being an outlaw turns out to be a kind of romantic questing with a comedic outcome. The reinstatement of the fertility of the family implied by the love interest turns quickly to comedy as the numbers of the rescued increase – outlawry is swamped by family values.

It is not very difficult to identify the main trajectory of Eastwood's film, either with or without the prompt from Twain. Its pre-credits sequence offers Josey Wales (Eastwood) as farmer, unable to protect his wife and young child. They are killed by Union guerilla fighters, and Wales joins a band of Confederate irregulars. In a montage sequence over which the credits are played, we see the Civil War. The central narrative begins when a massacre by Union troops leaves only Wales and another soldier (and symbolic son) Jaime (Sam Bottoms) alive. Pursued by the army, they move across Missouri towards the Indian nations, and Jamie now also dies, in the dark and the rain.

We see Wales alone only for one scene, his funeral oration over Jaime's body. The film's project now becomes the reconstruction of the family. Wales will be joined by a number of figures, whom he variously rescues or who simply decide to ride along with him. In order of their joining his party, they are an old Indian man, a young Indian woman, a dog, and a grandmother and granddaughter from Kansas. The last two are travelling towards an abandoned ranch, once owned by the older woman's son, who was killed in the Civil War. The party, with various hangers-on from a nearby town, make their new home in this place. The whole of this structure is also expressed in lighting – Eastwood has talked in interview about wanting an 'idyllic light' for the opening moments, the 'sombre tone' of the middle section and the movement back towards the idyllic towards the end. And what is lit is a landscape that passes from farmland to scrub to desert and finally back to farmland.

All this is quite clear, as it is that the film would have been read by its American audience in 1976 as making a specific case for reconstruction that addressed feelings about the Vietnam war. The connection is obvious in the final confrontation of the film, which resolves the plot in which Wales has been pursued by his old commander, Fletcher (John Vernon). Fletcher, pretending that he does not recognise his quarry, says that he will try to find Wales and 'tell him that the war is over'. Wales replies, 'I guess we all died a little in that damned war.' The reassurance here is achieved by looking at a specifically civil war, a period of conflict between different kinds of American rather than between Americans and another nation or culture, a seductive approach to the subject of war in the year after the Vietnam war finally ended with the fall of Saigon. The force of this can be judged by looking at Hal Ashby's *Coming Home* (1978), which adopts the same strategy in direct reaction to the Vietnam war, understanding the conflict as essentially between the kinds of American realised in the characters played by Jon Voight and Bruce Dern respectively, rather than between these two and any representation of the Vietnamese.

It could be argued that this has the status almost of a dominant tendency in films relating to the Vietnam war – that conflicts between Americans are more easily presented as 'tragic', and thus more obviously palatable, than accounts of imperialistic warfare. If we read *The Outlaw Josey Wales* in such a way, the interesting issue becomes what kind of reconstruction it offers, what movement is understood between the family at the beginning and the family at the end.

Two things emerge from the pre-credits sequence as important. One is that Wales is a father, and the father of a young male child – this is the first time in his career that Eastwood plays this role, although elements of it were present in the couple of Thunderbolt (Eastwood) and Lightfoot (Jeff Bridges) in Michael Cimino's 1974 film. The other is that the incident in which the wife and child are killed implies not just death but the rape of the wife by the soldiers. So the role of the father is linked with a failure of masculinity. Wales at this point is a family man, who does not have the skills to protect the family, a point made when we see him learning to shoot after their deaths.

We do no more than glimpse the wife and child, as if they (or Wales's state which allows them to be raped and killed) are almost an embarrassment. But the role of the father is emphasised and partly shifts in meaning during the next substantial relationship in the film, the sequences with Jaime. Although Wales, now fully competent with his pistols after the war years, can act as a protective father to Jaime, he cannot successfully fulfil the role of mother. Jaime has been wounded in the massacre, and the role of nursing the male back to health, which seems identified with women in Eastwood's westerns (the female leads of *Two Mules for Sister Sara* and *Hang 'Em High* both nurse Eastwood back to health), cannot be enacted here. The gendered nature of this subject first becomes specific in the river-crossing sequence, which distinguishes true care of the sick (Granny Hawkins and her poultices) from false (the male patent medicine seller). Later it is worked out in a conversation between Wales and Jaime – it is now fairly clear to the audience that he may be dying – in which Jaime talks about not having a mother, and about his father secretly sewing the embroidery on his shirt. At this point, Wales is being maternal (treating the wound), and the vulnerability resulting from this role appears when he is briefly captured by two hillbillies out for reward money. It is a situation from which Jaime rescues him in very Huck Finn-like manner, with a little act, pretending to be feverish and rambling on about stolen money. After they have killed the hillbillies, Wales again expresses gratitude by taking the role of Jaime's parent, threatening to 'whup you with a knotted plowline' if he fails to rest and so causes his wounds to bleed again.

Jaime dies in the next scene, just before he and Wales are about to attempt to pass through Union cavalry lines into the 'Indian nations'. Wales passes through the lines by tying the boy's dead body to a horse, and sending it through the cavalry camp. As the soldiers fire at the dead rider, Wales slips past unnoticed. This development, Wales given life, or an extension of his life, by the death of the other – the use he is able to put that death to – has dimensions of meaning that extend into the following sequence, in which Wales meets the Indian.

The two scenes are connected visually. We see the troops fire on the horse, its dead rider tied to appear as if he is crouched low in the saddle. In the next shot, it is dawn, and Wales is in the nations, riding in the mist through something that (with a musical score suggesting the strangeness of the Indian world) feels very like an enchanted wood. Its inhabitant is an old Indian man wearing a top hat. A horse on which a rider might be crouched low comes into view, and the man takes aim – but this time the horse is indeed riderless, and its owner has a pistol at the Indian's ear.

The association made here, the visual pun of the two horses, identifies Wales with the dead Jaime, and thus in turn suggests a reassignment of roles. In the scene which follows, the father/son couple of Wales and Jaime has been replaced by another father and son, now with the old Cherokee warrior Lone Watie (Chief Dan George) in the role of father and Wales in that of son.

Vulnerability: the hillbillies capture Wales (Eastwood) in The Outlaw Josey Wales.

The exposition which follows links Wales and Lone Watie in obvious ways. The activities of the Union have caused both of them to lose their families; both have declared war on the Union, and neither has surrendered. Connection to historical fact is close here – I assume the name Lone Watie was derived from Stand Watie, the Cherokee who was the last Confederate general officer to surrender in the Civil War.

Wales listens to Lone Watie's account of the loss of his family and of faith in the white man, but he is not interested in political history; the Indian's account of his visit to Washington and the encounter between the leaders of the 'Five Civilised Tribes' and the government is delivered to us as Wales falls asleep, and, before they leave together, Watie burns his top hat and frock coat, the costume he had worn to look like Lincoln.

What sort of a father figure, and what sort of an Indian, is Lone Watie? In the areas that we might think of as specific to the Indian, his skills are poor and the subject of irony – as a member of one of the 'civilised' tribes, he is easy to creep up on, both personally and politically. As always in the presentation of the Indian, language is important. Lone Watie has a certain gravity of speech, well modulated and grammatical English – he represents the wise father figure, just removed enough, by virtue of his nominal Indianness, from the anxieties and doubts surrounding the role of the father and the idea of the father's power or lack of it that have already been raised in the film.

As they prepare to leave together, Wales asks Lone Watie if he has any food. Lone Watie shows an object and replies, 'All I have is a piece of hard rock candy, but it's not for eating, it's just for looking through.' We may take the possession of some kind of a crystal ball to be a central attribute of any magician. What we have in Lone Watie is a version of a very familiar figure in comedy and romance, the wise father as magician, but a version of that figure steeped in irony, a magician who may have lost his powers, and whose ability to see is always ambiguous.

The role is related to Chief Dan George's earlier role as Chief Lionskins in Arthur Penn's *Little Big Man* (1970), in which the Indian father figure and his skills are also questioned. Penn treats the figure in terms closer to parody than irony, regarding his character's powers as a species of endearing foolishness. Lionskins is gifted with second sight, but his visions are unable to affect the destruction of the Indian world. The end of the film is exemplary. The old man's staging of his own death lapses into comedy, rather like a miscalculated shoot in a movie. He doesn't die, it begins to pour with rain, and the character acknowledges what a director might express: 'Well . . . sometimes the magic works, sometimes it doesn't.' Eastwood takes the role of the Indian patriarch more seriously, but perhaps because of this is less able to position him as a figure of authority.

The sequences that follow the meeting of Wales and Lone Watie are the reverse of the opening of the film. Wales successfully does what he failed to do earlier: protect women, which he manages on two occasions. The first reprises elements of the scene with the hillbillies and the dying Jaime. Here we are inside a trader's shack, where two thugs are raping a girl. They draw their guns and think, like the hillbillies, that they have captured Wales, but this time he needs no assistance in order to shoot them both dead. This does no more than very partially redress the loss of Wales's wife, for the rescued woman is another symbolic orphan, a Navaho girl, Little Moonlight (Geraldine Keams). She now considers

Wales and Laura Lee (Sondra Locke) in The Outlaw Josey Wales.

that she belongs to the man who rescued her, a 'Great Warrior'.

If this sounds familiar, it is because it seems like a rethinking, or re-use, of a plot in *The Searchers*. In John Ford's film, the search by Ethan Edwards (John Wayne) and Martin Pawley (Jeffrey Hunter) for Debbie (Natalie Wood), the white girl captured by the Indians, is interrupted by the appearance in the plot of a figure who is a kind of comedic parallel to Debbie. She is Look, the Indian girl whom Martin accidentally 'marries' – in effect, purchases without knowing that he is doing so. In Ford's film, this character speaks to the themes and taboos of national and racial pride. Debbie does not die, but Look does. The white girl taken by Indians can be implicitly redeemed into white society, but the Indian girl must die in order to leave the metaphorical 'son' of the hero free to marry his white sweetheart.

The woman in Eastwood's film combines elements of Debbie and Look. Little Moonlight's story is that she is a Navaho, captured by the Cheyenne. She bears the scar of a slit nose, and Lone Watie translates her story to Wales: '. . . their sign is the dirty-nose sign . . . [the Cheyenne Chief] figures that she didn't resist enough.' The anxiety about the sexual practice of other races and the myth of the pollution of the woman through sexual initiation by a member of a different race – the centre of the tension between white and Indian in *The Searchers* – is relocated here in such a way as to deprive it of its function as a source of violence or as a symbol of fear of racial and sexual otherness. This is clear in the treatment of actual desire for Little Moonlight, a further comedy of discomfiture for Wales

– he goes to wake her only to find her already making love with Lone Watie. This may possibly underline Watie's position as the father, but otherwise nothing is particularly at issue – the race of the girl is not even a minor taboo in sexual terms.

The next rescue combines a number of themes that seem to go further in restoring the structures in place in the film's opening shots. A band of 'pilgrims' making their way from Kansas to Texas are ambushed by Comancheros, and the men are killed. This offers a chance for Wales almost single-handedly to rescue the figures who will complete a reconstituted family: the grandmother (Paula Trueman) and granddaughter, Laura Lee (Sondra Locke).

Even if we leave aside her role as the partner of the Eastwood figure in later films – this is Sondra Locke's first film with him – the figure of Laura Lee has the qualities that locate her as the woman who will answer the loss of Wales's wife. She is white, and it is implied (both in the action here and by her costume later) that she is a virgin. But she is not quite as clearly positive a figure as we might expect. Most obvious is the detail that rather than representing woman as a source of culture or refinement, we learn that she is 'a little odd' – this is never more closely defined, but Locke's performance suggests that Laura Lee is almost simple-minded.

The effect here is to construct the character as sexually desirable but childlike, and this can possibly be linked with a trajectory in the film, in which the geographical move south becomes overlaid with other meanings; it becomes a movement in time, or rather can be read in terms of how the characters perceive their relationship to their times, to their history.

Consider the two towns through which the travellers pass. The first one looks, as we see it in long shot, a little like the set of *High Plains Drifter*, a spread of buildings in a vast, bright space. In contrast to the town of the earlier film, it is the repository of wild western energy. We are introduced to it by a couple of clichés, riders whooping down the main street on horseback and accompanying upbeat music on the soundtrack. There is activity both in the frame and implicit in the set design – an effective detail is the inclusion of a signmaker's workshop in the street, with a jumble of signs outside it, promises of building and businesses yet to come. There are also less positive suggestions: the first words that we see as the travellers enter town are 'Merchandise: Guns', the first hawker who addresses them is offering Indian scalps, and among the crowd are wounded Confederate veterans.

Once Wales moves into an interior, the interpretation of this energy is even darker. The central figure in the town sequence is the storekeeper, a cheery gossip with a broad smile on his face as he produces a photograph of the body of the last outlaw to be shot and hands it to Wales while – coincidentally, since he does not recognise him – speaking Wales's name.

A moment later, Wales is recognised, and there is the third attempt to bring him in, a shoot-out which implies both the inevitability of violence in a place like this and a reluctance to initiate it. Wales stands facing the men, his hands full of the parcels he has bought in the shop. Both sides are reluctant to start shooting – Wales says, 'Are you going to pull those pistols or whistle Dixie?'

After the shooting, our last view of the inhabitants of the town is of the storekeeper being photographed alongside the bodies of Wales's latest victims. As the posse hunting Wales moves off, we can read one of the signs outside the signwriting shop clearly, because, unlike the others, it is white script on black. It reads: UNDERTAKING.

Compare the signs of death, violence and new technology in this place with the town of Santa Rio, reached by the travellers as they near the ranch. It first appears as a ghost town, a huddle of dirty and abandoned buildings – on the soundtrack is a picked-out tune on a single guitar. Entering the saloon, Wales finds a set of western stereotypes in repose. If we ask what these people are doing, still in costume and role – the bartender, the faithful Mexican retainer, and Rose, the town floozie – there is no answer in terms of the film's realistic surface. The state of the town is explained: first, the silver ran out, then the people, then the whisky, then the beer. Wales's answer is to restore the saloon's function while inverting its commercial purpose; he exits for a moment and re-enters with a crate of bottles. Comanchero whisky might seem an unlikely candidate for reading as the water of life, but the moment does have obvious ritual suggestiveness.

The point of the clear contrast between the two towns is the preference for the values of a version of the West that is felt as an older world, centred on the saloon and the activities of eating, drinking and making love, but fallen into disuse, over the post-war bustling West centred in violence and commerce. The limits of the contrast between the two worlds is marked in the sequence when Wales is recognised and challenged in the Santa Rio saloon. A bounty hunter enters and Wales tries to dissuade him from fighting, telling him, 'This isn't necessary.' The man leaves but re-enters a moment later, saying, 'I had to come back.' Wales replies, 'I know.' Eastwood delivers the line sympathetically, almost in a whisper, which clearly recognises the man's condition as not so far from his own. They draw and Wales kills the man – the point seems to be that however reluctant he might be to acknowledge it, as an outlaw he is still locked inside a system of violence and money, a commodity in the world of bounty hunting.

The travellers now set up home at the abandoned ranch and the film celebrates this settlement with familiar rituals – lighting a fire, making music and dancing. The quality of these rituals is reserved, the players moving tentatively through a series of them that they remember from different contexts. When Laura Lee and Grandma are singing and playing the squeezebox, we see Little Moonlight, in the rear of the frame, executing a little shuffle that is clearly what remains of an Indian dance. It is the memory of Jaime that prompts Wales to ask the players to perform 'Rose of Alabama', and he and Laura Lee dance an unpractised, awkward step to it.

The rest of the action involves the defence of 'the family' against various attackers. The first group is the Indians, and again the film seems to be consciously returning to the past history of the West, as Wales gives instructions for defending the house – the slits in the window shutters point to the situation when it was originally built. Wales now goes to parley with the Comanche warriors led by Ten Bears (Will Sampson).

Visually, the Comanches are a total contrast to the Indians whom we have previously seen: Lone Watie and Little Moonlight. They might be thought of as the Indians of a much earlier tradition in the western; they are numerous, male and dressed in traditional costume – only perhaps a greater degree of nakedness distinguishes them from representations that go back to before sound film. The scene of confrontation between Wales and Ten Bears represents the romantic

Defending the family: Laura Lee at the window in The Outlaw Josey Wales.

individualistic pact of two warriors, revolving around phrases like 'my word of life' and a parallelism between Wales and his party and Ten Bears and his tribe, both of them in opposition to 'governments', a dramatic re-enactment of something that looks like an early encounter between white and Indian. This may be the climactic public moment of peace-making in the film, an answer to the massacre in its opening, but the scene is played in the knowledge that both sides are renegades, in retreat from a larger social violence which will destroy both their forms of life in the end.

After Wales has made peace with the Indians, returned in triumph to the homestead and made love with Laura Lee, he prepares to ride on. He is challenged by Lone Watie, and starts to make excuses, but Eastwood now repeats and reverses a move used in the first meeting between these two. When Wales looks up, he finds that Lone Watie hasn't stayed to hear his explanations.

He gallops away into the dawn light. The film could end here, but a scene follows in which Wales from outside the house and the family from within it successfully defend themselves against the forces that act against them – this time, a gang led by Terrill (Bill McKinney), the leader of the Union marauders who killed Wales's first family and his men. Following the pattern of the Callahan films, Wales does not kill Terrill in this fight, but tracks him to a sterile, disused space. Here he moves towards him, playing a version of the 'Russian roulette' routine of *Dirty Harry*. But it turns out that his pistols are entirely empty, and, again possibly in some acknowledgement of moving away from the role of the gunfighter, he uses Terrill's own sabre to kill him.

Two possible endings now present themselves – but the hero neither rides off immediately into the distance (as is the effect in the first three Callahan movies) nor do we see him with the family. Eastwood sets the last scene in the saloon of Santa Rio. As he enters, we hear a voice saying '. . . the bullets were flying, people running every which way . . .' – a story of the Old West is being told. It emerges that it is the mendacious story of Wales's death, told to protect him from identification by the Texas rangers accompanying Fletcher, his old commander. When Wales enters, he is addressed as Mr Wilson. All the parties to this deception assent to it, and, after the exchange acknowledging the cost of the war, Wales, or Wilson, rides off into the sun.

Clearly Fletcher recognises Wales; the inclusion of the Texas rangers in this final confrontation is the literal excuse for the invention of 'Mr Wilson' and enables Eastwood to give the pronouncement of the film's final chorus, the act of assigning Wales's life from the present social realm to the world of myth, to the three figures who represent the spirit of this place: Rose, the Bartender and Ten Spot. This acknowledges the role of the saloon as the crucial public space, the central stage on which the dramas of settlement are expressed in many of the westerns which deal with towns. Here it is presented in the light of a view of the West as already, after the brief moment of settlement, being in a state of irreversible decline, although it is a world that can be momentarily and locally benign. The effect depends partly on the use of strategically cast actors. Ten Spot, who tells the story of Wales's death, is played by Royal Dano, one of the group of 'supporting actors' whose presence in a wide range of westerns give the effect of a loosely defined stock company, where familiar faces repeatedly occur in related situations and settings, a practice that is central to John Ford's westerns. The distinction between such figures and the stars is that we cannot always name them, and it does not matter that we cannot. What is important is that we respond to the face: Dano's western credits include *Bend of the River, Johnny Guitar, Man of the West, Welcome to Hard Times*; among his many other films are two versions of *Huckleberry Finn* and the role of the Tattered Soldier in John Huston's film of Stephen Crane's *The Red Badge of Courage*. Writing about the stock company that inhabits the comedies of Preston Sturges, Penelope Houston has described it as 'an American chorus' – that is a more exact and narrow context, but the effect here, a combination of familiar actors and stereotypical roles, has something of that quality. Sending Wales off as Mr Wilson, they smile at each other, and cross the threshold to the inside of the saloon. This use of the chorus is one link with comedic structure; the most overt connection here is the changing of Wales's name, something that Northrop Frye, writing on comedic myth, has called 'the moment of ritual death'.

This sequence, with its use of saloon set and actors, expresses the emphasis in the film on aspects of the western that look back to a period, not only of historical fact, but of American movie-making, a time when the use of the western as a vehicle for the expression of loss and disillusion in America had not yet come to dominate the genre.

The emphasis that I am thinking of can be expressed in the treatment of technology. The movement in this film from weapons of mass destruction (a massacre

Not a gunman: Wales throws away his pistols and kills Terrill (Bill McKinney) with his own sabre in The Outlaw Josey Wales.

by machine gun) to Josey's pistols and to the final killing of Terrill with the sabre – with a striking parenthesis in the frontier town sequence on the subject of photography and the dead – expresses the belief in the possibility of a retreat or a withdrawal, or perhaps a refusal. This stands in opposition, which is to say, also in close relation, to those late westerns in which a movement is charted in the opposite direction, where the appearance of new, deadly technology – say, the machine gun and motor vehicle in Peckinpah's *The Wild Bunch* (1969) – announce the inevitability of historical change.

Can you, as one famous American hero (Jay Gatsby in F. Scott Fitzgerald's novel about another world experienced before and after a war) believes, repeat the past? I return to the final exchange of *The Outlaw Josey Wales*. Wales is being asked to acknowledge that something that the film calls a war has ended and to contemplate what the result of his accepting this could be. It seems to be suggested, through the not unsympathetic figure of Fletcher, that this involves an admission of a kind of diminution, the shift implied in the movement from Wales to Wilson, from pistol fighter to farmer, which means becoming again what he was before the war. Wales's final line – 'I guess we all died a little in that damned war' – acknowledges this subject, without exactly accepting the conclusion that Fletcher is pointing towards, and the consequences in the film remain obscure. The ending of Eastwood's source novel, Forrest Carter's *Gone to Texas*, reunites the family and redeems the deaths of the narrative, closing with two births and the note that Wales's new son is named Jaime. Eastwood's ending, in which Wales rides away but not necessarily 'home', suggests that the shattered agrarian stability of the opening sequence might still be irrecoverable, the movement from Wales to Wilson being one to which the film cannot give final confirmation.

Pale Rider

The hero as a man who is at the mercy of political and economic realities over which he has no control and who is in danger of interpreting his failures as compromising his masculinity has a particular context in Hollywood production of the period of *Pale Rider*. The economic problems of the early 'eighties were reflected in a group of films produced in response to the debt crisis that affected many American farmers at the time. These were *The River* (Mark Rydell), *Country* (Richard Pearce) and *Places in the Heart* (Richard Benton) – all three were released in 1984. The recurring figure, whose relationship to the farm is the central subject of the films, is the farmer's wife – played respectively in the three films by Sissy Spacek, Jessica Lange and Sally Field. In the first two cases, these women have husbands, played by Mel Gibson and Sam Shepherd – in *Places in the Heart*, the Field character is a widow, aided in her efforts by a black drifter.

In an able discussion of these films in the context of populist culture, Duncan Webster, in his book *Looka Yonder!*, argues that in them masculinity changes from being a spectacle into being a problem. Certainly, in *The River* and *Country*, the failure to hold on to the farm is seen as mainly a failure on the part of the man rather than the woman in the partnership – it is possible to speculate how far presenting their major male stars in this unflattering light made the films unpalatable commercially. *The River*, a contemporary narrative in which the impoverished farmer takes a job and finds that he is acting as a strike-breaker, was the most expensive film in the group to make at $21 million and commercially disastrous. *Country* was much cheaper to make, but again grossed slightly less than $5 million, about the same as *The River*. The commercially successful films of the group avoided placing their major male star in the role of the farmer and avoided direct confrontation with contemporary politics: *Pale Rider* is one of these. *Places in the Heart* is set in the Depression, and the commercially very successful *Witness* (Peter Weir, 1985), which grossed $28.5 million in the United States, moves between these subjects and the urban cop film, offering as its image of American farming the rural utopia of an Amish settlement.

We may define the subject here as essentially concerning the relationship of Americans to the land they own or exploit, and the threat from forms of usage or exploitation not conditioned by the framework of the family. These narratives are strongly related to a strain of westerns that metaphorically run together raising crops and raising children, that treat family life as emblematic of farm life. In these, the threat to the family comes from outside, from the Indians, or the banks. The argument is that the condition called family life is attacked by external forces rather than riven by internal tensions, that when we see an unhappy family, the unhappiness is the result of some force – political, economic, historical – that comes from outside the walls of the home.

In *Pale Rider*, benign order is represented by the community of Carbon Canyon, where a group of settlers pan a stream for gold. A short distance away is the industrialised and environmentally destructive version of the same search, in which the mountainside is blasted away by water under hydraulic pressure. The subject of the film is the attempt by the owner of the hydraulic process, Coy LaHood (Richard Dysart) to run off the settlers so that their canyon can be given the same treatment. The two groups are also distinguished socially – the gold panners of Carbon Canyon have families, while LaHood's miners are a malign all-male bunch – the only time a woman is among them is in a scene of attempted rape.

Of course, Eastwood's film is about mining rather than farming the land. In part the difference seems unimportant – the miners talk in language suggesting the same values as farmers – they see themselves as sinking roots, while LaHood's men are described as 'raping the land'. But there is a sense, related to the landscape of the film, in which the difference is significant.

In common with *High Plains Drifter* (and in contrast to *The Outlaw Josey Wales*), its landscape is that of a remote, inhospitable America. This is not a matter of historical date – the land here is not waiting for settlement, but inhospitable then as now – too cold, too high, too infertile for farming. Part of the difference between farming and mining as metaphors is that farming relates firmly to the hope of continuity, to a process that can theoretically at least be extended infinitely in time, while mining can be taken as an enterprise that always gives an ambiguous signal about the future, always moving towards a moment when the source of wealth will become exhausted or uneconomic to extract, or be overtaken by natural or man-made disaster. Some obvious visual detail in the film contributes to this quality. The mining town is tiny, at one point covered in snow, and weathered and faded in appearance.

The central woman in *Pale Rider* fits into the pattern of the farm debt films: here Carrie Snodgress as plain, strong pioneer mother Sarah Wheeler. The variation of the pattern begins with the father, who is not the major star and not the father of Sarah's daughter Megan (Sydney Penny). The two are clearly a couple, but we are shown not exactly a marriage, but a courtship, with the man doggedly pursuing the woman, who is resolved to take him in the end, but not just yet – a comic configuration with its roots in pastoral tradition and its famous American antecedent in the behaviour of Byron Bunch and Lena Grove in William Faulkner's novel, *Light in August*. Both this and the casting of Michael Moriarty as Sarah's suitor, Hull Barret, raise questions about masculinity. As a star and as a supporting actor, Moriarty has been cast in roles which question the adequacy of conventional routines of masculine behaviour. He is the traumatised war correspondent John Converse in Karel Reisz's Vietnam war film *Dog Soldiers* (1978). He also plays the central role as the rookie cop Beauregard Lockley in *Operation Undercover* a.k.a. *Report to the Commissioner* (Milton Katselas, 1975), a film which is of considerable interest in relation to Eastwood's work. Co-written by Ernest Tidyman, it puns on the Callahan films to the extent of including a Russian roulette sequence in which Lockley threatens a suspect with a rhetoric identical in intention to Callahan's. But the effect is opposite – the scene is played as an example of loss of control on the part of Lockley, who is as terrified as the man he is supposedly threatening. The film shows Lockley as both inadequate and trapped by the system, and it ends with his suicide.

Pale Rider clearly uses these aspects of Moriarty's persona. It begins with Carbon Canyon, which is half camp site, half rickety hillside village, being

Above: two types of masculinity – Megan (Sydney Penny) between the Preacher (Eastwood) and Hull Barret (Michael Moriarty) in Pale Rider. *Opposite: magical release – the Preacher rescues Hull from LaHood's men.*

raided by a group of LaHood's men whose primary object is to terrorise rather than to murder. They wreck a few dwellings, shoot a cow, and kill Megan's dog. At the end of the sequence, Eastwood expresses the problem of the masculine role in this 'family' – Sarah and Hull stand behind Megan as she mourns her pet. They neither look at each other nor speak. The shot of Hull's face invites us to read his awareness of his failure to protect these women, as does his next action – despite having been warned off, he chooses to take his wagon and go into town to collect supplies. As a man who cannot win a fight, he sustains his masculinity by putting himself in a position where he must confront LaHood's men, even though he knows he will at least be beaten up. He is set on with axe handles, and rescued from injury or worse only by the intervention of a stranger, played by Eastwood.

The rescue scene is played for comedy, or magical sleight of hand. It begins and ends with Eastwood delivering one-liners, and the fight itself is built around a comic routine – the stranger knocks the weapons out of the hands of his assailants. They watch them fly through the air, and while their attention is distracted, he slugs them, a device repeated several times with axe handles and twice with guns. Again, no-one is killed, and the stranger rides off with Hull to meet the family.

The implication at this point might be one of a happy conjunction of forces, the decentness of Hull complemented by the strength and power of a gunfighter, whose violence is thus cast in a benign form that will assure the defeat or containment of LaHood and leave the community of Carbon Canyon free to make a living and raise children. At its most benign, such a narrative might finally redeem the gunfighter from his isolation, allowing him to divest himself of his role and settle down.

Eastwood, interested, as elsewhere, in the quality of the isolation conferred by closeness to violence and death, constructs a different film, which is exemplified by the scene in which the principal characters eat together, the only extended domestic interior sequence in the film, almost the only one in any of Eastwood's westerns. It begins by reversing the comic quality of the fight sequence. Megan reads from *Revelations*, quoting the passage from which the film takes its title and which identifies the rider on the pale horse explicitly as 'Death, and Hell followed with him.' The women look out through the window at the sight of the stranger, and the music on the soundtrack confirms the ominousness of the identification. We now hear Sarah's argument that LaHood will inevitably defeat the settlers, and that, as a gunman, the stranger is only superficially different from LaHood's men. The appearance of the stranger dressed as a priest seems to counteract this, to make him acceptable to women. The point seems to be that only in his disguise as the Preacher can he be temporarily accepted into the family circle, eating the family meal.

In the Preacher's next confrontation, his role of fighter/priest is again essentially comic: the priest who enforces spiritual rhetoric with the power of his fists or his gun. It seems to be a scene – again the connection with the farm cycle is strong – about the dignity of work, the reassertion of masculinity for the men of Carbon Canyon. As it opens, we see Hull and the Preacher with sledgehammers, attempting to split a great rock in the river bed, and after LaHood's son and his

Above: an American dream – Hull shows a nugget to Megan and Sarah (Carrie Snodgress) in Pale Rider. *Right: absolute control, absolute isolation – the Preacher faces Stockburn.*

tame giant have been ousted, other men from the community appear with their own hammers and, accompanied by rousing music, set to work on the rocks.

The film does not offer any resolution via this newly found, or rediscovered, masculinity. The Preacher, after refusing a bribe from LaHood, acts as a negotiator for the community, obtaining an offer of $1,000 per claim. The men meet around a campfire, and Hull makes a speech stressing the claims of family and organic connection to the land – 'I sunk roots here' – over those of mere money. The men agree to refuse the offer, assuming that their stand will be led by the Preacher. His departure leads to a furious exchange between Sarah and Hull, she convinced that the men will now simply get themselves killed and he taking this as a reflection on his masculinity, which she does not deny. Despite their vote, the men seem to assume that the Preacher's departure means that in effect they have been defeated and will have to move on. Hull's exhortations, that they should behave as the Preacher would have done, is answered with an agreement to stay for a few more days, but nobody suggests that they can successfully confront LaHood or the gunfighters that he is hiring.

An incident here suggests the bleaker qualities of the whole enterprise of searching for gold. One of the miners turns up that American dream, a rock full of nuggets. This acts not as a liberation but as a prompt to a fatal misjudgement – he goes jubilantly into town, gets drunk and is shot dead in front of his sons by LaHood's professional gunmen, Marshal Stockburn (John Russell) and his

'deputies'. The good family man is shown to be no match for people for whom 'killing's a way of life' – they can be confronted only by a figure equally strongly associated with death. The Preacher, who now reappears as a gunfighter, kills the deputies one by one, and confronts Stockburn. After a moment of recognition – the implication is that the Preacher is somehow a supernatural presence, perhaps the ghost of a figure killed by Stockburn in the past – the Preacher shoots him dead, and rides off into the snow.

The point of the identification of the Preacher as a figure from the dead is not quite the same as in *High Plains Drifter*, where the Drifter had a connection, however sketchily established, with a character in the narrative. Here the reason is not to do with revenge – there is no suggestion that the Preacher comes to this place expecting to confront Stockburn. It is more to do with the establishment of the difference between Hull and the Preacher, a difference not unlike that between Callahan and some of his partners. The argument is that a man whose attitude to violence is one of diffidence about both his confidence and his skill can have a place within the community. The Preacher's absolute control of violence may apparently be more attractive from the viewpoint of assumptions about masculinity, but it actually places its possessor outside family or community life. He is in the end offered as Stockburn's double as well as his antagonist. The hint is the identical patterns, the arrangement of bullets that show as scars on the Preacher and as mortal wounds on Stockburn.

This is reflected in the side of the film that deals with the Preacher's relationships with Sarah and Megan. When he arrives in Carbon Canyon, it is clear that both women are attracted to him, or to the stereotype of masculinity he represents, in contrast to the questionable erotic qualities of Hull. Immediately after the scene in which the men decide to stand as a community and refuse LaHood's money is one in which Megan offers herself to the Preacher. Her age – she is about to turn fifteen, the age at which we have been told that her mother married – is not a problem in itself. The dialogue underlines a different issue: that for Megan sex is tied up with a vision of a future, the ongoing community of which the Preacher isn't a part. A related point is made in the opposite way towards the end of the film. Sarah tells the Preacher that she has agreed to marry Hull, who is, as they both assert for one of many times in the film, a good man. But the erotic possibilities of the Preacher cannot be ignored. Sarah kisses him and as she does this, a ghostly voice calls to him from the mountains. Her line – 'Who are you, who are you, really?' – is an implicit acknowledgement of his identification with the world outside the possibility of marriage, the space into which Megan's father disappeared. The Preacher's reply – 'It really doesn't matter, does it?' – both acknowledges his ultimate isolation from her (since he will never belong in her world it doesn't matter) and licenses the sexual act that implicitly follows. They can make love because Hull and the Preacher are not competing for the same role.

By the end of *Pale Rider*, Hull has armed himself with a rifle. It is a weapon associated by the Preacher with hunting rather than gun fighting; he uses a ruse to delay Hull's arrival in town so that he can face Stockburn alone. Hull appears just in time to shoot LaHood before he can fire at the Preacher, but this leads to no closeness between the two men. There are no exchanges of thanks or congratulation. The Preacher observes, 'Long walk . . .' Hull replies with a single word of assent. The last act in the film is Megan's arrival; she shouts declarations of love over the wind on the soundtrack, into empty space. Hull and Megan head home in the wagon. Although this is some kind of positive ending, it is achieved with a sense that the whole milieu of the film is marginal, a world where the costs and privations seem so great as to bring the whole subject of 'settlement' into question.

I mentioned earlier that the most famous images of the landscape used in *High Plains Drifter* and *Pale Rider* are those of the photographer Ansel Adams. His was one voice among many distinguished Americans in the early 'eighties to express concern at the effect on the environment of the policies of the Reagan administration. Adams wrote public letters of protest and even met with Reagan in June 1983 – he described this as a 'sour experience'. *Pale Rider* can be seen in this context, as a narrative expressing current anxieties that exploitation of the natural world was leading to irrevocable damage.

Central to this in the film is the role of Coy LaHood. In his one extended scene with the Preacher, he appears as a confused pioneer patriarch-turned-capitalist, a man who tells us that he 'opened up this country', and cannot understand why the logic of its exploitation is now driving him to acts of greater and greater violence towards both the people and the land itself. His hysteria as he thrusts fraudulent papers in the Preacher's face acknowledges his failure. LaHood's son Josh (Christopher Penn), a young, glamorous cowboy, clearly occupies the position that ought to have made him Megan's suitor, and so the agent of reconciliation. But when she goes to his hell-like camp, his only plan is to rape her. The Preacher, coming on this scene, does not kill Josh but delivers him from a career as a gunman by shooting him through the hand; elements of this relationship between old and young gunfighter appear again in *Unforgiven*.

Virtue protected: after LaHood's men have attempted to rape her, the Preacher returns Megan to her mother in Pale Rider.

CHAPTER FIVE
MEN AT WAR

Where Eagles Dare and Kelly's Heroes

Among the attempts made by studios to identify the exploitable elements of Eastwood at the end of the 1960s, we might compare *Where Eagles Dare* and *Two Mules for Sister Sara*. In both, Eastwood is placed alongside an established star and given second billing. In *Two Mules for Sister Sara*, he is the initiator of the action, but in *Where Eagles Dare*, as an American lieutenant under the command of a British commander played by Richard Burton, his role is simply to take orders, and his part consists of little more than lines which advance the narrative. The subject is a raid by a team of Allied commandos on a German fortress, supposedly to rescue an American general. Most of the English servicemen turn out to be double agents, and the climax is the predictable revelation that the chief of MI6 is working for the Germans. Eastwood's part is as the straightforward American, the observer of European duplicities on both a military level and a personal one. (The film makes some small use of Burton's persona as cynical and manipulative in relation to the women.) In retrospect, the film is remarkable only for how little of its interest relates to Eastwood – in effect, he is there to make it more approachable for its American audience, making the double-agent plot less remote, or at least providing the audience with a figure who expresses his distance from it.

Kelly's Heroes was produced by the same studio (MGM) and had the same director (Brian G. Hutton) as *Where Eagles Dare*, but makes much more substantial use of Eastwood. It belongs alongside a group of films released in 1969 and 1970 adapted from anti-war novels that dated (with one exception) from the early 'sixties but were filmed against the background of the escalation of the Vietnam war and of the movements protesting against the war. At this point, almost any war film had to present itself in part as an anti-war film. The films were *M*A*S*H** (Robert Altman, 1970, novel by Richard Hooker, 1968), *Castle Keep* (Sydney Pollack, 1969, novel by William Eastlake, 1965), and *Catch-22* (Mike Nichols, 1970, novel by Joseph Heller, 1961). All three express feelings about warfare via black or absurdist comedy. The most reassuring is *M*A*S*H**, in which the heroes' status as doctors is used as a way of placing them outside criticism of a war being fought elsewhere and connects the whole project to satires that are framed around medical culture. The contemplations of war in relation to high culture (in *Castle Keep*) and to capitalism (in *Catch-22*) are substantially more sombre; both films focus on war as a killer of young men. The sharpest contrast to these films was provided by *Patton, Lust for Glory* (Franklin Schaffner), winner of three major Oscars in 1970, which treated World War II as the end of the now-vanished tradition of martial glory expressed in the life of its officer hero.

Among the central planks of the anti-war satires is the subject of command, which raises matters of social class. It is not the officers' command and authority and the enlisted men's obedience and respect that are presented, but the officers' protected incompetence or despair and the men's desperate self-reliance. Officers are agonised intellectuals like Captain Beckman (Patrick O'Neal) in *Castle Keep* or incompetent bureaucrats like Major Major (Bob Newhart) in *Catch-22*.

The enemy is often conceived as an irrelevance, and not the only source of fear or violence – a recurrent trope both in the novels and the films is of being bombed by your own side. An attitude to technology is related to this. The fear of the technology of modern warfare is often expressed through the ironies of the murderous malfunction of weapons designed to deliver death to enemies but causing the deaths of comrades. When we do see the enemy, it is not especially as an alien or evil other, but as a mirror image – essentially similar, structured around the same absurdities.

Another important subject in the satires is sexuality, or at least the soldiers' desire for women. This might function in narratives about warfare as an opposite to fighting, as a sign of where these men would really like to be. Here, its traditional or legitimate form (desire structured around the family and dreams of girls back home) is replaced by what is felt as appropriate to the condition of warfare, the actual or imagined world of the prostitute and the brothel.

None of these elements is specific to a given conflict, and generally the anti-war satires are not interested in the causes or origins of a particular historical situation. Rather, they seem to function as complementary texts to the films that condemn warfare directly from a more conventional moral viewpoint as an abstract and intolerable horror, moving the same judgement towards comedy rather than tragedy. There is a paradox here, or at least a potential one. Apparently the audience is being offered a narrative set in an identified and familiar conflict, which might appear to be specific. Commonly, however, a historical setting in the recent past is used as an abstraction, as a period neither modern nor archaic, and in practice the films say nothing about that conflict's specificity. This can also be complicated by the presence of images of the military and anxieties about military power that relate not to the apparent setting but to a war being fought at the time of the film's production. In this, there has been a movement from the original anti-war novels, written largely before the escalation of the Vietnam war, to the films made in 1969 and 1970.

Kelly's Heroes contains many of the same elements as the overt anti-war satires, but to a greater extent these are combined with a more conventional treatment of a heroic raid behind enemy lines during the Allied invasion of France in World War II. The strategy is to establish the film as an anti-war satire in its opening sequence. In the first minutes, we see a platoon pinned down by a barrage from its own side, in spite of which the men's leader, Sergeant 'Big Joe' (Telly Savalas), is keen to press on to capture the next big town. He interrogates a captured German officer not about its defences but about its girls. Scenes of a soldier reading from the Michelin guide and of the commanding officer 'liberating' a yacht for transportation back to Paris confirm Big Joe's line, 'You've got to think of us as tourists.' All this clearly signals the satirical intention to the audience.

Eastwood is Kelly, a soldier in Big Joe's platoon who discovers from the German officer that a bank in a French town behind enemy lines holds $16 million in gold bars, and organises the platoon to capture it for themselves. The act of pushing forward into occupied territory ceases to be a matter of military heroics and becomes a 'bank job', an act of personal enterprise by its participants – Kelly explains, 'We're just a private enterprise operation.'

Or, rather, that is what has to be claimed, but the distinction turns out not to be simple either for the platoon or for the audience. The raid is not just presented as a covert business, sneaking into enemy territory and escaping with the money, but varies at different stages in the plot. Sometimes it is a caper operated by a few soldiers; sometimes it looks sufficiently identical to any other military push forward to have the commander, General Colt (Carroll O'Connor), jumping into his jeep to be with his heroic troops at the moment of liberation.

What is true for the members of the platoon also shapes the position of the audience: just as the troops will attempt something called a bank raid when they would not have followed a heroic mission, so the knowledge of the particular purpose of the mission allows an audience uneasy about warfare and its political motivations to accept a series of sequences similar in tone to many genre war films, with the main points being the rapid and massive despatch of the enemy and the spectacle of energetic destruction.

Sometimes, the film operates to distance itself from the war that America was currently fighting. The two major sequences of battle between American and German forces take place in towns, between uniformed troops. These show

Opposite: soldiers as hippies – the tank platoon's encampment in Kelly's Heroes.
*Above: absurdist showdown – Oddball (Donald Sutherland), Kelly (Eastwood) and
Big Joe (Telly Savalas) confront the German tank commander.*

a landscape unlike anything that might be reminiscent of the Vietnam war, and
no American dies in these places.

Against this, the film also reflects perceptions of the American military that
were emerging from the Vietnam war. The central figure here is Oddball, the
commander of the tanks Kelly uses for support. He is played by Donald
Sutherland as an icon of the soldier-as-hippie, recognisable by beard, long hair,
'beat' language. There are also a couple of details that seem to recall the
psychic aggression of Vietnam: the playing of music at full volume on the tanks
as they go into battle (at one point, the Germans are massacred to the sound of
Hank Williams's 'Sunshine') and the terrorising of the enemy with psychedelia
(shells full of paint). In Oddball, the breakdown of command has become
fearsome; the story of the death of his commander is told: 'The bastard had
been trying to get us killed for weeks.' At the time, Sutherland was becoming
known as a radical star – later, he campaigned alongside Jane Fonda, protesting
at American involvement in the war. In a characterisation that anticipates the later
cycle of films that were directly about Vietnam, Sutherland plays Oddball's
involvement in drug culture as an expression of protest against the military.
Nevertheless, he is not treated negatively: he is clearly an efficient soldier and
commander of his men, in contrast to many of the officers in the film.

A distance nonetheless remains between Oddball and the regular soldiers
who make up the bulk of Kelly's platoon, and he is not present in the film's
darkest sequence, when members of the platoon die. The imagery here can
again be loosely related to the context of Vietnam. The sequence begins with
the men fanned out on patrol through open country and one soldier suddenly

being killed by a landmine when the platoon finds that it has wandered into a minefield. It ends with two others dead, pinned down in the minefield during a shoot-out with a German patrol. The Americans move on, aware that they cannot cross the minefield again to check that their comrades are truly dead. There is a sense here of the treacherousness and brutality of the environment that can be loosely related to the feeling in the later Vietnam films that it is not only the enemy but the place itself, or what has been made of it, that is appalling.

Such subjects can be side-stepped again when the platoon arrives in the town. The strategy here is again to emphasise the connections with the anti-war satires. There is a battle in which all but one of the Germans die. The Americans now realise that they can demolish the doors of the bank only with the assistance of the last remaining German and his tank. They approach him, and he agrees to cooperate for a share of the booty. The effect is suddenly to wrench this figure, all of whose comrades have been killed by Americans, into the role of just another good guy in a uniform. This return to absurdist comedy is announced, as the Americans approach the tank, through a series of visual and soundtrack references to the Dollars trilogy.

The contradictions between the film's desire to show the platoon as traditional war heroes, and the insistence on the absurdity of the whole conflict, is never resolved. The final exchanges between the major players are minimal in substance, and an upbeat note has been added in the form of a final credits sequence using 'portrait' footage of the actors. Something of this may be reflected in Eastwood's comment in an interview on his disappointment with the film: 'It just ended up as the story of a bunch of American screw-offs.' Eastwood apparently argued that the film needed more work at the editing stage, but it seems unlikely that this could have resolved the problems of the war film genre and the attitude of its audience in 1970.

Escape from Alcatraz

Escape from Alcatraz links back to Eastwood's earlier work through Don Siegel's direction, and forward to *Tightrope* through Richard Tuggle, the director of that film and the writer of the screenplay here. The casting of Eastwood as a criminal rather than a cop offers only a partial reversal of terms. Eastwood is not a psychotic or corrupt figure, but a character very similar to Callahan, marked by his loneliness, or self-reliance. The exchange in his interview with the Warden of Alcatraz (Patrick McGoohan) about having no intimates or family, identifies him in a way that echoes the similarly placed exchange with the mayor at the beginning of *Dirty Harry*. Both films could be said to explore the space between the man without intimates and the world of those with attachments.

This contrast is worked out in *Dirty Harry* through an argument which establishes Callahan and the psychotic as two figures who move freely through the spaces of the city, in contrast to the more circumscribed family men. The reappearance of some of the same motifs in a prison film gives them a different meaning. Of the significant prisoners, three men are identified as having no ties with the outside; these are the three who break out of the prison. They are Frank Morris (Eastwood) and two who can take their one apparent family tie out with them, the brothers Clarence Anglin (Jack Thibeau) and John Anglin (Fred Ward). It is perhaps significant, even so, that very little is made of their being brothers.

A sterile world: Frank Morris (Eastwood) with English (Paul Benjamin) in Escape from Alcatraz.

Against them are posed the men who want to escape, but are trapped, not simply by iron and concrete but by their relationship to the world outside. They see life as it goes on outside the walls of the prison through their loved ones, and their perception of what that world is like depends on what they learn from those on the outside.

This is made explicit in a scene in which two prisoners who have been seen in some contact with Morris, and who might seem obvious candidates for participation in an escape attempt, are visited by their loved ones. They are English (Paul Benjamin), a black prisoner inside for murdering a white man, and Charley Butts (Larry Hankin), an ineffectual thief. They are seen respectively meeting a daughter and a wife. In both cases, the prisoners learn bad news – English's daughter intends marriage with a white man, and Charley learns that his mother is dying. When the breakout comes, English is not directly involved, and Charley, although he is part of the original group, arrives too late at a point on the escape route at which he would need the assistance of the others; he has to return to his cell.

Two characters stand between the poles of isolation and commitment; they are Litmus (Frank Ronzio) and Doc (Roberts Blossom). Litmus is the simpler case, a con whose attachment is to a concealed pet, a mouse. Litmus dies in Alcatraz, and the sole qualification of Morris's isolation in the film is that he takes the mouse out of Alcatraz with him, as if it, and thus perhaps the memory of a dead friend from inside, were the only unthreatening form of contact with another.

Doc is a convict whose attachment is not to another person, but to an activity. He is a painter, and functions in *Escape from Alcatraz* as the representative of what might be positive about these circumstances, the opportunity to give an intensity of study to a particular skill, which had been the central subject of John Frankenheimer's *The Birdman of Alcatraz* (1961), but here used in an opposite way. Doc functions as a confirmation of the viciousness of the system. After accidentally finding Doc's revealing portrait of himself, the Warden withdraws his painting privileges, and the artist mutilates his own hand in response. Apart from showing up sadism and declaring the prison to be fundamentally inimical to this kind of creativity (the connection with the Birdman is made explicitly in the last picture we see Doc painting in his cell), this gives us a minor plot involving a protagonist and antagonist. Another, in which Morris is sexually threatened by a psychopathic prisoner, surfaces at intervals in the film.

Here again, the comparison with the Callahan films is instructive. I have argued that those films commonly conclude with an action sequence in which the cop chases the hood to some large, sterile space, commonly associated with a disused or redundant industrial site, and the cop's triumph over the hood is presented through his domination and control of that space. Thus the hood might fall to his death (*Sudden Impact*) or drown (*Magnum Force*), or simply present an unmissable target (*The Enforcer*, in which the space is actually the abandoned site of Alcatraz).

One way of reading *Escape from Alcatraz* is that the whole film is concerned with this space – the distinction between it and the potentially more benign place that is inhabited by the society at large has disappeared (or almost disappeared, marginalised into the shots of brilliant red and orange sunrises and sunsets that Siegel opposes to the dominant blue of the prison sequences). In this space, what has also become largely marginal is the Eastwood character's antagonist. This function is not fulfilled by the Warden, who is closer to one of the inefficient bureaucrats, the mayors and chiefs of police, in the Callahan series. After their initial interview, Siegel gives us only two or three short and insubstantial scenes between them.

The breakout sequence, which concludes the film, demonstrates this lack of an antagonist. We are not shown a pursuit – the escape is not discovered until the men have got clean away, and once we see their pursuers we never see the convicts again. The interest in the sequence is focused entirely on the three escaping men and the physical spaces they are moving across – even here, the issue is less to do with avoiding guards and more with heights and depths and crossing physical barriers. In this respect, it is a continuation of the opening image of the escape attempt, which shows Morris minutely chipping away at the rotting concrete around the grille in his cell with a pair of stolen nail clippers.

The importance of this becomes clearer if we consider the matter of these men's guilt. It is clear that they are not criminals in the sense in which the term is understood in the Callahan films – the offences that they have committed have little or nothing to do with violence and are more like failed capers. The clearest case is the black comedy of the story of Butts, gaoled for stealing a prison guard's car. The exception to it is English, but it is implied that his violence was justified, and his conviction the result of racial prejudice. So what *Escape from Alcatraz* presents us with is a group of more or less sympathetic principals, whose wits are pitted, not against a human antagonist, but against a structure composed of elements that have to be dominated in order for them to survive/escape. This scenario is familiar from a cycle in which crime sometimes plays a peripheral part, the disaster movies of the 'seventies.

There are substantial discussions of the disaster cycle available elsewhere, and I will not examine it here in detail, but consider rather where connections might lead us. A common motif in the cycle is of entrapment, the unlucky group confined by the disaster to an environment the technology of which is suddenly acting against their interests. This phenomenon can have a human agent (the cheap wiring that starts the fires in the skyscraper in *The Towering Inferno*, John Guillermin, 1974) or a natural cause (the tidal wave in *The Poseidon Adventure*, Ronald Neame, 1972). The response is to attack the situation not by invoking a modern, high-technology solution, but by recourse to the skills and techniques associated with an earlier stage of development. Sometimes these are simply physical adeptness – climbing is important in many cases – and sometimes the taking of a technology from another context and adapting it to solve a problem for which it was not designed. Finally, as several writers on the cycle have pointed out, the films play on elemental threats, on death by fire and water.

One subject in the disaster cycle is the knowledge that there is a fragile division between the spaces we occupy socially and the milieu of the technology that supports them – the cellars and attics of gothic domestic space are replaced by ducts, ventilator shafts and access points – a world that only technicians know about, or into which only they can penetrate. The disaster plunges its participants into this world, and we see them, or rather some of them, survive its threat.

Let us take this as a point of departure and return to *Escape from Alcatraz*. Much of Siegel's film posits Alcatraz as a place of dark space: the arrival at night, the Warden's account of the prison's isolation in the freezing water, the windowless cells of D block. In such a place, the normal cell becomes a place of light and order, in which life is ordinarily spent. The film can be thought of as being like a disaster movie in which the principals voluntarily bring on the switch from light to darkness, from room to ventilation shaft, and put themselves in the position of surviving through their manipulation of that other world, using intelligence, physical prowess and 'low' technology – Morris's electric drill made up from a stolen fan is exemplary – in order to escape to freedom.

Two differences from the disaster cycle are suggestive. While the disaster movies generally crystallise anxieties about modern technology, Alcatraz is presented as a piece of penal technology surviving from the past. Morris's initial proposal to the other escapees stresses that the prison is already old: 'the moist air is corroding the concrete, the salt is rusting the metal'. The fact of the closure of Alcatraz in 1961, perhaps hinted at in the film's opening dateline and stated explicitly in its closing title, has a function not unlike the reassuring exchanges at the end of disaster movies to the effect that the particular faults which have led to this narrative will not be allowed to recur.

The major part of the disaster cycle was produced in the years 1972-76. By the end of the 'seventies, even disaster movies were moving away from positions of simple reassurance. The Canadian film *City on Fire* (Alvin Rakoff, 1979) clearly offers the survivors of near-holocaust as traumatised. A more useful comparison, though, is between *Escape from Alcatraz* and another feature released in 1979 that used aspects of the disaster cycle, Ridley Scott's *Alien*.

Certainly the disaster in *Alien* – allowing an immensely aggressive alien life form to enter the spaceship – has nothing whatsoever in common with Siegel's film. The interesting areas of comparison are the environments and the relationships to family/sexuality expressed in the two films. In both *Alien* and *Escape from Alcatraz*, the setting is a huge but confining space, surrounded by an environment of deadly hostility, which makes leaving immensely difficult. Within this space there are a few bright, unthreatening areas and a very large area dominated by heavy mechanical/hydraulic machinery; everything is connected by a complex web of ducts and vents. Part of the detail of *Alien*, the set of the lower holds of the ship, which seem to be full of miscellaneous mechanical junk, offers it as almost decrepit, not really in the control of those nominally in charge.

The different kinds of threat in the two films can be linked by the idea that they make the environment of the prison or spaceship literally or metaphorically deadly. In *Escape from Alcatraz*, the prisoners must escape or be effectively destroyed; there is no suggestion in the film that any of them will ever be released. In *Alien* the matter is simpler – the crew of the *Nostromo* must destroy the alien before it destroys them.

Similar strategies are deployed in *Alien* for tackling the alien to those in the disaster cycle – the construction of 'low' technology weapons, and the ability to move with skill through a set composed of hazardous spaces and physical challenges. The point at which the two films in some respects resemble each other, and depart from the disaster cycle, is in the conclusions to which their narratives move. The 'seventies disaster movies argue that survival as such is clearly desirable, because a return to the ordinary world – commonly the world of the family – is self-evidently worthwhile. In *Escape from Alcatraz*, there are only the three escapees, and the question of whether Morris and his companions survived in the freezing water or drowned is left open, in sharp contrast to the conclusions of the disaster cycle and the importance it places on showing a sufficient number of untraumatised survivors. In *Alien*, only Ripley (Sigourney Weaver) survives, and again we are never shown any sequence of arrival in another, better world.

The connection can perhaps be extended a little further. The disaster cycle displays 'good' masculinity in its depiction of men, in Richard Dyer's words, 'taking control of the elements'. In these films, made at the end of the cycle, sexuality remains important but understood in a different way. The films still make a distinction between strong and weak forms of masculine behaviour – the strong who try to escape or kill the alien, and the weak who stand and accept their fate: Charley Butts in Siegel's movie, and the physically not dissimilar figure of Brett (Harry Dean Stanton) in Scott's. The moment when Charley returns to his cell, knowing that his escape attempt has failed, can be linked to the point in *Alien* when Brett, just before his death, bares his head to the artificial rain in the hold of the ship. The two scenes are similarly expressive of the pathos in the situation of this kind of male.

Alien obviously goes further than *Escape from Alcatraz* in having masculinity completely fail – the alien kills all the men on the *Nostromo*. This fact, that *Alien*'s central figure and survivor is a woman, where *Escape from Alcatraz* offers the more 'conventional' man, may obscure the connection between the two. Both Morris and Ripley, presented as strong and benign examples of male and female, are figures whose sexuality, while clearly central, is always isolated, never placed in the context of family or lover. We might speculate that it is exactly this apartness that enables them to survive. We see both finally alone with a pet – Ripley's cat and Morris's mouse are simultaneously acknowledgements of indebtedness to the diasaster cycle and indications of the extent to which the reassuring elements of the cycle had become attenuated by 1979.

Firefox

Firefox (1982) was the first of two films that Eastwood was to make in the 'eighties directly invoking the presence or meaning or memory of Vietnam a decade and more after the United States's withdrawal. It is also part of a group of films made at around this time which take weapons technology as their subject: *Blue Thunder* (John Badham, 1983) is the closest parallel to this aspect of *Firefox*. The wider cycle of these films, considering both the nuclear and non-nuclear threat, has been discussed at length by Andrew Britton and others. (See, for example, Britton, 'Blissing Out: The Politics of Reaganite Entertainment', *Movie* 31/32.)

We learn in the opening moments of *Firefox* that the character played by Eastwood is a Vietnam veteran suffering from what is called later in the film 'delayed stress syndrome'. Airforce officers on a mission to find Major Mitchell Gant (Eastwood) in his remote rural retreat track him in a helicopter. The sight of the US military helicopter, which causes Gant to hallucinate a series of images of his experiences in Vietnam, would also have been one of the commonplaces of the representation of the American presence in Vietnam for any audience that had seen the Vietnam war films of the 'seventies. Strikingly, it is almost the only point in the film at which an image of the military directly invokes the imagery surrounding the Vietnam war.

This may seem to make the issue of Vietnam peripheral, and the lines of the main plot also appear to have nothing to do with the past, or rather the recent past. We learn that the Soviet Union has developed a new weapon, the MiG 31 or Firefox, and that it is proposed to smuggle Gant, a pilot who happens to speak fluent Russian, into the Soviet research base so that he can steal the plane and thus restore the 'balance' of power. There are several ways in which this scenario is made to seem reassuring. The two sides in the conflict are not entirely dissimilar to each other. America and American power are represented only minimally, in the figure of Gant's old subordinate Buckholz (David Huffman). Rather, the stress is on European culture; the planning of the raid takes place in London, and Aubrey, the leading Western planner, is played as an English boffin by Freddie

Jones. The set is a handsome period room with a discreetly lit Old Master in the background.

The plot requires Gant initially to be disguised as a European. He is supposed to be impersonating a drug dealer, and in his make-up looks a little like a particular icon of Europeanness to American audiences, Max von Sydow. When he arrives in Moscow, the city is presented – secret police apart – as a place not all that different from London or any other northern European capital. The object seems to be to signal similarity between the two sides, both as places and in their leaders, the balance disturbed only by the existence of the Firefox. This points to a contradiction, or paradox, in this film about the balance of power – it has simultaneously to make the statement that the two sides are alike and marry this to the argument that 'our' side is of course to be preferred to theirs. So alongside the presentation of the two powers as different versions of Europeanness, the film includes a number of scenes with secret police and implied torture by the Soviet military, and discussions of the freedoms of being an American.

Distinctions are also made around the idea of the hero. Across the division between westerners and Soviets, the film erects parallel figures – Gant and his Russian antagonist Voskov (Kai Wulff) – as men of action, contrasted with the generals and bureaucrats who watch display screens in darkened rooms on either side of the world. A detail of the plot, in which Gant refuses to kill Voskov as part of stealing the Firefox but dispatches him later when the stolen plane and another Firefox flown by Voskov meet in the climactic dogfight, offers a traditional image of military honour, the appropriateness of killing – or dying – in combat.

The kind of combat that is presented here is also significant, in that the dogfight differs very little in essentials from something we might have seen in a film about World War II. As a weapon, the Firefox is emphatically not a simple metaphor for a nuclear threat – it is shown as having only two elements that distinguish it from the technology of the 'forties – extreme speed and the fact that its weapon systems are launched via sensors which read the pilot's thoughts. The first of these serves to associate Gant with a traditional hero of technological advance dating back to the 'fifties, the test pilot – in *The Right Stuff* (1983), Philip Kaufman uses the historical figure of Chuck Yeager in a related way. The idea of thought-controlled weapons, and particularly the detail that in order to operate the systems Gant must think in Russian, seems potentially more interesting, but nothing of any substance comes of it beyond its use as a device to raise tension in the final scenes. It recalls – as do some of the visuals at this point – the climax of *Star Wars* (George Lucas, 1977), the reassuring concept that victory is always in the grasp of the right thinker, the figure possessed of 'the Force'.

The lack of interest in a device that requires the Eastwood character to think in Russian may point to another area of difficulty in the project. Clearly, one of the pleasures offered by *Firefox* is the slow emergence of the star's familiar persona from behind a series of masks, from traumatised war victim to uneasy European businessman to American tourist to American military hero. Insofar as one of the trajectories of the film is the movement to the point where American verve and know-how can be celebrated, *Firefox* is forced not to emphasise anything that might associate its star too closely with the Russian national culture, and thus

The European: Gant (Eastwood) in his disguise as a drug dealer in Firefox.

be seen to introduce any ambiguity into the image of the hero. Although Gant must be understood for plot reasons to speak Russian, the occasions for allowing us to see this happening have to be severely limited.

Little of this appears to be to do with Vietnam. Certainly, Gant has flashes of recollection of the war at intervals in the plot, but they seem to be devices to heighten tension, much as if he were subject to sudden attacks of, say, giddiness at crucial moments. The point seems to be that the Vietnam war has to all intents and purposes disappeared, except for something that happens inside the head of this character. It has no external existence in the sense that it cannot be seen to affect the behaviour or position of any other figure in the film and, as far as Gant is concerned, it exists as a nightmare that can be overcome by getting back to the kind of fighting at which he is truly skilled, where the antagonist is a reassuringly recognisable version of yourself, as opposed to the Asian woman of his hallucination.

If the project of *Firefox* is identifiable enough, the film's interest lies in the limitations to the success of this project in 1982, the year of arguably the most outspoken attempt to reinstate the figure of the military hero, Taylor Hackford's *An Officer and a Gentleman*. In implicit ways, the difficulty of Eastwood's project is very apparent. Its hero is a vet in retreat from America and wishing to remain so – the bribe that causes him to accept the mission is the offer of ownership of his remote hideaway. Its scene of American triumph, the landing of the Firefox, takes place not in a US base but in Antarctica, a landscape that has more in common with the science fiction of the period than with the places where military power had actually been exercised. At its close Gant says, conventionally enough, 'Let's go home.' But the film is substantially silent on the subject of home. Given the absence of the usual ways in which such a subject might be presented – there are, in clear contrast to the reactionary sexual politics of *An Officer and a Gentleman*, no significant women in *Firefox* – we cannot know very clearly what this line is to be taken to mean.

It is this that identifies *Firefox* sharply as an Eastwood film. The gesture towards the importance of home and its meanings, and the simultaneous awareness that this culture no longer supplies these meanings unambiguously, are what this film has in common with the Callahan cycle.

Heartbreak Ridge

The opening image of *Heartbreak Ridge* is the Warner logo in black and white. It is followed by a credits sequence, also in monochrome, which begins with a tank emerging from a tunnel, a shot of a sign locating the 38th parallel, and various images of men at war. Over this, martial music plays, at first *piano*, then growing in volume, finally giving way to Don Gibson singing 'Sea of Heartbreak'. These signs are a little difficult to read – an audience may or may not recall that the 38th parallel was the line along which the US divided Korea at the end of World War II, or exactly when the Don Gibson song was a hit (the answer is the early 1960s). The sense of time and place may not be quite clear, but the tenor of these images – tanks not helicopters, black-and-white not colour – confirms the reference made by the monochrome logo, that we are being asked to connect

The veteran: Gunnery Sergeant Thomas Highway (Eastwood) in Heartbreak Ridge.

this not so much with a specific war as with a particular kind of film, to look back past the last twenty years or so to films of wars that were able to present a defensible idea of military valour.

This is related to the perception of war as either a private or a public matter. If the opening of *Firefox* announces that the Vietnam war now exists essentially as a private trauma inside the heads of its veterans, the credits sequence of *Heartbreak Ridge* offers the memory of warfare as official history. The grainy images obviously evoke newsreel coverage – perhaps this is actually what they are – and a sense of the public, received image of war.

The impression here that warfare is a glorious tradition, cut off from any identification of the causes or effects of any particular war, is followed up in the introduction of the character played by Eastwood. The sequence after the credits takes place in jail, where Gunnery Sergeant Thomas Highway (Eastwood) has landed after getting drunk. We hear Highway before we see him – at this point the film shifts to colour footage. He is telling yarns – again, characteristic and unspecific soldier's tales of sex and squalor – to an appreciative young audience of fellow prisoners. In an incident strongly reminiscent of a comparable scrap in *Escape from Alcatraz*, a big goon takes exception to him and is duly defeated in the ensuing fight. In Highway's trial, we learn that he was arrested for urinating on a police car; outside the courthouse, there is nearly a fight with the police officer involved. As Highway walks away, the enraged policeman taunts him that his war record is 'ancient fucking history'.

There are echoes here. One detail – pissing on authority – points us towards the opening of one of Eastwood's 'seventies westerns, *Joe Kidd*. Another – the accusation that the Eastwood figure is a leftover from the past – links back to the name-calling (Dinosaur, Neanderthal) in the Callahan cycle. These are signposts pointing in opposite directions, or apparently so.

The reference to *Joe Kidd* suggests the end of something, the closing off of an era when heroics of a particular kind were felt to be possible or appropriate, and the anxiety that the hero of those earlier times might be turning into the sad, comic old man who misbehaves and tells tall stories to the young.

Alongside this we can place the different treatment of the past initiated when Eastwood is called a dinosaur or its equivalent in the Callahan cycle. There, the speaker represents a new order which is supposedly replacing the old skills or methods embodied by the Eastwood figure. The narrative shows him being demoted or shifted from his role, and then reinstated in it when it becomes apparent that his methods are the only effective ones. The most uncluttered version of this plot is found in *The Enforcer. Heartbreak Ridge* can be thought of as a variation of it in which the soldier rather than the cop bases his authority in the lessons of the past. Some elements are substantially identical. Highway's new commanding officer, Major Powers (Everett McGill), who tells him 'I haven't had the privilege of combat' and turns out to have moved over from a supply unit, recalls Captain McKay (Bradford Dillman), the new Homicide commander fresh from his years in Personnel in The *Enforcer*. In both films, the apparent stupidity of the new order is represented by Eastwood being forced to take as his partner in danger the young and putatively incompetent – the young cop from traffic division played by Tyne Daly in *The Enforcer*, the sloppy platoon of young men in *Heartbreak Ridge*. In both films, the pleasure is seeing the movement from mistrust to understanding, the young acquiring appropriate skills and acting bravely in a tight spot.

Here the cop cycle is in some respects on firmer ground than this variant. The probity of Callahan's fight against crime can be demonstrated easily enough in the hold-up sequences at the opening of the films, and the villainy of the central group of terrorists in *The Enforcer* is again beyond dispute. In *Heartbreak Ridge*, the experience that underwrites Highway's position, the equivalent to that opening hold-up sequence, is not directly shown and is certainly more difficult to present as beyond the need for justification or explanation. This is Highway's service in Vietnam. Or, rather, one particular incident in it, for the strategy is to move both to the particular – Vietnam seen not as a whole war but as a single engagement, the heroic defence of Heartbreak Ridge – and to the general – Vietnam seen not as a specific and unique war, but as part of a continuum of warfare stretching certainly back to Korea, implicitly to World War II, and forward into the contemporary plot of the film, the American invasion of Grenada.

One sequence demonstrates these strategies clearly. In the centre of the film, after bailing Highway out from his second spell in gaol, a group of central figures returns to the bar patronised by the Marine Corps. The setting is itself expressive of martial continuities – it is presided over by Mary (Eileen Heckart), who has 'served the marines in three wars'. Highway's old comrade from Vietnam, Master Sergeant Choozoo (Arlen Dean Snyder), and the young Stitch Jones (Mario Van Peebles), the leading figure in Highway's platoon, look at the photographs on the walls, and the story of Heartbreak Ridge is told. It is presented as unaffected by some larger (and less happy) consideration of history ('It ain't in any of the history books. It's just a little piece of war'). Yet, paradoxically, it is also a matter of public record: we learn that Highway won the Congressional Medal of Honor. The visual evidence here is the collection of Vietnam photographs on the walls. Again, black-and-white photography seems to offer them as of a piece with others, no doubt from earlier times, that stretch beyond our close vision.

Similar strategies operate in the presentation of the invasion of Grenada. Highway has said of Vietnam that 'we lost the war but we won the battles', and the invasion becomes another local action, with Highway's platoon liberating grateful (American) civilians and being given the opportunity to demonstrate their own heroics when pinned down by the enemy. As in *Firefox*, the representation of warfare leaps back over Vietnam to an earlier time. What we see looks in many respects like a part of the Allied offensive in Normandy – an amphibious landing in an unthreatening, unboobytrapped terrain, in which the enemy is represented by unproblematic Cuban regulars rather than local freedom fighters, the conflict becoming one between two professional forces. The representation of victory is interesting for its tacit insistence on the connection with the distant past. At the summit of the hill stormed by the platoon is a fort that clearly dates from the nineteenth century or earlier; the men scale its walls by attaching a line to an antique cannon. It is here that the final moves in the assertion of values are worked out, with the humiliation of the officer from Supply, and the assertion that what links the two vets (Highway and Choozoo) with the heroic general is their mutual history. As Highway put it earlier, in a conversation with the same general about Vietnam in 1968, 'We sure as hell chewed some of the same dirt.'

I argued in my discussion of the Callahan cycle that while the business of fighting crime is apparently easy to justify, the cop films generally find themselves taking up at best an ambiguous position regarding the wider public, those on whose behalf the war against crime is waged. This is reflected in the ends of the films, with the defeat of the criminal portrayed as an act of self-reliance on Callahan's part, almost a private matter, which receives no public applause and leaves him alone at the end of the movie. *Heartbreak Ridge* is at the opposite pole, seeing warfare as essentially a public spectacle and validating its justification of the martial by producing images of those for whom the war is fought. This covers both those at risk – the cheering liberated students in Grenada University – and the wider American public. The final sequence of the soldiers' return to America is essentially a visual melodrama organised around the reuniting of the family, taking place in public space.

But who was the Vietnam war fought for, who did it liberate or reunite? There is, of course, some difficulty in negotiating this element of the narrative, which in terms of images of the family offers only the destruction of the couple. There is loss (the mention of Stony Jackson, Mary's husband, a hero of Heartbreak Ridge but killed at Khe Sanh) or pain – the fear for Highway's life felt during the war years by his wife Aggie (Marsha Mason) that destroyed their marriage.

Redeeming this marriage is part of, or complementary to, the project of overcoming the legacy of the Vietnam war in the film. It is as if the war is seen as a moment of divorce from proper ideas of martial glory and proper ideals of marital loyalty. The connection is almost explicitly made in the scene in which Highway plays Santa Claus, assisting the one married member of his platoon with money out of his own pocket. Eastwood cuts directly from this to the most extended scene between Highway and Aggie, in which Highway's own description of his purpose is: 'I just want it to end as right as it was when I started.' At the point at which their differences are resolved, Eastwood cuts directly from their embrace to the anecdote of Heartbreak Ridge, and Aggie is there to greet Highway when he arrives home from Grenada at the close of the film.

Can this degree of redemption, this insistence that the present can be made as 'right' as the distant past, possibly work? Part of the interest of *Heartbreak Ridge* is in looking at what the film has to do in order to maintain its thesis and at the ways in which it inevitably acknowledges the limitations of what it attempts to assert.

Take the subject of modernity. The awareness that the world of 1983 is not the same as that of 1968 or 1944 is at its least threatening when modern technology is associated with fools and made to seem foolish – the exercise led by Major Powers and based around beepers triggered by laser guns is an example of this. That modernity might have an effect on the conduct of actual warfare can be admitted only as comedy. The incident in the Grenada invasion in which the platoon is saved by an air strike is exemplary. The strike is called in by the lieutenant telephoning the base in America, but the Air Force will not accept collect calls. Luckily Stitch Jones is prepared with his charge cards – 'I never travel into battle without my plastic' – and the call goes through. The comedy here is obvious and disarming, associating modernity with absurdity but not quite being able to dismiss it. It does, after all, save the lives of the platoon, but Stitch's line is a piece of juvenile cheekiness rather than any deeper acknowledgement of change.

There is an equivalent strategy in the treatment of the film's other subject. We see Highway reading magazine articles about the 'new' woman to further his courtship of Aggie. The function of this seems to be a signal to Aggie, a message that he is prepared to acknowledge or accept change, but there is a real uncertainty as to whether Aggie is best addressed through the language of feminism: if she herself is as uninfluenced by change as Highway, maybe that language will sound foolish or absurd to her. Like the charge cards, the magazines locate modernity negatively by associating it loosely with the trivia of modern culture.

There is a degree of unease in all of this, as if the assertion that things can be as they were cannot escape the occasional trace of anti-war satire. The liberation of the American 'hostages' – obviously an exorcism of a memory of one of the major military debacles of the 'eighties, the botched attempt to rescue the Americans held in Tehran – takes the form of an entirely conventional scene: troops burst into a room proclaiming themselves US Marines, and all dance for joy. But this is preceded by two other occasions in which Marines burst into rooms. The first is about fear, when the most nervous of the platoon shoots to pieces a skeleton in an anatomy classroom. In the second, which takes the image into the area of comedy, Stitch Jones encounters a naked co-ed taking a shower, and delivers his line identifying himself as a liberator with some embarrassment.

The unease also affects the presentation of the romance between Aggie and Highway. There is an apparently satisfactory movement, from the memory of the start of their relationship, of Aggie's senior prom and the first time they made love, to the new beginning emblematised in the pure white dress that Aggie wears in the final scene. But alongside this is the matter of class, and the wider context into which these two lives will have to fit.

Eastwood's casting as an officer in *Firefox* is not typical – here he returns to a role that casts him as the common man. Highway and Aggie, the career soldier on the point of retirement and the waitress with sore feet and dreams of an avocado ranch, are experienced as both the salt of the earth and potentially the dispossessed of this society, a paradox that echoes the couple in *The Gauntlet*. In Aggie's last significant line in the film, delivered to Highway as they enjoy a final moment of military glamour dancing together at a military party, she asks him why he wants her back: 'Is it because you can't be a Marine any more, and you've got no place to go?' The question cannot be answered; Aggie realises its tactlessness, but the plot takes Highway off to war in the middle of her apologies, and in the final sequence neither of them speaks.

It is possible to see the passionate attachment to an idealised version of military life in *Heartbreak Ridge* as part of a wider response to Reaganite America. In the dismissal of modern culture, there are hints of an anxious suspicion that once the characters move outside the base they will encounter an America that has almost nothing to offer them. The valorisation of the military goes along with the assumption of the bankruptcy of the civilian world, a feeling which associates the film with the attitudes to America found in *Bronco Billy* and *Honkytonk Man*. The film ends with the implication that the old man has successfully transmitted his skill and knowledge to the young one. On the other hand, Stitch Jones significantly announces his decision to choose to stay in the Marines rather than resume civilian life, and the benign image of the family and the couple never extends beyond the public reconciliations taking place on the tarmac.

CHAPTER SIX
EASTWOOD'S TRAVELS: THE ROAD MOVIES

In dealing with these films, I have to consider whether they are a group at all, or simply a random bundle of movies spread across the later part of Eastwood's career that appear here simply because they are not westerns, or Callahan films, or war films. In obvious respects, they are diverse. Eastwood's is always the central role, but he is variously a bank robber, a cop, a mechanic and part-time prize-fighter, the owner of a Wild West show, a country singer, and a skip tracer. Nor are the films all comedies, although all of them have comic elements. Probably nobody would call *Thunderbolt and Lightfoot*, in which all but one of the central characters die, a comedy, nor *Honkytonk Man*, in which it is obvious almost from the beginning of the movie that the character played by Eastwood is dying.

Is the quality that connects these films with one another just that they are set (that the majority of their action takes place) on something that we usually call 'the road'? A way of addressing the temptingly easy category of 'road movies' might be to consider again how the occupations of the figures played by Eastwood relate to space and freedom of movement. Answering questions at a press conference on *Bonnie and Clyde* in 1967, Arthur Penn made this point about the 'thirties:

'At that time, there was no national police force. They were all state-confined police forces. When Ford made the V-8, which was sufficiently powerful to outrun the local police automobiles, gangs began to spring up. And that was literally the genesis of the Clyde and Bonnie gang. And what happened was that they lived in their automobile . . .' *The Bonnie and Clyde Book*, p.7.

Whatever the actual relationship between local and national police forces in the United States, the idea of a force with purely local jurisdiction is still present in some movies. To be an officer of the law in, say, San Francisco is to have a status that is shown to relate exclusively to the city, and not to extend unaltered beyond its borders. One expression of this is in films that define their world as the city, in which no activity takes place beyond its borders, and the action will climax in a wasteland which accentuates qualities we think of as urban – the first three Callahan movies would fit this definition. The inverse but complementary case is the film in which a cop is landed in a context where his badge doesn't fit, where he represents law but is in a place where he is not a law officer – in Eastwood's work, this is the subject of *Coogan's Bluff* (an Arizona lawman in New York), the second half of *Sudden Impact* (a San Francisco lawman in a California small town) and *The Gauntlet* (an Arizona lawman sent to collect a prisoner from Las Vegas). There are other examples of this configuration outside

Out of place: Coogan (Eastwood) in New York in Coogan's Bluff.

Eastwood's work, among them *Black Rain* (Ridley Scott, 1989), in which a New York policeman travels to Japan.

Coogan's Bluff illustrates one of the possibilities of this situation. Coogan (Eastwood) is an Arizona Deputy Sheriff sent to collect a prisoner, Ringerman (Don Stroud), from New York. Coogan is a man who insists on being out of place, a western dandy who throughout the action sticks to his uniform – cowboy's hat, string tie, and boots – producing the film's running gag, in which every New Yorker assumes that he is from Texas. In the city, he is inept, trying to override police procedures and causing the fugitive to escape from custody.

Coogan can be allowed to triumph only by giving the film a geography in which the city is seen to have limits. Once free, Ringerman does not disappear into urban downtown Manhattan but takes unlikely refuge in nature, in the Cloisters – this north Manhattan park is a place in which the skills and authority that properly belong in Arizona can be found to apply, and Coogan can recapture him. But it is implied that Coogan will only succeed in this anomalous place, a setting from which the pastoral past of the city can be imagined. Coogan stands at a vantage point, 'trying to picture it the way it was, just the trees and the river . . .' The urban present, characterised here as hippie/drug culture, has no place or interest for him, and the film ends with him leaving the city to return to Arizona. Another thread of the plot allows him to find a girl in the city, but it is suggested that she will come to Arizona, not he to New York. In this, the film is like another narrative in which a girl falls for a cop from out of town, *Klute* (Alan J. Pakula, 1971), which ends with the couple leaving the city. We can see cop movies as usually showing a figure profoundly identified with a particular place, not a domestic space, but with the city or state which gives him his authority.

The movies in the group covered in this chapter speak to the opposite condition. The heroes are linked in that their occupation, or possibly what they make of their occupation, compels them to move from place to place, and these places will not often be large cities. Possibly the simplest case is that of Tommy Nowak (Eastwood) in *Pink Cadillac* who is employed by a bail bond company to trace offenders who have skipped bail, a kind of cop without the loyalties of being on a force. Then there are entertainers – Billy in Bronco Billy's Wild West Show and Red Stovall in *Honkytonk Man* scratch a living by moving across America with their 'live' entertainment shows. The point of Philo Beddoe's fights in *Every*

Urban hippie/drug culture: Coogan's antipathy shows in his treatment of Linny Raven (Tisha Sterling) in *Coogan's Bluff*.

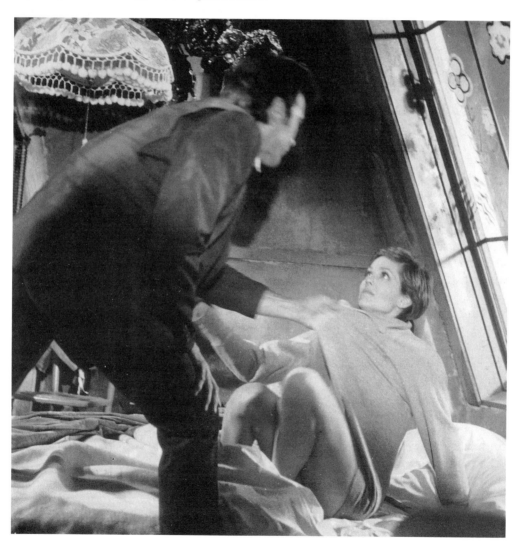

Which Way But Loose and *Any Which Way You Can* is similar: the bare-knuckle fist fight in the open air stands as a local entertainment in opposition to the professional boxing business. The second of these two films focuses on the anxiety that such fighting will become professionalised and be taken over by the mob and the rich gamblers.

Thunderbolt and Lightfoot seems to fit the model exactly, for Thunderbolt is a bank robber hiding from his old accomplices. In the opening minutes of the film he meets – is rescued by – Lightfoot (Jeff Bridges) driving a stolen car. Their drive across country seems to fit clearly into a group of films celebrating the identification of the outlaw with space and speed, the exact opposite of the constraints on the cop that I have described. But this only works as an account of the opening of the film. As the plot develops, it suggests the limits of these energies.

The Gauntlet is the only one of these films in which Eastwood plays a cop, and the only one which ends in the protagonist's home city, but after its opening few minutes, the film is set not in Las Vegas but on the road between Vegas and Phoenix. There, the Eastwood character discovers that he is a cop only in name, that he has none of the power and authority that being part of the larger force is supposed to confer.

Something is missing from an account of these films which suggests that their characters are travelling in America only in order to pursue their various occupations. This may be what they are doing, but it is not what we are waiting for them to do. At the beginning of *On the Road*, Jack Kerouac writes, 'Somewhere along the line I knew there'd be girls . . .', and this is what we know – or expect – too. Portrayals of the cop in the city in the significant Callahan movies include the difficulty of finding, or holding on to, the girl, but in the road movies the idea of pursuit and encounter moves from the adversarial pair of cop and hood couple to appear as the pursuit of and encounter with a woman.

To put it this way is to invite the possibility of reading the films as romances, films about finding an America which offers the opportunity to meet and win the girl, and perhaps to defeat forces associated with darkness or sterility. Along with this view go two questions: whether this America is in some sense utopian, and whether this feeling for a utopian place identifies it in traditional ways as the world outside the city and as evoking the past, a world without high technology, particularly a world without the new technology of entertainment. What we can find here is an image at the centre of American culture, the ideal combination of sexual happiness and contemplation of the land. Of course, there are ironies that attend our finding such a world in the movies and the use of film to celebrate and reproduce authenticity of this kind. The best discussion of this that I know is one of the greatest films on the subject, Preston Sturges's *Sullivan's Travels* (1941); its propositions as to what the ingredients of a film about this America might be may provide a context for Eastwood's road films.

Sturges's premise is that his central character, a rich and successful film director, John L. Sullivan (Joel McCrea), is tired of the kind of work that he does. He tells his producer that he wishes to make a film which is 'a commentary on modern conditions, stark realism, the problems that confront the average man'. In order to make such a film, he understands that he must learn about poverty, and suitably attired by the wardrobe department, he sets out on foot to find this other America. A few paces behind him is a studio land cruiser, equipped with a number of support systems – an evident reference to the business of filming, to what is necessary to film a supposedly simple event on location. He makes a deal with the crew in the cruiser, and goes off on his own. A series of accidents lands him back in a diner which we learn is in Hollywood, perhaps Sturges's way of reminding us that what we are looking at is also a set on a studio sound stage. There he meets a girl, just another hopeful extra – only this is Veronica Lake. Of course, the two go off together; if there is any residual danger of our mis-understanding what Sullivan has set out to find on the road, Sturges clears it up a few minutes later. The couple have been arrested, and Sullivan is being quizzed by the police: 'How's the girl fit in this picture?' This prompts the movie director to say: 'There's always a girl in the picture – haven't you ever been to the movies?'

The line implies Sullivan's unconscious recognition of what his travels are for, but Sturges also seems to be saying, or asking, if this is something we now (or then, in the great period of Hollywood sound comedy) learn from the movies. What he is also hinting is that cops might not go to the movies, or might not learn this from them, a problem raised in another way by Hawks in the jail scene in *Bringing Up Baby*, which takes us back to the particular isolation of cops.

So being on the road can offer an equivalent to the encounter with Veronica Lake in the diner – Kerouac, writing about meeting a girl in a Hollywood bus station in *On the Road*, locates the moment by referring specifically to this scene in Sturges's film. [This chapter was written some time before the release of *A Perfect World*, but Eastwood's latest road film seems clearly to acknowledge the Sturges. The landcruiser of *Sullivan's Travels* is visually not dissimilar to the mobile office used to support the police search for the escaped convict Butch Haynes (Kevin Costner) and the little boy Phillip Perry (T.J. Lowther). A sequence in which the latter vehicle takes off across country in pursuit of Haynes, with some physical comedy as its occupants are thrown in all directions inside, appears to be a direct quotation of Sturges. The relevant sequence is another image of a group of adults pursuing a man and a child, when Sturges's stock company of actors suffer similar physical effects in the landcruiser during a pursuit across rough country, after Sullivan has accepted a lift from a boy in a home-made jalopy.]

Thunderbolt and Lightfoot

Thunderbolt and Lightfoot begins with various kinds of apparent fun, and luck. We see Lightfoot (Jeff Bridges) con a car out of a gullible salesman in a used car lot, capping a taunt about whether he is man enough for a powerful machine with a line about having a wooden leg. The appearance of Thunderbolt (Eastwood) as a priest in the act of preaching to his congregation in a small Idaho church is an intriguing set-up, but one that lasts only briefly – a gunman enters, fires at the pulpit but misses. The subsequent chase ends with the man being killed by Lightfoot, who accidentally hits him fatally with the stolen car. The priest now manages to climb into the car, and the couple drive off together.

This is a film that positions the Eastwood character between his past (the bulky, suited hitman, seen arriving in a 'fifties car) and the zest of youth (Lightfoot in his stolen, almost new Transam). The pressures of past and possible future are already reflected in the credits; we know that we will encounter a character to be played by George Kennedy, but we are also promised a role to be played by a young woman – Catherine Bach is the fourth main credit, after Eastwood, Bridges and Geoffrey Lewis.

A way of contemplating past and future in the film is the idea of payment, of erasing your mistakes by paying for them. What Michael Cimino, who wrote and directed the film, intends us to understand by this is hinted at in an early scene in which Thunderbolt and Lightfoot pull into a filling station. The station attendant is an old man, played by Dub Taylor. Lightfoot asks him how the business is doing, and this is the speech in reply:

'Somewhere in this country there's a little old lady with seventy-nine dollars and twenty-five cents. The five cents is a buffalo nickel. If she cashes in her investment, the whole thing'll collapse, General Motors, the Pentagon, the two party system and the whole shebang . . . [*mumbles*] running downhill, got to keep running forward or we'll all fall down.'

The speech is punctuated by a piece of dramatic business. Another customer is trying to pay by credit card – at intervals, he offers different cards to the attendant, and is told 'That ain't it' until the right one is eventually produced.

The imagery here, where the difficulty of transacting a payment in the contemporary world is expressed by showing a world without real money, seems to date from another film about paying for past mistakes, John Boorman's *Point Blank* (1967). It is placed here next to an image of money and time, an old lady, an old coin, a strange piece of luck that is not benign, but rather a massive destabilising force from the past. All this can be related to the major plot, in which Thunderbolt is pursued by his former accomplices in a bank robbery, Red Leary (George Kennedy) and Goody (Geoffrey Lewis), who are seeking revenge, or payment.

Thunderbolt tells Lightfoot the story of the robbery, explaining that the stolen money was hidden in a place that was part of one individual's past, a one-room schoolhouse in a small Montana town, attended long ago by the oldest member of the gang. The two men go to this town, but the building has literally disappeared. They find a new school, and no sign of or reference to the old one. In response to Lightfoot's surprise, Thunderbolt simply replies, 'Progress'. The money has also been made to disappear in another sense: a conspiracy, intended to set the thieves at one another's throats, has been mounted by the police and newspapers claiming that the money has been recovered.

What is left appears simply to be the desire for revenge: getting even, no questions asked. At the beginning of the film, the directness, or simplicity, of this is offered as one of its forms of fun. The mood of the scene in which the hitman is blasting away at Thunderbolt in the pulpit is continued in the first car chase sequence, in which Leary and Goody shoot at Thunderbolt and Lightfoot as the two cars career across the landscape. When Leary's and Goody's car takes off over a ridge, Leary shouts 'Geronimo!', and Lightfoot fools around, taking his hands off the steering wheel.

The excitement of the chase is apparently only incidental to the satisfaction that Leary seeks in executing Thunderbolt. In due course, Thunderbolt and Lightfoot are captured by Leary and Goody and forced to drive to an isolated spot, apparently so that they can be shot. When part of Leary's rage at Thunderbolt is tweaked by Lightfoot into a joke about sexuality, Leary responds by discovering that he wants to take some of his revenge by demonstrating that he is still physically the dominant man. He puts his gun aside and disables Lightfoot with a single blow. Then he fights Thunderbolt, but loses; the fight ends when he wheezes, 'I can't breathe, I got asthma.' A little later, he is again about to shoot Thunderbolt, when a line from Lightfoot discloses that the money was never recovered, and this becomes an excuse to let the desire for revenge dissolve. The four men stagger down to a waterside. Leary mutters, 'I feel old.'

Indications of age and disability surround the robbers — one of the four has died of a heart attack, Leary suffers from asthma and hay fever, and Thunderbolt has a bad leg and scars dating from his service with Leary in Korea. Cimino also indicates visually that Leary and Goody are trapped in a possibly unconscious aversion to the world of the present. Like Dunlap, the dead hitman from the opening sequence, they dress in suits and ties, and their car is another 'fifties saloon. Leary's hatred of Lightfoot is clearly based on a jealous perception of him as a kid; both sexual potency and his freedom from the past are at issue.

We see the four men drive off together; it is not clear in any sense where they are going. But now Lightfoot suggests a way of producing, if not exactly re-covering, the money. The idea is to repeat the past, robbing the same bank vault in the same way. Paradoxically, this is both a repetition and an innovation – such a trick 'has never been done before'.

This robbery, presented as an efficient, traditionally exciting caper, occupies a substantial part of the second half of the film. The ways in which it resembles, and departs from, the previous robbery are significant. In the execution of the actual bank job, we see Thunderbolt, Leary and Goody fall into old routines – the breaking into the bank vault, which is effected by blasting a hole through its armour with a piece of military hardware stolen by Thunderbolt during his Korean war service, link this moment to their service in that war, to its loyalties and friendship, to a time when men could think of themselves as heroes; we will learn that Thunderbolt won the Silver Star.

At the level of plotting, the failure of the robbery can in part be attributed directly to the age and condition of the men. As they drive away, with Leary and Goody crammed into the boot of the saloon, Goody is complaining about his weak kidneys, and at one crucial moment, entering a drive-in movie theatre, Leary gives the game away with an asthmatic's sneeze. But more than this is at stake – Leary's response to being shut in the boot with Goody is to experience it as a sort of premature burial. He tells Thunderbolt, 'I'm dying in here' and 'I'm getting out of this coffin.'

After this, Leary tries to die the death of an old-time hood. He throws the rest of the gang out of the car and takes off alone, smashing through police roadblocks. But his final destruction is a moment of pointed irony. Before the robbery, the gang had taken jobs, temporarily entering the kind of dull workday world that none of them had been able to settle into. Leary had worked as a janitor in a store selling women's fashions. Now we see the front of the store, Le Paris, for the first time, just before Leary's car smashes through its window into a group of female dummies. As everything comes to rest, one such disembodied reminder of women, a hanger holding a hat and frock, falls into the car. An earlier sequence showed us that the store was guarded by ferocious dogs; in this setting, the dogs savage Leary.

Revenge: Goody (Geoffrey Lewis) holds Thunderbolt (Eastwood) at gunpoint in
Thunderbolt and Lightfoot.

To recognise the exact force of this event, it needs to be read in the context of another, highly developed thread in the film. Cimino uses the narrative to explore other possibilities for life in the America of this time, and the botched caper has to be seen against the defeat of these other possibilities, presented essentially as relationships with women.

The subject appears shortly after Thunderbolt and Lightfoot have met. Prompted by the sight of a hooker talking to a potential client, Lightfoot raises another version of the subject of payment:

Lightfoot: I never paid for it in my life.
Thunderbolt: Sometimes you have to pay for your pleasure.
Lightfoot: Not me. I'll never pay for it, I can tell you that.

Shortly afterwards, a scene with the two men and two girls picked up by Lightfoot addresses this distinction. Lightfoot finds Melody (Catherine Bach) by the device of aping the glamour of the movies, drawing up next to her in his car and shouting 'Quick. Get in. Quick!' Of course, she does so and comes back to the motel with him. We see Lightfoot's smile as they go to the bedroom – but we never see Melody again, as if Cimino wants to suggest how little can be made of an encounter like this.

Melody's friend Gloria (June Fairchild) is Thunderbolt's date. The scene shows her as sexually selfish – jumping off Thunderbolt as soon as she has come – and

expressing the indifference of youth to a history that seems hugely remote. Asking about his wounds, she responds to the mention of Korea, 'I've heard of that war.' Finally, he gives her money, nominally for a taxi, and she leaves. The sexual discomfiture of the scene is played as wry comedy, which was very much part of Eastwood's star persona at the time.

Neither woman will appear in the film again. Both relationships with women are inadequate; perhaps both Lightfoot's claim never to have paid for a woman and Thunderbolt's acceptance of the role of john are forms of pride, or isolation. Lightfoot's cheery assertions of his physical attractiveness, here and elsewhere, finally offer as little reward as Thunderbolt's belief that having a woman is a commercial transaction, a pleasure to be paid for.

One further incident demonstrates Cimino's sense of the brio, but also the limitations, of meeting a girl on the road. Lightfoot is again by himself in a vehicle, a borrowed van, when he pulls alongside a girl on a motorbike. An upbeat guitar number sets the mood. He delivers a come-on line to the girl – she produces a hammer and attacks the van, then pulls away. Lightfoot leans out of the van, whoops, and shouts, 'I think I love you.' Throughout the scene, the upbeat music is uninterrupted. Shortly after, asked about the dents on the van, Lightfoot replies with the word that had been used to him earlier, about the disappearance of the schoolhouse: 'Progress'. The point of this little sketch is to demonstrate that Lightfoot's behaviour expresses no particular expectations – indeed he can accept any response to it – although in the contemporary world of 'progress', disappointments are to be expected.

The anxieties about potency that emerge in the fight between Leary and Thunderbolt take a different, darker form when the four men live together, working at different jobs while planning the robbery. The jobs show Thunderbolt's and Lightfoot's work as occasions of blocked sexual temptation – the nude woman in the window watching Lightfoot work and the black secretary who speaks to Thunderbolt are isolated from the men by barriers of race and class. Related to these images is Leary's menial job in the store catering to an image of female glamour, not to mention the work of the least assertively masculine of the four, Goody's employment as an ice-cream van driver.

Leary's relationship to women is perhaps the least direct in the film, but is of obvious importance. The intensity of his response is expressed not in direct contact with women, which is significantly almost absent from his role, but in his fascination with the idea of sexuality, its image – a kind of voyeurism. This first appears in a sequence in which Lightfoot tells the story of the nude woman in the window. Leary's fascination with the implications of such a moment makes him vulnerable – Lightfoot responds to the last of Leary's questions by putting his hand over Leary's mouth and 'kissing' him. Leary's response is outrage; he tells Lightfoot, 'I'll kill you for that,' and the younger man laughs. As the scene concludes, Thunderbolt smiles.

In the light of the remaining action – in the aftermath of the robbery, Leary gives Lightfoot a beating which proves fatal – this scene implies an ignorance of Leary's character that links Thunderbolt with Lightfoot and relates back to their

Sexual discomfiture: Gloria (June Fairchild) after leaving Thunderbolt in Thunderbolt and Lightfoot.

Above: living together – Leary (George Kennedy), Lightfoot (Jeff Bridges) and Thunderbolt in Thunderbolt and Lightfoot. *Opposite: the offensive couple - the image of Thunderbolt and Lightfoot that provokes Leary.*

attitudes to women expressed in the sequence with Melody and Gloria. Their variously thin responses to women give the two men no access to the scale of Leary's rage, no sense of his fascination with women and the violence it unlocks.

Their attitude to sexual loneliness or inadequacy is expressed in the detail of the robbery. The only element of the original caper that has to be changed is the manner of disabling the alarm system. Previously this was done by Dunlap through technical know-how. Now the plot is to exploit another example of sexual inadequacy, the guard at the alarm station (Cliff Emmich). To do this, Lightfoot dresses as a girl; once inside the office, he can knock the guard out and fix the alarm when it trips. The idea is that a figure like the fat and unattractive guard is an easy mark, always more or less contemptible. Earlier Thunderbolt has listened, smiling, to an anecdote of a humiliation suffered by this man.

The direct connection between the guard and Leary is made through pornography. Behind his newspaper, the guard conceals girlie magazines. During the early part of the robbery, when Leary and Thunderbolt hold up the bank manager's family, they find his daughter making love with her boyfriend. Fascinated, Leary pulls off his stocking mask for a clearer look at the girl's nude body.

The second function of Lightfoot's disguise as a girl is in the escape – the idea is that Leary and Goody will remain concealed in the rear of the car while

Thunderbolt and his 'girl', apparently an unremarkable heterosexual couple, appear as inconspicuous patrons of the drive-in movie house. Consider Leary's position at this moment: to the image of Thunderbolt and Lightfoot as a 'couple' have to be added his awareness of Thunderbolt's commitment to Lightfoot (there is an exchange about this during the robbery) and the awareness of the drive-in as a location for sexual assignation, a detail that Cimino annotates briefly. When the plan goes wrong, Leary's revenge is on this couple. After ordering them out of the car, he savagely beats up the 'girl' of the pair. It is his response to Lightfoot's ignorance of the depth of his sexual feeling, and a punishment for the impersonation of the object of his fascination.

After the death of Leary, the film seems to move away from the previous realism of its surface. Lightfoot changes out of his dress into 'dead man's clothes' taken from the body of Goody, and the couple hitch a lift in the back of a truck of unlikely, remote pre-war vintage. Cimino shows us Thunderbolt now stripped to white vest and Lightfoot in Goody's suit. In these plain clothes, less 'modern' than any of their earlier costumes, they stumble across a field, and it is by now apparent to us that Lightfoot may be dying. Seemingly by chance, they come on the one-room schoolhouse, moved and preserved as a monument, in which the money from the first robbery is still concealed. Twice – on seeing the building and on finding that the money is still where it was left years before – Thunderbolt murmurs one word: 'Impossible'.

Thunderbolt takes some of the money to make a fantasy come true, the new white Cadillac that the men had once discussed. As they drive off, Lightfoot produces cigars – he says he has been saving them up, and we may notice that this is impossible, given that he is wearing Goody's clothes. With a line about feeling like a hero, Lightfoot dies, and the credits roll.

I do not mean to argue that these last scenes of the film are a dream sequence, but rather to point out the qualities that make them seem a little like one, as if the two men had dropped suddenly into a world with the logic of a fairy tale. The finding of the money is related to nothing except a fantastic chance (the 'buffalo nickel' speech is an intimation of it), as if somehow Thunderbolt and Lightfoot could magically translate themselves back into the past and avail themselves of its opportunities. But the limits of the fantasy are defined by the fact, insisted on at intervals in the sequence, that Lightfoot is dying from Leary's beating – the money cannot redeem this, just render it more ironic.

A way of understanding this is to connect it with the theme of dislocation. Had the result of the robbery been that Thunderbolt and Lightfoot were left with the proceeds, then that gain would at least have been produced by their crime – they would remain connected to society, as criminals or fugitives. But this money, now dislocated from any substantial link to a crime long in the past, connects the pair to nothing except a fantasy that somehow they are a success. Lightfoot's dying ramblings, about doing a job well, are the more ironic in that these riches have come from a robbery in which he took no part.

Thunderbolt and Lightfoot offers a vision of a post-Korea, post-Vietnam America, a civilisation with no redeeming qualities, in which the speed and glamour of the road – the Transam with which the film begins, the Cadillac with which it ends – offer the only moments of pleasure and freedom. Even then, the freedom has no purpose – the couple are caught between an inaccessibly remote past experienced only as violence and loss, a present experienced as dislocation and aversion (the two annotations of 'progress' speak of this) and a world without any future that can be formulated. Consider the linked moments of the pair driving off at the beginning and end of the film. In neither case can a destination be imagined; at the beginning, Lightfoot announces 'South', and, at the end, his 'See what's over the next mountain' takes its pathos from our knowledge that he may be dying. The characters cannot be reinserted into any other relationship to the world through women or the family – they remain, or come to understand that they are, utterly at the opposite pole from the idea of the couple. The scene in the schoolhouse, when the two men encounter the film's 'ordinary people', a harmless middle-aged married couple, is exemplary. Neither man says or does anything to confirm it, but the quality of apartness in the pair forces their instant identification by the couple as robbers, desperadoes of some kind. As the husband dumps his camera and the couple flee, Thunderbolt and Lightfoot watch in dumb amazement at this acknowledgement of their status.

Does the relationship of the two men to each other stand to some degree against this defeat? In a sympathetic consideration of the film in his *Hollywood from Vietnam to Reagan*, Robin Wood has argued that it does. My reading departs from Wood's at a number of points, largely in the importance I would place on the significance of women for the principal characters in the film. Wood argues that the film comes close to explicitness about the sexual nature of its central relationship, while 'coding' rather than 'dramatising' it. He suggests that the film 'celebrates the union of heroes' in the discovery of the hidden money, and that the death of Lightfoot is necessary because Lightfoot's sexuality represents 'the real threat to the culture'.

I would conclude that the film is not quite able to imply, in however encrypted a way, that the two men are, or could be, a gay couple. The proposition that might follow, that in a world where no possibility for heterosexual romance remains the pair might find some world in which they could exist as lovers, is an intuition of a radical future that the film seems equally unable to offer or imagine as the future in a 'straight' America. The closeness between the two men is limited by the difference of generation – a theme that begins with Thunderbolt telling Lightfoot that he is 'ten years too late', and which Cimino follows up, simply enough, with a series of details built around the offering and receiving of the gift of Thunderbolt's wristwatch, an insertion into time's limits that the younger man shows reluctance to accept.

Wood argues that the presentation of Thunderbolt is 'stoical, resolutely and unambiguously masculine' and confirms the point by saying that 'after all, he is played by Clint Eastwood'. But what is significant about Eastwood's role here, and not untypical, is that he expresses not routine sexual prowess and unambiguous masculinity but substantially the opposite. His sexual encounter I have already discussed, but even more crucial must be his complete inability to act to save Lightfoot from the fatal attack. There is no confrontation, just Leary dispatching Thunderbolt with a single blow before delivering a merciless beating to Lightfoot, and no recovery of the action hero to enact revenge – it is not Thunderbolt who finally kills Leary.

Why does Lightfoot die? His death can be seen as part of a pattern in films of this time, when the vulnerability of the younger of two men, his death or

Expendable: washed-up cop Shockley (Eastwood) and Las Vegas prostitute Mally (Sondra Locke) in The Gauntlet.

effective destruction, expresses the utter inability of a older generation to act in a way that might help the younger. The relationship of Baddusky (Jack Nicholson) and Meadows (Randy Quaid) in Hal Ashby's *The Last Detail*, made in the same year as Cimino's film, expresses the same sense of dislocation as the men move across America together. (The scenes with women in the two films are interestingly comparable.) For Eastwood, this role initiates a series of films in which he will be unable to save his younger 'partner'. The next Callahan film, *The Enforcer*, ends like this film with the death of the younger character, in that case a woman but not yet a lover, and my reading of *The Outlaw Josey Wales* considers a different, complex treatment of the same subject.

The Gauntlet

The Gauntlet is a heterosexual romance, but one in which the central couple, after they have discovered their feelings for each other, barely embrace. It is also a film with a reputation for non-stop violence in which the Eastwood character fires a gun only twice, once into the fuel tank of a motorcycle, and once to open a bathroom door lock. Although we continually see him threatening others with a gun, nobody in the film is directly harmed by him.

The premise of the film is that of a thriller. Blakelock (William Prince), the Commissioner of Police in Phoenix, Arizona, is a man with mob connections, who is intent on killing Gus Mally (Sondra Locke), a Las Vegas prostitute who can implicate him in her testimony at a forthcoming trial. The plan is to kill her on the road, while she is being escorted from Vegas to Phoenix by the cop sent to extradite her. A washed-up and thus expendable cop, who will be called a 'drunken bum' at one point, is chosen for the job – this is Ben Shockley (Eastwood).

The movie that follows from this offers obvious thrills, in which Mally and Shockley discover the plot and evade the various attempts to kill them as they flee across country. Some of these action sequences are entirely routine. Their hired car is booby trapped and explodes, they are pursued by hoods and shot at, and they are riding a stolen motorbike when they are attacked from the air by a helicopter gunman. In every case, the survival of the couple is determined not by superior skill but by a species of good fortune – the bomb goes off before they are close enough to the car, a lucky shot from Mally causes the hoods' car to crash, and Eastwood, who directed the film, uses a very familiar device – the helicopter crashes into live power lines.

This unremarkable material is not the only kind of violence in the film. There is another kind, which I will call, on the analogy of saturation bombing, saturation gunfire – there are three scenes in the film when an object is the deliberate target of a massive assault. The particular quality of these scenes is that the target is treated as if it were a homogeneous whole. No part of it is especially vulnerable, and the object of the exercise seems to be to make the interior of the target into a place in which nothing living can survive by shooting through its 'skin'. There is a thrill here, in the destruction of mundane things – the three targets are a house, a car and a bus – and the impersonality of execution by a version of the firing squad. The fact that the victims are inside serves the function of the blindfold, and the number of riflemen ensures that no one individual carries the guilt of causing death.

The first occasion demonstrates how this kind of violence can be used. The setting is Las Vegas; Shockley and Mally have taken refuge in the house to which she takes her clients. The police, acting on false information that the house is occupied by an armed gang, surround it and subject it to saturation gunfire. They are unaware that Mally has already left the building through a storm drain, and Shockley quickly follows her. As the firing ceases, the battered house seems to groan – as the cops watch, we see a sign in the frame: GOD MAKES HOUSE CALLS. The house collapses neatly and totally, and a watching cop has a one-liner: 'Cap'n, they should have surrendered.' The facetious sign, the punch line, and above all the physical vision and timing of the collapse – the crucial point is the few seconds of stasis before the event – connect it not with horror but with slapstick or silent comedy, where the wait for something whole but shattered to dissolve into its constituent fragments, for the energies holding it together suddenly to evaporate, is a familiar pleasure. It relates also to, say, the moments in Tom and Jerry cartoons when Tom stares at his shattered body for a second before it falls apart, an idea we might express by saying that we believe for a instant that in this world gravity itself is subject to comic timing.

Why is this comedy necessary? It is important here, as it will be in parts of the final sequence, that the massive and illegitimate use of firepower is the action of the supposed upholders of the law. Part of the film's premise, and the way that it differs from a vigilante movie like *Magnum Force*, is its cognisance – expressible after Watergate and Richard Nixon's resignation – that the system in which the hero is situated is corrupt not just in details or in particular places, but specifically at the point of high command. A Police Commissioner, as Shockley will later explain, can 'put an army on the streets if he wants to', and this army, in police uniforms, will simply follow orders and shoot. The comic elements of the two sequences of saturation gunfire by the police are an alibi for the anxiety about cops acting in this way, and nobody dies or is seriously hurt in either sequence.

The second saturation gunfire sequence is unlike the other two. Mally and Shockley hijack a patrol car driven by an unnamed constable (Bill McKinney), but they abandon it just before reaching the Nevada/Arizona border. It is now night, and the constable cheerily greets what he thinks are Arizona cops. The mobsters sent by Blakelock shoot the car to pieces, killing its occupant. The fact that the mob is responsible determines the different tone of the scene: it is the only occasion of saturation gunfire in which a character dies and it entirely lacks the comic quality of its predecessor.

The climax of *The Gauntlet* is a final vision of massive violence. Shockley's solution to the problem of the corrupt commissioner is to hijack a bus, convert it into a crudely armoured vehicle and drive into the city so that he can confront Blakelock on the steps of city hall – this is a move familiar in the cycle of films about paranoia made around this time, in which the only recourse after the discovery of a conspiracy is to publicity, to the idea that conspiracy can be defeated by exposure to public scrutiny, for example, to the press, the tactic of the characters played by Robert Redford in both *Three Days of the Condor* (Sydney Pollack, 1975) and *All the President's Men* (Alan J. Pakula, 1976).

Identification of the press as the recourse of the persecuted might be seen as a quality of the 'liberal' paranoia film. Here it is not an option; the only response that Shockley has to offer is self-reliance in the face of probable death. He expects to be killed by Blakelock's agents and can imagine no alternative to a showdown which he assumes that he is bound to lose.

The armoured bus drives into the city. The sequence opens with an incident in which Shockley's old partner and friend, Josephson (Pat Hingle), is killed by police marksmen. This figure, unambiguously the 'good cop', is presented as entirely powerless, an innocent easily gulled by his corrupt superiors. The police now subject the bus to saturation gunfire. Of course, Shockley and Mally survive it, and the way in which the bus suddenly 'collapses' on the steps of city hall reprises the comic elements of the destruction of Mally's house.

Some kind of denouement must now take place. The film employs the old device (the last minute of Frank Capra's *Mr Smith Goes to Washington*, 1939, is an example) of destroying the logic of the situation, which is that villainy will triumph, by having the central villain go mad. Blakelock bursts on the scene and wildly demands that the police shoot down the couple in cold blood. He then shoots his corrupt sidekick, who has just confessed to the conspiracy, and wounds Shockley. Mally picks up Shockley's gun and kills Blakelock.

The first and most striking quality of this scene is the sense that there is no longer any organisation or figure of higher or different authority that can be appealed to by the hero. When Shockley staggers from the bus, he delivers the 'heroic' line of the man who has finally got the job done: 'I've got a witness here for courtroom G . . .' But there is nobody in the scene to answer this line, nobody to whom it is said. This absence is related to the role of the police. When they cease firing, they stand in silent amazement as the couple emerge from the bus, and they are totally unable to prevent the subsequent shoot-out – Eastwood even shows a cop allowing Blakelock to snatch a gun in his final attempt to kill Shockley. It obviously signals the impotence of the police that it is Mally, and not Shockley, who kills the film's central villain.

Discussing the 1970s in his essay 'Law, Confidence and Disobedience in American Culture', Eric Mottram has written:

'It appears, then, that Americans live mythically in an unstable equilibrium between concepts of control and liberty established by a written Constitution, with floating dreams of lone anarchists and private eyes . . .'

It is this instability that *The Gauntlet* displays. In its understanding of control and liberty, it is locked into a commitment to 'law enforcement' at the same time as having the uneasy knowledge that the actual practice of this law enforcement has somehow gone horribly wrong, with the figures of command corrupt and the men in the field impotent as a result. It is to the idea of impotence that the saturation gunfire can be related, a performance designed to express both a huge relieving of frustration and an inability to imagine the defence of liberty other than with a gun. The social world of the film is indefensible; it cannot be re-formed, only abandoned – the couple walk away from it in the final shot.

Love on the road: Shockley and Mally in the cattle wagon in The Gauntlet.

Where are they going? Mottram's phrase 'floating dreams' seems particularly appropriate in view of the film's presentation of the couple's idea of their future, and it is to the romance that I will now turn.

In many ways, this aspect of the film is based in a familiar situation, the image of the man and woman handcuffed together – here not literally but by their roles as cop and prisoner – with their initial hostility melting as they endure the same privations and come to share the same goal of bringing their persecutors to justice. The first part of this configuration is clearly present, as Shockley comes to understand and accept that he is as much Blakelock's target and victim as Mally is. But consonant with the tone of *The Gauntlet*, this realisation seems for Shockley to go along with the sense that he and his ideas are washed up, hopelessly a thing of the past. After some dramatic action which prepares us for the romance – a scene in a cattle wagon in which they save each other from harm – the couple take a room in a motel. Shockley talks about his past and the reasons that he became a cop from the perspective of defeat – 'Now I finally break the big case, and I'm picked to go down with it.' His interest in Mally – he looks at her in the bath, thinks to order in some flowers along with their food – is entirely that of a man who assumes that he has no future. He announces his intention of returning to Phoenix to face Blakelock, seeing his inevitable death as a way to salvage his self-respect: 'At least, someone will know I tried . . . me'.

At this point the situation is shifted, not by the washed up man but by the younger woman. Mally articulates a dream, of marrying and settling down and having kids, even buying a place, 'Probably northern Arizona, maybe somewhere up near the canyon. It's supposed to be really beautiful there, and you can still get land . . .' But she cannot say these things directly to him. Her 'proposal' to Shockley takes the form of an assertion of the validity or reachability of the past. We see her making a telephone call to her mother, and the dream emerges piece by piece through this dramatic device, a conversation of which we hear only Mally's side. Shockley's only response to this is a muttered 'up near the canyon'. This is a grasping of the essential point, of the dream conceived of as a place, something like a frontier, where the America represented by the city can be evaded, where 'you can still get land'.

Despite its apparent commitment to a 'happy' ending, *The Gauntlet* is, in some respects, no less bleak than *Thunderbolt and Lightfoot*. Two details are indicative. When the couple is shown moving across the landscape, momentarily free of threat, the upbeat music which signifies brief accesses to freedom is absent. Also absent is the background of 'normal' life constituted by ordinary, benign characters or human gestures that the couple might hope to encounter on the road: in this film, the road is essentially hostile. The couple move across desert terrain with a goal in mind that the film cannot present directly – as they ride in their armoured bus into the centre of Phoenix, they elaborate the dream, talking of flowers, trees and horses. The clearest connection here seems to be to *The Outlaw Josey Wales*, which was Eastwood's immediately preceding film as director. The films share a vision of a journey to a place which is apart from the mainstream of the society around it. A life in such a place may be dreamed of, but not quite with the sense of how exactly it might be realised.

The violence of the film is not an indicator of control, but of anxiety about impotence on the part of both the police forces and the hero. The connection

Notorious: Philo Beddoe (Eastwood) and Clyde in Every Which Way But Loose.

with *Thunderbolt and Lightfoot*, and the distinction from the Callahan films, is that the hero does not kill the central villain. Such is the paralysis of the agents of the law that neither the cops in uniform, nor the cop out of it, can bring about the death of the villain. Mally can do so because through her a subject which is still morally unambiguous can be promoted – her ability to fire the gun relates back to her sexual violation by Blakelock, in which his gun played an unspeakable part. The revenge of the raped woman is a subject that will be taken up again, though in important respects treated differently, in *Sudden Impact*.

Every Which Way But Loose and **Any Which Way You Can**

These two films have a different notoriety from that of most of Eastwood's work. They are marked down as vulgar – they include a sequence in which the character played by Eastwood slips a pair of prop false teeth into a co-ed's chowder, and another in which comical 'Nazi' bikers are covered in road tar. There is a great deal of fighting, mostly fist fighting, but nobody dies in either film. The most notorious feature is the part played in both of them by an orang-utan. Neither

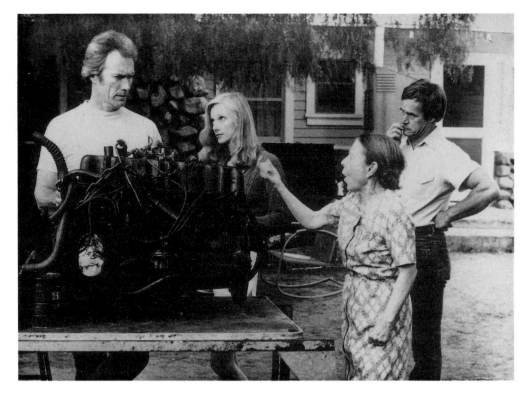

The utopian family: Philo, Ma (Ruth Gordon), Orville (Geoffrey Lewis) and Lynn Halsey Taylor (Sondra Locke) in Any Which Way You Can.

film is more than a relatively slight piece, but far from being predictable studio formula hit material – the first film was apparently made with some opposition from Warner Bros – they relate significantly to the themes and subjects of the films that lead up to and away from them.

The treatment of law in the films provides a useful starting point. *The Gauntlet* ends with a proposed, or imagined, retreat from the city, the police force and the work of law enforcement. Cops appear in both *Every Which Way* and *Any Which Way* (I will refer to the films by these shortened titles rather than continually reproduce them at their full length), but the function of the law and thus of cops is radically changed.

In *Every Which Way*, Philo Beddoe (Eastwood) is involved in a bar fight and mutters to the bartender, 'Better call the cops'. The reply is, 'They are the cops'. This institutes a plot in which two of the cops try to track Philo down, not to bring him to public justice, but to exact a private revenge. When they finally do so, he defeats them, and sinks their truck in a lake.

They appear in the closing moments of the film in the cab of their filthy truck, which is now being towed home. What we have here is not crime and punishment, but misbehaviour and humiliation; the central image is comic defilement.

Another kind of dirt is a feature of the cops' place in the second film. The opening sequence is a fight between their champion and Philo. While all attention is on the fight, Philo's pet orang-utan Clyde does something that we gather he has done before – Philo has said, 'You know how he likes to crap in squad cars.'

This mischief happens again a little later; in both cases, Philo and Clyde make a quick getaway.

What is hinted at in these sequences comes close to being explicit later in the film. The gang of comical bikers, whose humiliations at Philo's hands are a strand running through both films, are riding on the open highway when they are pulled in by the cops. An earlier piece of comic business has resulted in their wearing wigs – when they are stopped, the sight is evidently risible. The cops cannot bring themselves to book the bikers – when their leader declares, 'We've earned those tickets,' one cop replies through his laughter, 'You're a walking violation of the laws of nature, but we don't enforce them laws . . .'

Earlier Eastwood films have continually dealt with the violation and enforcement of Federal law. It is a premise of these two films that this subject is taboo – their world contains no such thing as the kind of crime and criminality that has any relevance to policing. The 'laws' that are being followed here are those of supposed 'nature': a form of utopian release exactly because the film asserts that those who live by such laws can place themselves outside any form of regulation – cops 'don't enforce them laws'.

This is related to other forms of utopian imagination in *Every Which Way*. The setting is the family: a house, somewhere outside the city, in which Philo lives with Ma (Ruth Gordon) and his brother Orville (Geoffrey Lewis). Or perhaps Orville is his friend – part of the benign character of this world is that it does not have to be clear whether these people are blood relatives or not. The film's world is shown to be one in which a big animal is charming and graceful, and his anarchy is comical and never seen as dangerous, while old people, the roles taken by distinguished American players (Ruth Gordon as Ma in both films, Hank Worden as the Trailer Court Manager in *Every Which Way*), are presented as feisty, witty and triumphant.

It is also a world in which work is largely benign, consisting not of paid employment but of a secure form of gambling: Philo is a fist fighter, and he and Orville set up contests and make their money by placing bets. Again, this is anticipated in *The Gauntlet*, where we see Mally supply the money that will enable her and Shockley to realise their utopian dreams by betting on their survival against high odds offered by the mob. Both *Every Which Way* and *Any Which Way* begin with bare-knuckle fights in the open air and in the daytime; none of the audience seems to have to go to work. And the treatment of the fights is as a set of stunts and sound effects which magically involve no serious injury, or apparent risk of it, to any party.

It is on the subject of bare-knuckle fighting as a form of utopian work that the plots of the films express different degrees of anxiety. After the first open-air contest, the next fight in *Every Which Way* takes place in a cold store, and the losers are reluctant to pay up. The third and final bout, virtually at the end of the film, takes place at night, and the visual treatment of the audience is considerably more negative. It is the point at which Philo is about to beat the famous champion of the area, 'Tank' Murdoch. Philo hears himself referred to as 'the new Tank Murdoch', and there is a sotto voce exchange between two punters: 'Boy, are we going to make money on this guy.' The result of this insight into what winning might possibly mean is that Philo's concentration wavers for a moment, and Murdoch lands the blow that wins the fight.

Utopian work: Philo in bare-knuckle combat in Every Which Way But Loose.

This anxiety becomes the major plot of *Any Which Way*, the idea that what was once a form of pleasure or self-reliance is being turned into a piece of mass entertainment and money-making for mobsters. A bout is proposed between Philo and Wilson (William Smith), a fighter controlled by New York mobsters. The fighting now appears briefly to promise real violence, both because Wilson has seriously injured opponents before and because bare-knuckle fighting is 'strictly illegal, no referee, and the fight won't end until one or the other's half dead'. But the film's actual use of Wilson is quite unlike this, continuing to observe the convention that fist fighting is not seriously injurious, and offering the actions of the mobsters in kidnapping Philo's girl at gunpoint and wounding Orville as the film's real violence.

The final fight between Philo and Wilson, which is the climax of *Any Which Way*, is symptomatic of the change of tone which takes place between the two films. Although the two boxers wish to disappoint the mob, they still want to fight, both for the satisfaction of emerging the victor and for the little men and women in their audience: 'a lot of people bet money on me. Not all of them are rich.' This suggests that the fight will return to the quality of the fights which opened the films. But the convention that no injury is possible in a fist fight is more extreme, and has to be confronted much more as a convention, in the enormously protracted fight that follows. Similarly the convention that the hero will necessarily win is met, but in a way which marks it as unreal – at a late stage, Philo is completely disabled in one arm, but defeats Wilson nonetheless. And so strong is the insistence that neither of these men can truly hurt the other simply with his fists that even the arm injury is inflicted when a blow lands as Philo falls against an iron stove.

The shift I am describing might be seen as a move from a certain kind of anxiety in the first film to a degree of hysterical insistence in the second. In *Every Which Way*, Philo's utopian existence can be threatened, but the status quo can be maintained without too much difficulty, by losing a fight and losing a girl. *Any Which Way* moves towards a climax in which the various groups represented in the film – bikers, mobsters, tourists, punters – are witnesses to a ritual the point of which seems to be to insist that there must be a form of violence between men that is not malign.

Analogous movements between the two films occur in other contexts. I have already mentioned dirt and cops, and the shift from mud to shit is suggestive. It is matched in the treatment of the bikers. A comic set piece in the first film concludes with the victims in a car wash, the men and their bikes covered in suds. The comparable moment in *Any Which Way* has the bikers riding through a road-tarring machine, emerging so covered in tar that they set solid as it cools. This might recollect the rusted tin man of *The Wizard of Oz*, but the difference is in the implicit violence. Recalling elements of *The Gauntlet*, the connection is again with cartoons, with the kind of violence – or, rather, its results – that we associate with a world in which a gross attack on the body leaves no trace, or only a simple comic sign – as in the case of the bikers, who are bald when we next encounter them.

A similar change takes place in the use of Clyde. In *Every Which Way*, Clyde's strength is rarely at issue, and this is part of his benignness. We see him lift up the end of a car, as an enormously strong man might do. But in *Any Which Way*, Clyde's strength is allied to cartoon violence. When a car has to be scrapped, an instruction given to Clyde is followed by shots of the parts of the car flying through the air, and this routine is repeated later in the film, with a terrified mobster cowering as Clyde wrecks his Cadillac.

The treatment of sexuality in the films requires a fuller discussion. In *Every Which Way*, the road seems to offer a utopian world in which desires can be effortlessly met. Orville finds his girl, Echo (Beverley D'Angelo), at a roadside fruit stall. The mention of 'her place down by the wash' associates her with the country world, and a comic reference to fertility is made in a piece of classical low comedy, a pun on melons and breasts. Even Clyde can be used as a reminder of the conventions that love stories can use in the movies – Philo breaks into a zoo for his benefit, and the shot of a door closing on the 'happy couple' is a reference to a world where we cannot question the positive resolution of romantic contacts.

But this is the background – the central romance in *Every Which Way* is treated in terms that are more negative and follow closely on from *The Gauntlet*. Philo's girl, Lynn Halsey-Taylor, is played by the same star, Sondra Locke, now in a role which initially seems benign – she is a country and western singer. Her meeting with Philo takes place not on the road, but when he hears her sing in a local club. Here Eastwood plays Philo as an artless westerner whose idea of a good joke is the prop teeth and chowder gag, and Locke's part is the more poised and ironic, the knowing girl teasing the simple man – again this seems to relate closely to the playing of the couple in *The Gauntlet*. This quality governs the whole of their first meeting; Beddoe ends it sitting in his truck with the words 'slightly advanced' – a man who wonders if he is being obscurely hustled. (In fact he is quoting. Thunderbolt used these same words as his comment on the Bill McKinney character, a madman, in *Thunderbolt and Lightfoot*.)

Every Which Way lacks the romantic resolution of *The Gauntlet*. After their first meetings, Lynn disappears and Philo takes to the road in pursuit. They finally re-encounter each other – not in a bar but on the open road – and a love scene follows, but he still knows little about her. In their final scene, she is shown to be involved in some kind of hustling with her 'boyfriend' Skyler (Bruce Scott), and she rejects Philo as an interfering simpleton.

This side of the film is not very clear – Lynn's motives and attitudes never emerge very precisely – but it seems to relate to the larger anxieties in the two films which refer to the city, and in this film to commercialised entertainment. The most telling contrast between the two young women in the film is a brief sequence showing Lynn alone in a bowling alley, fantasising about her commercial success as an entertainer as she bowls, then picking up a man – the film cuts directly from this to Echo by the riverside, washing a pan.

The contrast between the world of the road and the alienation of the city is the point of a sequence in which Philo, accompanied by Clyde – and a ballad on the film's soundtrack – searches for Lynn in the bars of Albuquerque. The sequence uses familiar images of hooker, stripper and sex film theatres to signal the world of commodified sex, while Philo and Clyde – the shooting of the sequence strongly emphasises Clyde's dependent role, so he appears very much as Philo's symbolic child – search for a woman to make their 'family' complete. That the narrative does not conclude in this way, but ends with a retreat, or movement home, with Orville, Echo, Philo and Clyde on the road back to Ma, may reflect Eastwood's sense of the inflexibility of this utopian world, where the woman from outside brings with her the taint of a place where entertainment is about the commercial utilisation of emotion. Utopian simplicity can be preserved here only by rejecting the lures of public reputation and commercial success.

In *Every Which Way*, a piece of comic business shows Echo at first terrified by the sight of Clyde. She then comes to accept him, and the kind of naturalness or simpleness which he represents. Part of the contrast between the two women is that Lynn never encounters Clyde in the first film, another way in which Eastwood expresses the distance between her and Philo's world. There is a lapse in continuity between the two films, as we see Lynn in the opening scenes of *Any Which Way* on familiar terms with Clyde. The shift expresses something of the different focus of the sequel. The figure of Lynn and the world of entertainment of which she is again a part now seem entirely favourable – the appearance of Fats

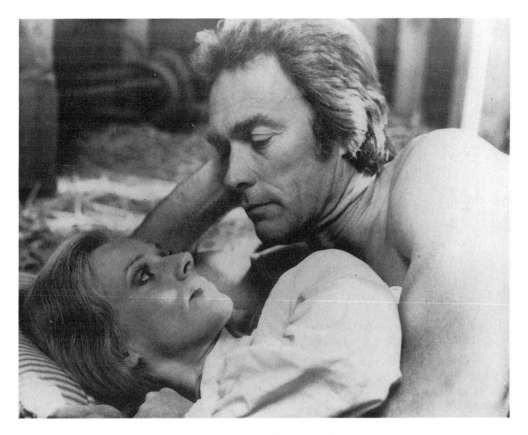

The lovers: Philo and Lynn in Any Which Way You Can.

Domino in the early part of the film looks like a way of stating this. The anxieties surrounding the commercialisation of entertainment are now located in the images of mobsters, and no difficulties exist in establishing Philo and Lynn as a couple early in the film, with Clyde as their wild child, or pet.

The sequence in which this is achieved sets out the second film's very different attitude to sexuality. Philo invades the YWCA to find Lynn. The police are called to deal with this male intruder. When a cop arrives, one woman comments, 'They all think we moon around all day lusting after their bodies.' The punch line is delivered by another woman: 'Some of us do, Rita.' The speaker now triumphantly kisses the cop.

This initiates a narrative in which sex is treated as a dominant form of activity, but one which can have nothing other than good consequences. At the centre of this is Clyde, and the anarchic, festive rumbustiousness with which the animal's sexuality is shown is seen as affecting all expressions of sexuality in the film's world. Hence the sequence in which the two orang-utans in one room of a motel 'inspire' imitative sexual behaviour in Philo and Lynn in another room, and in the film's low comedy couple, a middle-aged pair from Iowa, in yet another. The motel sequence – which includes smashed furniture and cars, and human and animal characters hanging from light fixtures – anticipates the final fist fight in its complete insistence that serious damage of any kind is unthinkable. Sexual activity in the film is another form of action sequence, like fist fighting;

Imitative behaviour: Philo swings from the light fitting in Any Which Way You Can.

both are forms of activity celebrated as expressions of cartoon-like brio outside the controls of the society. (This may be a reflection of the different directors of the two films: *Every Which Way* was directed by James Fargo, who had directed *The Enforcer*, and the director of *Any Which Way* was Buddy Van Horn, who had worked as the stunt coordinator on films such as *Thunderbolt and Lightfoot*.)

The point, or a point, of the insistence on unconstrained action is hinted at in the song with which *Any Which Way* opens. 'Beers to You', a duet by Eastwood and Ray Charles, remembers service in Vietnam as a matter of meeting 'foreign ladies' and drinking 'lukewarm beer'. A mood in which the American experience in the Vietnam war can be celebrated in such terms depends on the construction of a world in which a fantasy of freedom is essentially one of freedom from consequence, where no physical act, of sex or violence, causes a permanent effect.

Bronco Billy

It is possible to take *Bronco Billy* as the exemplary film with which to make a case against Eastwood. In a section of his *Hollywood from Vietnam to Reagan* subtitled 'Hollywood Antifeminism: The 80s', Robin Wood compares it with another film released in 1980, *Urban Cowboy*, linking them through their use of 'the tradition of the Western . . . as a means of putting assertive women back where they belong'. The telling detail from the film used in Wood's argument is the fact that Miss Antoinette Lily (Sondra Locke) is a good shot but nonetheless ends up 'spread-eagled on a revolving wheel, as Bronco Billy's target in his travelling Wild West show' (p.206). The meaning of this image clearly depends on why Miss Lily chooses to conceal her skill, what this Wild West show is and what it means in 1980, which then leads us to the meaning of the specific act: the woman on the wheel as the focus of danger and suspense.

Miss Lily is a New York heiress, whose money is subject to one of those quirky wills found in comedy – she must marry by her thirtieth birthday or lose her inheritance. We first see her when she is marrying, making a convenience of a penniless acquaintance, John Arlington, played with some enjoyably leering gestures by Geoffrey Lewis. She carries this through with sufficient irritation and self-disgust for Arlington to leave her stranded in a small town. When she fails to make contact, her stepmother and lawyer in New York conspire with Arlington to attest that he has murdered Miss Lily so that the three can claim her estate. It is at this point that she finds herself becoming assistant to Bronco Billy (Eastwood) in his Wild West show.

As so often in Eastwood's work, the broad outlines of plot do little to tell us how the film works. A crucial issue is whether Miss Lily's move from heiress to cowgirl is something done to her despite her assertiveness, or something in which she colludes. The mechanisms produced in the film to annotate the ways in which it is possible suddenly to drop out of an urban culture – a broken radiator in the limousine, not having the correct change for a pay phone, finding that a New York number is busy when you do finally make a call – are minor frustrations that would not be difficult for Lily to overcome, if New York were truly where she wanted to go. At first, her involvement in the Wild West show is something between a bargain (she agrees to act as Billy's assistant for one show, in exchange for a lift to the next town) and a dream (as she walks to his van, she murmurs to herself, 'This isn't happening').

But the crucial choice is made a little later. Lily is delivered to the next town after a brief and confrontational sequence as Billy's assistant. It is in this sequence that we learn that she can shoot, and this is the first time that we see her as Billy's target on the revolving wheel. Now she is about to walk back to her old life. Two steps from a telephone callbox, she sees the newspaper headline announcing her supposed murder. She takes a paper, which has her photograph on it. Lefty LeBow (Bill McKinney), a member of the show, asks her for the sports section of the paper but sees the front page – he recites the headline: 'Heiress Murdered'. A sequence involving Arlington and the fraud plot intervenes, and then we see Billy find Miss Lily in the cab of his van, where she signs on as his assistant.

This uses a familiar convention of comedy, in which the heroine is released through the agency of apparent death or disguise into a role in another world. To understand exactly what this world is, and thus why Miss Lily might choose it, we need to consider the character of the Wild West show.

The opening sequence of the film establishes the show as threadbare, scarcely surviving as a form of commercial entertainment in contemporary America. Its

calamities are part of the establishing of the show's marginality; it begins with a snakebite and ends with Billy wounding his assistant (Edye Byrde) on her first night with the show. Leonard James (Sam Bottoms) is the only performer who does not in some way fail in the ring; his act is the only one not associated with physical risk.

The other keynote is the lack of authenticity. This Wild West show is not the last refuge of representatives of a vanished world, of actual westerners reduced to entertainers, but an imaginary world created out of western myth by a crew of refugees from different situations in a degraded modern America. This is related to the insistence on 'correctness' exemplified when Chief Big Eagle (Dan Vadis) is bitten by a rattlesnake in his opening act because he will not use gopher snakes. Billy's explanation is the deadpan statement that Big Eagle is a 'proud Indian'. In *The Adventures of Huckleberry Finn*, Mark Twain points out through the figure of Tom Sawyer that an attachment to the inauthentic goes with a determined reliance on the 'authorities'. The world of Bronco Billy is one of Tom Sawyers, a landscape from which the Huck Finns have vanished.

It is this world into which Miss Lily chooses to insert herself, and the dialogue, as she chooses, is suggestive. Miss Lily is sitting in the troupe's van, Bronco Billy is looking in at the door.

Billy: What are you doing here?
Antoinette: Why, you still need an assistant, don't you?
Billy: I'm the head ramrod, I give the orders?
Antoinette: Yes, Bronco Billy.
Billy: All-right, get out of this truck.
Antoinette: Why, aren't we heading down the old trail?
Billy: First you've got to prove you can work hard, before you can ride with the head ramrod.

This conversation turns on qualities of tone. The heavy sarcasm that Miss Lily brings to the words 'old trail' is utterly absent from Billy's references to himself as 'head ramrod'. In the middle of this is Sondra Locke's performance of Miss Lily abasing herself: 'Yes, Bronco Billy'. It is hard to read this – perhaps it is another piece of sarcasm, perhaps an experiment with the adoption of a role. It seems to have the deadpan quality which occurs a few other times in the film, where a line is not so much delivered as quoted ('The only good Indian is a dead Indian'; 'These wide open spaces, where the deer and the buffalo roam'), with a sense that it is no longer clear in this America what authority the speaker retains, what kind of self might once have supplied any given line with authenticity.

These lines must be read against the film's account of contemporary America, the America, as it were, outside Bronco Billy's tent. Here the grimness of the film's vision is striking. Its New York is clearly corrupt, with William Prince (as Edgar Lipton, Lily's lawyer) playing a version of his earlier role as the corrupt father figure, Blakelock, in *The Gauntlet*, and looking forward to the mafiosi of *Any Which Way You Can*. But at least Edgar and New York are offered as rather clumsy comedy. The small-town America seen here is exemplified by the bar fight footage, which is much more violent than anything in the Beddoe films,

The heiress: Miss Antoinette Lily (Sondra Locke) at the opening of Bronco Billy.

with an explicit emphasis on the glass in the face as a form of combat. This is followed by the attempted rape of Lily by two men in the bar's parking lot, and a piece of plotting which brings Billy into confrontation with the local lawman, Sheriff Dix (Walter Barnes).

As in the Beddoe films, it is not crime and the enforcement of law that are at stake in this meeting. Here the issue is a fantasy about power. The sheriff has arrested Leonard, and the price for releasing him (in addition to a bribe) is ritual humiliation of Billy. It is typical of the vision of this film that the sheriff unambiguously triumphs – the sequence is not followed by any kind of comeuppance.

Leonard's crime – he was a deserter from the army at the time of the Vietnam war – is not condemned by any member of the show. Billy, Lefty and Big Eagle are themselves outsiders, ex-convicts whose crimes centred around women and money, and who met in prison. In the conversation with Lily in which these histories are revealed, Billy's story is that he found his wife in bed with his best friend. Asked what he did next, Billy calmly replies, 'I shot her.' Lily's astonished 'And what about him?' draws only the reply, 'He was my best friend.' This is more than just a crude attempt to shock or joke. Its force can be measured by the degree to which it works against the grain of the bulk of Eastwood's work, in which violence against women is the index of corruption. In the world outside

Below: the exercise of power – Sheriff Dix humiliates Bronco Billy. Opposite: a grim vision – the rain falls on Bronco Billy (Eastwood), Leonard James (Sam Bottoms) and Lorraine Running Water (Sierra Pecheur) in Bronco Billy.

the tent, such behaviour results in 'seven years in Folsom for attempted murder', a verdict that Billy does not dispute. But it also shows him as a man incapable of living in a world in which the response to real adultery was real violence, and emphasises the function of the Wild West Show, and in particular his construction of himself as Bronco Billy, as forms of retreat.

The retreat is to a site where the crucial event in Billy's past is subject to ritual re-enactment. Billy's act is a licensed occasion for the subordination of a woman: tied to the 'wheel of fortune', she is spun around and shot at, and in the climax of the act Billy throws a knife which is intended to land between her spread legs. The interest of this spectacle is, or perhaps ought to be, its 'safe' relocation of violence and eroticism – it resembles any circus magician's trick where the object of ritual violence is a woman but where the promise is that the 'victim' will emerge from the ordeal unhurt. The use of a blindfold makes the connection clear; the girl is offered and refuses it, whereupon Billy blindfolds himself. This locates the act firmly as a piece of magic – in the way in which he shoots the sequences, Eastwood gives no indication that there is any form of cheating involved, and thus any form of ordinary skill that Billy can be understood to be exercising as he aims at the target.

We are not the audience within the film and there is, of course, no difficulty for us in identifying what kind of magic this is. We know that what enables the violence to be seen to have a specific effect, or no effect, is that this is a sequence in a movie. And the film is never far from acknowledging the connection between a Wild West show, which is directed by Bronco Billy, and a movie called by that name which is directed by Clint Eastwood.

Above: ritual violence – Miss Lily on the 'wheel of fortune' in Bronco Billy.
Opposite: a form of containment and a barrier – Bronco Billy's tent.

I have touched on this subject elsewhere, and it will emerge in a different form in *White Hunter, Black Heart,* in which Eastwood actually plays a film director. Here the connection is pervasive, built around Billy's and Eastwood's dual roles as star and boss of the show/film. We see him negotiating with his cast over money, experiencing 'special effects' that go wrong, having a dressing-room row with a female star who wants to change her lines, dealing with promotion and disaster – all this is obvious enough. The film also uses gags about the notorieties of Eastwood's roles to date. The sequence in which Billy foils a bank robbery has a little joke reprised from *Coogan's Bluff,* the shot of Billy when he is addressed as 'Tex'. Perhaps the connection also extends to the area of power – the singleness of vision and self-reliance of Billy as the director's way of holding show/film together.

But if the film is aware of similarities between the Wild West show and more technological forms of showmanship, it is also aware of differences. The show represents a simple, low-technology world that is part of the past not simply in the material performed but in the type of performance itself, so that its audience simultaneously experiences two types of nostalgia, for the West and for the circus. The tent becomes a space where an older America, both in history and of enter-tainment, can be remembered and celebrated, but at the cost of a rejection of the contemporary world, related to the individual retreat that I have already discussed. The plotting of the central part of *Bronco Billy* outlines the violence of the confrontation between the world inside the tent and the America outside it. In a film that shares with the Callahan films the effective absence of positive images of a home, it is suggestive that this subject is initiated by a pregnancy. The news from Big Eagle's wife causes the troupe to 'go into town and raise some hell', the beginning of a chain of events which includes the near-rape of Miss Lily and the arrest of Leonard. This contact with the outside ends with

Cowboys and Indians: the members of the Wild West show prepare to rob a train in Bronco Billy.

the destruction of something that is symbolically both a form of containment and a barrier, the tent itself – Billy's late return from his humiliation by Sheriff Dix is the indirect cause of the fire that destroys it.

Deprived of the tent, the troupe is paradoxically brought more immediately into contact with America – it is now that Billy quotes the line: 'Don't you just love these wide open spaces, where the deer and the antelope roam.' This openness, which also contains the threat of emptiness, introduces an important sequence in which Billy announces a solution to their situation – they are going to rob a train.

The contemplation of this act is the opportunity for clear statements of position. Miss Lily appeals to the fact of contemporary America: 'There are no more cowboys and Indians. That's in the past.' This is Billy's speech in reply: 'Miss Lily, I was raised in a one-room tenement in New Jersey. As a kid, I never even saw a cowboy, much less the wide open spaces, except when I could scrounge up a quarter for a picture show. I was a shoe salesman till I was thirty-one years old. Deep down in my heart I always wanted to be a cowboy. One day I lay down my shoe horn and swore I'd never live in the city again. You only live once – got to give it your best shot.'

Clearly, the understanding of freedom as flight from the city and the status of cinema as a vision of that freedom are important here. The speech gives a context for the behaviour of the troupe in Billy's car (Big Eagle is actually going to shoot at the train with bow and arrows). The whole caper, viewed as train robbery, might be hopeless or foolish, but it can be comprehended if we see it as another act in the Wild West show orchestrated by Billy, a ritual of confrontation between his invented world and an icon of America, penetrating, ruthless, unstoppable and heroic, part of a thread of imagery in American culture running from the writing of Nathaniel Hawthorne and Henry David Thoreau to the present day. It is important that Eastwood does not present the train to us negatively. The shots of the troupe and the music on the soundtrack define the mood as one of celebration, of the fact that the confrontation between man and locomotive is still enactable. Rather than getting the troupe arrested or killed, it confirms their status as American dreamers, romantic outlaws inscribing themselves in myth, part of the America that roars past them.

Eastwood presses the point home with a simple detail. He takes us inside the train, to a vision of civilised life: a table laid for a meal, at which a young child sits opposite his mother. The connections are with Billy's reference to himself as a child at the movies and Miss Lily's comment about the past. The child, looking out through another kind of screen, the window of the carriage, watches Billy and the troupe and announces, 'Cowboys and Indians'. So naturalised is this mythology, so clearly is this what a little boy might expect to see, or imagine, as a train crosses the plains, that his mother agrees with him without even opening her eyes.

In the vision of the train, the viewer has always been both part of the tableau and divided from the machine itself. In *Walden*, Thoreau refers to himself as an 'employee' of the railroad, and yet says, 'I must get off the track and let the cars go by.' This is the situation of the would-be train robbers – the train roars into the distance, and their situation is unchanged.

Given the vision of America up to this point, the film has a clear difficulty in providing an ending that goes beyond this moment. There is no possibility that the troupe can be found a place within the literal America of the film, and this leaves the other potential solution, of returning them to their earlier situation, in other words their finding – in a metaphorical as well as literal sense – a new tent. The film does this by adopting a comic version of the strategy of the end of *The Gauntlet*, deploying the idea of madness. The action now moves to an old port of call for Billy's show, a home for the criminally insane, where the plot of Miss Lily's marriage to Arlington can be picked up again and a new tent can be produced in a suitably unlikely way, by the sewing together of American flags. At best, this is a deeply ironic vision of a benign America – the insane inmates listen in total silence to Billy's speech of thanks.

The intervention of the outside world in the form of the law and the media breaks up even this. Lily returns to New York, and faced with having to attend court in the city, the rest of the troupe take flight. The problem of an ending is almost directly articulated a little later when Doc (Scatman Crothers) suggests ironically, 'Maybe we can live happily ever after in this bar.'

The actual ending is a retreat to the show, to the inside of the tent. The film ends with a utopian performance – well attended, successful, the occasion of reconciliation between Billy and Miss Lily. The climax of the performance is the final wheel-of-fortune sequence. The act has appeared twice before in the film – in the opening sequence, where the result is actual injury, and in Miss Lily's first performance with the show, when her sarcastic 'Must you, Bronco Billy?' in reply to Billy's line about wearing a blindfold defeats the act's insistence on magic and provokes a furious row. At the end, the magic finally works, the cast take their bow, and the movie concludes.

It concludes in the tent, with a speech from Billy addressed to children, promoting the values of prayer, obedience to parents, telling the truth. Is this simply an expression of Eastwood's conservative values? I believe that the film makes two claims regarding this world of pieties. First, that in the contemporary world they can exist only in this space, an America contained inside a bizarre iconography of patriotism, the tent of flags sewn by the insane. Second, that they are the values that this ex-shoe salesman – in interview, Eastwood described him as a 'naive messiah' – has chosen to give to the creature of his invention. That Billy can articulate them is part of his naivety, which runs right through the film. It is expressed exactly in his response to Miss Lily being a good shot, a fact that other members of the show know and comment on, but which Billy himself doesn't know how to accept, sticking to the end to his image of himself as patient transmitter of skills.

Billy is still, of course, a salesman, with the resonances the word has for his culture. In the closing moments of the most famous treatment of this subject, Arthur Miller's *Death of a Salesman*, a player makes the essential point: 'A salesman is got to dream, boy. It comes with the territory.'

Honkytonk Man

This is the second of the two movies to date in which the character played by Eastwood dies – the other is *The Beguiled*. An obvious reading of this is to take the film as a possible end-point of the visions of America that I have mapped out in the other movies in this chapter, a vision in which the American hero is finally destroyed by the conditions of this culture, although the force of the film is not entirely in this direction, being complicated both by the period setting, and the particular reason for the death of Red Stovall (Eastwood).

The film begins with a piece of careful period reconstruction: a sharecropper's farm in the Oklahoma dust bowl in the early 1930s on the day of the destruction of the family's crop by a storm, which leads to their decision to set out for California. The meaning of this in 1982 is partly determined by its reference not just to a historical occurrence but to a famous novel and film. The image of the heroic family, centrally represented here by Emmy (Verna Bloom), a figure of benign motherhood preserving the group at the moment when the father is losing his sense of purpose and effect, calls to mind the Joad family in John Steinbeck's novel and John Ford's film of *The Grapes of Wrath*. But *Honkytonk Man* does not follow the journey to California, nor is it concerned with a political account of loss – there are no references to banks here, only dust, so that the disaster is seen entirely as an effect of nature. The evocation of *The Grapes of Wrath*, not as realism but as costume drama, carries a paradoxical message. The farm world is offered both as the benign context from which values emerge and as a world that must be fled from, one which offers no opportunity.

As the storm breaks, we see the family singing together. The idea of music as a celebration of the values of country and family but also as a route of escape from the world of those values has roots in American culture as far back as Willa Cather's novel *The Song of the Lark* (1915), but its film antecedent at this time was Michael Apted's *Coalminer's Daughter* (1980), a biopic of Loretta Lynn which

Sharecroppers: Red Stovall (Eastwood) with Grandpa (John McIntire), Emmy (Verna Bloom), Whit (Kyle Eastwood) and Arnspringer (Matt Clark) in Honkytonk Man.

was a box office hit, grossing $35m in the United States. This film was one of the earliest of the cycle of 'eighties films about country values that I considered briefly in my discussion of *Pale Rider*.

Here the country music star is Red Stovall, Emmy's brother, who arrives at the farm just as the storm is breaking. He represents both the privations of country life (he is penniless and dead drunk) and the image of potential success (his car and guitar as we see them after the storm, with their gleaming surfaces restored, in a setting covered in dust). It is also quickly made clear that he is ill with tuberculosis.

Writing about the imagery of disease in her *Illness as Metaphor*, Susan Sontag considers tuberculosis at length, linking it to ideas of creativity and the image of the bohemian life that was pervasively present in nineteenth and early twentieth century depictions of the artist. Red's illness has this traditional function. It expresses the toll taken by a life cut off from domestic pleasures and implies that this is the price to be paid for his devotion to singing. Rather than being seen as something done to him, the disease is a recurrent occasion for the expression of Red's self-reliance, his determination to live 'on my own terms' or not at all.

The date also affects this. We see his illness from the perspective of the development of treatments for tuberculosis in the 'forties and 'fifties. It needs no precise knowledge on the part of the audience to be aware of Red's condition as a historically specific component of the heroic imagery characterising the sensitive artist. His tuberculosis (or rather its meaning) is another aspect of a world about to disappear.

The travellers in this road movie are Red, his father-in-law, Grandpa Wagoneer (John McIntire), and his nephew Whit (Kyle Eastwood). The casting of John McIntire, an actor with a distinguished career in supporting roles in westerns as well as other genres (he appears in *Psycho* and *The Asphalt Jungle*), has something in common with the use of Ruth Gordon and Hank Worden in the Beddoe films and of Royal Dano in *The Outlaw Josey Wales*. His function here is to recall an event from history, a race for land, the opening up of the Cherokee strip in 1893. This is first dismissed, then taken up again – Grandpa Wagoneer mentions it at the family dinner table, producing a reaction of impatience in Whit's father (Matt Clark), then he tells the full story to Whit as the pair look at the horizon where the race commenced. It is described very much as a moment of American promise, offering something more than the literal prize: 'It wasn't just the land, it was the dream.' That the idea of promise remains despite the fact or likelihood of literal disappointment – the Cherokee strip is now 'turned to dust' – links with other ambitions in the film, the family's dream of life in California and Red's hope for success at the Grand Ole Opry in Nashville.

Much of the narrative of *Honkytonk Man* is a series of incidents on the road which are jokes about the committing of crimes and the humiliation of cops, not unrelated to those in the Beddoe movies. The references to dirt – here it is chickens that make a mess in cars – and to big animals which are comical rather than seriously threatening – here a bull — are the direct parallels. Where the film differs from the Beddoe movies is in the treatment of sexuality. There is no role that corresponds to the Sondra Locke parts in the earlier films – the portrayal of the hero's relations with women as essentially lost in the past, a measure not of contact with the world but of the loss of it, recalls the mood of *Thunderbolt and Lightfoot*. Red tells a story of love, but it is strikingly downbeat – the girl was married and finally returned to her husband, and Red had, or may have had, a daughter who never knew of his existence.

The film's direct attention to sexual activity is no more positive. The sexual initiation of Whit is another incident on the road: Red and Whit visit a brothel, and Red buys Whit a woman. The sequence, even down to exactly the same piece of comic business about premature ejaculation, is a reprise of the scene in *The Last Detail* (Hal Ashby, 1973), in which Meadows (Randy Quaid) is initiated, paid for by the sailors who are escorting him to prison. Both sequences place the limited positive experience of the initiates alongside the mood of the father-figures, who pay for the boy but do not themselves take a girl. In *The Last Detail*, the occasion is a cue for Baddusky (Jack Nicholson) to talk about his failed marriage. In Eastwood's film, after a moment of wavering, Red settles for music, providing the scene with its honkytonk piano soundtrack.

The other direct treatment of sex is through Marlene (Alexa Kenin), a girl in her late teens who joins the travellers on the road. Her character represents a comic inflation of adolescent aspirations – although she cannot sing, Marlene dreams of becoming a star, of 'destinies intertwined'. She finally sleeps with Red, but the incident is treated as a minor comedy of entrapment, and her main function seems to be to reappear in the final part of the movie as an implicit partner for Whit, enabling the movie to end with the image of a new couple.

Sexual histories and erotic dreams enter the film in another way, as the lyrics of country music. As Grandpa Wagoneer tells the story of the Cherokee Run, Eastwood cuts between the old man and Red, who is not listening but playing guitar as accompaniment to a love song. Even the story of Red's lost love becomes a song in recitative, or raw material for a lyric. As Red tells it to Whit, the story is given a guitar accompaniment *piano* on the soundtrack. The country music offers us different effects according to where Eastwood shows it being played, in the light and space of open country, as Grandpa Wagoneer and Whit contemplate the Tennessee line, or in the car at night, immediately before Red's disastrous try-out at the Grand Ole Opry in Nashville.

The Nashville sequence shows us one of the ways in which *Honkytonk Man* is related to the other films in this group, through the subject of flight from the city. Here the point is reversed in a narrative of a journey to the city, to the grim tenement room in Nashville – Eastwood specifically annotates this with some exterior shots – in which Red will die. The tension between country and city is another element of the mythology of tuberculosis. Listing the destinations proposed as places of cure, Sontag points out that 'their very diversity suggests what they have in common: the rejection of the city'.

The movement from country to city is expressed as a critique of different qualities of entertainment. The bar in which Red sings at the opening of the film is an entirely benign setting, the place where country folk – again in an iconography borrowed from the famous earlier images of rural America in the Depression – come to listen and dance. The next setting is a club in Memphis, a place where sexual energies and racial tensions are much closer to the surface, but where the suggestion that this is a place of illegitimate pleasures is dissipated in a piece of comedy, the joke that Whit becomes high just by passively taking in the smoke of the reefers being used around him.

This is still clearly a celebration of the city as a site of anarchic pleasure. The opposite is true of Nashville, or rather of the Opry, where entertainment is commercial – a show with a national radio hook-up, and subject to censorship. Eastwood makes the point in several ways, explicitly in the rejection of Red's songs about drinking and boogie-woogie; he is told, 'Ours is a clean, wholesome family show, Red.' It is also implicit in the imagery of the whole sequence that the Opry is devoted to the promotion of the couple – a woman sits with the producer as he judges the songs, and Red's act is framed by others performing numbers honouring the family. As he arrives, the melodrama of divorce is the subject ('Mummy's gone again') and, as he leaves, we glimpse in the background of the shot a couple taking the stage for a love duet ('Let's put our pride aside'). Against this background, the explosion of tubercular coughing in the middle of Red's song, rendering him unusable as a star on live radio, is not just a failure but a clear statement of how different he is, how he is not wholesomely devoted to family values.

Red is rescued from total collapse by an entertainment form that is to the Opry as movies are to live theatre, an opportunity to record his songs on disc. It is possibly not surprising that Eastwood treats the recording studio positively, as somewhere that final performances can be given by the dying Red to an

The all-male setting: Red in the recording studio in **Honkytonk Man**.

audience of sympathetic figures, fellow musicians and technicians. An obvious aspect of this is the studio's function as an all-male setting – the scenes there are unique in the film in that they momentarily recreate the sense of shared values and common purpose that we might recognise in a western or a war film. The studio becomes a place where Red's illness can be acknowledged but also camouflaged, where the physical cost of performance is not denied (Eastwood offers a striking shot of Red's ravaged face as he collapses in a corner at the climax of the final song), but the demands of the medium control the melodrama. A stand-in finishes the last verse, and this is offered as comradeship rather than usurpation.

The person who stands slightly apart from the group, Whit, is the only one who is not an adult male. It is Whit who is given a line that sounds like the cry of the protective woman: 'Let him go, can't you see he's had enough.' This ends the final recording sequence, and Red dies shortly afterwards.

I have had little to say in this account of *Honkytonk Man* of what we might expect to be one of its obvious subjects, the transmission of traditions or skills from father to son. The treatment of this elsewhere, particularly in *The Outlaw Josey Wales*, suggests a degree of reserve, and here Eastwood avoids the easy assumption of it as a meaning of this narrative. The matter of skills is exemplary.

Nothing can be transmitted through the symbol of the car, as Whit is already a better driver than his uncle. The most obvious and potent skill, that of playing the guitar, is treated in a strikingly negative way. Instead of the scene in which Red might have taught Whit to play, we see a bad-tempered refusal brought on by 'fever' and only minimally redeemed later on. The age of the 'son' is perhaps crucial – Whit is fourteen, and despite rituals such as his sexual initiation, he is not presented as taking over any very significant adult role from his uncle.

The final sequence of the film, at Whit's graveside, sums up the limitations of what has been transmitted. A note of dimmed western tradition rather than religious observance is stressed, as Marlene, Whit and a black gravedigger sing a few lines of 'Swing low, Sweet Chariot'. As they walk into long shot, Marlene is proposing an 'act' in memory of Red, but we already know that she cannot sing, and the point seems again to be the persistence of dreams of success in the face of possible realities. The concluding note is one of optimism, but sounded by a couple who are little more than children.

Pink Cadillac

Pink Cadillac is a road movie which uses some elements of the Beddoe films and *Bronco Billy* – Eastwood's role as Tommy Nowak, a 'skip-chaser' employed by a bail-bond company to track and bring in fugitives, gives him a chance to engage in the fun of disguise, and there is yet another comedy sequence about animals defiling cars. The film is also linked to *Bronco Billy* by its extremely negative view of contemporary America, the America that surrounds the film's symbol of a more benign past, a 'fifties Cadillac convertible. The urban world is represented by the garish casinos of Reno, and the place of the disaffected male group – the comic Black Widow bikers of the Beddoe films – is filled by 'The Birthright', a group of fascist white supremacists practising wargames in the hills. (This was a topical subject and had been treated in Costa-Gavras's *Betrayed*, released in the previous year, 1988.) A difficulty in the film is that it cannot decide whether the fascists are 'a bunch of jerk-offs' to be treated comically, or a more serious expression of the bankruptcy of militarism and of some aspects of masculinity in American culture.

The grimness of the America presented in *Pink Cadillac* is caught in two moments in Tommy's romance with the girl he finds on the road, Lou Ann McGuinn (Bernadette Peters). Talking to her about a previous lover, Tommy mentions that they parted when the girl won the title of Miss AmCo Transmission of Turlock, California, and needed a man to stand by her while she 'performed all her queenly duties, like cutting the ribbon on a new muffler shop'. This recollection of the demeaning use to which sexuality can be put in a consumer culture is followed shortly by the sequence in which Tommy and Lou Ann first make love. When they arrive at a motel, the owner volunteers that he is going to give them the 'Hawaiian Luau Room'. As they look around the grim space, Lou Ann remarks dryly, 'It's eerie how much this place looks like Hawaii, isn't it?'

There is a loose parallel here with a famous scene in American cinema, from a film that I have argued is important to Eastwood. This is the wedding night sequence in Frank Capra's *It's a Wonderful Life*, when the dilapidated Granville home becomes, with the help of some simple props and Hawaiian music, a place that will stand in for the South Sea setting that George Bailey (James Stewart) had wanted for his honeymoon. There, Capra's triumphant point was about the transforming power of imagination, something that George and Mary Bailey and their friends were shown to be able to achieve for themselves. Eastwood's subdued echo of that scene marks the distance between Capra's world of the 'forties and contemporary America – his lovers live in a culture in which the props that are thought to signify Hawaii are produced for sordid motels and provide a hopelessly threadbare image that denies not only physical but also imaginative release from the mundane world.

The ending of the film, in which the narrative leaves the couple's future unclear – maybe they will settle down, or maybe they will have to keep running – expresses a vision of a world where neither moving on nor staying put seems a possible way of life. A little like Bronco Billy's tent or the Army in *Heartbreak Ridge*, the pink Cadillac becomes a refuge from the rest of America.

In this group of films, there is usually a girl in the picture, at least in the comedies; their common feature is that they conclude with the production, or celebration, of the couple. *Thunderbolt and Lightfoot* is the exception, and *Every Which Way* and *Honkytonk Man* are muted examples, both ending with couples with supporting roles rather than principal ones. The comedies take as their subject the relocation of the girl from the place in which she is originally encountered to the new context which she shares with the hero, expressed by a place that seems more benign. They share the movement from an interior – a gaol cell, a grim gambling den — to a place of space and light. Often that space is simply the road itself – almost all the films (*Bronco Billy* is a partial exception) end with an image of travelling, a couple in a car or truck, or on foot.

The films conclude by implicitly questioning the kind of future to which the couple is travelling. If they conclude with a departure, where are they departing for? The films are more various in their answers to this. There is retreat to the family (the group returning in *Every Which Way*). There is the acknowledgement that no future can be identified, only the unstoppable movement across country. This is the link between the film that most hysterically asserts the couple, *Any Which Way* – Philo's last word is 'onwards' – and the film which acknowledges its loss, *Thunderbolt and Lightfoot*. More positive, but still ambiguous, are the two films which end with the couple imagining a future, and thus with our calculation of the possibility of triumph or defeat for these dreams in the America we have seen – *The Gauntlet* and *Honkytonk Man*.

At the end of *Sullivan's Travels* the director, after his ritual death and restoration to life and love, announces his return to Hollywood, the abandonment of his 'deep dish movie' project and his commitment to the kind of comedies with which he started out. The sense of accepting that you are back where you started is the connection with *Bronco Billy*, where the couple find themselves in a place quite unlike any other, a place which is not fixed and is not exactly 'home', but which they create for themselves using fragments and patches of a national mythology to make 'entertainment'. This is both the same place as where the hero started out, and a different one. Despite all the ways in which the film illustrates the sense that such a place is marginal or threatened in contemporary America, it is not surprising that Eastwood has described *Bronco Billy* as the film that 'came closest to what I wanted to do'.

CHAPTER SEVEN
AMERICAN LIVES

Bird

There is a simple distinction between *Bird* and *White Hunter, Black Heart* and Eastwood's other work. Charlie Parker, the subject of *Bird*, and John Huston, in a way at the centre of *White Hunter, Black Heart*, are the names of actual Americans of whom it can be assumed that audiences will probably have heard. But there is also a distance between these famous men and what we are seeing on the screen. We know that the person has, or had, an existence outside the film that presents him to us, and that this is not just a matter of a historical past, of there being those alive who spoke to or lived with this man. It is also a matter of the future, that Forest Whitaker as actor and Eastwood as director, in offering us their vision of Charlie Parker, are not necessarily having the last word. 'Charlie Parker' is a role that exists free of a text – less like Hamlet, more like 'Marilyn Monroe' – that another actor and director could explore in very different terms.

What we mean when we invoke the figure of Charlie Parker is certainly not a fixed, or elaborate, or complete, narrative. We start with the aspects of Parker that we know before we see the film: these are not necessarily the same subjects as those that the film may wish to explore, or may teach us about, or remind us of.

I will suggest a minimum of what the film seems to expect us to know, basing this on its unquestioning presentation of the following points: that Charlie Parker was black, that he was an American genius, that he died young some little time ago, and that his death was in part due to drink and drugs. We know that the field of his genius is jazz, although this is a difficult area, at once popular and the subject of erudite learning. More important than any one of these elements is what they mean when taken together. Jazz, associated both with music as an art form and with the social and political deprivations of black Americans, offers the brutally short life of a Charlie Parker (or a Billie Holliday) as a site of a myth, that of the artist as martyr. This is the word used of Parker by Eastwood in an interview, and it is also used to describe him at one point in the film.

Against this list we may place another, of matters of which the film is aware, but in which it is largely uninterested. At its head might be the technicalities of influence, or the trajectory of a career. Eastwood does not show us how Parker's music relates to, grew out of, or influenced, the music of others. He is only tangentially interested in Parker's status as a worker in the music industry, how he participates in, and is excluded from, its rewards. We see enough for it to be implied that Parker has financial good times and bad times, that the owners and producers and agents make – or hold on to – more money than he does, and that he and other heroin addicts are part of another local economy, in which corrupt narcotics cops take their rake-off from the earnings of the addicts. But these subjects surface only briefly, and in the service of other matters.

Alongside the subjects in which the film is uninterested are those which it rejects: explanations or explanatory myths circulating around the view of the artist as martyr. We are not shown a man whose genius is crucially dependent on, or released by, the use of drugs. Equally, we are not looking at a man whose relationship to the central woman of the narrative is one of Artist to Muse. The film does consider both drug-taking and a relationship to a woman, but its concerns lie elsewhere: in exploring the ways in which these things operate outside dominant myths of the artist, and in questioning the idea that the functions of women or narcotics in this context are only as routes to art viewed as romantic excess.

This can be put more generally by saying that the film is interested in the relationship between discipline and excess, with Parker's music considered as a form of discipline, not as an expression of excess. Talking about Parker in an interview on the BBC arts programme, *Arena*, Eastwood commented that 'it's hard to understand why a person could be so disciplined with playing an instrument, and not be disciplined . . . [*breaks off*]' He goes on to say, 'I don't try to tell the answer in the film . . . it's just there.' The last three words are repeated a moment later. The insistence is important; what Eastwood is looking at are not the local causes, but the conditions operative in American culture by which Parker's life was determined.

After two very short sequences in the rural world, one preceding and one interrupting the credits, and establishing shots of Parker playing in a club, Eastwood opens the film with a long night sequence in which Parker (Forest Whitaker) comes home to his wife Chan (Diane Venora). The sequence, in which the couple move around their apartment quarrelling, physically fight and embrace, and which ends with Parker's attempt at suicide, is searing. The disorientation and pain, the

Not the last word: Eastwood directing Forest Whitaker and Sam Wright in Bird.

defeat felt by both parties, is clear but made more difficult (although also possibly more bearable) because we are not yet familiar with the history to which this scene alludes. We learn, for example, that they have lost a child, but we know nothing about the circumstances of the loss. We see that Parker is beginning to acknowledge, or rather to find ways of rendering speakable, the possibility of his imminent death – he tries to talk about his will to Chan, and he stares into the bathroom mirror remembering a relevant expression in literature. (He does not speak, but his voice-over quotes Edward Fitzgerald's lines about the 'bird of Time' from *The Rubáiyát of Omar Khayyám*). Eastwood's direction of the sequence acknowledges its harshness, emphasising the physical awkwardness and dissonance between the two bodies in the spaces of these rooms – the camerawork emphasises the degree to which they seem to get in each other's way.

This is the sequence that the rest of *Bird* has to answer, to explain or account for. There is an analogous opening, in which a sequence which is the end but not quite the literal last scene of the chronological narrative, plays at the very beginning behind the credits. This is in *Written on the Wind* – 'you start with an end situation', in Sirk's words. He goes on to describe the effect as one in which 'The spectator is supposed to know what is waiting for him. It is a different type of suspense, or antisuspense.'

According to Sirk, the effect of this is to turn the attention of the audience to 'structure instead of plot'. The form of explanation being rejected here is that implied in a chronologically sequential biography or biopic, in which succeeding events are to be interpreted as cause and effect. This rejection is behind the time scheme of *Bird*, in which a narrative largely covering a few days at the end of Parker's life is interrupted by flashbacks from his consciousness and Chan's to different periods, and briefly, within a flashback, by a further retreat through the mind of a minor character. The relationship of flashback to 'present' narrative is not obscure – that the flashbacks themselves are mainly in chronological sequence assists the audience – but the threads of remembered past and the present day of the film do not meet until almost its end, when what had been the present at the beginning (Parker's suicide attempt) is repeated, reappearing at the end of a long series of remembered events.

Perhaps the function of flashback, presented as our entry into the memory of specific characters, is to emphasise an insistence, an urge to communicate which may not be desired, but cannot be resisted. This is the difference between our entering the consciousness of the remembering mind (as in all the flashbacks in *Bird*) and those occasions where the material is introduced by a character deliberately beginning to speak of the past to others.

The subject of causation in the film is taken up in the first flashback. It takes place shortly after the opening apartment sequence, as Parker lies, held down by physical restraints, in a bed at Bellevue. To use Sirk's words again, its subject is knowing what is waiting for you. Eastwood takes us to a city morgue. The sequence begins with a high-angle longshot as light floods through an opening door and two men enter. One is speaking: 'Yeah, Charles Christopher Parker Junior, August 29th 1920 . . .' The qualities of this moment, the formality of the spoken names, the evocation of the past, and the place itself – all of these recall another account of a representative American life, Orson Welles's *Citizen Kane*. The connection is generally with the moments when the reporter's various informants begin their stories. More specifically – this is largely to do with the lighting of the shot and the set – it is with the Vault Room of the Thatcher Memorial Library, which Herman Mankiewicz's shooting script for *Citizen Kane* describes as a room 'with all the warmth and charm of Napoleon's tomb.'

The sequence in *Bird* to develops differently. It emerges that the man accompanying the speaker is the young Charlie Parker, brought here, by the doctor who had delivered him as a baby, to view the corpse of a heroin addict. So this is not Parker's body, but it will be – the man on the slab is a message, and the subjects of the communication are the inevitability of an early death and an unanswered question about room for choice.

This is not unrelated to Welles's film. There, the sequence points out that Kane is the product of the particular intersection of financial power and emotional need represented in the meeting of the lost world of his childhood and Mrs Kane with that of his metaphorical father, the banker Walter Parks Thatcher, an occasion on which a child was given no choice. It is also about the ineradicability of the urge to tell, the impulse which has made Thatcher write his memoir of Kane like a novelist, and then lock it away like a banker.

That Eastwood's film is concerned with the nature of communication, between artist and public, man and wife, one musician and another, and with the links and divisions between private and public worlds is clearly signalled as the sequence ends. Parker's last line to the doctor in the flashback is taken in the world of the present as addressed to another doctor, the young intern at Bellevue who awkwardly hands him an album – 'I haven't done anything remotely resembling this in my life' – and asks him to sign it. Suddenly Parker is Bird, the focus of a fan's homage and professional discourse; his agent turns up bearing chocolates and offers of work. Yet he is still subject to the practices of the institution – Eastwood ends the sequence with a verbal reminder of the restraints that hold Parker to the bed.

Eastwood's exploration of the relationship of public to private lives, the nature and the difficulty of privacy, is centred on his presentation of Parker's courtship of Chan Richardson and their married life. (Chan Parker's recollections of the marriage seem to have been the starting point for the script of the film.) Much of this can be read as dramatising how Parker communicates, the kind of language – when he is not playing the saxophone – such a man has at his disposal. We see his directness in the courtship scene, when Chan has told him about her father, 'Broadway Ben', and her 'sweet sixteen party at the Cotton Club' and asks him in turn for some kind of parallel confession. He offers, entirely without irony, a message about what is going to happen to him that is the verbal equivalent of the addict's corpse, the story of his first finding himself 'strung out' on drugs. Immediately afterwards, he tells her that 'you make me feel very peaceful', the first example of what Chan will come to call his 'George Brent dialogue'.

What she is describing in this is the difficulty that Parker continually experiences in finding actions and a vocabulary that will express his feeling towards Chan, and later towards his role as paterfamilias. The subject is tellingly presented in the actual seduction —- remembering her story of being serenaded on her sixth birthday by her father's band, he sets up two buddies to play the saxophone outside her window and himself turns up on a white horse – as they ride away the couple are arguing about the one past they seem to share, about Rudolph

Married life: Charlie Parker (Forest Whitaker) and Chan Richardson (Diane Venora) in Bird.

Valentino and Vilma Banky, stars of (significantly) silent scenes of seduction. The reference to the western here is not entirely irrelevant. Given the essentially male companionship of musical performance as we see it, Parker's desire for Chan can be seen as a version of the awkward desire for the woman and the settled life found in the western hero, not a surprising connection for Eastwood to make, or wish to expound.

These hesitancies are related to the two American utopias, or perhaps we should call them utopian possibilities, explored in the film. One involves the all-male bebop group, and has at its core the friendship between Parker and Red Rodney (Michael Zelniker), the white trumpeter. In the two sequences that express it, the musicians play to an audience that dances, in the Jewish wedding sequence and on the trip to the deep South. In the first, racial and religious differences are reconciled: 'These are not Jewish boys, but good.' On the deep South trip, the racial prejudice of the South is turned into a confidence trick, in the presentation of Rodney as 'Albino Red' and in his singing of the blues. A line from Parker in the script explicitly links this honorary 'blackness' with Parker's honorary 'jewishness' earlier.

These pleasures, even the more extended sequence of the deep South trip, are only temporary and unstable. They are interrupted by the pressures of drug addiction – the positive energy of the deep South sequence, expressed in the melody played over part of it, dissipates in a scene in which Rodney obtains drugs from a local doctor, and the group is finally destroyed when Rodney is busted in New York.

What replaces it is another piece of American dreaming, the utopia of the domestic world: 'Charley Parker with Strings'. A motif from the beginning of the film, this title was on the record sleeve which Parker signed in Bellevue. Now the pun on the words is insistently made – a montage sequence over the David Raksin melody 'Laura' includes the positioning of the Strings poster on the wall of the family apartment that we see Parker and Chan making into a home. The sensuousness and pleasure of these moments is clearly indicated, but so is the reservation: this music felt as something slick, as lesser work than the bebop. This is expressed and linked with domesticity in the dialogue that ends the re-cording session for the album (Eastwood shows that it involves a woman wielding strings, a harpist). As the number ends, another musician assures Parker that 'you're still the greatest', and he replies, 'I've been away too long.' This is followed by an innocent enquiry about Chan, that 'chick you used to run with'. Parker replies with discernible irony that 'she's the mother of three lovely children'.

The reservation felt here becomes clear in the use of an important configur-ation in domestic melodrama, which we have already encountered in the opening sequence, the man's return to the home. Parker's return to the family apartment here begins with something that looks like jollity, or fun. We see him throwing open the door and mugging to Mario Lanza's vocals of 'Be My Love', and tangling on the floor with the children. Perhaps even here there is an awkwardness, as if Parker needs the jokey excess of Lanza's emotion and the rowdiness of the moment to conceal something that he does not know how to express. We now find this emerging in the plot – Chan takes Parker to another room, to see his sick daughter. The famous precedent for this, for the near-intolerable strain of family life being expressed through a father's reaction to the illness of a daughter, is Frank Capra's *It's a Wonderful Life*. The row between Chan and Parker over whether or not he should kiss the sleeping child (and thus risk waking her up) is analogous to the row over the furious telephone calls made by George Bailey (James Stewart) in Capra's film. What the sequences have in common is that the emotional commitment of the husband and wife to each other is not in question – that this commitment offers no solution to the actual problems of their situation is intolerable to them. Both men flee the domestic space and the family, George to the river and his attempted suicide, Parker to a heroin dealer.

As Parker leaves, he underlines this impasse with a heartbreaking irony – going out of the door, he sings the three words that we have heard at the beginning of the sequence, but revealing the functionlessness of such a plea in a situation like this: 'Be My Love . . .' Like his note on the refrigerator in the opening sequence of the film – 'I love you . . . think about it' – its directness is eloquent, but solves nothing.

There is another aspect through which 'home' is understood in the film, and which is important in the resolution of the sub-plot in which the daughter dies in New York while Parker is playing in California. This is the film's treatment of space. I have argued in previous chapters that this is an important subject in Eastwood's work; *Bird* continues to stress the importance of place as a condition governing American lives.

The film covers a considerable range of physical spaces. There is the initial journey, in the two sequences before and during the credits, to the city from the remoteness of the countryside in which Parker's life begins. New York is initially presented as a positive experience, notably in the sequence of Chan's first memories of 52nd Street, where Eastwood's camerawork, both in montage and in long takes, expresses the energy and good humour of the time, the sense of figures able to move through and control the spaces. (Through three appropriately costumed figures, there seems to be a reference to the zest of the city seen in the cinema of the times, to the sailors of *On the Town*). This sharply contrasts with the presentation of Los Angeles through camera angles and lighting as 'unfamiliar' space. The point is made metaphorically through minor characters as well, in the contrast between the doorman's progress down 52nd Street and the silent drug-pusher in a wheelchair on the West coast.

The effect is to present an America where it is too easy, in every sense, to lose touch. Hence the moments when the musicians urge each other to keep in contact, or admit the loss of it; at one point Parker says, 'I owe Dizzy [Gillespie] everything – except a phone call.' The image of a self strained over huge physical spaces, whether within America or outside it, seems to be the point of the Paris sequence; the possibility of living and working permanently in Europe is taken by Parker as a kind of defeat, an abandonment of his own country. The ironies of this feeling being expressed by a Black American at this time are explicitly pointed out here.

At the opposite pole from the experience of the foreign as alien is the dream in which the artist can cross international barriers and settle successfully in a foreign land. In the first California sequence, Parker listens to a list of European immigrants to Los Angeles: Igor Stravinsky, Arnold Schoenberg, Jascha Heifetz, Aldous Huxley, Thomas Mann. Suddenly – the slight unreality here is obviously intentional – Parker arrives at the gate of Stravinsky's home. He rings the bell, and a couple come to the door. We glimpse someone who might be Stravinsky, but Parker turns away – the vision of this coherence can't be directly confronted. We can link this with the flashback to Parker's first audition, and another musician's comment that Parker will always be damned by his own self-description, Charlie from 'just around'. The film's use of Stravinsky is continued in the figure of Baroness Nica (Diane Salinger), the European aristocrat to whose house Parker retreats at the end of the film. He dies there in a domestic scene, in a living room, watching television – in one of the film's starkest ironies, he is in a gracious home, but one that is not his own. Just before the end, the Parker family has moved from the city apartment to a house in the country. Hours before his death, he speaks to Chan on the telephone, nominally about painting the garage, saying, 'If you have a home, the least you can do for that home is maintain it.' This might recall the similar pieties famously expressed by Arthur Miller's Willy Loman – is Eastwood deliberately echoing a text contemporary with Parker's times here?

Eastwood's film demonstrates the impossibility of holding the family together by keeping them in the same space, a vision of a desolate America where the domestic milieu disintegrates in the face of distances that are both metaphorical

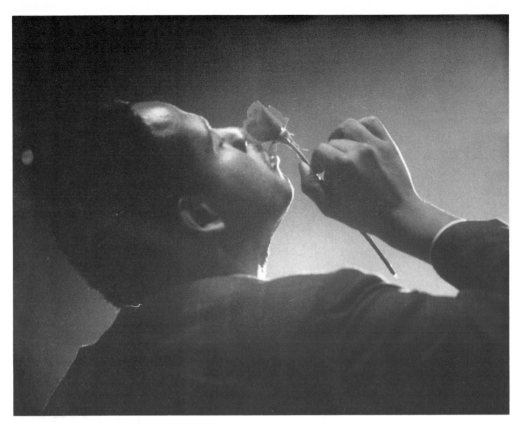

Genius: Parker receiving applause in Bird.

and literal, and cannot be bridged. The sequence at the time of the daughter's death, in which Parker sits by a telephone in Los Angeles, sending telegram after telegram to Chan, expresses this perfectly. Rather than curing or ameliorating it, the technology of the telegram brings Parker horribly into confrontation with the inadequacy of the words he has to offer and the distances he cannot cross. The opposite vision is expressed by Capra in the suggestion that the home can be maintained only by packing more and more into the domestic interior, so that the climax of *It's a Wonderful Life* does indeed 'solve' the problem, by bringing the entire cast into the Bailey house – in Capra's original version of the script, even Potter, the film's villain, was to be included. It is difficult to take much comfort from either version.

The final sense of disintegration charted by the film is historical, the fact that Parker's music was possible in a specific historical period of which the film observes the rise (the 52nd Street montage in Chan's memory) and fall (the arrival of rock'n'roll). Here, too, the film can be seen as rethinking some elements of Capra's masterpiece. The sequence in which, after leaving the city, Parker comes back to 52nd Street to find the clubs converted into strip joints clearly recalls the 'dreamland' sequence of *It's a Wonderful Life*, a connection that is even clearer when we see Parker, simply dressed, quite alone and the subject of no attention, walk down the aisle through the audience of the rock'n'roll concert, rendered momentarily invisible, not by enchantment but by 'progress'.

But this does not last – the end of the film returns, albeit in the spirit of remembering something past, to Parker's music. The sense of disintegration and pain stands throughout the film alongside something much more difficult to characterise or discuss, the achievement of the music as we hear it on the soundtrack. (It is important that Eastwood in his detailing of Parker's destruction never uses the strategy of suggesting that his playing deteriorates in any significant way. Even when he admits to a mistake, in the opening sequence, he says, 'Wouldn't nobody have noticed except maybe Dizzy Gillespie.' The choice of playing 'with strings' is clearly a different issue.) The American conditions that the film presents destroy Parker, but they also enable him to produce his music, and we are not asked to look at the defeat of the American dreams in the film as being apart from the achievement of that music, but as intimately related parts of a whole. This is what Chan Parker means when she replies to the Bellevue doctor's question about wanting a husband or a musician, with the words 'they do not separate'.

White Hunter, Black Heart

In *Bird*, Eastwood is interested in an American life which spans many different locations, both inside and outside America. The period of time evoked is relatively short – from Parker's first fame in 1945 to his death in 1955 – and we have a film which inevitably treats this period from the perspective of the 1980s. In *White Hunter, Black Heart*, these interests are in part pursued but approached very differently. I will begin with chronology, because this is the easiest way of locating the origins of the film, or the origins that it alludes to.

The nominal present of *White Hunter, Black Heart* is the early 'fifties. The subject is an expedition made by an American film director, John Wilson, to Africa. A film, entitled 'The African Trader' is to be shot there, starring 'Kay Gibson' and 'Phil Duncan'.

In the transparency of these pseudonyms, there is an invitation to intimacy, to being in the know. What Eastwood's film itself nominally disguises is made explicit in just one clue that enables the decoding of the rest. To know that 'The African Trader' is *The African Queen*, gives us enough to identify John Huston as its director, Katharine Hepburn and Humphrey Bogart as its stars. And there are treats for the initiate – another level of knowledge may be called upon to produce the name Sam Spiegel for the producer character Paul Landers (George Dzundza), or the knowledge that the newly wed bride of 'Phil Duncan' represents Lauren Bacall. A comparable experience – the same historical period is involved – is reading the novels of Jack Kerouac. Again, knowledge of the actual names of the historical figures concealed behind the pseudonyms – knowledge which is not at all obscure or difficult to acquire – gives a paradoxical sense of closeness, of inwardness with a milieu, and makes for an apprehension of the figures that seems strangely more direct than if they were rightly named. This impulse, to find, or believe in, some privileged access to the 'reality' of stars is both complex and well-known; in Richard Dyer's phrase, in the study of Joan Crawford in his *Heavenly Bodies*, 'it is the insistent question of "really" that draws us in'.

What is this background, the 'really' that *White Hunter, Black Heart* invites us to disinter? In 1935, C.S. Forester published his novel *The African Queen*; it

dealt with the river voyage made by an unlikely couple, an alcoholic trader and a spinster missionary. The novel is set during World War I, in 1915. The successful book was considered by more than one studio (Columbia, for Elsa Lanchester and Charles Laughton, and Warners for Bette Davis). Finally, the rights were sold to Spiegel and Huston, who shot the film, largely in Uganda and the Belgian Congo, in 1950. It was released with considerable financial and industrial success in 1951 ($4.1 million domestic gross, one Oscar and three other nominations). In 1953, Peter Viertel, who had worked as a scriptwriter on the film, published a novel entitled *White Hunter, Black Heart* dealing with the events that preceded the actual shooting and thinly masking characters through pseudonyms. Other direct accounts covering some of the same events appeared later, in Huston's autobiography, *An Open Book*, in 1980, and in Katharine Hepburn's memoir *The Making of the African Queen*, which was published in 1987, the year before Huston's death. Her subtitle is 'How I went to Africa with Bogart, Bacall and Huston and almost lost my mind'. Eastwood's film, based on the Viertel novel and using its title and its pseudonyms, was released in 1990.

The complexity of layers of the past appears to be in play here. In 1990, the audience is looking at a narrative of 'fifties Africa, and a memory of 'fifties Hollywood, in which a cast and crew are about to film a 'thirties novel which deals with the events of the early part of the century. (Such a pattern is not unique – a parallel case is Sydney Pollack's 1985 feature *Out of Africa*, a filming of Karen Blixen's memoir of her life in Kenya in the period 1914-31, originally published in 1937 and issued in paperback in Britain in 1954.)

The different decades, which might seem more clearly distinct if we were looking at, say, Chicago at various points in the century, blur in the presentation of Africa into a more generalised sense of the past. Without specific signposts, the Africa of 1910 might be difficult for an audience to distinguish from that of 1930, or even a late colonial context of 1950, which is itself looking backwards to its own past. If this is so, then the important remaining distinction must be between the 'fifties and the 'eighties, a period in which colonial Africa turned into a subject of memory and nostalgia. We can investigate this, or begin to do so, by asking in what ways Eastwood's film, which is a recognisable adaptation of Viertel's novel (retaining the main strands of the plot and taking over many scenes and passages of dialogue), differs from the novel, and perhaps from any film that might have been made of it in the 'fifties.

The novel begins in London. Wilson summons his old wartime friend Peter Verill (Jeff Fahey) with a proposal for a trip to 'the very darkest bloody corner of Africa that we can find'. The nominal purpose is to make a movie, and Verill, who is a writer, is told by Wilson, 'There's a little work to be done on the script, and then you can stay on and we'll hunt.' The body of the novel is concerned with the effect of Africa on Wilson and the resulting reversal of the order of events – Wilson postpones the start of the film in order to hunt. The hunt becomes reduced to Wilson's pursuit of a particular quarry, the 'big tusker', and the climax is a confrontation in which Wilson shoots his bull elephant but Kivu, his chief native hunter, is killed. The novel ends here, although we learn that Wilson, now 'a gaunt silent scarecrow', goes on to make 'The African Trader'.

The effect of Africa: Eastwood as John Wilson in White Hunter, Black Heart.

Above: impersonations – Kay Gibson (Marisa Berenson), Phil Duncan (Richard Vanstone) and Mrs Duncan (Jamie Koss) in a publicity shot for 'The African Trader' in White Hunter, Black Heart. *Opposite: American confidence – Wilson and the film's steamboat.*

An important quality of Viertel's novel, linking it with other writing popular at the time, is the suggestion of elegy, a mode being seen as appropriate to a period of massive political uncertainty about the future. Probably the most concise expression of this is in Jean-Paul Sartre's contemporary comment on William Faulkner's writing: 'For him, as for all of us, the future is closed.' This feeling surfaces directly in the novel in a brief reference to the atomic bomb, more metaphorically in a number of references to the difficulty of finding a suitable ending to the script – Wilson wants all the characters to die. The hunt is finally represented as an undertaking that fails to leave the participants with a future – 'We stood there in the hot dust, and everything seemed pointless and lost.'

Eastwood's film reinflects this source material in several ways. Most clearly, from the point of view of 1990, the world of 1950 is seen less as a contemporary order poised on the brink of self-destruction and more as a matter of the nostalgia of costume drama – 'fifties England is as eclipsed a world as 'fifties Africa. The idea of Wilson's insertion of himself, as an American, into exotic milieux – here the English upper classes – is presented in the novel as an expression of the man's successful cosmopolitanism and part of his ruthlessness. In the opening sequences of the film, it feels like a gag, an evident awkwardness, as if we were being given a signal that this scene is about to dissolve into something else, say, that it will turn out to be a sequence in a film within the film. This may have largely to do with our knowledge of what is 'really' evoked behind the pseudonyms of the film, our sense that this is an impersonation of a manner, which we measure against our familiarity with Huston's appearance or his voice. But it also depends on the assertion, from his earliest starring features, of Eastwood not as cosmopolitan, but as associated as an actor or director exclusively with America.

This is further accentuated by the rest of the casting of the film. Jeff Fahey, as Verrill, is nominally another American, but almost no stress is laid on his nationality, and he is shown as prepared to fit into European stereotypes of the cultured – that is, Europeanised – American. One of the changes that Eastwood makes to the novel is that Kay Gibson (Marisa Berenson) is played as English, and Phil Duncan (Richard Vanstone) and Mrs Duncan (Jamie Koss) are Americans only in their nominal impersonations of Bogart and Bacall, which are given no prominence by Eastwood. The major crew parts are taken by English actors, and George Dzundza's performance reminds us that Paul Landers is Hungarian. The effect, particularly marked when the action shifts to Africa, is to emphasise by contrast Wilson's Americanness. His qualities of ruthlessness and outspokenness become less those of a particular individual, as they are in Viertel's presentation of them in the novel, than those of a representative American democrat.

This is also the force of his love of action involving open spaces and technology, which we see in two action sequences, the white-water testing of the boat that will figure in the movie, and the stunt flying sequence. Both of these are presented as forms of teasing, of his cautious English unit manager Ralph Lockhart (Alun Armstrong) and of Verrill, respectively. As expositions of American freedom and fun, they can be compared with the stunt-flying episode at the beginning of Capra's *State of the Union*, where Spencer Tracy's credentials as an American democrat are very much at issue.

The contrast between Verrill and Wilson is expressed in the early sequences in Africa, in which we see Verrill assume the habits of the colonial community, playing tennis in whites, and joining in the football match. Wilson's role is of the defender of rights; we see the rhetorical demolition of an antisemitic female dinner guest and an actual fight with a racist hotel manager. Although he literally loses the fight, these sequences are essentially celebratory, of Wilson's American brio and confidence. Like the Jewish wedding and southern tour sequences of *Bird*, they are a temporary and local triumph over religious and racial intolerance.

The fight sequence raises another issue. It is made clear that Wilson's moral triumph lies in taking on a fight that he is bound to lose against a much younger man. The Wilson of the novel is implicitly Huston's age at the time, in his mid-forties, and loses the fight because he is drunk. Eastwood, who is not made up to look particularly young, was in his sixtieth year when the film was released. In the hunting sequences, this subject is emphasised – at one point, Wilson actually collapses after a gruelling safari. We can relate this diminution of individual potency to something that suggests another ending, Eastwood's presentation, from the perspective of 1990, of the end of colonial rule in Africa. Part of this is expressed through the dramatising of the embattled quality of this last generation of colonial whites, and part through visual material, the impression of the white presence as invasions of technology. Early in the African footage, we see Lockhart cursing as he drives a car down a crowded track, forcing the native pedestrians off the road. Towards the end, the cast and crew of 'The African Trader' appear in longer and longer convoys of vehicles, moving across country.

All these subjects could be considered by locating them within a wide context of American cultural representation: the adventure of hunting, male companionship, the relationship to a member of another race, the hero's awareness of his own relationship to time, the invasion of a natural world by technologies, and the confrontation between man and beast as a moment of particular grandeur because behind it lies some sense of a unique loss of opportunity, of a moment that cannot be infinitely extended or repeated. The literary resonances of such material are not obscure. The very heavily travelled circuit of American literature and of discussions of it relevant here would have to include James Fenimore Cooper, Herman Melville, Mark Twain and William Faulkner, as well as Ernest Hemingway. Among literature popular in the early 'fifties, the specific context for Viertel's novel is to be found in the most famous of Hemingway's African stories, 'The Short, Happy Life of Francis Macomber' and 'The Snows of Kilimanjaro' – like Forester's *The African Queen* originally published in the 'thirties but substantially reprinted at this time – and Faulkner's story of hunting in the Mississippi delta that came to be known as 'The Bear'. Again, the earliest version of the latter, a short story called 'Lion', falls into an identical period, appearing in 1935.

At least some salient points about the film's position, and the distance it places between itself and Viertel's novel, can be divined by looking at one of these writers, whose presence in the background of novel and film is unavoidable, simply through the connection of hunting as subject and Africa as setting. This is Hemingway, a figure who exists both as the author of a set of texts and as a heavily mythologised life story and set of ideas that extend beyond any one text. Viertel's novel accepts the terms of Hemingway's hunting narratives, in which

Wilson is challenged by Landers (George Dzundza) in White Hunter, Black Heart.

hunting provides a way for spiritual renewal or triumph to coexist with loss or death. This is the basis of Hemingway's story 'The Short, Happy Life of Francis Macomber' (Macomber finds his courage but is shot dead in an 'accident') and the novella *The Old Man and the Sea* (the fisherman catches the great fish, then loses it to sharks) – the latter published to huge acclaim in the year before Viertel's novel. Viertel includes a brief direct mention of Macomber, and he uses the surname of the Shakespeare-quoting white hunter in Hemingway's story as his pseudonym for the Huston character.

In the novel, Wilson kills the bull elephant, acting against his white hunter's advice – the elephant is surrounded by 'cows and young ones'. In the ensuing melee, Kivu is killed, and this converts the kill into a matter of 'uselessness', failing in its purpose of offering spiritual renewal. Even the language in which this defeat is expressed is very close to Hemingway's; Viertel's 'everything seemed pointless and lost' recalls 'It makes everything wrong' (*The Old Man and the Sea*). The other important perspective on the episode is Verrill's – the potential of the hunt is expressed in Verrill's view of the spiritual cost to himself of refusing to be part of it:

'. . . I knew that what I felt was a desire to be there among the elephants with the others. . . It was envy and despair, and the feeling of having lost something eternally, as if a death had occurred inside me, a death that had been a long time in coming.'

Finally, Verrill says of the making of the film that it is 'foolish make-believe', as opposed to 'the reality he [Wilson] could not stamp out'.

Eastwood's film retains a little of this plotting, but makes several major changes. We are shown Wilson acting against advice, but this is reinflected by

American innocent? Wilson in his safari suit in White Hunter, Black Heart.

the presentation of him as an older man: just before the final move into the bush, we see him exhausted, clinging to a tree for support. His insistence on moving forward with Kivu – the line in the script, which is not in the novel, is 'Of course he'll go, he's got guts' – feels not like a piece of mysticism but a slightly petulant insistence that this situation is really a simple one. We then see Wilson face the bull elephant, but he does not shoot; we see the barrel of the gun in focus, then Wilson's face, then the safety catch being applied. Wilson watches a baby member of the herd and nods to himself. The control thus exercised is almost immediately exploded with Kivu (Boy Mathias Chuma) running forward to head off the bull – it is not clear if it is charging to protect its young – and being killed by the elephant.

The sequence has almost none of the novel's interest in the mystical qualities of the hunt, of the proof of masculinity through bravery or cowardice. Apart from Wilson's choice not to shoot, this is most clearly marked in the role of Verrill. Whereas in the novel the two were implicitly of the same age, in the film Verrill is a much younger man than Wilson and sees Wilson simply as foolish and unprofessional in view of his responsibility to the cast and crew of the film. The novel's discourse about eternal loss is reduced to Wilson twitting Verrill briefly about his guts. Verrill is part of the final hunt, present as a shocked witness at the death of Kivu.

What is presented in the novel as a ritual that goes wrong has here become a piece of naivety; Wilson's attitude to the hunt contains a refusal to acknowledge any serious danger until somebody is actually hurt. In his neat safari suit, Wilson is an American innocent – possibly his innocence consists partly in believing in his earlier Hemingwayesque justifications of hunting as a great 'sin'. In the end, he is satisfied with a moment of apparent control, expressed in the choice of not shooting the beast, but seeing it clearly, in detail. Eastwood acknowledges this with a self-conscious device, the sudden change of focus within the shot, from tip of gun barrel to Wilson's face, which expresses the shift from the weapon to the eye.

I am conscious of an apparent parallel here with the moment towards the end of Cimino's *The Deer Hunter* when Mike (Robert De Niro) makes a similar decision not to shoot the deer. This would seem to express a movement in 'eighties (that is, post-Vietnam) cinema in which the American hero is seen to have lost, in Robin Wood's phrase, his 'sense of his divine right' as a hunter. In Cimino's film, the sequences of shooting and then not shooting the deer are separated by the Vietnam war footage. The other connection seems to be the implication that while the hero can exercise control over this specific act of violence, a wider chaos flares up again almost immediately.

Eastwood offers an image of the arrival of the film crew as an invasion of technology. This is particularly true of the scenes in Kivu's village – we see the machinery of cinema being erected in the middle of the village, and this continues even when the hunting party returns with the news of Kivu's death. The final moments of the film oppose two rituals. The mourning and drum messages of the native world give way to the presentation of a series of professional roles – the actors, grips, sound men, camera operators – as the business of filmmaking begins. Alongside this is the opposition of two figures, Wilson and a young African boy, now presented in parallel shots as they watch each other over an unbridgeable gap.

The purpose of this does not seem to be to deride what the white world is doing, although it may be to remind the audience that its culture conceals rituals quite as strange, as theatrical, as those of this African village. It certainly serves to remind us, more sharply than anything else in the film, of the other realities, or fantasies, that are scattered around it: *The African Queen* (the principals are in recognisable costume now), Huston's roles as actor and his films as director, Eastwood's films and his own roles, the fact that what we are watching is a film. Wilson's penultimate line – the novel has nothing like it – is to Verrill: 'You were right, Pete, the ending is all wrong.' He is talking about the script of 'The African Trader', the subject of previous discussions between the two, but he is also talking about the 'ending' that we have just seen, the power that his own naive fantasy of an encounter has turned out to have in affecting a reality.

The last word seems to be about the status of film. Wilson is now about to function as the director of the film, although the evocation of the other two directors in play is clear at this point. Eastwood seems to gesture to this in the shot here of the back of the chair, which reads, not 'Mr Wilson', but 'DIRECTOR'. Nothing will happen until Wilson initiates it – the tableau-like treatment of these last shots, the sense of stillness anticipating the break into movement, is very strong. In the final shot, the camera moves slowly in towards Wilson's face, in which the shame and grief of the events we have seen are registered. These emotions carry through to his delivery of his single, final word, which makes, and breaks, a spell: 'Action'. The word is both a command and a reminder that a filmed event is an action, an act of the imagination transferred into the physical world. So it is a reminder of the power of fantasy to change whatever reality is, not to be separable from it.

The status of film: Eastwood directing White Hunter, Black Heart.

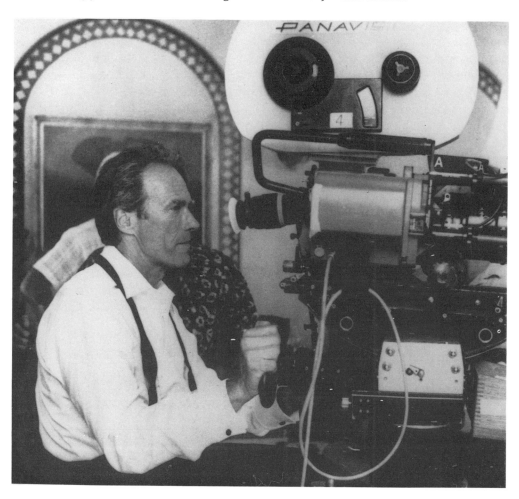

CHAPTER EIGHT
THE IDEA OF ORDER AT BIG WHISKEY

Both *Bird* and *White Hunter, Black Heart* were films that in Eastwood's characteristically calm phrase 'failed to find an audience'. A little earlier, *Pink Cadillac* had been the first recent Eastwood feature to be so unsuccessful that it received no theatrical release in the UK. It is important to remember that *Unforgiven* was conceived and made in the light of these apparently uncertain commercial omens; Eastwood has said that he was 'shocked' when the film started doing good business. The commercial success of the film (*Variety* reporting an American box office gross of over $100 million in July 1993) was substantial even by current standards.

At the Academy Awards in the Spring of 1993, *Unforgiven* was the subject of a string of nominations and lost in the minor, but won in the major categories – crucially both Best Picture and Best Director. Obviously, its already considerable commercial success ($81 million gross in the US by the end of March) was being acknowledged here, as no doubt was the industry's desire to compliment Eastwood at this stage in his career. A more difficult factor to evaluate would be the part played by Eastwood's use in supporting roles of substantial male stars, Gene Hackman, Morgan Freeman and Richard Harris, very much in contrast to the main balance of his work to that point.

Another issue that is pertinent to the status of the film is the matter of genre, the fact that *Unforgiven* is a western. Much of the praise heaped on the film has had the effect, intended or otherwise, of foregrounding Eastwood primarily as a director of westerns, as if the westerns were self-evidently his most important, best, or most enduring work. This is not only a matter of polemics, the argument for the historical depth and intense Americanness of the genre. It may also be a way of pushing other material, which for various reasons fits current views of Eastwood less comfortably – say, *Bronco Billy*, or *Bird*, or *Heartbreak Ridge* – into the background.

I do not wish to avoid considering *Unforgiven* as a western. Part of its appeal lies in the very accessible way in which it explores familiar western themes through the Eastwood and Hackman characters. But in important respects, it is quite unlike Eastwood's earlier uses of the western, which are themselves by no means a homogenous group. To understand it we need to look both inside and outside the genre.

I will begin at a point which stresses the generic western subjects of settlement and social order, a sequence which takes place some way into the running time of the film. It opens with an image that could be taken as a bow in the direction of the late Sergio Leone, with his taste for American history – the film is dedicated to 'Sergio and Don'. The shot is of a Northwestern Railroad locomotive making its way through Wyoming in 1881. We move into the train's interior, and into something that is historically identifiable, a discussion of the assassination of President Garfield. The argument is about democracy – a European voice is claiming the superiority of monarchy over democratically elected office. As a cowboy hastily shuts up his aggressive partner, it emerges that the speaker is English Bob (Richard Harris), a deadly gunfighter now employed 'to shoot China-men' by the railways. We know enough of the plot of the film by this point to assume that English Bob is travelling to the Wyoming town of Big Whiskey as an assassin, to kill two men and collect a bounty of $1,000.

After a little teasing of these democrats, English Bob disembarks from the train and boards the crude stagecoach that will take him into Big Whiskey. He is still describing America, and his topic is the enduring one of assassinations: '. . . it's the climate that does it, that and the infernal distances . . . induces people to shoot persons in high places . . . it's a savage country, really.' As the stagecoach pulls into town, Eastwood includes a shot which is a visual expression of similar feelings. The stagecoach is framed between the buildings on either side of main street at the point at which the street dissolves into open country, the whole image dominated by the vast mountain ranges in the background (Eastwood is actually using Alberta to stand in for Wyoming).

The connection can be made with the town (not the mining settlement) that we see in *Pale Rider*, and with Lago in *High Plains Drifter*, not places that are presented as destined to grow into the cities of twentieth-century America, but marginal settlements, hanging on in the face of hostile conditions to semblances of civilisation, having a sense of themselves as remote, on the edge of uninhabitable high mountain country.

The idea of order in such a place is shown to turn on the difference between the armed and the defenceless. We see the confrontation between English Bob and Little Bill Daggett (Gene Hackman), the town's sheriff, in which Bob is encircled by guns, disarmed and then violently beaten by Daggett as a warning to other bounty hunters not to come to Big Whiskey. Law here is enforced not by a high degree of skill with a weapon, the quick draw or the accurate aim, but by crude firepower, the fact of being surrounded by a body of armed men. (The point is made earlier through a gag about one of Daggett's deputies, a man with one arm and three guns.)

The film opens with another version of the confrontation between the armed and the defenceless. We are in the whorehouse, on a gothically terrible night. An imagined slight to his masculinity causes a local trailhand, aided with some reluctance by another, to use a knife to slash the face of the woman who has offended him. The other whores are helpless to prevent this, and the attack ends only when the brothel owner, Skinny (Anthony James) puts a pistol to the attacker's head. Daggett now prepares to bull-whip the men, but abandons this when Skinny points out that what is at stake is not blood vengeance but property rights. The spoiled whore Delilah (Anna Thomson) represents an 'investment of capital' on his part that must be the subject of restitution. Daggett's proposal, a number of ponies to be given to Skinny by each man according to the gravity of his offence, is met by outrage from the spokeswoman of the whores, Strawberry Alice (Frances Fisher), in an unsurprising enough response: 'Maybe we ain't nothing but whores, but we – by God, we ain't horses.'

After an intervening sequence with the Eastwood character, we see the two men return to town with the ponies for Skinny on a bright spring day – one of the few breaks in the hostile climate. The sequence begins by continuing the previous mood, with the whores – Delilah apart – expressing their rage at the cool camaraderie of the exchange between the men by pelting them with dirt. Quick Mike (David Mucci), the trailhand who actually attacked Delilah, now rides off, and there is a plot twist. It emerges that the younger man, Davey (Rob Campbell), has brought another of his ponies, the best of them all, as a gift for 'the lady that my partner cut'.

This is an important moment in *Unforgiven*, expressive of the limit to which a plea for forgiveness can be taken, of how far the social order which we are seeing here is capable of change. The tempo of the sequence slows in a series of close-ups as the whores consider the possibility of a world based on impulses other than bodily urges and property rights – a gesture expressive of the difficulty of this moment is when one young woman lifts a muddied hand to her brow. But the offer is doomed – behind the young trailhand is an unlikely but appropriate sign – its message reads 'Meat Market'. It is Strawberry Alice who speaks in furious rejection of the gift, and again – now Delilah and another girl are exceptions – the whores throw dirt at the retreating cowhand. Eastwood ends the sequence with another series of close-ups, as the women recognise that they are trapped within the closed categories of their society.

The importance of the sequence is that it expresses the paradox at the heart of the presentation of Big Whiskey, a place in which it seems that a movement away from a degraded and barbarous order cannot actually be achieved, but where the possibility of something better is persistently sensed, and felt to be perhaps only just out of reach. It remains an intensely violent world surrounded by dreams of reason and order, which sounds like a metaphor for a view of America.

Such feelings are to be found not only in the traditional embodiment of an impulse towards civilisation in westerns, that is, in women. They are also to be found in Little Bill. Consider his biography. We learn that he came out of 'Kansas and Texas . . . he worked those tough towns', the west of some past period of turmoil. In his conversation with English Bob, he acknowledges that he has changed his appearance since that time and even suggests that moving across America can amount to believing that you are reborn: 'Hell, even I thought I was dead, till I found out it was just that I was in Nebraska.' His belief that his new life as sheriff of Big Whiskey expresses a desire for settlement and order is contained in the obvious metaphor of his building himself a home on the edge of town, and particularly a porch where he imagines himself in domestic repose, drinking coffee and watching the sunset. The gag here is that Little Bill, for all the coolness and skill developed during his time as a gunfighter, is an inept pioneer – 'He don't have a straight angle in that whole goddamn porch.' But rather than being a crude expression of failure, of ineptitude as representing the thinness of the fantasy, this perhaps expresses the intensity of the otherwise inarticulate impulse contained in constructing the house at all, Little Bill's unselfconscious pride in his own single-handed achievement. This is a man who can imagine the domestic only in this way; there is no sign even of the idea of a sexual partner.

Little Bill's belief that he is making Big Whiskey into a place that can be civilised stretches from the private dream of individual repose to an idea of civic order. The basis of this is a familiar line of American thinking, that the town can be protected from invasions from outside, from the disorder that would be imported by outsiders with no attachments to the place. This is clearly the point of the ordinance forbidding the carrying of guns in Big Whiskey, which is applied to strangers only. Within the town, the other men that we see are Daggett's heavily armed 'deputies', and we have seen in the opening sequence that Skinny has access to a pistol. Some related thinking also appears in Bill's explanation to Strawberry Alice of why he is not going to whip the two trailhands:

'It ain't like they was tramps, or loafers, or bad men . . . you know, they were just hard-working boys that was foolish. If they was given over to wickedness in a regular way . . .'

The opposition here between 'tramps' and 'hard-working boys' acknowledges that the decision has nothing to do with Delilah, and everything to do with Bill's judgements being based in estimates of worth drawn from the public world, the exterior stage which is the dominant realm of Big Whiskey. The detail of set and costume emphasise this here, in one of several scenes where the qualities of the world of exteriors intrude into the film's interior spaces. Bill's words are spoken on the dimly lit set of the bar of the saloon/brothel, and Alice, like the other women, is wearing a peignoir; Little Bill stands over her, still wearing his soaking waterproofs.

The point is recast later in the only scene set inside Bill's unfinished house, when he again speaks of disorder, of tramps in the saloons, as the water pours in through the ineptly made roof of the dwelling. In the next scene, he gives an example of this feeling in action, with a rhetoric referring to 'prosperous communities' as he disarms and beats up a sick old man in the saloon, and sends him crawling out into the storm. (This is the third occasion in the film when we see an attack presented through the image of the bloody, injured head of the victim, as if it is not the body, but what is represented by the brain or the senses, that this community feels as a threat.)

The sadism of this scene, the fact that this victim is obviously ill, the relish in the cruelty of allowing him to crawl out into the hellish weather, is marked on the faces of the audience in the saloon. This horror is carried out in the light of the belief that Bill has about himself, that he is a reformed man, the saviour of the town. The belief never essentially wavers – as he is dying, he will say to the Eastwood character: 'I don't deserve this, to die like this; I was building a house.' There is probably no intentional echo here of one of the last comments made by Charlie Parker in *Bird* on the duty to maintain a home properly. The point is only that such sentiments express the way in which such a character might imagine himself, in the end, to be a good American, a settler.

Readers familiar with *Unforgiven* will be aware that I have omitted one fact from the previous discussion. This is that the sad, sick old man who is the subject of Bill's violence is the character played by Eastwood. I have omitted it because I wished to look at the scene as it appears from Bill's perspective, and he has not at this point identified the Eastwood character. But to understand what this man is seeking in the scene, why he might allow himself to be so

'I ain't like that no more' – Eastwood as William Munny in Unforgiven.

terribly beaten, we must explore what kind of man he is – or thinks or hopes he is – for, as with Little Bill, the film is deeply involved here with the possibility of changing one's life, or imagining a changed life.

William Munny (Eastwood) is 'a known thief and murderer, a man of notoriously vicious and intemperate disposition', according to the written titles that interrupt the opening credits. We learn that he is civilised by a woman, and becomes a farmer – the film's first image, in long shot, establishes the fact of the wife's death. The film then takes us to Big Whiskey, to the night of the attack on Delilah and the whores' subsequent decision to offer a reward for the punishment of her attackers. This is followed by the Kansas sequence in which the Eastwood character first appears; he is visited by a young gunslinger, the Schofield Kid (Jaimz Woolvett). We see a pen in which a man is tussling in the mud with pigs. It is the Kid who is given the authority of being introduced by the device of being heard before he is seen. His line is an irony, or a puzzled challenge: 'You don't look like no rootin' tootin' son-of-a-bitch killer.' Eastwood – we can see now who it is – looks up from the filth to this icon of romance, a rider on horseback. Munny acknowledges reluctantly that he was once a gunman, but he rejects the Kid's proposal that they form a partnership to kill the two trailhands: 'I ain't like that no more . . . my wife cured me of drinking and wickedness.'

The configuration of the older man called out of retirement to perform one further, final office in the trade that he once practised is not specific to a genre. Not only gunfighters, but private eyes, cops, hoods, spies, even magicians can find themselves in this position, sometimes, as here, as the result of a call from a younger man who is privy to the past but not part of it. It is also interesting to recognise it as a device in war movies – elements of it are present in two previous war films with Eastwood as both star and director, *Firefox* and *Heartbreak Ridge*.

One element of this configuration is that a substantial period of time has elapsed since the act of 'retirement' (which distinguishes it from narratives that consider the last raid, the last patrol, a final caper that is supposedly going to precede retirement). The meaning of any given version of the configuration obviously depends on the past being returned to, the reasons for the original retirement, and how we understand the period since then to have been spent. Where the past world is remembered as benign, retirement may represent the assertion that older, better times have been overtaken by a new order and new methods, which leave no place for the hero, whose retirement is prompted by a sense that he is now out of fashion. But where the past is malign and the retirement is in the nature of a flight or a concealment, the point may be the impossibility of escaping the past and the dream of doing so.

A good example of the latter is the opening of a *film noir*, Jacques Tourneur's *Out of the Past*, in which Jeff Markham (Robert Mitchum) has fled a past that includes gangsters, a murder, and betrayal by a woman. He is now, under another name, running a gas station in a small town. Every day, he goes fishing with his new love, a local girl, and Tourneur includes a scene between these two in which dreams of a future, of a house by a lakeside, are interrupted by the news of the appearance of a man with business from the past.

Compare this with Munny's situation. His past appears as names or places and incidents recited by the Kid. This is not done in the service of presenting any one of them as unfinished business – it exactly expresses the anarchy of the past times that nobody has come to seek out Munny in a spirit of vengeance, and the plot will not involve this. It is, rather, a matter of telling him who he is. Quoting his uncle, a companion from the past who has sent him to Munny, the Kid says, 'if I ever wanted a partner for a killing, you were the worst one [*a pause, and an interpolated shot of Munny follow here*] meaning the best'.

But while the past does not return literally in a plot or character, there is ample evidence that it has not been escaped. Eastwood's film contains a trope identical to Tourneur's – that is, redemption by a woman – but where Tourneur offers the presence of the woman, the pathos of an escape into a new life that is almost palpable, Eastwood's film opens with the woman already dead, and the resonances of the images here are sombre. It does not need deep sensitivity to the use of animals as symbols to recognise that the fact that Munny farms pigs, not sheep or cattle, can be placed alongside the loneliness of the farm (Munny says, 'We don't see no one out here'), and the fact that the animals are ill underlines this place as a site of penance, a self-imposed sentence of hard labour rather than a rural idyll. The opening shot of the whole sequence, of a little girl in a pinafore running across the Kansas prairie to the pig-pen, seems to be prompting us to recollect a famous cinematic image of the American Depression, the Kansas sequence of *The Wizard of Oz*.

This sequence ends almost exactly where it began, with the hero in the mud, looking from the pigpen at the image of the rider on horseback on the horizon. When we return to the farm it emerges that Munny has decided to follow the Kid. The possible reasons include collecting the money, enough to end the penitential era of the pigfarm and give his two children a better start. This is the reason that Munny gives to himself, and to Ned Logan (Morgan Freeman), his old partner. Another may be simply to ride again, and ride with Ned – the shots of the two on horseback heavily emphasise the sensuousness of unfettered movement across the open spaces of America, and, of course, another important American myth is being tacitly re-enacted here, the racial reconciliation implied as black and white partners travel together.

There is a further, more specific reason. When Munny dismissively asks what crime the trail hands have committed, the Kid replies: '. . . cutting up a lady. They cut up her face, cut her eyes out, cut her ears off, hell, they even cut her teats.' When Munny is persuading Ned into the expedition, he repeats this list almost verbatim, ending it with '. . . cut her teats . . . everything but her cunny, I suppose.' Ned's response is a formula which will emerge almost as the tag-line of the movie: 'I guess they've got it coming.' Later in the film, it will be repeated by Strawberry Alice and then by the Kid, and turned, in a shift very typical of the Eastwood persona, from a local judgement into a statement of acceptance of a condition: 'We've all got it coming, Kid.'

We know, of course, that the accounts of Delilah's maiming are not true, but more is at stake than the exaggerations of rumour and distance. In order to mount the expedition, the older men have to understand themselves to be avenging womanhood, which is imagined as being subject to terrible carnal atrocity. Their own past crimes, or at least their image of them, are centred around the killing of men, and thus the distinction can be preserved between their earlier deeds and the image of themselves as defenders of womanhood, men reformed by the love of good women. (It is significant that no comment is made about this exaggeration when the men arrive in Big Whiskey.)

This is part of a more widely felt attitude to women in the film. In a world from which intimacy between men and women is entirely absent (I am not thinking of the basic physical kind, which certainly happens), many of the men preserve fragments of a fantasy of the sacredness of womanhood, and the duty owed to it, as their fragile proof to themselves that they are not barbarians but participants in a civilised order. Daggett's professed reluctance to hurt women, or the common consent to the euphemism of 'billiards' for prostitution are minor examples of this. The scene in which Munny prepares to leave for Wyoming is exemplary of the fragility. His advice to his children is a melange of practical instruction and pious admonition, on killing chickens and remembering 'how the spirit of your dear departed Ma watches over you'. But the flat way in which this line is delivered recalls some of the qualities of the character played by Eastwood in *Bronco Billy*, a delivery that seems to acknowledge the possibility that the line is only a formula, almost a quotation or a magic charm, of uncertain application to the particular situation. We might link this to the ambiguous role of religion in *Unforgiven* – it is never really clear if Munny's belief is much more than superstition, and a major image of civilisation in westerns is reduced to a subdued echo: the only crosses in Big Whiskey are holding up the whores' washing lines.

As the three bounty hunters approach Wyoming, various conversations include Munny's assertion that he is a changed man, defining himself through denial of the body. He tells Ned that he has no sexual relations with women: 'I don't miss it that much.' But he is also haunted by the past, not only by guilt but by its horror, by images of violent destruction of the body. His insistence that he is no longer the man he was is expressed in the film's use of whiskey, which here, as in *The Outlaw Josey Wales*, has a ritual significance. Refusing to drink in the pouring rain as they approach the town causes Munny to develop a fever, like his hogs. His first line to Daggett is 'I ain't drunk', and by this time he has taken on the identity of one of the men that he killed – he tells Daggett that his name is William Hendershot. This seems like atonement – identifying with his victim and causing himself to be punished. These visions of horror come to a climax in the sequences in the abandoned building outside town where the three take refuge after Munny's beating by Daggett. There, even the memory of Munny's wife Claudia becomes only an image of horror, and the life of this apparently dying man is acknowledged as a matter of shame: 'Don't tell my kids none of the things I done.'

These details are important because they so clearly set the scene for a drama of redemption, a film in which Munny would return from this ritual death free of the past, and with a new relationship to the present. In fact, his recovery offers only the most temporary redemption. He awakes, in what is I think the central scene of *Unforgiven*, face to face for the first and only time with Delilah, who is nursing him. The scene is immaculately performed by both actors. Their exchanges touch on her scars and his, the killing of the two trailhands, the payment for the killing, and the advances against the payment – the use of two of the prostitutes by Logan and the Kid for sex. Delilah calls these encounters 'free ones'; she shyly asks Munny if he would like a 'free one'. When he declines, she stumbles for a moment with embarrassment: of course, she did not mean to imply that he would want her – the other unscarred women would gladly oblige. Munny replies with a speech about her being a beautiful woman, but he must be faithful to his wife, 'watching over my little ones' in Kansas. This speech is accompanied by the guitar melody that opens and closes the film.

Is this just sentimentality? The scene can be approached by considering what is at stake in the way in which Eastwood has chosen to present Delilah's scars. Given the current state of technical expertise in such matters, a wide range of possible effects could have been shown, from minimal to severe disfigurement, or a horror implied through the device of concealment of the face. However, Delilah's scars are presented to our vision almost as if they were make-up, marks on the face painted on as a sign of difference – a little like the marks on the face of a woman captured by Indians in another kind of western. (As in so many seminal American films of the last two decades, there is a strong echo of *The Searchers*, that is, of a journey ending in an encounter with a woman who is both desirable and proscribed.) The scars do not conceal Delilah's desirability, but they are seen by the rest of Big Whiskey as massively disfiguring, rendering her untouchable for sexual purposes. Alice's line as she throws mud at the younger trailhand is: 'She ain't got no face left – you're going to give her a god-damn mangy pony?' And Skinny believes that Delilah can be made desirable only by turning her mutilation into a mystery, by the wearing of a veil.

Temporary redemption: Munny is nursed by Delilah (Anna Thomson) in Unforgiven.

Then there is Delilah's view of herself. On the one hand, the two trailhands are to be killed, $1,000 will be paid, Ned and the Kid enjoy their 'free ones' – for all this to be the case, and the conversation with Munny confirms it as unalterably true, her scarred face must somehow represent the violence and rage that is about to be unleashed again. But part of the paradox of her status is that the scarring has removed her from the category of prostitute. In this scene, she is dressed in demure grey, and as Munny assures her of her desirability, she puts on an elaborate bonnet which completes the iconography of a Victorian heroine – the Jane Eyre of Wyoming.

I do not mean the connection facetiously. Munny's telling Delilah that he would want her if he were not married is an invitation to put herself in the position not of whore but of a heroine without money or great beauty, who is denied by circumstance intimacy with a man but whose worth is expressed through her holding on to an ideal of marital fidelity which will have to determine both their positions. This sounds not unlike the plot of *Jane Eyre* at the point of Jane's aborted marriage. The difference is equally suggestive – in Charlotte Brontë's novel, the woman who prevents the union exists, and it is the work of that narrative to dispose of her so that the lovers can be united. The pathos of Munny's and Delilah's position is that the 'other woman' here is harder to dispose of, an internalised fantasy of the good wife and mother which Munny can offer, and Delilah can share. By sharing it, they can briefly participate in a little bit of imagined civilisation.

It is a civilisation that exists only in the imagination. The rigorousness of *Unforgiven* is indicated by the cut from this sequence to the killing of Davey, a messy and fumbled business enacted on the same pattern as one of Hemingway's African hunting stories, with its roles of confused onlooker (the Kid), unhappy marksman with no stomach for the kill (Ned), and cool white hunter (Munny), and its code of the 'good kill' expressed in lines like 'Better finish him before he gets clear . . . he gets in those rocks, we ain't going to get him, unless we go down there.' It is followed by Ned's departure and the killing of Quick Mike, shot at point-blank range by the Kid as he sits in what will later be referred to as a shit-house. We might assume that the use of this place is a modern, uncensored annotation of the 'reality' of the West, a reminder that western lives included bodily imperatives. But this has become old news, and the setting here addresses other issues. It is yet another stark example of how the executions in the world of this film consist not of gunfights but of brutal encounters between the armed and the defenceless, and have nothing to do with skill.

It is here that the whole matter of the Kid's short-sightedness becomes clear. The fact that the Kid cannot see more than a short distance is taken by Ned, apparently the only good shot of the three, to render his role as gunfighter, particularly with an accurate weapon, ironic or foolish. This of course has its possibly redemptive side; it is obvious from the start that the Kid's claims to be a killer are lies, mere adolescent boasting. But now it becomes clear that the Kid is in truth a gunfighter, in the sense that the film defines one. He is a man possessed not of skill, but of the preparedness to destroy others, a situation in which seeing clearly – think of the film's constant references, from all its principal gunmen, to being drunk – might be a positive disadvantage.

The plot now begins to unravel. As he rides back towards Kansas alone, Ned is captured, tortured by Little Bill and dies. (The scene between Ned and Dagget here is interestingly unsuccessful, as if there were a problem in imagining what a man with Daggett's proved urges to violence might do once provided with a real victim. Perhaps this is one of the occasions in the film where race matters – the conventions governing the presentation of the punishment of black by white may restrict what can be thought of here.)

The scene in which Munny learns of Ned's death extends and inverts the earlier scene between Munny and Delilah. Again the imagery seems to be of romance, the pretty girl in her cloak sitting on horseback – this time it is Little Sue (Tara Dawn Frederick), the whore who joined Delilah in not throwing mud at Davey. She has come not only to tell of Ned's death but to underline Munny's identity. There follows an unmissable device – exactly as she speaks the words, 'You was really William Munny out of Missouri', we see the character lift the whiskey bottle to his lips for the first time.

Munny's opening line in the final scene in the saloon – 'Who's the fellow owns this shit-hole' and his subsequent execution of the unarmed Skinny echo the killing of Quick Mike, and the shoot-out with Daggett and the deputies is a visual re-run of a story that Daggett has told earlier about a fight in the old days – the rifle misfires, Munny throws it at Daggett, the deputies struggle to draw and aim. We see how little skill and speed have to do with gun fighting, and how large a part is played by coolness, preparedness to kill, and chance.

To the end, Munny preserves some part of his understanding of himself as a figure charged with regulating gross barbarities, rather than committing them. Leaving town, he shouts instructions to the cowering townsfolk. They must bury Ned right, and had 'better not cut up or otherwise harm no whores'. The slight formality of 'or otherwise harm', suggests a lawgiver. What is insisted on is that Munny has to believe that all this violence is for something, that it can be made part of a dream of order. It is a dream related, of course, to Little Bill's beatings of outsiders, and to the fascination of both Little Bill and English Bob with the figure of the pulp writer, the man whose particular speciality is turning occasions of violence into the ordered categories of popular narrative.

When the fight is over, Munny speaks with this character, the writer W.W. Beauchamp (Saul Rubinek). Beauchamp tries to insist on a logic in gunfighting, but Munny replies 'I was lucky in the order, but I've always been lucky when it comes to killing folks.' There is no irony here, or none intended by the speaker – David Webb Peoples's unswervingly intelligent script contains a number of lines of this kind, in which a vocabulary that might have had positive associations (the words 'free', 'innocent', 'trust', 'mercy', 'hospitality', 'desire') is used in contexts that deny the values potentially implicit in it.

The final question about *Unforgiven* is the nature of the loss and the horror that lie in the background and that cannot be escaped. Consider one subject about which the characters never speak – that Ned is black – and add to it one moment in the action. Ned is stitching a wound, Munny's cut eye, by candlelight. When the Kid observes that he has obviously done this before, Ned replies, 'plenty of times . . .' What might be hinted at here is that in the distant past, ending sixteen years before these events, there was a brutal civil war fought between Americans. For Eastwood's contemporary audience, the America of 1992 buries its images of another peculiarly terrible war under something like the same distance of time travelled, from 1975 to 1992. (It appears that David Webb Peoples's original script was written in the late 1970s, much closer to the trauma of the Vietnam war.)

I do not mean to argue anything so crude as that *Unforgiven* really refers to the Vietnam war. Indeed, part of its force comes from the lack of specificity, the veil drawn over all but a corner of the terrible history shared by Munny and Ned, the legacy of a vision of horrific violence to the body, the knowledge of the

English Bob (Richard Harris) and W.W. Beauchamp (Saul Rubinek) in Unforgiven.

destruction (at the distances made possible by weapons technology) of women and children, and, lurking behind these, even more terrible atrocities.

It may be possible to express the connection more exactly by considering the two films directed by Eastwood that directly invoke the Vietnam war. We find the figure of the traumatised veteran, subject to flashbacks from the past, in *Firefox* (1982). By 1985, in *Heartbreak Ridge* we find another strategy, the attempt to locate the war, or such elements of it as are amenable to this treatment, within a tradition of martial honour, symbolised by the framed black-and-white still photograph. Is it perhaps that these strategies may reflect changing attitudes and impulses in the 1980s – ways in which it was desired, or ways in which it had become possible, to think of this particular American past?

Unforgiven might be taken as relating similarly to the quality such memories have assumed by the early 1990s. What it presents is a past that has retreated to a set of names, essentially geographical place names. These are not horrors that are in the mind – no flashbacks here – but rather acknowledgements of the horror and shame that lie behind a bare name or date that we could recall if we wanted to, or could bear to. The connection to Vietnam is this reproduction of how that war (but not, of course, only that war) might now be experienced.

The film ends with a divergence between image and narrative. The closing titles tell us of a positive impulse that is loosely related to other narratives of warfare, a mother's difficult journey to her child's grave. They also indicate the limits of understanding, the puzzle of why Claudia married Munny, in a story that ends, in appropriate American fashion (precedents are as various as Herman Melville's 'Bartleby' or F. Scott Fitzgerald's *Tender is the Night*), by fading into rumour and vague report. But Eastwood does not show us on screen, say, a woman bending over a grave. Instead a line of washing dissolves into nothing, and the final image – not freeze-frame, but with the camera left, as it were, running – is of the empty house in Kansas. It has not collapsed, nor is it re-occupied; it remains as a promise, or a monument, the one material structure that symbolises settlement.

In the Line of Fire

In *In the Line of Fire*, Eastwood plays the part of Frank Horrigan, a Secret Service agent. Thirty years before, on duty by the limousine in which President Kennedy was assassinated, he had been unable to react fast enough to place himself in the path of the second, fatal bullet. Now a new assassin threatens, and Horrigan will redeem the past by taking the bullet meant for the President.

Wolfgang Petersen's successful thriller celebrates the glamour of technology – a fingerprint library search on computer, and a modernised version of the old routine of a telephone conversation that carries on as technicians scramble to identify the location of the line – and combines it with the spectacle of the sheer scale of superpower agencies. The reassuring plot is that, after all, the solution to threat turns out to depend on one man, his perseverance and his alertness to detail. Typically, the hero sees something that everyone else has missed (here it is another old device – a casual remark prompts Horrigan to decipher the code that indirectly reveals the assassin's alias) and has the luck and self-reliance to arrive in the nick of time. It is a reassuring fable in which paranoia plays no part – this time, the assassin really is a lone gunman, defeated by a single agent.

Implicit comparisons are made in the film between the Kennedy assassination and the present time. Some elements remain unchanged – the impossibility of adequately protecting a President against a determined gunman in a public space, particularly when the imperatives of electioneering require that he expose himself to public view and touch. In contrast, there are small ways in which the presentation of the assassin signifies the modern. He is a technocrat, outwitting security systems with a weapon made of a material invisible to scanning devices. But, in an echo of *Dirty Harry*, he is also reassuringly a psychotic, enjoying murder and craving publicity and the 'game' of the assassination attempt.

The main interest is the characterisation of his past. As a rogue CIA officer, trained to kill by the American government, Leary (John Malkovitch) represents some minimal acknowledgement of American guilt for the covert operations of the post-Vietnam period; as the photographs of his past indicate, his is an American bourgeois life gone wrong. That this fact is an uncomfortable one for Americans who would prefer to believe that assassins must come from a racial or economic underclass is suggested by the reaction to his various disguises. Early in the film, Horrigan instantly spots Leary masquerading as a city derelict in denims and long hair. He fails to recognise him in the role of a rich American businessman chatting casually about the Japanese trade threat, and the photofit pictures used by the secret service stress the image of Leary as worker or hippie, not as bourgeois.

The greatest difference between the views of past and present in the film lies in the attitude to the presidency itself. A current cycle of films touching on this subject emphasises the importance of the President's role as public icon, the manipulations of the power brokers who determine and control it, and the distance between his public and private qualities. This can be inflected as outright comedy, as in *Dave* (Ivan Reitman, 1993), in which the President is a shallow womaniser, but even in *The Pelican Brief* (Alan J. Pakula, 1993), a thriller not too far in genre from Petersen's film, the President is shown as a pawn, absorbed in trying to teach his dog a new trick – rolling over for its owner – while the agencies around him govern and manipulate power.

Petersen's purposes are not quite satirical, but he portrays the President as an anonymous middle-aged icon. The systems of protection or promotion operate around him, and he functions within them almost as a passive object. A good example of this is the climactic assassination attempt, in which Petersen shows his flair for very fast action sequences as the secret servicemen whisk the President out of the building at top speed and bundle him into his limousine.

Horrigan characterises times past with the words 'he [Kennedy] was different', and the difference is symbolised by Kennedy's sexual energies. An anecdote of a sexual escapade in which Horrigan took the blame and protected the President from odium is told as a positive example of the zest of youth – implicitly Horrigan's as well as Kennedy's. Now Horrigan will put himself in the line of fire, but he is defending an abstract principle – that of doing his job properly – rather than any personal loyalty. It is through the insistence on this point that the part is related to Eastwood's roles as Harry Callahan.

There is another way of reading Eastwood's role in the film, or rather, his presence in it. This is through the moments of punning on the connection between Eastwood's life – or the life of a film director and actor rather like Eastwood – and the experience of the character whom he plays in this film. Consider these facts about Horrigan. He is over fifty and has been doing the same job for thirty years, in spite of recent suggestions that he might retire. In the early years of that job, he has appeared in a movie which very large numbers of Americans have seen. (It is supposedly the Zapruder film of the Kennedy assassination, which is credited.) In the course of his working life, he has had contact with more than one President of the United States; he tells agent Lilly Raines (Rene Russo), the woman whom he courts during the film, that he once played a passable duet with Nixon. He is a lover of jazz, as both a listener and a pianist. He refers to himself at one point as a 'living legend', and at another as representing a sup-posedly marginal but powerful group – white heterosexual males over fifty. At the beginning of one of the telephone calls to Horrigan, Leary tells him that he has been watching some of Horrigan's old movies – of course, Leary is referring to Kennedy material, but this is the moment when the punning is closest to becoming overt in the film. In order to make love with Lilly, Horrigan has to divest himself of a whole load of technical junk relating to his job – he is depressed by the thought of taking it all up again.

These details suggest that Eastwood wants to remind us of who he is, the fêted Oscar-winning director, and this is supported by references to the subject of acting and direction. The most obvious is the sequence on the steps of the Lincoln Memorial, where Horrigan has been sitting with Lilly, and apparently annoying her – his way of wooing her. As she walks away, he tells himself, and so us, that if she turns to look back at him 'she's interested'. Of course, she turns; later on in the film, she will repeat the gesture, and we will know what it means. There is an analogous piece of business, this time a neatly paced repeated detail to do with the opening of car doors, in Robert De Niro's *A Bronx Tale* (1993). It seems that these actor/directors want to remind us of what Stanley Cavell called 'the power of film to materialise and satisfy . . . human wishes that escape the satisfaction of the world as it stands' (*Themes out of School*, p.180).

This can be connected with the opening sequence of the film, in which we see Horrigan in an undercover operation, forced to prove his genuineness as a criminal. He is handed a gun; he must place it to his partner's temple and pull the trigger. (There is a dim echo here of a related moment early in *Dirty Harry*.) The gun turns out not to be loaded; after the occasion has been satisfactorily resolved, there is a moment close to comedy when the partner anxiously inter-rogates Horrigan as to whether he knew it was empty – 'You knew from the weight, right?' Horrigan won't exactly confirm this. It is as if something else were at stake, some other answer, an understanding of the incident as something that happens on film, something that the character cannot convey.

At the very end of the film, Eastwood's sense of having fun with this condition is uppermost. The lovers are back on the steps of the Lincoln Memorial, and there is a gag about Horrigan's knowing which of the pigeons that they are watching will fly away first (we cannot see them). He has spoken about his knowledge of the world several times in the course of the film and now closes it with a version of this, a boast to Lilly: 'I know about pigeons'. What does he know – what is this drollery trying to tell us? At the risk of being heavy-handed, I suggest that he is reminding us where we are – in the cinema – and saying that what he knows is what can be made of things like these when they are filmed and put on the screen for us.

CHAPTER NINE
THE RAGGED PROMISED LAND

There is one persistent configuration in Eastwood's work which can be established most clearly by means of two lists, both of women, but in neither case the female leads of the movies. The first is of women who do not appear at all on the screen and have no direct relationship to the plot. Their existence is part of the condition of the Eastwood character; they inform his view of the world and influence what he does or can imagine. They are: the woman whom the hero remembers he knew when 'there was no-one there to help' in *A Fistful of Dollars*; Harry's wife, who died – 'there was no reason for it, really' – before the action of *Dirty Harry*; the unfaithful wife whom a shoe salesman shot in an earlier time, before he took on the identity of Bronco Billy; the 'raw-boned okie girl', the lost love whose story Red Stovall tells in *Honkytonk Man*; Claudia Feathers Munny, dead of smallpox – the husband's digging of his wife's grave is part of the image that opens *Unforgiven*. The only image on screen of any of these women is a framed photograph of Claudia.

Alongside this list we could place another, of women whose death or loss forms part of the events that initiate or develop the plot of the film, but who are not substantial characters in it. These women appear only briefly: Colonel Mortimer's raped sister in flashback in *For a Few Dollars More*; the female swimmer, who dies in the pre-credits sequence of *Dirty Harry*; Ann Mary Deacon, whose body is seen in longshot in *Dirty Harry*; Josey Wales's wife, murdered in the opening seconds of *The Outlaw Josey Wales*; the woman injured by Billy in the circus act at the opening of *Bronco Billy*; the catatonic rape victim of *Sudden Impact*; the wife who has left Wes Block before the opening of *Tightrope*. Possibly I should add Sally Two Trees, the Indian woman who Munny believes has given him the 'evil eye' in *Unforgiven*.

None of these women plays more than a minor part. I mention them to establish how widely distributed in Eastwood's work (although of course not exclusive to it) is the idea that the deficiencies of the worlds portrayed in the films can be expressed through failures that have to do with women. These can be either the absence of proper relationships between men and women, or failure to prevent women becoming the victims of violence. The anonymity of this army of dead or lost women is important. As I have mentioned, what happens to them is the result not of freak or anomalous occurrences but of a milieu characterised by its treatment of women. This may be demonstrated either in the antagonists to Eastwood or in the impulses of the Eastwood figure himself. Again, the relative anonymity (the exception is John Malkovitch in *In the Line of Fire*) of the actors who play villains in Eastwood's work is important. Not using stars as the villains stresses not the uniqueness, but the typicality, almost the anonymity, of the roles they play.

Some of these issues are taken up in *Play Misty for Me*. The first half of the film, at least, makes clear that the failure of Dave and Evelyn in their dealings with each other belongs to both of them, and springs from their view of themselves, of their public and private roles, of what an appetite is and how such a thing might be satisfied, and the uselessness of their mutual violence. This is presented without having to dump either character into the category of the psychopath – the man or woman defined as being essentially unlike anyone else, as somehow outside society. This is what the second half of *Play Misty for Me* does with Evelyn. *Dirty Harry* is a simpler case, identifying the antagonist as a psychopath and the protagonist as his professional opponent, a homicide cop.

What does such professionalism consist of? Clive Bush, exploring the development of the view of professionals as the 'arbiters of the social in Western Society' in the early decades of the century, has summed up the figure in a list that echoes Callahan's qualities: the hostility to 'political' issues, the claim to objectivity, the pride in knowing more than his masters. Bush continues:

'[A profession] could distinguish itself from the mass of working class people on the double basis of the moral superiority of its regularised lifestyle while offering those same working people 'help'. Its watchword was service, not profit.' (*Halfway to Revolution*, p.427)

Dirty Harry explores the way in which this view of a cop's role might sustain him, while also revealing its limits – limits both to Callahan's actions against the psychopath (the intrusion of emotion) and also to Callahan's understanding of what he is. His objectivity, negatively felt, becomes an inability to explain, when pressed, why he carries on as a cop at all.

The reassurances, if such they are, of *Play Misty for Me* and *Dirty Harry* reside in seeing a character put into the category of psychopath, and then in seeing the psychopath dispatched, literally falling from a height in both cases. This does nothing for the world, leaving it minus only one individual who expresses its violence; *Play Misty for Me* is very different from the kind of horror film which is firmly convinced of the perfection of its surviving couple.

The vision is even more bleak in *High Plains Drifter* and *Magnum Force*. The social worlds of both films are presented as almost entirely worthless – the difference lies in the way in which cleansing them is metaphorically represented. The town of Lago can be shattered with explosives, burned, painted – as a settlement at a primitive stage of development its existence as a canvas suggests the possibility of renewal – it could perhaps become something else, and thus conceivably better. But the contemporary city as we see it in *Magnum Force* is an unreformable melange of crime, money and violence. The other strong link between the two is that the cleansing and revenge are carried out by a man who is utterly without the possibility that his act could in its turn release or redeem him from this bleakness. He is part of it, appearing as a dead man in the plot of *High Plains Drifter*. In *Magnum Force*, Callahan defends, partly from behind dark glasses, a social realm from which the idea of service has all but disappeared. The deadness, or the attitude for which deadness is a metaphor, is expressed in the sexual encounters that take place between the woman and Eastwood in the two films and have the blankness and apparent simplicity of emotional numbness. They figure as dimmed echoes of past loves and lovers, of Sarah Belding's possible feelings towards the dead Duncan in *High Plains Drifter*, and of the putative history of the unidentified woman, again seen only in a still photograph, by Callahan's bedside in *Magnum Force*.

In his subsequent career, Eastwood has opened up spaces for a degree of escape from this intolerable position. While *Breezy* is violently critical of both the milieux it examines, it is interested in the idea that in these circumstances what makes the couple work is their very oddity. Their difference in age and circumstance can prompt them to detach themselves from milieux into which they would otherwise fit more or less uneasily, and which would – of this the film is clearly certain – destroy them. So *Breezy* offers a couple who are the inheritors of a famous American tradition – mutually in flight from versions of what is termed civilisation, they exist in a condition not unrelated to that of Huck Finn and Jim drifting down the river – the same image of space and openness, the same sense of limitation, of having sooner or later to touch dry land. The final exchange of the film, the suggestion that as a couple they might last a year, expresses this space and this limitation.

The idea of oddity, of the odd couple or the group of oddities, who are able to escape from the terms of a hostile world because they refuse to assign themselves to any part of it, is important to two of Eastwood's best and most successful films of the 'seventies: *Thunderbolt and Lightfoot* and *The Outlaw Josey Wales*. The films share the remembering of a war and the image of a journey (not exactly of a literal kind) into the past. The groups in both films find themselves repeating a project (bank robbery, settlement) that previously ended in failure for others; at the ends of both journeys, the Eastwood figure finds himself in a place associated with the pieties of long ago, where it seems that some version of those pieties can still be remembered, or imagined. The image of visionary escape becomes associated not with the future but with the past, and with the quality of vision with which the past can be encountered.

In other ways, the films are widely divergent. Michael Cimino's exploration of the sexual tensions and frustrations, both heterosexual and homoerotic, which destroy the all-male group of his film, feeds into his argument that his characters are destroyed partly because they have no point of reference from the past to the sort of stability that is associated with a particular place, and no ambition except to keep moving. The conversation between Thunderbolt and Lightfoot as they wait for the 'Idaho Dream' is the film's most concise expression of this. The nicknames, from which the characters cannot detach themselves, are the film's indication of cramped identities. We might see Eastwood's film, with its movement from 'Josey Wales' to 'Mr. Wilson', as the opposite of Cimino's – re-discovering the site of the past becomes a deliberate project, as opposed to something stumbled into. This might be expressed through the difference between the places, the one-room schoolhouse in *Thunderbolt and Lightfoot* expressive of the appropriation of the past into the categories of 'heritage', and the abandoned homestead of *The Outlaw Josey Wales* as something soiled and broken that can be made, with enough physical and imaginative effort, into a world.

The presentation of this in both films has elements of a dream. In *The Outlaw Josey Wales*, what I might call its staged or ritual quality is possibly Eastwood's particular contribution. He wants to remind us that an act of vision inside the film is also an act of imagination in the world outside it, the world in which films are made and watched. This is not just coy reflexiveness, but a matter of acknowledging that one of the sources of knowledge for how to go about reconstructing a home – a potent subject in mid-'seventies America – is something we have been taught by, or learnt from, other American films that address the emotions accompanying the end of a war.

The contemporary worlds of *The Enforcer* and *The Gauntlet*, Eastwood's next two films, can be linked by the image of flight from the city in the company of a woman. In the earlier film this is only a brief allusion, a drink on a windy hillside, before the woman dies. *The Gauntlet* is a film in which the paranoid view of power in America, the realisation that there exists no incorruptible final court of appeal, is fully developed. Here the motif of flight is in the imagination, as its couple speak (in circumstances in which they cannot look at each other) of what this other world might be like.

The Gauntlet may be read as the narrative of a man who supposed that he was a professional, a policeman finding out why he does not wish to be one. The four country movies made in the next few years – the two films with the pet orang-utan, *Bronco Billy* and *Honkytonk Man* – take up this subject. What links them, politically speaking, is a horror of professionalism, an impulse to celebrate the amateur, the local, the activity without certificate or permit. (It is indicative that the cycle begins with a routine gag about sociology, the only reference to it, I think, in Eastwood's work.) One of the projects of these films is an attempt to shift the view of violence and sexual activity away from that of the earlier films. The central device is playing both the violence and the sexuality of animals for comedy. Clyde, the orang-utan, is a creature without certificate or permit, a means of rejecting scientific – professional – definitions of nature. To save such acts for comedy is to rescue them from the categories of professionalism, of laws broken or kept, and to remind us that they may be stunts or tricks. To see just how successful this can be I recommend the reader to look at the moment in *Every Which Way But Loose* when Eastwood points his finger at Clyde and 'shoots' him (with the single word 'bang'). The animal drops 'dead' in a piece of perfect mugging.

The worlds of the country movies are under threat, constantly in tension with destructive forces at their borders. There is the danger that the desire to relocate acts of sex and violence can take on the potentially hysterical, uneasy brio of a cartoon, as in *Any Which Way You Can*; in *Bronco Billy*, the grim nature of much of the literal America outside Billy's tent threatens to overwhelm the film. In the first three country comedies this sense of being under threat is complicated by being associated with the figure that the film wishes to redeem, played in each case by Sondra Locke. It fails – with unusual obscurity of plotting for a Malpaso film – to redeem her in *Every Which Way But Loose*, and achieves this rather mechanically in *Bronco Billy*. In *Any Which Way You Can*, the problem is avoided by the simple route of relocating the enemy as the mafia. *Honkytonk Man*, the least comedic of the four, could be said to admit to the destructiveness of the world directly. It is a film in which being finally back in the city is associated with being surrounded by professionals – musical and medical – and with death.

Escape from Alcatraz was made between the first and second country movies, and *Firefox* between the third and fourth. They can be seen as complementary to the cycle, being films in which masculinity, defined as competence and discipline as well as the ability to exercise control through the operation of technology, is successfully expressed, but only within conditions of cramped technological efficiency – the world has shrunk to the dimensions of the walls and fences of Alcatraz in the first film, and finally to the cockpit of a jet in the second.

The return to the contemporary city and the Callahan cycle in *Sudden Impact* is mostly a continuation of the attitudes of *The Gauntlet*. The city is simply the site of frustration, and the assumption that it is unreformably corrupt is stated even more clearly. The plot of the hunt for the single psychopath with which the Callahan cycle started is now replaced with the equally reassuring figure of the woman revenging rape, who is assumed to be as absolutely right as the other was utterly wrong.

The need to externalise villainy in the form of the psychopath reappears in *Tightrope*, but it is now pushed to the sidelines. The villain functions here as a Hitchcockian McGuffin, a device which enables the film to ask how the Eastwood hero functions when placed in a city that refuses to acknowledge its manners and practices as corruption, but lays claim to them in a different, less moralistic way, expressed through the New Orleans setting, with its historical depth and association with foreignness. What is it like to be a cop in such a place? Again, we can think of the film as an interrogation of the idea of professionalism – as a breaking down of the aloofness, the claims to a scientific, objective attitude exposed through a need or desire to control women. The central symbol of this in *Tightrope* is the handcuffs, which represent both professional equipment and sexual accessory. The film pushes its analysis of the difficulty of acting, or knowing how to act, for someone stripped of the professional role almost to the point of breakdown. The hero is saved, not simply by the love of a good woman, but by the reconstitution of his professional role, the identification of a villain for him to chase and combat.

Eastwood's next film as director was *Pale Rider*. The fact that it has another hero who appears in some way to have returned from the dead might suggest a link with *High Plains Drifter*, but this is a very different, much more positive world. In his preface to *The Faithful Shepherdess* (c.1610), the playwright John Fletcher claimed of tragicomedy that 'a god is as lawful in this as in a tragedy, and mean people as in a comedy'. The Eastwood figure in *Pale Rider* is such a god, a kind of wizard with powers that enable him to defeat the forces of violence but, by the same token, leave him isolated, allowed only limited contact with the human world. In its subjects, good and bad relationships to nature and the growth to sexual maturity of a young woman, it is engagingly close, for a western, to Shakespearean romance.

Pale Rider was followed by *Heartbreak Ridge*, which might seem to spring from exactly the opposite impulse, a different version of professionalism, in which the old soldier takes the group of raw recruits and turns them into professionals, from something heterogeneous to something homogeneous. I have discussed the anxieties surrounding this project, the ways in which it uneasily acknowledges the modernity of its present-day setting. The danger of such a film is that we will think of it as if it were simply believing in a world of some earlier time, in which an impersonal tradition of martial valour is expressed, as if Eastwood had made it in 1945.

This might be the movie we would see if we were shown only something which claimed to be the American invasion of Grenada in a film which ignored Vietnam. But the insistence on the memory of Vietnam casts the Grenada footage in a specific light – the myth that late twentieth-century warfare can look like this, like ideal, 'just' warfare as it can only exist in the movies, is related to understanding the Vietnam war in the particular way offered in the film. *Heartbreak Ridge* becomes a film about the proposition that the way in which the past is imagined influences the possibilities for behaviour in the present. A number of writers on the Vietnam war have commented on 'John Wayne movie preconceptions' as part of what accompanied young Americans into that war, and on their subsequent disillusionment. *Heartbreak Ridge* can be seen as a right-wing response to this, imagining a war where these preconceptions would not be out of place. It can also be thought of as a film in which, trying to leave behind a memory of a past failure, you find yourself enacting something which feels not like a modernisation of it, but like a reproduction of the conditions which existed in some lost time predating the disaster – a reframing of the situation in *The Outlaw Josey Wales*.

The film acknowledges the fragility of its position, acknowledges that it can be sustained only within the world of the armed forces, another isolated kind of America. It is a perfectable world, but only within the movie; watching it can be compared to being inside Bronco Billy's tent.

Eastwood's next two films consider protagonists who act on the world in other ways, who cannot be put in the category of the professional with certificate or permit, but who are not magicians or gods, at least not outside a very local context – the creative artists of *Bird* and *White Hunter, Black Heart*. In these two films, the central character is one whose acknowledged achievement in his creative field (authenticated indirectly by both men being historical figures) exists alongside a desire to act on the world in ways that involve taking on other roles, respectively paterfamilias and hunter – both famous and mythologically charged in American culture. The intolerable difficulty of occupying these roles, which are so laden with fantasies of what successful masculinity ought to consist of, is expressed in a death – of Bird's daughter in *Bird*, of the black tracker in *White Hunter, Black Heart*. (It is worth putting this in the wider context of Eastwood's work. The subdued note of an inadequate relationship to a younger or more vulnerable dependent figure, often but not always a child, runs through a number of films – different inflections of it are to be found in *Dirty Harry*, *The Beguiled*, *The Outlaw Josey Wales*, *Honkytonk Man* and *Tightrope*, and it is a substantial subject in *A Perfect World*.)

The movement from *Bird* and *White Hunter, Black Heart* to *Unforgiven* feels in some respects like a descent into darkness and loss. There is no equivalent here to what is implicit in Parker's music, or Wilson's film-making. As the film begins, we are looking at a world in which the only person to operate against its pervasive violence, as usual in Eastwood's work a woman, has just been destroyed, not by an antagonist who can be tracked down and killed, but by the random attack of a fatal disease.

Something else is at stake here that would not be at issue if the film had been made thirty years earlier, and relates to the particular conditions of viewing a western in 1992. Eastwood's earlier westerns had seemed to need to insist on the comedic possibilities of the genre. Here the presentation of material as a western is felt very strongly as a return, not just to a genre but to an earlier point in that genre, a point before the western comedies of the 'sixties, in which the western's function as a vehicle for considering the impulses behind the settlement of America and the costs involved in that settlement are treated with complete seriousness. *Unforgiven* is entirely free of knowingness, of any invitation to be superior to generic conventions or situations. This rediscovery is complemented in its plot, which is not about the linear progress of American civilisation, a dramatisation of a particular episode in the process of settlement, but about a new start, about men who have lived through a period of anarchic violence now believing that it is possible to reincarnate themselves, to make a civilised order that is constructed not by reforming the present one, but by going back past it and trying again from scratch.

Of course, it fails – Munny's last cry to the townsfolk of Big Whiskey, that he'll come back and kill them all if they do not respect his 'civilising' instructions, resembles nothing so much as Kurtz's final scrawl across his programme for civilising the native world in Joseph Conrad's *Heart of Darkness*: 'Exterminate all the brutes.' But Eastwood's interest is not in the success or failure of a specific attempt at founding America again – rather it is in the persistence of the impulse. We can find in *Unforgiven* a subject of which I have traced variations in some earlier films – *The Outlaw Josey Wales, White Hunter, Black Heart*, even a subdued version of it in *Heartbreak Ridge*. The subject is that of a journey that is not exactly anticipated or charted to a place in which something is rediscovered. (It is the opposite of tracking your antagonist to a sterile space and killing him, the dominant shape of the cop films – both *The Outlaw Josey Wales* and *White Hunter, Black Heart* are in part dramatised debates between the two subjects.)

The form that this rediscovery takes, on film, is fittingly the form of vision, of seeing something that you have seen before but not with the same clarity or attention. In *Unforgiven* it is the setting, the bright blue day, the last of the winter snows, of which Munny speaks to Delilah: 'I wouldn't normally pay no notice to high country like this . . . trees . . . but I sure notice 'em now . . . thought I was dying for sure.' A dying man is given back the world. In the scene which follows we see, briefly and obliquely, the kind of relationship between Munny and a woman that exists nowhere else in the film but points, although nothing can come of this, towards his lost relationship with the dead woman, and thus towards the promise – nothing more – of the creation of a civilised world. None of the three principals of these last films finds anything more than fragments of that world, although they all contemplate the prospect of it in the past and in the future. Freud's famous comment, that the finding of an object is in fact the re-finding of it, seems to receive its echo in Eastwood's films, in the hero's search for America, the ragged promised land.

FILMOGRAPHY

A FISTFUL OF DOLLARS (*Per un pugno di dollari*) Italy/West Germany/Spain 1964.
100 minutes

Jolly Film (Rome)/Constantin (Munich)/Ocean (Madrid). Distributed by United Artists. Post-synchronised – English-language version with Eastwood speaking his own dialogue.

Directed by Sergio Leone [credited as Bob Robertson]. Produced by Arrigo Colombo [Harry Colombo] and Giorgio Papi [George Papi]. Production managers: Franco Palaggi, Günter Raguse. Script by Sergio Leone and Duccio Tessari, based on *Yojimbo* (1961) by Akira Kurosawa and Ryuzo Kikushima. English version by Mark Lovell. Photographed in Techniscope and Technicolor by Massimo Dallamano [Jack Dalmas]. Edited by Roberto Cinquini [Bob Quintle]. Art Direction by Carlo Simi [Charles Simons]. Music by Ennio Morricone [Dan Savio]. Titles by Luigi Lardini. Sound by Elio Pacella and Edy Simson.

With: Clint Eastwood (The Stranger), Gian Maria Volonté [John Welles] (Ramon Roho), Marianne Koch (Marisol), Pepe Calvo (Silvanito), Wolfgang Lukschy (John Baxter), Sieghardt Rupp (Esteban Roho), Antonio Prieto (Benito Roho), Margherita Lozano (Consuela Baxter), Daniel Martin (Julian), Bruno Carotenuto [Carol Brown] (Antonio Baxter), Benito Stefanelli [Benny Reeves] (Rubio), Richard Stuyvesant (Chico), Josef Egger (Piripero), Mario Brega.

FOR A FEW DOLLARS MORE (*Per qualche dollari in più*) Italy/Spain/West Germany 1965.
130 minutes

P.E.A. (Rome)/Arturo Gonzales (Madrid)/Constantin (Munich). Distributed by United Artists. Post-synchronised – English-language version with the English-speaking actors recording their own dialogue.

Directed by Sergio Leone. Produced by Alberto Grimaldi. Production Manager: Ottavio Oppo. Assistant Director: Tonino Valerii. Script by Sergio Leone and Luciano Vincenzoni, based on a story by Leone and Fulvio Morsella. Photographed in Techniscope and Technicolor by Massimo Dallamano. Edited by Alabiso Serralonga and Georgio Serralonga. Art Direction by Carlo Simi. Music by Ennio Morricone, directed by Bruno Nicolai. Costumes by Carlo Simi. Sound by Oscar De Arcangelis.

With: Clint Eastwood (The Stranger), Lee Van Cleef (Colonel Mortimer), Gian Maria Volonté (Indio), Klaus Kinski (Hunchback), Josef Egger (Old Man), Mara Krup (Hotel Keeper's Wife), Rosemary Dexter (Mortimer's Sister), Mario Brega, Aldo Sambrel, Luigi Pistilli, Benito Stefanelli, Panos Papadopoulos, Roberto Camardiel, Luis Rodriguez, Diana Rabito, Giovanni Tarallo, Mario Meniconi, Lorenzo Robledo.

THE GOOD, THE BAD, AND THE UGLY (*Il buono, il brutto, il cattivo*) Italy, 1966.
180 minutes

Produzioni Europee Associate (Rome). Distributed by United Artists. Post-synchronised – English-language version with the English speaking actors recording their own dialogue.

Directed by Sergio Leone. Produced by Alberto Grimaldi. Production Manager: Fernando Cinquini. Assistant Director: Giancarlo Santi. Script by Leone and Luciano Vincenzoni, based on the story 'The Magnificent Rogues' by Age-Scarpelli, Vincenzoni and Leone. English version by Mickey Knox. Photographed in Technicolor and Techniscope by Tonino Delli Colli. Edited by Nino Baragli and Eugenio Alabiso. Art Direction by Carlo Simi. Special Effects by Eros Bacciucchi. Music by Ennio Morricone, directed by Bruno Nicolai. Costumes by Carlo Simi. Titles: Ardani.

With: Clint Eastwood (Joe), Eli Wallach (Tuco), Lee Van Cleef (Angel Eyes/Setenza), Aldo Giuffré, Mario Brega, Luigi Pistilli, Claudio Scarchelli, Livio Lorenzon, Antonio Castale, Rada Rassimov, Enzo Petito, Sandro Scarchelli, Benito Stefanelli, Silvana Bacci, Antonio Casas, Aldo Sambrell, Chelo Alonso, Al Mulock.

THE WITCHES (*Le Streghe*) Italy/France, 1966. 110 mins.

Dino De Laurentiis (Rome)/Les Productions Artistes Associés (Paris). Distributed by United Artists. A film composed of five unconnected segments by five different directors, all featuring Silvana Mangano. The piece in which Eastwood appears was directed by Vittorio De Sica; the other directors are Luchino Visconti, Pier Paolo Pasolini, Mauro Bolognini and Franco Rossi.

Segment: *A Night Like Any Other* (*Una sera come le altre*) 19 minutes

Directed by VittorioDe Sica. Produced by Dino De Laurentiis. Script by Cesare Zavattini, Fabio

Carpi and Enzo Muzzi. Photographed in Technicolor by Giuseppe Rotunno and Giuseppe Maccari. Music by Piero Piccione and Ennio Morricone.

With: Silvana Mangano (Giovanna), Clint Eastwood (Mario), Armando Bottin, Gianno Gori, Paolo Gozina, Angelo Santi, Valentino Macchi, Piero Torrizi, Franco Moruzzi.

HANG 'EM HIGH USA, 1967. 114 minutes

Leonard Freeman Productions/Malpaso. Distributed by United Artists.

Directed by Ted Post. Produced by Leonard Freeman. Associate Producer: Robert Stampler. Production Manager: Frank Mayer. Assistant Directors: Richard Bennett and Don Klune. Script by Leonard Freeman and Mel Goldberg. Photographed in De Luxe Color by Leonard South and Richard Kline. Edited by Gene Fowler, Jr. Art Direction by John B. Goodman. Set Decoration by Arthur Krams. Music by Dominic Frontière. Sound by Franklin Milton and Al Strasser Jr. Special Effects by George Swartz and Dewey Grigg.

With: Clint Eastwood (Jed Cooper), Inger Stevens (Rachel), Ed Begley (Captain Wilson), Pat Hingle (Judge Adam Fenton), Arlene Golonka (Jennifer), James MacArthur (Priest), Bruce Dern (Miller), Alan Hale Jr (Stone), James Westerfield (Prisoner), Charles McGraw, L.Q. Jones, Jack Ging, Dennis Hopper, Ben Johnson, Ruth White, Michael O'Sullivan, Joseph Sirola, Russell Thorsen, Bob Steele, Bert Freed, Ned Romero, Jonathan Lippe, Rick Gates, Bruce Scott, Richard Guison, Todd Andrews, Mark Lenard, Roy Glenn, Hal England, Robert B. Williams, Tony Di Milo, Paul Sorenson, Richard Angarola.

COOGAN'S BLUFF USA, 1968. 94 minutes

A Universal Production.
Distributed by Universal.

Directed and produced by Don Siegel. Executive Producer: Richard Lyons. Associate Producer: Irvin Leonard. Production Manager: Robert Larson. Assistant Director: Joe Cavalier. Script by Herman Miller, Dean Riesner and Howard Rodman, based on a story by Herman Miller. Photographed in Technicolor by Bud Thackery. Edited by Sam Waxman. Art direction by Alexander Golitzen. Set Decoration by John McCarthy and John Austin. Music by Lalo Schifrin. Costumes by Helen Colvig. Sound by Waldon Watson, Lyle Cain and Jack Bolger. Dialogue coach: Scott Hale.

With: Clint Eastwood (Coogan), Lee J. Cobb (Detective McElroy), Susan Clark (Julie), Tisha Sterling (Linny Raven), Don Stroud (Ringerman), Betty Field (Mrs Ringerman), Tom Tully (Sheriff McCrea), Melodie Johnson (Millie), James Edwards (Jackson), Rudy Diaz (Running Bear), David Doyle (Pushie), Louis Zorich (Taxi Driver), Meg Myles (Big Red), Marjorie Bennett (Mrs Fowler), Seymour Cassell (Young Hood), John Coe (Bellboy), Skip Battyn (Omega), Albert Popwell (Wonderful Digby), Conrad Bain (Madison Avenue Man), James Gavin (Ferguson), Albert Henderson (Desk Sergeant), James McCallion (Room Clerk), Syl Lamont (Manager), Jess Osuna (Prison Hospital Guard), Jerry Summers (Good Eyes), Antonia Rey (Mrs Amador), Marya Henriques (Go-Go Dancer).

WHERE EAGLES DARE GB, 1968.

155 mins.

Winkast Productions (Jerry Gershwin/Elliott Kastner). Distributed by MGM.

Directed by Brian G. Hutton. Produced by Elliott Kastner. Production supervised by Ted Lloyd. Second Unit Production Manager: Tom Sachs. Second Unit Director: Yakima Canutt. Assistant Director: Colin Brewer. Script by Alistair MacLean, based on his own novel. Photographed in Panavision 70 and Metrocolor by Arthur Ibbetson. Second Unit Photography by H.A.R. Thomson. Special Photographic Effects by Tom Howard. Edited by John Jympson. Art Direction by Peter Mullins. Set Decoration by Arthur Taksen. Special Effects: Richard Parker and Fred Hellenburgh. Music by Ron Goodwin. Sound Editing by Jonathan Bates. Sound Recording by John Bramall.

With: Richard Burton (John Smith), Clint Eastwood (Lieutenant Morris Schaffer), Mary Ure (Mary Ellison), Patrick Wymark (Colonel Turner), Michael Hordern (Vice-Admiral Rolland), Donald Houston (Olaf Christiansen), Peter Barkworth (Berkeley), Ferdy Mayne (German Officer), Neil MacCarthy (Torrance-Smythe), William Squire (Lee Thomas), Brook Williams (Sergeant Harrod), Ingrid Pitt (Heidi), Robert Beatty (Cartwright-Jones), Anton Diffring (Colonel Kramer), Derren Nesbitt (Major von Hapen), Victor Beaumont (Colonel Weissner), Richard Beale (Telephone Orderly), Ivor Dean (German Officer), Lyn Kennington (German Woman), Nigel Lambert (Young German Soldier), Michael Rooney (Radio Operator), Ernst Walder (Airport Control Officer).

PAINT YOUR WAGON USA, 1969.

164 minutes

Paramount/Alan J. Lerner Productions. Distributed by Paramount.

Directed by Joshua Logan. Produced by Alan J. Lerner. Associate Producer: Tom Shaw. Second Unit Directors: Tom Shaw and Fred Lemoine. Assistant Director: Fred Roe. Script by Paddy

Chayefsky, based on the musical *Paint Your Wagon* (book and lyrics by Alan Jay Lerner, music by Frederick Loewe.) Photographed in Panavision 70 and Technicolor by William A. Fraker. Edited by Robert Jones. Production Designer: John Truscott. Art Direction by Carl Braunger. Set Decoration by James Berkey. Special Effects: Maurice Ayers and Larry Hampton. Costumes by John Truscott. Music by Frederick Loewe, with music for additional songs by André Previn. Choral arrangements by Joseph Lilley, conducted by Roger Wagner. Musical direction by Nelson Riddle. Songs: 'I'm on My Way', 'I Still See Elisa', 'The First Thing You Know', 'Hand Me Down that Can o'Beans', 'They Call the Wind Maria', 'A Million Miles Away Behind the Door', 'There's a Coach Comin' in', 'Whoop-Ti-Ay!', 'I Talk to the Trees', 'The Gospel of No Name City', 'Best Things', 'Wand'rin Star', 'Gold Fever' by Lerner and Loewe, Lerner and Previn. Sound by William Randall. Titles: David Stone Martin.

With: Lee Marvin (Ben Rumson), Clint Eastwood (Pardner), Jean Seberg (Elizabeth), Harve Presnell (Rotten Luck Willie), Ray Walston (Mad Jack Duncan), Tom Ligon (Horton Fenty), Alan Dexter (Parson), William O'Connell (Horace Tabor), Ben Baker (Haywood Holbrook), Alan Baxter (Mr Fenty), Paula Trueman (Mrs Fenty), Robert Easton (Atwell), Geoffrey Norman (Foster), H.B. Haggerty (Steve Bull), Terry Jenkins (Joe Mooney), Karl Bruck (Shermerhorn), John Mitchum (Jacob Woodling), Sue Casey (Sarah Woodling), Eddie Little Sky (Indian), Harvey Parry (Higgins), H.W. Gim (Wong), William Mims (Frock-coated man), Roy Jenson (Hennessey), Pat Hawley (Clendennon).

TWO MULES FOR SISTER SARA USA, 1969. 116 minutes
Universal/Malpaso productions.
Distributed by Universal.

Directed by Don Siegel. Produced by Martin Rackin and Carroll Case. Production Managers: William Davidson and Alfonso Sanchez Tello. Assistant Directors: Joe Cavalier, Manuel Munoz. Script by Albert Maltz from the story *Two Guns for Sister Sara* by Budd Boetticher. Photographed in Panavision and Technicolor by Gabriel Figueroa. Second Unit Photography: Gabriel Torres. Edited by Robert Shugrue and Juan Marino. Art Direction by José Granada. Set Decoration by Pablo Galvan. Special Effects: Frank Brendel and Leon Ortega. Music by Ennio Morricone. Costumes by Helen Colvig and Carlos Chavez. Sound by Waldon Watson, Jesus Gonzalez Gancy and Ronald Pierce.

With: Shirley MacLaine (Sara), Clint Eastwood (Hogan), Manolo Fabregas (Colonel Beltran), Alberto Morin (General Leclair), Armando

Silvestre (First American), John Kelly (Second American), Enrique Lucero (Third American), Pedro Armendariz (Young French Officer), David Estuardo (Juan), Ada Carrasco (Juan's Mother), Poncho Cordoba (Juan's Father), José Chavez (Horacio), Pedro Galvan, José Espinosa.

KELLY'S HEROES USA/Yugoslavia, 1970. 143 minutes
The Warriors Company (USA)/Avala Films (Belgrade). Distributed by MGM.

Directed by Brian G. Hutton. Produced by Gabriel Katzka and Sidney Beckerman. Associate Producer: Irvin Leonard. Production Supervisor: Basil Somner. Production Managers: Terry Lens (USA) and Milenko Stankovic (Yugoslavia). Second Unit Director: Andrew Marton. Assistant Dirctors: John Chulay (USA) and Stevo Petrovic (Yugoslavia). Script by Troy Kennedy Martin. Photographed in Panavision and Metrocolor by Gabriel Figueroa. Second Unit Photography by H.A.R. Thompson. Edited by John Jympson. Art Direction by Jonathan Berry. Set Decoration by Mike Ford. Special Effects by Karli Baumgartner. Music by Lalo Schifrin. Songs: 'Burning Bridges' by Lalo Schifrin and Mike Curb, sung by The Mike Curb Congregation, 'Si tu me dis' by Lalo Schifrin and Gene Lees, sung by Monique Aldebert. 'Sunshine' sung by Hank Williams. Sound by Cyril Swern and Harry Tetrick. Technical Advisor: Major Alexander Gerry.

With: Clint Eastwood (Kelly), Telly Savalas (Big Joe), Don Rickles (Crapgame), Donald Sutherland (Oddball), Carroll O'Connor (General Colt), Gavin MacLeod (Moriarty), Hal Buckley (Maitland), Stuart Margolin (Little Joe), Jeff Morris (Cowboy), Richard Davalos (Gutowsky), George Savalas (Mulligan), David Hurst (Colonel Dankhopf), John Heller (German Lieutenant), Gene Collins (Babra), Perry Lopez (Petchuko), Dick Balduzzi (Fisher), Harry Stanton (Willard), Len Lesser (Bellamy), Michael Clark (Grace), George Fargo (Penn), Dee Pollock (Jonesy), Shepherd Sanders (Marvin), Frank J. Garlotta (First Tank Commander), Sandy Kevin (Second Tank Commander), Phil Adams (Third Tank Commander), Read Morgan (ADC Driver), Robert McNamara (Roach), James McHale (Guest), Ross Elliott (Booker), Tom Signorelli (Bonsor), Karl Otto Alberty (German Tank Commander), Hugo de Vernier (French Mayor), Harry Goines (Supply Sergeant), David Gross (German Captain), Donald Waugh (Roamer), Vincent Maracecchi (Old Man).

THE BEGUILED USA, 1971. 105 minutes

A Universal/Malpaso production.
Distributed by Universal.

Directed and produced by Don Siegel.
Executive Producer: Julian Blaustein. Associate Producer: Claude Travers. Production Manager and Second Unit Director: Joe Cavalier. Assistant Director: Burt Astor. Script by John B. Sherry and Grimes Grice [pseudonyms for Albert Maltz and Irene Kamp], based on Thomas Cullinan's novel. Photographed in Technicolor by Bruce Surtees. Edited by Carl Pingitore. Production Design by Ted Haworth. Art Direction by Alex Golitzen. Set Decoration: John Austin. Music by Lalo Schifrin. Costumes by Helen Colvig. Sound by Waldon Watson and John Mack.

With: Clint Eastwood (John McBurney), Geraldine Page (Martha Farnsworth), Elizabeth Hartman (Edwina Dabney), Jo Ann Harris (Carol), Mae Mercer (Hallie), Pamelyn Ferdin (Amy), Darleen Carr (Doris), Melody Thomas (Abigail), Peggy Drier (Lizzie), Pattye Mattick (Janie), Charles Briggs, George Dunn, Charles Martin, Matt Clark, Patrick Culliton, Wayne 'Buddy' Van Horn.

PLAY MISTY FOR ME USA, 1971.

102 minutes

A Universal/Malpaso production.
Distributed by Universal.

Directed by Clint Eastwood. Produced by Robert Daley. Associate Producer and Assistant Director: Bob Larson. Script by Jo Heims and Dean Riesner, based on a story by Jo Heims. Photographed in Technicolor by Bruce Surtees. Edited by Carl Pingitore. Art Direction by Alex Golitzen. Set Decoration: Ralph Hurst. Music by Dee Barton. Songs: 'Misty', written and performed by Erroll Garner, 'The First Time Ever I Saw Your Face' sung by Roberta Flack. Titles: Universal Title. Sound by Waldon Watson, Robert Martin and Robert Hoyt.

With: Clint Eastwood (Dave Garver), Jessica Walter (Evelyn Draper), Donna Mills (Tobie Williams), John Larch (Sergeant McCallum), Jack Ging (Frank Dewan), Irene Harvey (Madge Brenner), James McEachin (Al Monte), Clarice Taylor (Birdie), Donald Siegel (Murphy), Duke Everts (Jay Jay), Britt Lind (Angelica), Ginna Paterson (Madelyn), George Fargo (Man), Mervin Frates (Locksmith), Tim Frawley (Deputy Sheriff), Otis Kadani (Policeman), Paul Lippman (Second Man), Jack Kosslyn (Cab Driver), Malcolm Moran (Man in Window). The Johnny Otis Show and the Cannonball Adderley Quintet appear as themselves.

DIRTY HARRY USA, 1971. 101 minutes

A Warner Bros/Malpaso production. Distributed by Warner.

Directed and produced by Don Siegel.
Executive Producer: Robert Daley. Associate Producer: Carl Pingitore. Production Manager: Jim Henderling. Assistant Director: Robert Rubin. Script by Harry Julian Fink, Rita M. Fink and Dean Riesner, based on a story by the Finks. Photographed in Panavision and Technicolor by Bruce Surtees. Edited by Carl Pingitore. Art Direction by Dale Hennessy. Set Decoration: Robert DeVestel. Music by Lalo Schifrin. Sound by Willian Randall.

With: Clint Eastwood (Inspector Harry Callahan), Harry Guardino (Lieutenant Bressler), Reni Santoni (Chico), John Vernon (The Mayor), Andy Robinson (Scorpio), John Larch (Chief of Police), John Mitchum (DiGeorgio), Mae Mercer (Mrs Russell), Lyn Edgington (Norma), Ruth Kobart (Bus Driver), Woodrow Parfrey (Mr Jaffe), Josef Sommer (Rothko), William Paterson (Bannerman), James Nolan (Liquor Store Proprietor), Maurice Argent (Sid Kleinman), Jo de Winter (Miss Willis), Craig G. Kelly (Sergeant Reineke).

JOE KIDD USA, 1972. 87 mins.

A Universal/Malpaso production.
Distributed by Universal.

Directed by John Sturges. Produced by Sidney Beckerman. Executive Producer: Robert Daley. Production Manager: Ernest Wehmeyer. Assistant Director: Jim Fargo. Script by Elmore Leonard. Photographed in Panavision and Technicolor by Bruce Surtees. Edited by Ferris Webster. Art Direction by Alex Golitzen and Henry Bumstead. Set Decoration by Charles S. Thompson. Music by Lalo Schifrin. Titles by Universal Title. Stunts: Buddy Van Horn. Sound by Waldon Watson and James Alexander.

With: Clint Eastwood (Joe Kidd), Robert Duvall (Frank Harlan), John Saxon (Luis Chama), Don Stroud (Lamarr), Stella Garcia (Helen Sanchez), James Wainwright (Mango), Paul Koslo (Roy), Gregory Walcott (Mitchell), Dick Van Patten (Hotel Manager), Lynne Marta (Elma), John Carter (Judge), Pepe Hern (Priest), Joaquin Martinez (Manolo), Ron Soble (Ramon), Pepe Callahan (Naco), Clint Ritchie (Calvin), Gil Barreto (Emilio), Ed Deemer (Bartender), Maria Val (Vita), Chuck Hayward (Eljay), Michael R. Horst (Deputy).

HIGH PLAINS DRIFTER USA, 1972.

105 minutes

A Malpaso production.
Distributed by Universal.

Directed by Clint Eastwood. Produced by Robert Daley. Executive Producer: Jennings

Lang. Production Manager: Ernest Wehmeyer. Assistant Director: Jim Fargo. Script by Ernest Tidyman. Photographed in Panavision and Technicolor by Bruce Surtees. Edited by Ferris Webster. Art Direction by Henry Bumstead. Set Decoration by George Milo. Music by Dee Barton. Sound by James Alexander. Stunts: Buddy Van Horn.

With: Clint Eastwood (The Stranger), Verna Bloom (Sarah Belding), Mariana Hill (Callie Travers), Mitchell Ryan (Dave Drake), Jack Ging (Morgan Allen), Stefan Gierasch (Major Jason Hobart), Ted Hartley (Lewis Belding), Billy Curtis (Mordecai), Geoffrey Lewis (Stacey Bridges), Scott Walker (Bill Borders), Walter Barnes (Sheriff Sam Shaw), Paul Brinegar (Lutie Naylor), Richard Bull (Asa Goodwin), Robert Donner (Priest), John Hillerman (Bootmaker), Anthony James (Cole Carlin), William O'Connell (Barber), John Quade (Jake Ross), Jane Aull (Townswoman), Dan Vadis (Dan Carlin), Reid Cruickshanks (Gunsmith), James Gosa (Tommy Morris), Jack Kosslyn (Saddlemaker), Russ McCubbin (Fred Short), Belle Mitchell (Mrs Lake), John Mitchum (Warden), Carl C. Pitti (Teamster), Chuck Waters (Stableman), Buddy Van Horn (Marshal Jim Duncan).

BREEZY USA, 1973. 107 minutes

A Universal/Malpaso production. Distributed by Universal.

Directed by Clint Eastwood. Produced by Robert Daley. Executive Producer: Jennings Lang. Associate Producer: Jo Heims. Production Manager: Donald Roberts. Assistant Directors: Jim Fargo and Tom Joyner. Script by Jo Heims. Photographed in Technicolor by Frank Stanley. Edited by Ferris Webster. Art Direction by Alex Golitzen. Set Decoration by James Payne. Music by Michel Legrand. Song: 'Breezy's Song' by Michel Legrand and Marilyn and Alan Bergman, sung by Shelby Flint. Sound by James Alexander.

With: William Holden (Frank Harmon), Kay Lenz (Breezy), Roger C. Carmel (Bob Henderson), Marj Dusay (Betty Tobin), Joan Hotchkis (Paula Harmon), Jamie Smith Jackson (Marcy), Norman Bartold (Man in Car), Lynn Borden (Frank's Overnight Date), Shelley Morrison (Nancy Henderson), Dennis Olivieri (Bruno), Eugenie Peterson (Charlie), Lew Brown (Police Officer), Richard Bull (Doctor), Johnnie Collins III (Norman), Don Diamond (Maitre D'), Scott Holden (Veterinarian), Sandy Kenyon (Real Estate Agent), Jack Kosslyn (Driver), Mary Munday (Waitress), Frances Stevenson (Saleswoman), Buck Young (Paula's Escort), Priscilla Morrill (Customer).

MAGNUM FORCE USA, 1973. 122 minutes

A Malpaso production. Distributed by Warners.

Directed by Ted Post. Produced by Robert Daley. Production Manager: John G. Wilson. Assistant Director: Wes McAfee. Second Unit Director: Buddy Van Horn. Script by John Milius and Michael Cimino, based on a story by Milius. Photographed in Panavision and Technicolor by Frank Stanley. Edited by Ferris Webster. Art Direction by Jack Collis. Set Decoration by John Lamphear. Music by Lalo Schifrin. Sound by James Alexander.

With: Clint Eastwood (Harry Callahan), Hal Holbrook (Lieutenant Briggs), Mitch Ryan (Charlie McCoy), Felton Perry (Early Smith), David Soul (Davis), Robert Urich (Grimes), Tim Matheson (Sweet), Kip Niven (Astrachan), Christine White (Carol McCoy), Adele Yoshioka (Sunny), Richard Devon (Carmine Ricca), Tony Giorgio (Frank Palancio), Albert Popwell (Pimp), John Mitchum (DiGeorgio), Margaret Avery (Prostitute), Jack Kosslyn (Walter), Clifford Pellow (Lou Guzman), Maurice Argent (Nat Weinstein), Bob March (Eastabrook), Bob McClurg (Cab Driver), Russ Moro (Ricca's Driver).

THUNDERBOLT AND LIGHTFOOT USA, 1974. 115 minutes

A Malpaso production. Distributed by United Artists.

Directed by Michael Cimino. Produced by Robert Daley. Production Manager: Abner Singer. Assistant Directors: Charles Okun, David Hamburger and Arnie Schmitt. Script by Michael Cimino. Photographed in Panavision and DeLuxe Color by Frank Stanley. Edited by Ferris Webster. Art Dirction by Tambi Larsen. Set Decoration by James Berkey. Special Effects: Sass Bedig. Music by Dee Barton. Song 'Where Do I Go From Here' by Paul Williams, sung by Paul Williams. Titles: Wayne Fitzgerald. Sound Editing: Keith Stafford. Sound Recording: Bert Hallberg and Norman Webster. Stunt Co-ordinator: Buddy Van Horn.

With: Clint Eastwood (Thunderbolt), Jeff Bridges (Lightfoot), George Kennedy (Red Leary), Geoffrey Lewis (Goody), Catherine Bach (Melody), Gary Busey (Curly), Jack Dodson (Bank Vault Manager), Burton Gilliam (Welder), Roy Jenson (Dunlop), Claudia Lennear (Secretary), Bill McKinney (Crazy Driver), Vic Tayback (Mario), Dub Taylor (Gas Station Attendant), Gregory Walcott (Used Car Salesman), Erica Hagen (Waitress), Virginia Baker and Stuart Nisbet (Couple at gas station), Gene Elman and Lila Teigh (Tourist Couple), Alvin Childress (Janitor), Irene K. Cooper (Cashier), Cliff Emmich (Fat Security Man), June Fairchild (Gloria), Ted Foulkes (Little Boy), Karen Lamm (Girl on motorcycle), Leslie

Oliver and Mark Montgomery (Teenagers), Luanne Roberts (Suburban Housewife), Tito Vandis (Counterman).

THE EIGER SANCTION USA, 1975.

128 mins.

A Universal/Malpaso production. Distributed by Universal.

Directed by Clint Eastwood. Produced by Robert Daley. Executive Producers: Richard D. Zanuck, David Brown. Production Managers: Fred Simpson (USA) and Wallace Worsley (Switzerland). Assistant Directors: Jim Fargo (USA), Craig Hughes (Switzerland) and Victor Tourjansky. Script by Warren B. Murphy, Hal Dresner and Rod Whitaker, based on the novel by Trevanian. Photographed in Panavision and Technicolor by Frank Stanley. Mountain sequences photography by John Cleare, Jeff Schoolfield, Peter Pilafian and Pete White. Edited by Ferris Webster. Art Direction by George Webb (USA) and Aurelio Crugnola (Switzerland). Set Decoration by John Dwyer. Special Effects: Ben McMahan. Music by John Williams. Sound Recording: James Alexander. Climbing Advisor: Mike Hoover.

With: Clint Eastwood (Jonathan Hemlock), George Kennedy (Ben Bowman), Vonetta McGee (Jemima Brown), Jack Cassidy (Miles), Heidi Bruhl (Mrs Montaigne), Thayer David (Dragon), Reiner Schoene (Freytag), Michael Grimm (Meyer), Jean-Pierre Bernard (Montaigne), Brenda Venus (George), Gregory Walcott (Pope), Candace Rialson (Art Student), Elaine Shaw (Miss Cerberus), Dan Howard (Dewayne), Jack Kosslyn (Reporter), Walter Kraus (Kruger), Frank Redmond (Wormwood), Siegfried Wallach (Hotel Manager), Susan Morgan (Buns), Jack Frey (Cab Driver).

The Eiger Sanction relates closely to Eastwood's war films. A cold-war spy thriller, it takes the political cynicism of the genre to an extreme: the mission is a pointless fake, both sides being equally corrupt. The exercise of masculinity in the second half of the film has almost nothing to do with the thriller plot and becomes an encounter between man and extremely hostile nature (the north face of the Eiger). In a suggestive anticipation of *Escape from Alcatraz*, Eastwood's presentation of the mountain stresses not romantic landscape but cramped, difficult movement, space that is restricting rather than liberating. And the appalling conditions on the mountain directly result in the deaths of all of the climbers apart from the Eastwood figure.

THE OUTLAW JOSEY WALES USA, 1976.

134 minutes

A Malpaso production. Distributed by Warner.

Directed by Clint Eastwood. Produced by Robert Daley. Associate Producers: Jim Fargo and John G. Wilson. Assistant Directors: Jim Fargo, Win Phelps and Alan Brimfield. Script by Phil Kaufman and Sonia Chernus, based on the novel *Gone to Texas* by Forrest Carter. Photographed in Panavision and DeLuxe Color by Bruce Surtees. Edited by Ferris Webster. Production Designer: Tambi Larsen. Set Decorator: Chuck Pierce. Special Effects: Robert MacDonald and Paul Pollard. Music by Jerry Fielding. Sound Editing: Keith Stafford. Sound Recording: Bert Hallberg. Stunt Co-ordinator: Walter Scott. Titles/Optical effects: Pacific Title.

With: Clint Eastwood (Josey Wales), Chief Dan George (Lone Watie), Sondra Locke (Laura Lee), Bill McKinney (Terrill), John Vernon (Fletcher), Paula Trueman (Grandma Sarah), Sam Bottoms (Jamie), Geraldine Keams (Little Moonlight), Woodrow Parfrey (Carpetbagger), Joyce Jameson (Rose), Sheb Wooley (Travis Cobb), Royal Dano (Ten Spot), Matt Clarke (Kelly), John Verros (Chato), Will Sampson (Ten Bears), William O'Connell (Sim Carstairs), John Quade (Comanchero Leader), Frank Schofield (Senator Land), Buck Kartalian (Shopkeeper), Len Lesser (Abe), Douglas McGrath (Lige), John Russell (Bloody Bill Anderson), Charles Tyner (Zukie Limmer), Bruce M. Fischer (Yoke), John Mitchum (Al), John Chandler (First Bounty Hunter), Tom Roy Lowe (Second Bounty Hunter), Clay Tanner (First Texas Ranger), Madeline T. Holmes (Grannie Hawkins), Erik Holland (Union Army Sergeant), Cissy Wellman (Josey's Wife), Faye Hamblin (Grandpa), Danny Green (Lemuel).

THE ENFORCER USA, 1976. 96 minutes

A Malpaso production. Distributed by Warner.

Directed by James Fargo. Produced by Robert Daley. Production Manager: John G. Wilson. Assistant Directors: Joe Cavalier, Joe Florence and Billy Ray Smith. Script by Stirling Silliphant and Dean Riesner, based on a story by Gail Morgan Hickman and W. Schurr. Photographed in Panavision and DeLuxe Color (prints by Technicolor) by Charles W. Short. Edited by Ferris Webster and Joel Cox. Art Direction by Allen E. Smith. Set Decoration by Ira Bates. Special Effects: Joe Unsinn. Music by Jerry Fielding. Titles: Pacific Title. Sound Recording: Bert Hallberg. Sound re-recording: Les Fresholtz. Stunt Co-ordinator: Wayne Van Horn.

With: Clint Eastwood (Harry Callahan), Tyne Daly (Kate Moore), Harry Guardino (Lieutenant Bressler), Bradford Dillman

(Captain McKay), John Mitchum (DiGeorgio), DeVeren Bookwalter (Bobby Maxwell), John Crawford (Mayor), Samantha Doane (Wanda), Robert Hoy (Buchinski), Jocelyn Jones (Miki), M.G. Kelly (Father John), Nick Pellegrino (Martin), Albert Popwell (Big Ed Mustapha), Rudy Ramos (Mendez), Bill Ackridge (Andy), Bill Jelliffe (Johnny), Joe Bellan (Freddie the Fainter), Tim O'Neill (Police Sergeant), Jan Stratton (Mrs Grey), Will MacMillan (Lieutenant Dobbs), Jerry Walter (Krause), Steve Boff (Bustanoby), Tim Burrus (Henry Lee), Michael Cavanaugh (Lalo), Dick Durock (Karl), Ronald Manning (Tex), Adele Proom (Irene DiGeorgio), Glenn Lee Marshall (Army Sergeant), Robert Behling (Autopsy Surgeon).

THE GAUNTLET USA, 1977. 109 mins.

A Malpaso production. Distributed by Warner.

Directed by Clint Eastwood. Produced by Robert Daley. Associate Producer: Fritz Manes. Production Manager: Joe Cavalier. Assistant Directors: Richard Hashimoto, Lynn Morgan, Peter Bergquist and Al Silvani. Script by Michael Butler and Dennis Shyrack. Photographed in Panavision and DeLuxe Color by Rexford Metz. Edited by Ferris Webster and Joel Cox. Art Decoration by Allen E. Smith. Set Decoration by Ira Bates. Special Effects: Chuck Gaspar. Music by Jerry Fielding. Jazz Soloists: Art Pepper, Jon Faddis. Costumes by Glenn Wright. Titles: Pacific Title. Sound Recording: Bert Hallberg. Stunt Co-ordinator: Wayne Van Horn.

With: Clint Eastwood (Ben Shockley), Sondra Locke (Gus Mally), Pat Hingle (Josephson), William Prince (Blakelock), Bill McKinney (Constable), Michael Cavanaugh (Feyderspiel), Carole Cook (Waitress), Mara Corday (Prison Guard), Douglas McGrath (Bookie), Jeff Morris (Policeman), Samantha Doane, Roy Jenson and Dan Vadis (Bikers), Carver Barnes (Bus Driver), Robert Barrett (Doctor), Teddy Bear (Lieutenant), Mildred J. Brion (Old Woman on bus), Ron Chapman (Old Cop), Don Circle (Bus Clerk), James W. Gavin, Tom Friedkin (Helicopter Pilots), Darwin Lamb (Police Captain), Roger Lowe (Ambulance Driver), Fritz Manes (Helicopter Marksman), John Quiroga (Taxi Driver), John Rainer, Al Silvani (Policemen), Art Rimdzius (Judge).

EVERY WHICH WAY BUT LOOSE USA, 1978. 114 mins.

A Malpaso production. Distributed by Warner.

Directed by James Fargo. Produced by Robert Daley. Assistant Directors: Larry Powell, Wendy Shear, Al Silvani and Alain J. Silver. Script by Jeremy Joe Kronsberg. Photographed in DeLuxe Color by Rexford Metz. Edited by Ferris Webster and Joel Cox. Art Direction by Elayne

Ceder. Set Decoration by Robert de Vestel. Special Effects: Chuck Gaspar. Musical Supervision by Snuff Garrett, conducted by Steve Dorff. Songs: 'Every Which Way But Loose' by Dorff/Garrett/M. Brown, performed by Eddie Rabbit; 'I'll Wake You up when I Get Home' by Dorff/Brown, performed by Charlie Rich; 'Behind Closed Doors' by K. O'Dell, performed by Charlie Rich; 'Coca Cola Cowboy' by S. Pinkard/I. Dain/Dorff/S. Atchley; 'Send Me Down to Tucson' by C. Crofford/T. Garrett, performed by Mel Tillis; 'Ain't Love Good Tonight' by G. Sklerov/R. Cate/G. Howe, performed by Wayne Parker; 'Don't Say You Don't Love Me No More' by P. Everly/J. Paige, performed by Sondra Locke and Phil Everly; 'Honky Tonk Fever' and 'Monkey See, Monkey Do' by C. Crofford/T. Garrett, performed by Cliff Crofford; 'I Seek the Night' performed by Sondra Locke; 'Red Eye Special' by S. Collins/S. Pinkard/T. Garrett, performed by Larry Collin; 'Salty Dog Blues' and 'Under the Double Eagle' adapted by Dorff/Garrett; 'Six Pack To Go' by Thompson/Lowe/Hart performed by Hank Thompson. Costumes by Glenn Wright. Titles: Pacific Title. Sound Recording: Bert Hallberg. Stunt Co-ordinator: Wayne Van Horn.

With: Clint Eastwood (Philo Beddoe), Sondra Locke (Lynn Halsey-Taylor), Geoffrey Lewis (Orville), Ruth Gordon (Ma), Beverly D'Angelo (Echo), Walter Barnes (Tank Murdoch), George Chandler (DMW employee), Roy Jenson (Woody), James McEachin (Herb), Bill McKinney (Dallas), William O'Connell (Elmo), John Quade (Cholla), Dan Vadis (Frank), Gregory Walcott (Putman), Hank Worden (Trailer Court Manager), Jerry Brutsche (Street Sweeper Driver), Cary Michael Cheifer (Manager), Janet Louise Cole (Girl at Palomino Club), Sam Gilman (Fat Guy's Buddy), Chuck Hicks (Truck Driver), Timothy Hervin (M.C.), Tim Irwin (Musician), Billy Jackson (Bettor), Joyce Jameson (Sybil), Richard Jamison (Harlan), Jackson Kane (Man at Bowling Alley), Jeremy Kronsberg (Bruno), Fritz Manes (Bartender), Michael Mann (Church's Manager), Lloyd Nelson (Bartender), Bruce Scott (Schyler), Al Silvani (Tank Murdoch's Manager).

ESCAPE FROM ALCATRAZ USA, 1979. 112 minutes

A Paramount/Malpaso production. Distributed by Paramount.

Directed and produced by Don Siegel. Executive Producer: Robert Daley. Associate Producer; Fritz Manes. Assistant Directors: Luigi Alfano, Mark Johnson and Richard Graves. Script by Richard Tuggle, based on the book by J. Campbell Bruce. Photographed in Panavision and DeLuxe Color by Bruce Surtees.

Edited by Ferris Webster. Production Designer: Allen Smith. Set Decorator: Edward MacDonald. Special Effects: Chuck Gaspar. Music by Jerry Fielding. Song: 'D Block Blues' by Gilbert Thomas Jr. Costumes by Glenn Wright. Titles: Pacific Title. Sound Recording: Bert Hallberg.

With: Clint Eastwood (Frank Morris), Patrick MacGoohan (Prison Warden), Roberts Blossom (Doc), Jack Thibeau (Clarence Anglin), Fred Ward (John Anglin), Paul Benjamin (English), Larry Hankin (Charley Butts), Bruce M. Fisher (Wolf), Frank Ronzio (Litmus), Fred Stuthman (Johnson), David Cryer (Wagner), Madison Arnold (Zimmerman), Blair Burrows (Guard), Bob Balhatchet (Medical Assistant), Matthew Locricchio (Guard), Stephen Bradley (Guard), Don Michaelian (Beck), Ray Gorman (Cellblock Captain), Jason Ronard (Bobs), Ed Vasgersian (Cranston), Ron Vernan (Stone), Regie Bagg (Lucie), Hank Brandt (Associate Warden), Candace Bowen (English's Daughter), Joseph Miksak (Police Sergeant), Gary Goodrow (Weston), Ross Reynolds (Helicopter Pilot), Al Dunlap (Guard), Don Siegel (Doctor).

BRONCO BILLY USA, 1980. 115 minutes

A Warner Bros/Second Street Films production. Distributed by Warner.

Directed by Clint Eastwood. Produced by Dennis Hackin and Neal Dobrofsky. Executive Producer: Robert Daley. Associate Producer: Fritz Manes. Assistant Dirctors: Tom Joyner, Stanley J. Zabka, Richard Graves and Fritz Manes. Script by Dennis Hackin. Photographed in Panavision and DeLuxe Color by David Worth. Cameraman: Jack N. Green. Edited by Ferris Webster and Joel Cox. Art Direction by Gene Lourie. Set Decorator: Ernie Bishop. Musical Supervisor: Snuff Garrett. Music conducted by Steve Dorff. Songs: 'Cowboys and Clowns' by Dorff/Garrett/G. Harju/L. Herbstritt, and 'Bronco Billy' by M. Brown/Dorff/Garrett, both performed by Ronnie Milsap; 'Misery and Gin' by J. Durrill/Garrett, performed by Merle Haggard; 'Barroom Buddies' by M. Brown/C. Crofford/Dorff/ Garrett, performed by Merle Haggard and Clint Eastwood; 'Bayou Lullaby' by Crofford/Garrett, performed by Penny De Haven. Costumes by Glenn Wright. Titles: Pacific Title. Sound Recording: Bert Hallberg.

With: Clint Eastwood (Bronco Billy), Sondra Locke (Antoinette Lily), Geoffrey Lewis (John Arlington), Scatman Crothers (Doc Lynch), Bill McKinney (Lefty LeBow), Sam Bottoms (Leonard James), Dan Vadis (Chief Big Eagle), Sierra Pecheur (Lorraine Running Water), Walter Barnes (Sheriff Dix), Woodrow Parfrey (Dr Canterbury), Beverlee McKinsey (Irene Lily), Douglas McGrath (Lieutenant Wiecker),

Hank Worden (Garage Mechanic), William Prince (Edgar Lipton), Pam Abbas (Mother Superior), Edye Byrde (Eloise), Douglas Copsey (Reporter at Bank), John Wesley Elliott Jr (Sanatorium Attendant), Chuck Hicks, Bobby Hoy (Cowboys), Michael Reinbold (King), Tessa Richarde (Mitzi Fritts), Tanya Russell (Doris Duke), Valerie Shanks (Sister Maria), Sharon Sherlock (Licence Clerk), James Simmerhan (Bank Manager), Chuck Waters and Jerry Wills (Bank Robbers), Jefferson Jewell (Boy at Bank), George Orrison (Cowboy).

ANY WHICH WAY YOU CAN USA, 1980.

115 minutes

A Malpaso production. Distributed by Warner.

Directed by Buddy Van Horn. Produced by Fritz Manes. Executive Producer: Robert Daley. Production Manager: Larry Powell. Assistant Directors: Tom Joyner, Stan Zabka, David Valdes and Fritz Manes. Script by Stanford Sherman. Photographed in DeLuxe Color by David Worth. Cameramen: Jack Green and Douglas Ryan. Edited by Ferris Webster, Ron Spang. Production Design: William J. Creber. Set Decoration: Ernie Bishop. Special Effects: Chuck Gaspar and Jeff Jarvis. Musical supervision by Snuff Garrett. Musical direction by Steve Dorff. Songs: 'Beers To You' by Dorff/J. Durrill/S. Pinkard/Garrett, performed by Ray Charles and Clint Eastwood; 'Any Which Way You Can', by M. Brown/Dorff/ Garrett, performed by Glen Campbell; 'Whiskey Heaven' by C. Crofford/Durill/Garrett, performed by Fats Domino; 'Cow Patti' by and performed by Jim Stafford; 'Acapulco' by L. Collins/M. Leath, performed by Johnny Duncan; 'Any Way You Want Me' by L. Offman, performed by Gene Watson; 'One too Many Women in Your Life' by Durrill/P. Everly; 'Too Loose' by M. Brown/Dorff/Garrett, performed by Sondra Locke; 'Cotton-Eyed Clint' adapted by Dorff/Garrett; 'You're the Reason God Made Oklahoma' by Collins/Pinkard, performed by David Frizzell and Shelly West; 'Orangutan Hall of Fame' by Crofford/Garrett, performed by Cliff Crofford; 'The Good Guys And the Bad Guys' by Durrill/Garrett, performed by John Durrill. Costumes by Glenn Wright. Titles: Pacific Title. Sound Recording: Bert Hallberg.

With: Clint Eastwood (Philo Beddoe), Sondra Locke (Lynn Halsey-Taylor), Geoffrey Lewis (Orville), Wiliam Smith (Jack Wilson), Harry Guardino (James Beekman), Ruth Gordon (Ma), Michael Cavanaugh (Patrick Scarfe), Barry Corbin (Fat Zack), Roy Jenson (Moody), Bill McKinney (Dallas), Dan Vadis (Frank), William O'Connell (Elmo), John Quade (Cholla), Glen Campbell as himself, Al Rusco (Tony Paoli), Camila Ashlend (Hattie), Julie Brown (Candy), Lynn Hallowell (Honey Bun),

Ken Lerner (Tony Paoli Jr), Anne Ramsey (Loretta Quince), Logan Ramsey (Luther Quince), Jerry Brutsche, Orwin Harvey, Larry Holt, John Nowak, Walt Robles and Mike Tillman ('Black Widow' Bikers).

HONKYTONK MAN USA, 1982, 123 minutes

A Malpaso production. Distributed by Warner.

Directed and produced by Clint Eastwood. Executive Producer: Fritz Manes. Production Manager: Steve Perry. Assistant Directors: Tony Brown, Tom Seidman. Script by Clancy Carlile, based on his novel. Photographed in Panavision and Technicolor by Bruce Surtees. Cameraman: Jack N. Green. Edited by Ferris Webster, Joel Cox and Michael Kelly. Production Design: Edward Carfagno. Set Decoration: Gary Moreno. Special Effects: Wayne Edgar. Musical supervision by Snuff Garrett. Musical direction by Steve Dorff. Costumes by Glenn Wright. Titles: Pacific Title. Sound Recording: Don Johnson.

With: Clint Eastwood (Red Stovall), Kyle Eastwood (Whit), John McIntire (Grandpa), Alexa Kenin (Marlene), Verna Bloom (Emmy), Matt Clark (Arnspriger), Jerry Hardin (Snuffy), Tim Thomerson (Highway Patrolman), Macon McCalman (Dr Hines), Joe Regalbuto (Henry Axle), Gary Grubbs (Jim Bob), Rebecca Clemons (Belle), John Gimble (Bob Wills), Linda Hopkins (Flossie), Bette Ford (Lulu), Jim Boelsen (Junior), Tracey Walter (Pooch), Susan Peretz (Miss Maud), John Russell (Jack Wade), Charles Cyphers (Stubbs), Marty Robbins (Smoky), Ray Price (Bob Wills Singer), Shelly West and David Frizzell (Singers at Grand Ole Opry), Porter Wagoner (Dusty), Peter Griggs (Mr Vogel), Julie Hoopman (Whore), DeForest Covan (Gravedigger), Lloyd Nelson (Radio Announcer), Roy Jenson (Dub), Sherry Allurd (Dub's Wife).

FIREFOX USA, 1982. 124 minutes

A Malpaso production. Distributed by Warner.

Directed and produced by Clint Eastwood. Executive Producer: Fritz Manes. Associate Producer: Paul Hitchcock. Production Managers: Steve Perry, Fritz Manes (USA) and Dieter Mayer (Europe). Assistant Directors: Steve Perry, David Valdes (USA), Don French and Charles Furth (Europe). Script by Alex Lasker and Wendell Wellman, based on the novel by Craig Thomas. Photographed in Panavision and DeLuxe Color by Bruce Surtees. Cameraman: Jack N. Green. Special Visual Effects: John Dykstra. Special Effects Supervisor: Robert Shepherd. Edited by Ferris Webster and Ron Spang. Art Directors: John Graysmark and Elayne Ceder. Set Decorator: Ernie Bishop. Special Effects: Chuck Gaspar (USA) and Karl Baumgartner (Europe). Music

by Maurice Jarre. Costumes by Glenn Wright. Titles: Pacific Title. Sound Rcording: Don Johnson.

With: Clint Eastwood (Mitchell Gant), Freddie Jones (Kenneth Aubrey), David Huffman (Buckholz), Warren Clarke (Pavel Upenskoy), Ronald Lacey (Semelovsky), Kenneth Colley (Colonel Kontarsky), Klaus Lowitsch (General Vladimirov), Nigel Hawthorne (Piotr Baranovitch), Stefan Schnabel (First Secretary), Thomas Hill (General Brown), Clive Merrison (Major Lanyev), Kai Wulff (Lieutenant Voskov), Dimitra Arliss (Natalia), Austin Willis (Walters), Michael Currie (Captain Seerbacker), James Staley (Lieutenant Commander Fleischer), Ward Costello (General Rogers), Alan Tilvern (Air Marshal Kutuzov), Oliver Cotton (Dimitri Priabin), Bernard Behrens (William Saltonstall), Richard Derr (Admiral Curtin), Woody Eney (Major Dietz), Bernard Erhard (KGB Guard), Hugh Frazer (Police Inspector Tortyev), Neil Hunt (Richard Cunningham), Wolf Kahler (KGB Chairman), Fritz Manes (Captain), George Orrison (Leon Sprague), John Yates (Admiral Pearson).

SUDDEN IMPACT USA, 1983. 117 minutes

A Malpaso production. Distributed by Warner.

Directed and produced by Clint Eastwood. Executive Producer: Fritz Manes. Associate Producer: Steve Perry. Assistant Directors: David Valdes and Paul Moen. Script by Joseph C. Stinson, based on a story by Earl E. Smith and Charles B. Pierce. Photographed in Panavision and Technicolor by Bruce Surtees. Cameraman: Jack N. Green. Edited by Joel Cox. Production Design: Edward Carfagno. Set Decoration: Ernie Bishop. Special Effects: Chuck Gaspar. Music by Lalo Schifrin. Music Editor: Donald Harris. Song: 'This Side Of Forever' by Lalo Schifrin and DeWayne Blackwell, performed by Roberta Flack. Costumes by Glenn Wright. Titles: Pacific Title. Sound Recording: Don Johnson. Stunt Co-ordinator: Wayne Van Horn.

With: Clint Eastwood (Harry Callahan), Sondra Locke (Jennifer Spencer), Pat Hingle (Jannings), Bradford Dillman (Captain Briggs), Paul Drake (Mick), Audrie J. Neenan (Ray Parkins), Jack Thibeau (Kruger), Michael Currie (Lieutenant Donnelly), Albert Popwell (Horace King), Mark Keyloun (Bennett), Kevin Major Howard (Hawkins), Bette Ford (Leah), Nancy Parsons (Mrs Kruger), Joe Bellan (Detective Burly), Wendell Wellman (Tyrone), Mara Corday (Coffee Shop Waitress), Russ McCubbin (Eddie), Robert Sutton (Carl), Carmen Argenziano (D'Ambrosia), Lisa Britt (Elizabeth Spencer), Bill Reddick (Police Chief), Lois DeBanzie (Judge), Matthew Child (Alby), Lloyd Nelson (Desk Sergeant), Christopher Pray

(Detective Jacobs), James McEachin (Detective Barnes), Lisa London (Young Hooker),Eileen Wiggins (Hysterical Customer), John Novak (Robber).

TIGHTROPE USA, 1984. 114 minutes

A Malpaso production. Distributed by Warner.

Directed by Richard Tuggle. Produced by Clint Eastwood. Production Manager: Fritz Manes. Assistant Directors: David Valdez, Paul Moen and L. Dean Jones Jr. Script by Richard Tuggle. Photographed in Panavision and Technicolor by Bruce Surtees. Cameraman: Jack Green. Edited by Joel Cox. Production Design: Edward Carfagno. Set Decorator: Ernie Bishop. Special Effects: Joe Unsinn. Music by Lennie Niehaus. Main and end title themes performed by The James Rivers Movement. Costumes: Glenn Wright. Titles: Pacific Title. Sound Recording: William Kaplan. Stunt Co-ordinator: Wayne Van Horn.

With: Clint Eastwood (Wes Block), Geneviève Bujold (Beryl Thibodeaux), Dan Hedaya (Inspector Molonari), Alison Eastwood (Amanda Block), Jennifer Beck (Peggy Block), Marco St John (Leander Rolf), Rebecca Perle (Becky Jacklin), Regina Richardson (Sarita), Randi Brooks (Jamie Cory), Jamie Rose (Melanie Silber), Margaret Howell (Judy Harper), Rebecca Clemons (Woman with whip), Jannet MacLachlan (Dr Yarlovsky), Graham Paul (Luther), Bill Holliday (Police Chief), John Wilmot (Forensic Surgeon), Margie O'Dair (Mrs Holstein), Joy N. Houck Jr (Massage Parlor Owner), Stuart Baker-Bergen (Surfer), Donald Barber (Shorty), Robert Harvey (Lonesome Alice), Ron Gural (Coroner Dudley).

CITY HEAT USA, 1984. 97 minutes

A Malpaso/Deliverance production. Distributed by Warner.

Directed by Richard Benjamin. Produced by Fritz Manes. Assistant Director: David Valdes. Script by Sam O. Brown [pseudonym of Blake Edwards] and Joseph C. Stinson, based on a story by Sam O. Brown [Blake Edwards]. Photographed in Panavision and Technicolor by Nick McLean. Edited by Jacqueline Cambas. Art Direction by Edward Carfagno. Set Decoration by George Gaines. Special Effects: Joe Unsinn. Music by Lennie Niehaus. Songs: 'City Heat' by Irene Cara and Bruce Roberts, performed by Joe Williams; 'Million Dollar Baby' by Billy Rose, Mort Dixon, Harry Warren, performed by Al Jarreau; 'Between the Devil and the Deep Blue Sea' by Ted Koehler, Harold Arlen, performed by Eloise Laws; 'Embraceable You' by George and Ira Gershin; 'Get Happy' by Ted Koehler, Harold Arlen, peformed by Irene Cara; 'Let's Do It' by Cole Porter,

performed by Rudy Vallee; 'Montage Blues' by Lennie Niehaus, performed by Mike Lang, Pete Jolly, Clint Eastwood. Costumes by Norman Salling. Titles: Pacific Title. Sound Recording: C. Darin Knight. Stunt Co-ordinator: Wayne Van Horn.

With: Clint Eastwood (Lieutenant Speer), Burt Reynolds (Mike Murphy), Jane Alexander (Addy), Madeline Kahn (Caroline Howley), Rip Torn (Primo Pitt), Irene Cara (Ginny Lee), Richard Roundtree (Dehl Swift), Tony Lo Bianco (Leon Coll), William Sanderson (Lonnie Ash), Nicholas Worth (Troy Roker), Robert Davi (Nino), Jude Farese (Dub Slack), John Hancock (Fat Freddie), Tab Thacker (Tuck), Gerald S. O'Loughlin (Counterman Louie), Bruce M. Fischer and Art La Fleur (Bruisers), Jack Nance (Aram Strossell), Dallas Cole (Redhead Sherry), Lou Filippo (Referee), Michael Maurer (Vint Diestock), Preston Sparks (Keith Stoddard).

Largely written by Blake Edwards, who was apparently the original choice to direct, *City Heat* constructs the Eastwood and Reynolds characters as male rivals, respectively tough cop and dandified private eye, in a comedy which places them between opposing sets of mobsters. The emphasis on the period setting, expressed through set decoration and a score involving George Gershwin and Cole Porter, can be read as an attempt to distance the film's violence from that of the modern city, to reduce it to harmless slapstick. But this succeeds hardly at all; Benjamin fails to find an appropriate way of presenting relentless brutality and cannot integrate it with the comedic elements of the script.

PALE RIDER USA, 1985. 113 minutes

A Malpaso production. Distributed by Warner.

Directed and produced by Clint Eastwood. Executive Producer: Fritz Manes. Assistant Director: David Valdes. Script by Michael Butler and Dennis Shryack. Photographed in Panavision and Technicolor by Bruce Surtees. Cameraman: Jack Green. Edited by Joel Cox. Art Direction by Edward Carfagno. Set Decoration by Ernie Bishop. Special Effects: Chuck Gaspar. Sound Recording: C. Darin Knight. Music by Lennie Niehaus. Costumes: Glenn Wright. Titles: Pacific Title. Stunt Co-ordinator: Wayne Van Horn.

With: Clint Eastwood (The Preacher), Michael Moriarty (Hull Barret), Carrie Snodgress (Sarah Wheeler), Christopher Penn (Josh LaHood), Richard Dysart (Coy LaHood), Sydney Penny (Megan Wheeler), Richard Kiel (Club), Doug McGrath (Spider Conway), John Russell (Stockburn), Charles Hallahan (McGill), Marvin J. McIntyre (Jagou), Frank Ryan (Matt Blankenship), Richard Hamilton (Jed

Blankenship), Graham Paul (Ev Gossage), Chuck LaFont (Eddie Conway), Jeffrey Weissman (Teddy Conway), Allen Keller (Tyson), Tom Oglesby (Elam), Herman Poppe (Ulrik Lindquist), Kathleen Wygle (Bess Gossage), Terrence Evans (Jake Henderson), Jim Hitson (Briggs), Loren Adkins (Bossy), Tom Friedkin (Miner Tom), S.A. Griffin, Billy Drago, Jeffrey Josephson and John Dennis Johnston (Deputies).

HEARTBREAK RIDGE USA, 1986.

130 minutes

A Malpaso production in association with Jay Weston Productions. Distributed by Warner.

Directed and produced by Clint Eastwood. Executive Producer: Fritz Manes. Assistant Directors: Paul Moen and L. Dean Jones Jr. Script by James Carabatsos. Photographed in Panavision and Technicolor by Jack N. Green. Cameraman: Stephen St. John. Edited by Joel Cox. Art Direction by Edward Carfagno. Set Decoration by Robert Benton. Special Effects: Chuck Gaspar. Music by Lennie Niehaus. Songs: 'Sea Of Heartbreak' by Hal David, Paul Hampton, performed by Don Gibson; 'Secret Love', 'A Very Precious Love' by Sammy Fain, Paul Webster; 'How Much I Care' by Clint Eastwood, Sammy Cahn, performed by Jill Hollier; 'I Love You, but I Ain't Stupid' by Mario Van Peebles, Desmond Nakano, performed by Mario Van Peebles; 'Bionic Marine', 'Recon Rap' by Mario Van Peebles. Costumes by Glenn Wright. Titles: Pacific Title. Sound Recording: William Nelson. Stunt Co-ordinator: Wayne Van Horn.

With: Clint Eastwood (Sergeant Thomas Highway), Marsha Mason (Aggie), Everett McGill (Major Powers), Moses Gunn (Sergeant Webster), Eileen Heckart (Little Mary), Bo Svenson (Roy Jennings), Boyd Gaines (Lieutnant Ring), Mario Van Peebles ('Stitch' Jones), Arlen Dean Snyder (Master Sergeant Choozoo), Vincent Irizarry (Fragetti), Ramon Franco (Aponte), Tom Villard (Profile), Mike Gomez (Quinones), Rodney Hill (Collins), Peter Koch ('Swede' Johanson), Richard Venture (Colonel Meyers), Peter Jason (Major Devin), J.C. Quinn (Quartermaster Sergeant), Begoña Plaza (Mrs. Aponte), John Eames (Judge Zane).

BIRD USA, 1988. 160 minutes

A Malpaso production. Distributed by Warner.

Directed and produced by Clint Eastwood. Executive Producer: David Valdes. Assistant Director: L. Dean Jones Jr. Script by Joel Oliansky. Photographed in Technicolor and Panavision by Jack N. Green. Edited by Joel Cox. Art Direction by Edward Carfagno. Set Decoration: Thomas Roysden. Special Effects:

Joe Day. Costumes by Glenn Wright. Sound Recording by Willie D. Burton, Bobby Fernandez.

Music supervised by Lennie Niehaus. Music/songs: 'Maryland, My Maryland' arranged and performed by Lennie Niehaus; 'Lester Leaps In' by Lester Young; 'I Can't Believe that You're in Love with Me' by Clerance Gaskill, Jimmy McHugh; 'All of Me' by Seymour Simon, Gerald Marks; 'This Time the Dream's on Me' by Harold Arlen, Johnny Mercer, performed by Charlie Parker, Monty Alexander, Ray Brown, John Guerin; 'Reno Jam Session' by Lennie Niehaus, performed by Lennie Niehaus, James Rivers, Red Rodney, Pete Jolly, Chuck Beghofer, John Guerin; 'Young Bird' by Lennie Niehaus, performed by James Rivers, Pete Jolly, Chuck Berghofer, John Guerin; 'Why Do I Love You?' by Jerome Kern, Oscar Hammerstein II, performed by James Rivers, Lennie Niehaus; 'Moonlight Becomes You' by Johnny Burke, Jimmy Van Heusen, performed by Ronnie Lang, Gary Foster, Bob Cooper, Pete Christlieb, Chuck Findley, Conte Candoli, Rick Baptist, Dick Nash, Bill Watrous, Barry Harris, Chuck Berghofer, John Guerin; 'Moose the Mooche' by Charlie Parker, performed by Charles McPherson, Jon Faddis, Walter Davis Jr, Ron Carter, John Guerin; 'Ornithology' by Charlie Parker, Bennie Harris, performed by Charlie Parker, Jon Fadis, Mike Lang, Chuck Domanico, John Guerin, Charlie Shoemaker; 'Lover Man' by Jimmy Davis, Roger Ramirez, Jimmy Sherman, performed by Charlie Parker, Charles McPherson, Jon Faddis, Walter Davis Jr, Ron Carter, John Guerin; 'April In Paris' by Vernon Duke, E.Y. Harburg; 'Laura' by David Raskin; 'Parker's Mood' by Charlie Parker, performed by Charlie Parker, Barry Harris, Chuck Berghofer, John Guerin, plus strings; 'Jewish Wedding' by Lennie Niehaus, performed by Charles McPherson, Red Rodney, Walter Davis Jr, John Guerin; 'One for Red' by Lennie Niehaus, performed by Red Rodney, Mike Lang, Chuck Domanico, John Guerin; 'Now's the Time' by Charlie Parker, performed by Charlie Parker, Charles McPherson, Red Rodney, Walter Davis Jr, Ron Carter, John Guerin; 'Albino Red Blues' by Lennie Niehaus, Joel Oliansky, performed by Red Rodney, Walter Davis Jr, Ron Carter, John Guerin; 'Cool Blues', 'Ko Ko' by Charlie Parker, performed by Charlie Parker, Walter Davis Jr, Ron Carter, John Guerin; 'Be My Love' by Nicholas Brodszky, Sammy Cahn, performed by Mario Lanza; 'Parker's Mood' by Charlie Parker, performed by King Pleasure, John Lewis, Percy Heath, Kenny Clarke; 'Buster's Last Stand' by Lennie Niehaus, performed by Ronny Lang; extract from the Firebird Suite by Igor Stravinsky performed by the Vienna Symphony Orchestra, conducted by Wolfgang Sawallisch.

With: Forest Whitaker (Charlie 'Yardbird' Parker), Diane Venora (Chan Richardson), Michael Zelniker (Red Rodney), Samuel E. Wright (Dizzy Gillespie), Keith David (Buster Franklin), Michael McGuire (Brewster), James Handy (Esteves), Damon Whitaker (Young Bird), Morgan Nagler (Kim), Arlen Dean Snyder (Dr Heath), Diane Salinger (Baroness Nica), Sam Robards (Moscowitz), Penelope Windust (Bellevue Nurse), Glenn T. Wright (Alcoholic Patient), Bill Cobbs (Dr Caulfield), Chris Bosley (Doorman), Joey Green (Gene), John Witherspoon (Sid), Tony Todd (Frog), Jo De Winter (Mildred Berg), Richard Zavaglia (Ralph the Narc), Anna Levine (Audrey), Billy Mitchell (Billy Prince), Jason Bernard (Benny Tate), Ann Weldon (Violet Welles), Richard Jeni (Chummy Morello), Don Starr (Doctor at Nica's).

THE DEAD POOL USA, 1988. 91 minutes

A Malpaso production. Distributed by Warner.

Directed by Buddy Van Horn. Produced by David Valdes. Assistant Director: L. Dean Jones Jr. Script by Steve Sharon, based on a story by Sharon, Durk Pearson and Sandy Shaw. Photographed in Panavision and Technicolor by Jack Green. Edited by Joel Cox and Ron Spang. Art Direction: Edward Carfagno. Set Decoration by Thomas Roysden. Special Effects: Chuck Gaspar. Music by Lalo Schifrin. Song: 'Welcome To The Jungle' written and performed by Guns 'n' Roses. Costumes by Glenn Wright. Titles: Pacific Title. Sound Recording: Richard S. Church and Bobby Fernandez. Stunt Co-ordinator: Richard Farnsworth.

With: Clint Eastwood (Harry Callahan), Patricia Clarkson (Samantha Walker), Liam Neeson (Peter Swan), Evan C. Kim (Al Quan), David Hunt (Harlan Rook), Michael Currie (Captain Donnelly), Michael Goodwin (Lieutenant Ackerman), Darwin Gillett (Patrick Snow), Anthony Charnota (Lou Janero), Christopher Beale (DA Thomas McSherry), John Allen Vick (Lieutenant Ruskowski).

PINK CADILLAC USA, 1989. 116 minutes

A Malpaso production. Distributed by Warner.

Directed by Buddy Van Horn. Produced by David Valdes. Assistant Directors: Matt Earl Beesley, Frank Capra III and Jeffrey Wetzel. Script by John Eskow. Photographed in Panavision and Technicolor by Jack N. Green. Production Design by Edward Carfagno. Set Design: Judy Cammer. Musical supervision by Clint Eastwood and David Valdes. Songs: 'Two Doors Down' by and performed by Dolly Parton; 'Born under a Bad Sign' by Booker Jones, William Bell, performed by Robben Ford; 'Any Which Way The Wind Blows' by John

McFee, Andre Pessis, performed by Southern Pacific; 'Rollin' Dice' by Dennis Robbins, John Sherill, Bob Di Perlo, performed by Billy Hill; 'Beneath the Texas Moon' by J.C. Crowley, Jack Wesley Roth, performed by J.C. Crowley; 'Drive All Night' by Bryan Adams, performed by Dion; 'Let It Roll' by Bill Payne, Paul Barrere, Martin Kibbee, performed by Little Feat; 'Card Carryin' Fool' by Byron Hill and Tim Bays, performed by Randy Travis; 'There's A Tear In My Beer' by Hank Williams, performed by Hank Williams Sr and Hank Williams Jr; 'Never Givin'' up on Love' by Michael Smotherman, performed by Michael Martin Murphey; 'If it Wasn't for the Heartbreak' by Chris Walters and Kix Brooks, performed by Jill Hollier; 'Have You Ever Been Mellow' by John Farmer; 'Baby Let's Play House' by Arthur Gunter; 'Boola Boola' by Alan M. Hirsch; 'Hawaiian War Chant' by Ralph Freed, Johnny Noble; 'Blue Suede Shoes' by Carl Lee Perkins. Stunt Co-ordinator: Richard Farnsworth. Titles: Pacific Title.

With: Clint Eastwood (Tommy Nowak), Bernadette Peters (Lou Ann McGuinn), Timothy Carhart (Roy McGuinn), Michael Des Barres (Alex), John Dennis Johnston (Waycross), Jimmy E. Skaggs (Billy Dunston), Bill Moseley (Darrell), Michael Champion (Ken Lee), William Hickey (Mr Burton), Geoffrey Lewis (Ricky Zee), Gary Klar (Randy Bates), Gary Leffew (John Capshaw), Julie Hoopman (Waitress), Paul Benjamin (Judge), Cliff Remis (Jeff), Frances Fisher (Dinah), Mara Corday (Stick Lady), Bill McKinney (Bartender), Bob Feist (Rodeo Announcer), Wayne Storm (Jack Bass), Richie Allen (Derelict), Roy Conrad (Barker).

WHITE HUNTER, BLACK HEART USA, 1990. 112 minutes

A Malpaso/Rastar production. Distributed by Warner.

Directed and produced by Clint Eastwood. Executive Producer: David Valdes. Assistant Directors: Patrick Clayton, Chris Brock, Tim Lewis and Isaac Mabhikwa. Script by Peter Viertel, James Bridges and Burt Kennedy, based on the novel by Viertel. Photographed in Panavision and Technicolor by Jack N. Green. Edited by Joel Cox. Art Direction by Tony Reading. Set Decoration by Peter Howitt. Special Effects: John Evans. Music by Lennie Niehaus, performed by Emil Richards, Efrain Toro, Bill Perkins. Song: 'Satin Doll' by Duke Ellington, Johnny Mercer, Billy Strayhorn. Costumes by John Mollo. Titles: Pacific Title. Sound Recording: Peter Handford. Stunts: George Orrison.

With: Clint Eastwood (John Wilson), Jeff Fahey (Pete Verrill), Charlotte Cornwell (Miss

Wilding), Marisa Berenson (Kay Gibson), Richard Vanstone (Phil Duncan), Timothy Spall (Hodkins), George Dzundza (Paul Landers), Boy Mathais Chuma (Kivu), Edward Tudor Pole (Reissar), Roddy Maude-Roxby (Thompson), Richard Warwick (Basil Fields), John Rapley (Gun-shop Salesman), Norman Lumsden (Butler George), Catherine Neilson (Irene Saunders), Jamie Koss (Mrs Duncan), Anne Dunkley (Scarf Girl), Geoffrey Hutchings (Alec Laing), Christopher Fairbank (Tom Harrison), Alun Armstrong (Ralph Lockhart), Clive Mantle (Harry), Mel Martin (Margaret MacGregor), Martin Jacobs (Dickie Marlowe), Alex Norton (Zibelinsky), Eleanor David (Dorshka), Andrew Whalley (Photographer), Conrad Asquith (Ogilvy).

THE ROOKIE USA, 1990. 121 mins.

A Malpaso production. Distributed by Warner.

Directed by Clint Eastwood. Produced by Howard Kanzanjian, Steven Siebert and David Valdes. Assistant Directors: Matt Earl Beesley, Frank Capra III, Jeffrey Wetzel, D. Scott Easton and George Fortmuller. Script by Boaz Yakin and Scott Spiegel. Photographed in Panavision and Technicolor by Jack N. Green. Edited by Joel Cox. Art Direction by Ed Verreaux. Sets designed by John Berger and Dawn Snyder. Special Effects: John Frazier. Music by Lennie Niehaus. Songs: 'All The Things You Are' by Jerome Kern, Oscar Hammerstein II; 'Red Zone' by Kyle Eastwood, Michael Stevens. Costumes by Glenn Wright and Deborah Hopper. Titles: Pacific Title. Sound Recording: Don Johnson. Stunt Co-ordinator: Terry Leonard.

With: Clint Eastwood (Nick Pulovski), Charlie Sheen (David Ackerman), Raul Julia (Strom), Sonia Braga (Liesl), Tom Skerritt (Eugene Ackerman), Lara Flynn Boyle (Sarah), Pepe Serna (Lieutenant Ray Garcia), Marco Rodriguez (Loco), Pete Randall (Cruz), Donna Mitchell (Laura Ackerman), Xander Berkeley (Blackwell), Tony Plana (Moralles), David Sherrill (Max), Hal Williams (Powell), Matt McKenzie (Wang), Joel Polis (Lance), Anthony Charnota (Romano), Paul Ben-Victor (Little Felix), Jeanne Mori (Connie Ling), Anthony Alexander (Alphonse), Paul Butler (Captain Hargate), Seth Allen (David as a Child), Coleby Lombardo (David's Brother), Roberta Vasquez (Heather Torres), Robert Harvey (Whalen), Nick Ballo (Vito), Jay Boryea (Sal), George Orrison (Detective Orrison).

The parodic elements of *The Dead Pool* are taken to a further extreme in *The Rookie*. Dominated by different kinds of spectacular action sequence, it is marked by an inability to arrive at a consistent approach to its world – in this respect it resembles another unsuccessful film,

Pink Cadillac, which relates to the road films much in the way that *The Rookie* relates to the Callahan cycle. While the level of stunt action, in which cars, lorries and finally planes are destroyed, tends towards cartooning, there is also a commitment to showing us a demonic world, exemplified in the explicit physical punishment of the principal villains: we watch all three die of gunshot wounds, in two cases shots to the head. Alongside this are comedic elements in a 'new partner' plot using the Eastwood and Sheen characters, and a subdued melodrama built around the family of the Sheen character. The result is entirely incoherent, arguably Eastwood's least succesful movie.

UNFORGIVEN USA, 1992. 131 mins.

A Malpaso production. Distributed by Warner.

Directed and produced by Clint Eastwood. Executive Producer: David Valdes. Assistant Directors: Scott Maitland, Bill Bannerman, Grant Lucibello, Tom Rooker and Jeffrey Wetzel. Script by David Webb Peoples. Photographed in Panavision and Technicolor by Jack N. Green. Edited by Joel Cox. Production Design by Henry Bumstead. Art Direction by Rick Roberts, Adrian Gorton. Set Design by James J. Murakami. Special Effects: John Frazier. Music by Lennie Niehaus. Costumes by Glenn Wright. Titles: Pacific Title. Sound Recording: Rob Young. Technical Consultant: Buddy Van Horn.

With: Clint Eastwood (William Munny), Gene Hackman ('Little Bill' Daggett), Morgan Freeman (Ned Logan), Richard Harris (English Bob), Jaimz Woolvett (the 'Schofield Kid'), Saul Rubinek (W.W. Beauchamp), Frances Fisher (Strawberry Alice), Anna Thomson (Delilah), David Mucci (Quick Mike), Rob Campbell (Davey Bunting), Anthony James (Skinny Dubois), Tara Dawn Frederick (Little Sue), Beverley Elliott (Silky), Liisa Repo-Martell (Faith), Josie Smith (Crow Creek Kate), Shane Meier (Will Munny), Aline Levasseur (Penny Munny), Cherrilene Cardinal (Sally Two Trees), Robert Koons (Crocker), Ron White (Clyde Ledbetter), Mina E. Mina (Muddy Chandler), Henry Kope (German Joe Schultz), Jeremy Ratchford (Deputy Andy Russell), John Pyper-Ferguson (Charley Hecker), Jefferson Mappin (Fatty Rossiter), Walter Marsh (Barber), George Orrison (the Shadow).

IN THE LINE OF FIRE USA, 1993.

129 minutes

A Columbia Pictures production. Distributed by Columbia Tristar.

Directed by Wolfgang Petersen. Produced by Jeff Apple. Assistant Directors: Peter Kohn, Lee Cleary and David Katz, Michael Grillo. Script by Jeff Maguire. Photographed in Panavision and Technicolor by John Bailey and Mark Vargo. Edited by Anne Coates and Steven Kemper. Production Design: Lilly Kilvert. Art Director: John Warnke. Set Design: Jann K. Engel. Special Effects: Rocky Gehr. Music by Ennio Morricone; 'Willow Weep for Me' by Anne Ronell; 'All Blues' by and performed by Miles Davis; 'As Time Goes By' by Herman Hupfield; 'I Didn't Know what Time It Was' by Richard Rogers, Lorenz Hart; 'I only Have Eyes for You' by Harry Warren, Al Dubin. Costumes by Erica Edell Phillips. Sound Recording: Willie Burton. Stunt Co-ordinator: Buddy Van Horn. Titles: Pacific Title.

With: Clint Eastwood (Frank Horrigan), John Malkovitch (Mitch Leary), Rene Russo (Lilly Raines), Dylan McDermott (Al D'Andrea), Gary Cole (Bill Watts), Fred Dalton Thompson (Harry Sargent), John Mahoney (Sam Campagna), Greg Alan-Williams (Matt Wilder), Jim Curley (the President), Sally Hughes (the First Lady), Clyde Kusatsu (Jack Okura), Steve Hytner (Tony Carducci), Tobin Bell (Mendoza), Bob Schott (Jimmy Hendrickson), Juan A. Riojas (Raul), Elsa Raven (Leary's Landlady), Patrika Darbo (Pam Magnus), Mary Van Arsdel (Sally), John Heard (Professor Riger), Alan Toy (Walter Wickland).

A PERFECT WORLD USA, 1993.

138 minutes

A Malpaso/Warner Bros. production. Distributed by Warner.

Directed by Clint Eastwood. Produced by Mark Johnson and David Valdes. Assistant Directors: L. Dean Jones, Bill Bannerman and Sarah Shields. Script by John Lee Hancock. Photographed in Panavision and Technicolor by Jack N. Green. Edited by Joel Cox and Ron Spang. Production Design by Henry Bumstead. Art Director: Jack Taylor Jr. Set Design: Charlie Vassar and Antoinette Gordon. Music by Lennie Niehaus. Songs: 'Ida Red' performed by Bob Wills and his Texas Playboys; 'Abilene' by John D. Loudermilk, Lester Brown, Bob Gibson, performed by George Hamilton IV; 'South' by Bennie Moten, Thamon Hayes, performed by Bob Wills and his Texas Playboys; 'Please Help Me', I'm Falling (In Love With You)' by Don Robertson, Hal Blair, performed by Hank Locklin; 'Blue Blue Day' by and performed by Don Gibson; 'Catch a Falling Star' by Paul Vance, Lee Pockriss, performed by Perry Como; 'Guess Things Happen that Way' by Jack Clement, performed by Johnny Cash; 'Night Life' by Willie Nelson, Walt Breeland, Paul Buskirk, performed by Rusty Draper; 'Sea of Heartbreak' by Hal David, Paul Hampton, performed by Don Gibson; 'Dark Moon' by Ned Miller and 'The Little White Cloud that Cried' by Johnnie Ray, performed by Chris Isaak; 'Funny How Time Slips Away' by and performed by Willie Nelson; 'Don't Worry' by and performed by Marty Robbins; 'Big Fran's Baby' by Clint Eastwood. Costumes by Erica Edell Phillips. Titles: Pacific Title. Sound Recording: Jeff Wexler, Bobby Fernandez. Stunt Co-ordinator: Buddy Van Horn.

With: Kevin Costner (Butch Haynes), Clint Eastwood (Red Garnett), Laura Dern (Sally Gerber), T.J. Lowther (Phillip Perry), Keith Szarabajka (Terry Pugh), Leo Burmester (Tom Adler), Paul Hewitt (Dick Suttle), Bradley Whitford (Bobby Lee), Ray McKinnon (Bradley), Jennifer Griffin (Gladys Perry), Leslie Flowers (Naomi Perry), Belinda Flowers (Ruth Perry), Darryl Cox (Mr Hughes), Jay Whiteaker (Superman), Taylor Suzanna McBride (Tinkerbell), Christopher Reagan Ammons (Dancing Skeleton), Mark Voges (Larry), John M. Jackson (Bob Fielder), Connie Cooper (Bob's Wife), George Orrison (Officer Orrison).

BIBLIOGRAPHY

This bibliography lists books and articles that are referred to or quoted in the text. A much fuller listing of work on Eastwood can be found in the bibliography of Christopher Frayling's valuable *Clint Eastwood* (Virgin Books, 1992).

1. Entirely or mainly on American cinema

Bach, Steven *Final Cut: Dreams and Disaster in the Making of 'Heaven's Gate'*, Cape, London, 1985

Biskind, Peter 'Any Which Way He Can' in *Premiere* vol.6, no.8, April 1993

Britton, Andrew 'Blissing Out: The Politics of Reaganite Entertainment' in *Movie* 31/32, 1986

Carney, Raymond *American Visions: The Films of Frank Capra*, Cambridge University Press, 1986

Cavell, Stanley *Themes out of School: Effects and Causes*, University of Chicago Press, 1988. Includes the essay on *North by Northwest* and 'The Fact of Television'

Cavell, Stanley *The World Viewed: Reflections on the Ontology of Film* (enlarged edition), Harvard University Press, 1979

Dyer, Richard *Heavenly Bodies: Film Stars and Society*, Macmillan, London, 1987

Dyer, Richard 'The Towering Inferno' in *Movie* 21, 1975

Frayling, Christopher *Spaghetti Westerns*, Routledge, London, 1981

French, Philip *Westerns: Aspects of a Movie Genre*, Secker & Warburg, London, 1973

Guérif, François (translated by Lisa Nesselson) *Clint Eastwood*, Roger Houghton, London, 1986

Halliday, Jon *Sirk on Sirk*, Secker & Warburg, London, 1971

Hepburn, Katharine *The Making of 'The African Queen'*, Century Hutchinson, London, 1987

Houston, Penelope 'Preston Sturges' in *Sight & Sound*, Summer 1965

Huston, John *An Open Book*, Macmillan, London, 1981

Penn, Arthur '*Bonnie and Clyde*: Private Integrity and Public Violence' in *The Bonnie and Clyde Book*, edited by Sandra Wake and Nicola Hayden, Lorrimer, London, 1972

Pye, Douglas '*Ulzana's Raid*' in *Movie* 27/28, 1980-81

Rosen, Marjorie *Popcorn Venus: Women, Movies and the American Dream*, Peter Owen, London, 1975

Thompson, Richard, & Hunter, Tim 'Clint Eastwood, Auteur' in *Film Comment*, January/February 1978

Wood, Robin *Hollywood from Vietnam to Reagan*, Columbia University Press, New York, 1986

2. On American culture, and other background material

Bush, Clive *Halfway to Revolution: Investigation and Crisis in the Work of Henry Adams, William James and Gertrude Stein*, Yale University Press, 1991

Freud, Sigmund *The Interpretation of Dreams*, Penguin, Harmondsworth, 1976

Frye, Northrop *Anatomy of Criticism*, Princeton University Press, 1971

Josephy, Alvin M., Jr *The Indian Heritage of America*, Penguin, Harmondsworth, 1975

Marc, David *Demographic Vistas: Television in American Culture*, University of Pennsylvania Press, 1984

Matthiesen, F.O. *American Renaissance: Art and Expressionism in the Age of Emerson and Whitman*, Oxford University Press, New York, 1941

Mottram, Eric *Blood on the Nash Ambassador: Investigations in American Culture*, Hutchinson Radius, London, 1989

Platt, John Clark *Vietnam Voices: Perspectives on the War Years 1941-82*, Viking Penguin, New York, 1984

Sartre, Jean-Paul (translated by Annette Michelson) *Literary and Philosophical Essays*, Rider, London, 1955

Sontag, Susan *Illness as Metaphor*, Penguin, Harmondsworth, 1983

Viertel, Peter *White Hunter, Black Heart*, Penguin, Harmondsworth, 1990. First published by Doubleday, New York, 1953. The Penguin edition includes an afterword by Viertel written in 1989

Webster, Duncan *Looka Yonder! The Imaginary America of Populist Culture*, Routledge/Comedia, London, 1988

INDEX

Academy Awards (Oscars) 29, 138, 209, 217, 230
Adams, Ansel 119, 137
Adventures of Huckleberry Finn, The (Richard Thorpe, 1939; Michael Curtiz, 1960) 128
Adventures of Huckleberry Finn, The (Twain) 27, 119-120, 185, 233
Africa 209, 212
African Queen, The (Forester) 207-209, 212
African Queen, The (John Huston, 1951) 207, 215
Alcatraz 51, 53, 142, 144, 145, 234
Aldrich, Robert 74, 86, 104
Alien (Ridley Scott) 146-147
All that Heaven Allows (Douglas Sirk,1955) 92, 93, 94, 97
All the President's Men (Alan J. Pakula, 1976) 172
Allen, Woody 89
Altman, Robert 138
Angel of Vengeance (Abel Ferrara, 1981) 56
Any Which Way You Can (Buddy Van Horne, 1980) 159, **175-182**, 185, 198, 234
Apted, Michael 192
Arness, James 12
Ashby, Hal 121, 170, 194
Asphalt Jungle, The (John Huston, 1950) 194

Bacall, Lauren 207, 209, 210
Bach, Steven 103
Badham, John 147
Baker, Roy Ward 74
Ballad of Cable Hogue, The (Sam Peckinpah, 1970) 103
Banky, Vilma 203
Bartleby (Melville) 228
Bear, The (Faulkner) 212
Beddoe films **175-182**, 186, 194, 197
Beggar's Opera, The (Gay) 29, 32
Beguiled, The (Don Siegel, 1971) 22, 73, 74, **75-82**, 82, 100, 101, 192, 236
Bend of the River (Anthony Mann, 1952) 128
Benjamin, Richard 9, 247
Benton, Robert 130
Bergman, Marilyn and Alan 90
Betrayed (Costa-Gavras, 1988) 197
Big Sleep, The (Chandler) 71
Billy Budd (Melville) 107
Bird (Clint Eastwood, 1988) 73, **199-207**, 217, 220, 236
Birdman of Alcatraz, The (John Frankenheimer, 1961) 144
Black Rain (Ridley Scott, 1989) 157
Blixen, Karen 209
Blue Thunder (John Badham, 1983) 147
Bogart, Humphrey 207, 209, 210
Bonanza 12
Bond, James 60
Bonnie and Clyde (Arthur Penn, 1967) 156
Boorman, John 161
Boston Strangler 65
Boyer, Charles 24
Breezy (Clint Eastwood, 1973) 73, 74, **90-100**, 101, 233
Brennan, Walter 26
Brent, George 202

Bringing Up Baby (Howard Hawks, 1938) 160
Britton, Andrew 147
Bronco Billy (Clint Eastwood, 1980) 8, 155, **182-192**, 197, 198, 217, 223, 231, 234
Brontë, Charlotte 95, 225
Bronx Tale, A (Robert De Niro, 1993) 230
Bujold, Geneviève 62
Buono, il brutto, il cattivo, Il see *The Good, the Bad and the Ugly*
Burton, Richard 138
Bush, Clive 232
Bush, George 8

California 73, 75, 82, 192
Callahan films 20, 24, **35-61**, 62, 64, 71, 72, 73, 74, 112, 127-128, 131, 142, 144, 152, 154, 156, 159, 175, 189, 235
Capra, Frank 9, 70, 100, 172, 197-198, 204, 206
Carney, Raymond 100
Carrie (Brian De Palma, 1976) 74
Carter, Forrest 129
Carter, Jimmy 8
Casablanca (Michael Curtiz, 1942) 89, 90
Castle Keep (Eastlake) 138
Castle Keep (Sydney Pollack, 1969) 138, 139
Cat Ballou (Elliot Silverstein, 1965) 26
Catch-22 (Heller) 138
Catch-22 (Mike Nichols, 1970) 138, 139
Cather, Willa 192
Cavell, Stanley 8, 12, 34, 101, 230
Chandler, Raymond 71
Charles, Ray 182
Cherokee Strip 194
Cheyenne 12
Cheyenne Autumn (John Ford, 1964) 25
Cheyenne Social Club, The (Gene Kelly, 1970) 26
Cimino, Michael 9, 44, 103, 121, 161, 163, 165, 168, 169, 170, 215, 233
Cinecittà 21
Citizen Kane (Orson Welles, 1941) 201-202
City Heat (Richard Benjamin, 1984) 9, 247
City on Fire (Alvin Rakoff, 1979) 146
Civil War (American) 26, 29, 74, 75, 120, 123
Clift, Montgomery 13
Coalminer's Daughter (Michael Apted, 1980) 192
Cold War 18
Columbia 209
Coming Home (Hal Ashby) 121
Confidence Man, The (Melville) 27
Conrad, Joseph 119, 237
Conway, Tim 26
Coogan's Bluff (Don Siegel, 1968) 30, 60, 102, 156, 157-158, 189
Cooper, James Fenimore 13, 110, 212
Costa-Gavras 197
Country (Richard Pearce, 1984) 130
Crane, Stephen 128
Craven, Wes 56
Crawford, Joan 207
Crosby, Bing 28
Curtiz, Michael 89

Daly, Tyne 52
Dano, Royal 128, 194
Dassin, Jules 29
Dave (Ivan Reitman, 1993) 229
Davis, Bette 209
De Niro, Robert 230
Dead Pool, The (Buddy Van Horne, 1988) 35, **60-61**, 250
Death by Hanging (Nagisa Oshima, 1968) 106
Death of a Salesman (Miller) 192, 205
Death Wish (Michael Winner, 1974) 56, 57
Death Wish II (Michael Winner, 1981) 56, 57
Deer Hunter, The (Michael Cimino, 1978) 215
Depression, the 130, 222
Dern, Bruce 106
DeSalvo, Albert 65
Devine, Andy 26
Diddling Considered as One of the Exact Sciences (Poe) 27, 34
Dirty Harry (Don Siegel, 1971) 35, 36, 37, **38-43**, 44, 45, 46, 48, 49, 50, 52, 53, 54, 55, 56, 60, 64, 65, 82, 127, 142, 228, 230, 231, 232, 236
disaster movies 145-147
Dog Soldiers (Karel Reisz, 1978) 131
Dollars films **11-34**, 73, 102, 142
Domino, Fats 180
Dr Jekyll and Sister Hyde (Roy Ward Baker, 1971) 74
Dyer, Richard 9, 146, 207
Dzundza, George 211

Eastlake, William 138
Edwards, Blake 247
Eiger Sanction, The (Clint Eastwood, 1975) 243
Emerson, Ralph Waldo 9
Enforcer, The (James Fargo, 1976) 35, 36, 37, **48-53**, 54, 55, 60, 144, 152, 153, 160, 182, 234
Escape from Alcatraz (Don Siegel, 1979) 62, **142-147**, 152, 234-235
Every Which Way But Loose (James Fargo, 1978) 159, **175-182**, 198, 234
Faithful Shepherdess, The (Fletcher) 235
Fargo, James 9, 182
Faulkner, William 22, 75, 131, 210, 212
Ferrara, Abel 56
film noir 86
Firefox (Clint Eastwood, 1982) 8, **147-150**, 152, 155, 222, 228, 234-235
Fistful of Dollars, A (Sergio Leone, 1964) 7, 11, **14-20**, 20, 21, 22, 24, 25, 26, 27, 231
Fitzgerald, Edward 201
Fitzgerald, F. Scott 129, 228
Flack, Roberta 59, 85
Fleischer, Richard 79
Fletcher, John 235
Fonda, Henry 26
Fonda, Jane 141
For a Few Dollars More (Sergio Leone, 1965) **20-25**, 26, 32, 112, 113, 231
Ford, John 25, 104, 109, 124, 192
Forester, C.S. 207, 212
Frankie and Johnny (Garry Marshall, 1991) 82
Frayling, Christopher 21
Freeman, Morgan 217

French Connection, The (William
Friedkin, 1971) 112
French, Philip 103
Freud, Sigmund 69, 237
Friday the Thirteenth I-III (1980-82) 57
Friedkin, William 112
Frye, Northrop 128

Garfield, James Abram 218
Garner, Erroll 89
Garner, James 11, 26
Gauntlet, The (Clint Eastwood, 1977)
155, 156, 159, **170-175**, 175, 177,
179, 180, 185, 191, 198, 234, 235
Gay, John 29, 32
Gene Autry Show, The 12
Gershwin, George 247
Gibson, Don 150
Gillespie, Dizzy 205, 207
Glass Menagerie, The (Williams) 79,
81, 82
Gone to Texas (Carter) 129
Good Guys and the Bad Guys, The
(Burt Kennedy, 1969) 26
Good, the Bad and the Ugly, The
(Sergio Leone, 1966) 20, **25-33**, 41
Gordon, Ruth 177, 194
Grand Ole Opry 194, 195
Grapes of Wrath, The (John Ford,
1940) 109, 192
Grapes of Wrath, The (Steinbeck) 109,
192
Great Gatsby, The (Fitzgerald) 129
Grenada 153, 154, 236
Guérif, François 116
Guillermin, John 145
Gunsmoke 12

Hackford, Taylor 150
Hackman, Gene 217
Halloween I-III (1978-82) 57
Hamlet (Shakespeare) 199
Hammer 74
Hang 'Em High (Ted Post, 1967) 102,
103, **103-109**, 112, 121
Harris, Richard 217
Have Gun Will Travel 12
Hawks, Howard 13, 160
Hawthorne, Nathaniel 191
Hearst, Patty 44
Heart of Darkness (Conrad) 237
Heartbreak Ridge (Clint Eastwood,
1986) **150-155**, 198, 217, 222, 228,
235-236, 237
Heaven's Gate (Michael Cimino, 1981)
103
Heifetz, Jascha 205
Heims, Jo 90
Heller, Joseph 138
Hemingway, Ernest 212, 213, 215, 225
Hepburn, Katharine 52, 207
High Noon (Fred Zinnemann, 1952)
15, 22, 104, 113
High Plains Drifter (Clint Eastwood,
1972) 17, 73, 103, **112-119**, 125, 131,
136, 137, 218, 232, 233, 235
hippies 90, 92, 93, 141, 157, 229
Hitchcock, Alfred 101, 235
Holden, William 90, 100
Holliday, Billie 199
Honkytonk Man (Clint Eastwood,
1982) 73, 155, 156, 158, **192-197**,
198, 231, 233, 236
Hooker, Richard 138
Hope, Bob 28
Hopper, Dennis 106
Houston, Penelope 128
How the West Was Won (Henry
Hathaway, John Ford, George
Marshall, 1962) 26
How to Steal a Million (William Wyler,
1966) 27
Hughes, Howard 99, 108
Huston, John 128, 199, 207, 209, 211,
212, 213

Hutton, Brian G. 138
Huxley, Aldous 205

I Spit on Your Grave (1980) 56, 57
In the Line of Fire (Wolfgang Petersen,
1993) 7, **228-230**, 231
Indians (North American) 104, 122-
124, 126-127, 185
It's a Wonderful Life (Frank Capra,
1946) 70, 72, 197-198, 204, 206

James, Henry 15, 117-119
Jane Eyre (Brontë) 95, 225
Joe Kidd (John Sturges, 1972) 102,
109-112, 152
Johnny Guitar (Nicholas Ray, 1954)
128
Johnson, Lamont 56
Jolly Corner, The (James) 117-119
Jones, Freddie 147-148
Jones, L.Q. 106
Jourdan, Louis 24
Kelly's Heroes (Brian G. Hutton, 1970)
138-142
Kennedy, George 26, 160
Kennedy, John 229, 230
Kerouac, Jack 6, 159, 207
King Lear (Shakespeare) 71
King, Stephen 74
Kiss Me, Deadly (Robert Aldrich, 1955)
86
Klute (Alan J. Pakula, 1971) 82, 158
Knotts, Don 26
Korea 150, 153, 162, 168

Lanchester, Elsa 209
Lanza, Mario 204
Last Detail, The (Hal Ashby, 1974)
170, 194
Last House on the Left (Wes Craven,
1973) 56, 57
Laughton, Charles 209
Laura (Otto Preminger, 1944) 82
Legend of Lylah Clare, The (Robert
Aldrich, 1968) 74
Leonard, Elmore 110
Leone, Sergio 9, 11, 16, 20, 21, 24, 27,
29, 30, 32, 34
Lewis, Geoffrey 183
Light in August (Faulkner) 75, 131
Lincoln, Abraham 123
Lion (Faulkner) 212
Lipstick (Lamont Johnson, 1976) 56,
57
Little Big Man (Arthur Penn, 1970)
104, 123
Locke, Sondra 125, 180, 194, 234
Logan, Joshua 102-103
Lone Ranger, The 12
Long Goodbye, The (Robert Altman,
1973) 93
Lucas, George 148
Lust for a Vampire (Jimmy Sangster,
1971) 74
Lynn, Loretta 192

McIntire, John 194
McQueen, Steve 11
Mafia/mob 55, 170, 172, 178, 185, 234
Magnificent Seven, The (John Sturges,
1960) 26
Magnum Force (Ted Post, 1973) 35,
36, 37, **44-48**, 48, 49, 50, 54, 55,
111, 144, 171, 232, 233
Major Dundee (Sam Peckinpah, 1965)
15, 103
Malkovitch, John 231
Malpaso 9, 234
Man of the West (Anthony Mann,
1958) 128
Man Who Shot Liberty Valance, The
(John Ford, 1962) 22, 34, 104
Mandingo (Richard Fleischer, 1975)
79
Mankiewicz, Herman 202

Mann, Anthony 128
Mann, Thomas 205
Marshall, Garry 82
Marvin, Lee 26
M*A*S*H (Hooker) 138
M*A*S*H (Robert Altman, 1970) 138
Matthiessen, F.O. 9
Maverick 11, 12, 26
Measure for Measure (Shakespeare) 28
Meet John Doe (Frank Capra, 1941)
100
Melville Herman 27, 107, 117, 212
Merry Wives of Windsor, The
(Shakespeare) 29
Mexico 15, 21 24, 25, 27, 102
MGM 138
Milius, John 44
Miller, Arthur 192, 205
Misfits, The (John Huston, 1961) 26
Mitchum, Robert 26
Monroe, Marilyn 199
Moriarty, Michael 131
Morricone, Ennio 16, 26, 32, 102
Mottram, Eric 173-174
Mr Smith Goes to Washington (Frank
Capra, 1939) 100, 172
Ms 45 (Abel Ferrara, 1981) 56
Munch, Edvard 58
My Darling Clementine (John Ford,
1946) 25, 104

Neame, Ronald 145
New Mexico 109
New Orleans 62, 235
New York 157, 185, 191, 205
Nichols, Mike 138
Night of the Living Dead (George
Romero, 1968) 109
Nixon, Richard 100, 172, 230
North by Northwest (Alfred Hitchcock)
101
Nostromo (Conrad) 119

O'Brien, Pat 26
Officer and a Gentleman, An (Taylor
Hackford, 1982) 150
Oklahoma 102, 107, 192
Old Man and the Sea, The
(Hemingway) 213
On the Road (Kerouac) 6, 159
On the Town (Stanley Donen and
Gene Kelly, 1949) 205
Once upon a Time in the West (Sergio
Leone, 1968) 27
Operation Undercover (Milton Katselas,
1975) 131
orang-utan (Clyde) 175, 176, 179,
180-181, 234
Oshima, Nagisa 106
Othello (Shakespeare) 71
Out of Africa (Sydney Pollack, 1985)
209
Out of the Past (Jacques Tourneur,
1947) 222
Outlaw Josey Wales, The (Clint
Eastwood, 1976) 103, **119-130**, 131,
160, 174, 175, 192, 196, 224, 231,
233-234, 236, 237
Outlaw, The (Howard Hughes, 1943)
108
Over the Hill Gang, The 26
Over the Hill Gang Rides Again, The 26

Page, Geraldine 80, 81
Paint Your Wagon (Joshua Logan,
1969) 7, 17, 102-103
Pakula, Alan J. 158, 172, 229
Pale Rider (Clint Eastwood, 1985) 103,
130-137, 193, 218, 235
Paleface, The (Norman Z. McLeod,
1948) 26
Palm Beach Story, The (Preston
Sturges, 1942) 99
Parker, Charlie 199, 200

Pat Garrett and Billy the Kid (Sam Peckinpah, 1973) 103
Patton, Lust for Glory (Franklin Schaffner, 1970) 138
Pearce, Richard 130
Peckinpah, Sam 56, 100, 103, 129
Pelican Brief, The (Alan J. Pakula, 1993) 230
Penn, Arthur 104, 123, 156
Peoples, David Webb 227
Per qualche dollari in più see For a Few Dollars More
Per un pugno di dollari see A Fistful of Dollars
Perfect World, A (Clint Eastwood, 1993) 160, 236
Petersen, Wolfgang 9, 228, 229
Pink Cadillac (Buddy Van Horne, 1989) 158, **197-198**, 217, 250
Pioneers, The (Cooper) 13, 110
Pistols 'n' Petticoats 26
Places in the Heart (Robert Benton, 1984) 130
Play It Again, Sam (Herbert Ross, 1972) 89
Play Misty for Me (Clint Eastwood, 1971) 73, 74, **82-90**, 90, 100, 101, 232
Poe, Edgar Allan 27, 34, 117
Point Blank (John Boorman, 1967) 161
Polanski, Roman 109
Pollack, Sydney 138, 172, 209
Porter, Cole 247
Poseidon Adventure, The (Ronald Neame, 1972) 145
Post, Ted 102
Preminger, Otto 82
Pretty Woman (Garry Marshall, 1990) 99
Production Code 106
Psycho (Alfred Hitchcock, 1960) 194
Pye, Douglas 104

racial prejudice 145, 212
Rakoff, Alvin 146
Raksin, David 204
Rango 26
Rawhide 11-14, 20, 102, 103
Ray, Nicholas 128
Reagan, Ronald 8, 137, 147, 155, 182
Red Badge of Courage, The (Crane) 128
Red Badge of Courage, The (John Huston, 1951) 128
Red River (Howard Hawks, 1948) 13
Reisz, Karel 130
Reitman, Ivan 229
Report to the Commissioner (Milton Katselas, 1975) 131
Restless Gun, The 12
Revelations, Book of 132
Reynolds, Burt 247
Rifleman, The 12
Right Stuff, The (Philip Kaufman, 1983) 148
Rio Bravo (Howard Hawks, 1959) 15
Ritt, Martin 20
River, The (Mark Rydell, 1984) 130
road movies (with Eastwood) **156-198**
Romero, George 109
Rookie, The (Clint Eastwood, 1990) 250
Rosemary's Baby (Roman Polanski, 1968) 109
Rosen, Marjorie 74
Ross, Herbert 89
Rubáiyát of Omar Khayyám, The (Fitzgerald) 201
Rydell, Mark 130

San Francisco 35, 156
Sangster, Jimmy 74
Sartre, Jean-Paul 210
Saxon, John 110
Schaffner, Franklin 138

Schoenberg, Arnold 205
Schroeder, Barbet 82
Scott, Ridley 146, 157
Searchers, The (John Ford, 1956) 104, 124, 224
Shaft (Tidyman) 112
Shaft films (1971-73) 112
Shakespeare, William 28, 29, 71, 213
Shakiest Gun in the West, The (Alan Rafkin, 1968) 26
Sheridan, Ann 26
Short, Happy Life of Francis Macomber, The (Hemingway) 212, 213
Siegel, Don 9, 38, 39, 43, 73, 77, 78, 81, 82, 83, 102, 142, 145, 147
Single White Female (Barbet Schroeder, 1991) 82
Sirk, Douglas 9, 92, 95, 97, 201
Sisters (Brian De Palma, 1973) 74
Snows of Kilimanjaro, The (Hemingway) 212
Song of the Lark, The (Cather) 192
Sontag, Susan 193
South (American) 74, 75, 77, 79, 81, 203-204
Spain 15, 21
Spanish-Americans 109-110, 111
Specimen Days in America (Whitman) 6
Spiegel, Sam 207, 209
Spy Who Came in from the Cold, The (Martin Ritt, 1966) 20
Stagecoach (John Ford, 1939) 11, 17
Star Wars (George Lucas, 1977) 148
State of the Union (Frank Capra, 1948) 100, 211
Steinbeck, John 109, 192
Stewart, James 25, 26
Stravinsky, Igor 205
Straw Dogs (Sam Peckinpah, 1971) 56
Streetcar Named Desire, A (Williams) 82
Sturges, John 102, 110, 111
Sturges, Preston 6, 128, 159-160
Sudden Impact (Clint Eastwood, 1983) 35, 36, 37, **54-60**, 60, 113, 144, 156, 175, 231, 235
Sullivan's Travels (Preston Sturges, 1941) 6, 159-160, 198
Support Your Local Sheriff (Burt Kennedy, 1968) 26
Sutherland, Donald 141

Taylor, Dub 161
Tehran 155
television 11-14, 26
Tender Is the Night (Fitzgerald) 228
Thackeray, William Makepeace 6, 7
Thoreau, Henry David 9, 92, 191
Three Days of the Condor (Sydney Pollack, 1975) 172
Thunderbolt and Lightfoot (Michael Cimino, 1974) 48, 121, 156, 159, **160-170**, 174, 180, 198, 233
Tidyman, Ernest 112, 131
Tierney, Gene 82
Tightrope (Richard Tuggle, 1984) 37, **62-72**, 142, 231, 235, 236
Tom and Jerry cartoons 171
Topkapi (Jules Dassin, 1964) 29
Tourneur, Jacques 222
Towering Inferno, The (John Guillermin, 1974) 145
Tracy, Spencer 52, 211
tuberculosis 193, 195
Tuggle, Richard 62, 66, 71, 142
Twain, Mark 9, 27, 119-120, 185, 212
Two Mules for Sister Sara (Don Siegel, 1969) 102, 121, 138

Ulzana's Raid (Robert Aldrich, 1972) 104
Unforgiven (Clint Eastwood, 1992) 17, 103, 137, **217-228**, 231, 236-237

Urban Cowboy (James Bridges, 1980) 183
Ustinov, Peter 29

Valentino, Rudolph 203
Van Cleef, Lee 21, 22, 26
Van Doran, Charles 12
Van Horne, Buddy 182
Vanity Fair (Thackeray) 6, 7
Vertigo (Alfred Hitchcock, 1958) 8
Viertel, Peter 209, 210, 211, 212, 213
Vietnam 8, 20, 29-30, 44, 45, 48, 50, 55, 75, 100, 111, 120-121, 139, 140-142, 147, 150, 152, 153, 154, 168, 182, 215, 227-228, 229, 236
Volonté, Gian Maria 17, 22, 24
von Sydow, Max 148

Wagon Train 12, 13
Walden (Thoreau) 191
Wallach, Eli 26
Walter, Jessica 84
Wanted: Dead or Alive 11, 12
war films (with Eastwood) **138-155**, 156
Warhol, Andy 61
Warner Bros 150, 175, 209
Watergate 44, 172
Watie, Stand 123
Wayne, John 11, 12, 236
Webster, Duncan 130
Weir, Peter 130
Welcome to Hard Times (Burt Kennedy, 1967) 128
Welles, Orson 201-202
westerns (with Eastwood) **11-34**, 73, 74, **112-137**, 156, **217-228**, 236
Wharton, Edith 15
Where Eagles Dare (Brian G. Hutton, 1968) 138
Whitaker, Forest 199
White Hunter, Black Heart (Clint Eastwood, 1990) 8, 189, 199, **207-216**, 217, 236, 237
White Hunter, Black Heart (Viertel) 209, 210
Whitman, Walt 6
Wild Bunch, The (Sam Peckinpah, 1969) 15, 103, 129
Williams, Hank 141
Williams, Tennessee 79, 81, 82
Winner, Michael 56
Witness (Peter Weir, 1985) 130
Wizard of Oz, The (Victor Fleming, 1939) 179, 222
Wood, Robin 169, 182-183, 215
Worden, Hank 177
World War II 138, 139, 148, 153
Wright, Frank Lloyd 97
Written on the Wind (Douglas Sirk, 1956) 201

Yeager, Chuck 148

Zapruder, Abraham 230
Zinnemann, Fred 104